Convergence of Deep Learning In Cyber-IoT Systems and Security

Scrivener Publishing
100 Cummings Center, Suite 541J
Beverly, MA 01915-6106

Artificial Intelligence and Soft Computing for Industrial Transformation

Series Editor: Dr. S. Balamurugan (sbnbala@gmail.com)

Scope: Artificial Intelligence and Soft Computing Techniques play an impeccable role in industrial transformation. The topics to be covered in this book series include Artificial Intelligence, Machine Learning, Deep Learning, Neural Networks, Fuzzy Logic, Genetic Algorithms, Particle Swarm Optimization, Evolutionary Algorithms, Nature Inspired Algorithms, Simulated Annealing, Metaheuristics, Cuckoo Search, Firefly Optimization, Bio-inspired Algorithms, Ant Colony Optimization, Heuristic Search Techniques, Reinforcement Learning, Inductive Learning, Statistical Learning, Supervised and Unsupervised Learning, Association Learning and Clustering, Reasoning, Support Vector Machine, Differential Evolution Algorithms, Expert Systems, Neuro Fuzzy Hybrid Systems, Genetic Neuro Hybrid Systems, Genetic Fuzzy Hybrid Systems and other Hybridized Soft Computing Techniques and their applications for Industrial Transformation. The book series is aimed to provide comprehensive handbooks and reference books for the benefit of scientists, research scholars, students and industry professional working towards next generation industrial transformation.

Publishers at Scrivener
Martin Scrivener (martin@scrivenerpublishing.com)
Phillip Carmical (pcarmical@scrivenerpublishing.com)

Convergence of Deep Learning In Cyber-IoT Systems and Security

Edited by

Rajdeep Chakraborty
Anupam Ghosh
Jyotsna Kumar Mandal
and
S. Balamurugan

Scrivener
Publishing

WILEY

This edition first published 2023 by John Wiley & Sons, Inc., 111 River Street, Hoboken, NJ 07030, USA and Scrivener Publishing LLC, 100 Cummings Center, Suite 541J, Beverly, MA 01915, USA
© 2023 Scrivener Publishing LLC
For more information about Scrivener publications please visit www.scrivenerpublishing.com.

Wiley Global Headquarters
111 River Street, Hoboken, NJ 07030, USA

For details of our global editorial offices, customer services, and more information about Wiley products visit us at www.wiley.com.

Limit of Liability/Disclaimer of Warranty

Library of Congress Cataloging-in-Publication Data

ISBN 978-1-119-85721-1

Cover image: Pixabay.Com
Cover design by Russell Richardson

Set in size of 11pt and Minion Pro by Manila Typesetting Company, Makati, Philippines

Printed in the USA

10 9 8 7 6 5 4 3 2 1

Contents

Part II: Innovative Solutions Based on Deep Learning 99

Part III: Security and Safety Aspects with Deep Learning

Preface

Deep learning (also known as deep structured learning) is part of a broader family of machine learning methods based on artificial neural networks with representation learning. Learning can be supervised, semi-supervised or unsupervised. Deep-learning architectures such as deep neural networks, deep belief networks, deep reinforcement learning, recurrent neural networks and convolutional neural networks have been applied to fields including computer vision, speech recognition, natural language processing, machine translation, bioinformatics, drug design, medical image analysis, material inspection and board game programs, where they have produced results comparable to and in some cases surpassing human expert performance. Artificial neural networks (ANNs) were inspired by information processing and distributed communication nodes in biological systems. ANNs have various differences from biological brains. Specifically, artificial neural networks tend to be static and symbolic, while the biological brain of most living organisms is dynamic (plastic) and analogue. The adjective "deep" in deep learning refers to the use of multiple layers in the network. Early work showed that a linear perceptron cannot be a universal classifier, but that a network with a nonpolynomial activation function with one hidden layer of unbounded width can. Deep learning is a modern variation which is concerned with an unbounded number of layers of bounded size, which permits practical application and optimized implementation, while retaining theoretical universality under mild conditions. In deep learning the layers are also permitted to be heterogeneous and to deviate widely from biologically informed connectionist models, for the sake of efficiency, trainability and understandability, whence the "structured" part.

Deep learning approaches are now used in every aspect of cyber systems and IoT systems. The main goal of this book is to bring to the fore unconventional cryptographic methods to provide cyber security, including cyber-physical system security and IoT security through deep learning techniques and analytics with the study of all these systems.

Thus, the book covers the evolution of deep learning from machine learning in the very first section. It also provides innovative projects and implementation on deep learning-based solutions in Cyber-IoT systems as well as detailed aspect on deep learning-based security issues in Cyber-IoT systems. Finally, this book also covers cyber physical system concepts and security issues. Therefore, we feel the book is well suited for students (UG & PG), research scholars, and enthusiastic readers who wants a good domain knowledge on deep learning.

Part I: Various Approaches from Machine Learning to Deep Learning

Chapter 1 discuss a method using web-assisted non-invasive detection of oral submucous fibrosis using IoHT. Oral cancer is another big threat and disease of human race. The early detection of oral cancer is of the upmost importance. This chapter starts with a detailed literature on oral cancer then it gives all the primary concepts to understand the proposed system of the authors. Then the chapter gives a proposed model to detect non-invasive oral submucous fibrosis which is web-assisted and for IoHT.

Chapter 2 provides a performance evaluation of machine learning and deep learning, the case study used in this chapter is house price prediction. After the introduction, the chapter starts with a detailed literature review of machine learning and deep learning. The authors used a very standard research methodology to carry out this study, which is discussed next. Authors used Gradient Boosting Regression, Support Vector Regression (SVM), Support Vector Regression (SVM), Multi Output Regression, Regression using Tensorflow – Keras and various classification models for their study. The authors concluded with very good performance analysis and results in both tabular and graphical forms.

Chapter 3 gives why it is important to study cyber physical systems, machine learning & deep learning. First, the author discusses cyber physical systems, machine learning & deep learning in detail. Then the author gives a detailed academic program in cyber physical systems, machine learning & deep learning throughout the world and in India. Finally, the author concludes with the importance to study cyber physical systems, machine learning & deep learning.

Chapter 4 proposes a hybrid model using machine learning techniques and semantic attribute to detect fake news, which is one of the important applications in this cyber and social media world. It uses NLP and applied to various datasets from Facebook, Twitter, Whatsapp, etc. The results are finally compared with existing literature and the proposed model is found to be 93% accurate.

Part II: Innovative Solutions based on Deep learning

Chapter 5 gives an online assessment system using Natural Language Processing (NLP) techniques. It starts with the importance of online assessment in the 'home from work' scenario due to the COVID-19 pandemic. The chapter then moves to a detailed literature on online assessments. Thereafter, the authors discuss some algorithms for online assessments. In the next section it proposes a system design for online assessment. Finally, implementation is shown and concluded with it's novelty.

Chapter 6 gives a reference architecture to build deep Q learning-based intelligent IoT edge solutions. The chapter starts with a detailed overview of machine learning and deep learning. Then the chapter moves to dynamic programming features and deep Q learning in IoT and Azure. Thereafter, the authors give a proposed model and detailed result and analysis.

Chapter 7 provides an improved fuzzy logic-based solutions for air conditioning systems. Then the authors give a proposed system which is composed of Fuzzy variables, Fuzzy base class, Fuzzy Rule Base and Fuzzy rule viewer. The chapter then gives the simulated results of the proposed system and conclusion is drawn based on it's novelty.

Chapter 8 has an important implementation to detect masked face to combat the pandemic situation. The chapter starts with a detailed related work on masked face recognition. Then it gives all the mathematical preliminaries required to understand the proposed system. Thereafter, it moves to the proposed system with algorithms, methods and applications followed by experimental results. It concludes with the novelty of the proposed system.

Chapter 9 is another deep learning approach to encounter COVID-19 pandemic situation. The chapter starts with the introduction of COVID-19 situation and the need of deep learning-based solutions to encounter it. Here, the authors propose a medical imaging solution using deep learning where images of lungs are taken and COVID-19 infection positivity is predicted. The chapter also provides the method of COVID-19 variant tracing and biological protein structure. Moreover, this chapter gives selection drugs combination for a particular COVID-19 patient. It ends with detailed result and analysis of the proposed model.

Chapter 10 provides another online question answering system using Bengali language. It starts with the discussion on the existing literature then it moves towards a problem statement. The authors discuss the proposed model in a very structured way with algorithms. Thereafter, a detailed result and analysis is given and compared with existing work.

The chapter ends with analysis of error, some close observations, applications of the proposed model and scope for improvement as future work.

Part III: Security and Safety Aspects with Deep Learning

Chapter 11 gives a secure access mechanism for smart homes using biometric authentication and RFID authentication which can be implemented for IoT systems. The authors give a structured approach and framework for smart home access method with biometrics. The authors then discuss the same using RFID followed by proposed Control Scheme for Secure Access (CSFSC). The proposed system is discussed with mathematical equations and then it provides result of the proposed system.

Chapter 12 is a MQTT-based implementation of home automation system prototype with integrated Cyber-IoT infrastructure and also discusses deep learning-based security issues. After the introduction, literature review and importance of home automation, the author starts with proposed system architecture of home automation. Then it discusses the various security issues in home automation. Thereafter, the author moves to the implementation part of the proposed system and gives the detailed results with discussion.

Chapter 13 gives a malware detection framework using deep learning. Malware is a risk to the privacy of computer users which can cause an economic loss to organizations. Deep Learning is a subfield of machine learning which concentrates on human brains using artificial intelligence result analysis and conclusion.

Chapter 14 gives an application for women safety, namely "Patron for Women". The authors first give relative research where the first application is a mobile-based women safety application. Secondly, the authors refer to another application which is android-based. Thirdly, it gives another android-based application namely, "Lifecraft" and, finally, "Abhaya and Sakshi", another two-women safety applications are discussed. Then it provides a new methodology, system and model with deep learning for women safety. The chapter concludes with result and analysis and novelty.

Chapter 15 discusses concepts & techniques in deep learning applications in the field of IoT systems and security. The chapter starts with a detailed introduction and concepts on deep learning. Then it discusses various techniques used in deep learning such as CNN, RNN, GAN, SOM, autoencoders etc. Thereafter, it gives various deep learning applications followed by a detailed concept on IoT system and it's applications. Next the authors show the amalgamation of deep learning with IoT. The chapter concludes with the author's finding deep learning applications in the field of IoT systems and security.

Chapter 16 is an implementation of efficient detection of bioweapons for agriculture sector using narrow band transmitter and composite sensing architecture. The authors start with a detailed literature review and understanding of pest and insects to be discovered using deep learning techniques. Then the authors give a structured working methodology and proposed algorithm followed by block diagram of the proposed method.

Chapter 17 gives a deep learning-based malware and intrusion detection framework. After a detailed literature survey author moves to the proposed work with problem description, working model, data set for deep learning application, deep learning algorithms. Then it gives the implementation with python libraries. Thereafter, a detailed result and analysis is provided and concludes with the accuracy of the system and future work.

Chapter 18 gives phishing URL detection-based on deep learning techniques. This chapter focuses on detecting phishing URL using Convolutional Neural Network. The phishtank dataset is considered and the features of the URL are extracted. Finally, the deep learning classifiers is used to detect the URL is phishing or legitimate URL. The performance of the classifier is evaluated based on the accuracy, precision, recall and F1 score.

Part IV: Cyber Physical Systems

Chapter 19 is an overview and understanding of Cyber Physical System (CPS). After a short introduction the authors start with the architecture and design of the CPS and move to reliability and distribution management in CPS. Thereafter, the authors discuss the security issues in CPS with the role of machine learning and deep learning for providing security in CPS. Finally, the authors conclude with various applications of CPS.

Chapter 20 is dedicated to the security issues, threats and solutions in Cyber Physical Systems. With the introduction of CPS, the author gives the motivation of this work. Then the authors discuss the various characteristics of CPS followed by a detailed understanding of threats in CPS. The authors then give various security mechanism aspects to achieve in CPS. The chapter concludes with how to overcome security issues in CPS, with and without deep learning, and discussion with probable solutions.

The Editors
August 2022

Part I

VARIOUS APPROACHES FROM MACHINE LEARNING TO DEEP LEARNING

1

Web-Assisted Noninvasive Detection of Oral Submucous Fibrosis Using IoHT

Animesh Upadhyaya[1*], Vertika Rai[2], Debdutta Pal[1], Surajit Bose[3] and Somnath Ghosh[2]

[1]Department of Computer Science and Engineering, Brainware University, Kolkata, India
[2]Department of Allied Health Sciences, Brainware University, Kolkata, India
[3]KSD Dental College & Hospital, Kolkata, India

Abstract

Today's world is connected with the Internet. In our daily life, we are also connected with many things that are connected through the Internet, and that is the way that "Internet of Things" evolves. In every aspect of life, we have applications of IoT, smart home, smart city, smart transport, and many more. Healthcare is also required to be smart to reach maximum patients in minimum time. In this chapter, we focus on a chronic unbearable disease of the oral cavity characterized by infection and progressive fibrosis. This disease may cause an inability to open the mouth, but it is absolutely curable. The faster the disease is diagnosed the rate of curability is high. Our aim is to develop a model with the help of IoHT device for the detection of oral submucous fibrosis in the early stage.

Keywords: Internet of HealthcareThings, noninvasive, oral submucous fibrosis, ThinkSpeak, MQTT, ESP8266

1.1 Introduction

Early 1926, Nikola Tesla envisioned a "Connected World." He told Colliers Magazine in an interview: "When Wireless is perfectly applied, the whole world will be converted into a huge brain, which in fact it is, all things

---

*Corresponding author: upadhyayaanimesh12@gmail.com

Rajdeep Chakraborty, Anupam Ghosh, Jyotsna Kumar Mandal and S. Balamurugan (eds.) *Convergence of Deep Learning In Cyber-IoT Systems and Security*, (3–20) © 2023 Scrivener Publishing LLC

particles of a real and rhythmic whole and the instruments through which we shall be able to do this will be amazing simple compared with our present telephone, A man will be able to carry one in his vest pocket" [1].

In 1999, Kevin Asthon coined the phrase "Internet of Things" to refer to supply chain management with RFID-tagged or barcoded item (things) bringing increased efficiency and accountability to the organization. As Ashton said in an RFID journal article (June 22, 2009): "If we had computers that knew everything there was to know about things—using data they gathered without any help from us—we would be able to track and count everything and greatly reduce waste, lost and cost. We would know when things needed replacing, repairing, or recalling and whether they were fresher past their best" [1].

Oral cancer (OC) in today's world is now a menacing health problem and is now accepted as Indian disease, despite advances in oral cancer therapy, it remains as a disease of later diagnosis [2]. Oral submucous fibrosis (OSF) is the sixth most common cancer with the highest malignant transformation rate. Diagnosis of OSF currently consists of clinical examination, followed by biopsy [3]. There is a requirement for minimal invasive markers for the disease that are specific for risk assessment [4]. To achieve this goal, better understanding of complex molecular events that regulate the progression of this disease is required [5]. Early detection not only decreases the incidence and mortality rate but also improves the survival of oral precancer [6]. With the increasing number of OC patients reported, the need for a continuous and throughout observation system is the need of the hour. Pathologists find it difficult to diagnose OC patients at early stages due to overlapping symptoms. In fact, the information medical practitioners get from a patient's visit is usually very limited [7]. Till now, there is no gadget available that can be utilized to screen oral well-being at an early stage of the disease. The 21st century has become a century of new digital technologies. Digital technologies have started playing a vital role in the medical healthcare sector [8]. Digital technologies are nowadays are used in dentistry to help in the treatment system, enabling the healthcare practitioners for early diagnosis and detection [9]. While using a wide range of sensors protocols, the IoT-based healthcare system delivers the data collected from cancer patients and monitors them in real-time, it becomes easy for patients and oncopathologists, to screen the OC patients, and differentiate between the stages of cancer for early diagnosis. IoT-based systems reduce the workload demanded by the conventional biopsy [10]. Digital technologies have started playing a vital role in the medical healthcare sector [9]. Digital technologies are now a day are used in dentistry to help in the treatment system, enabling the healthcare practitioners for early diagnosis and detection [10]. Many sensors are easy to install to monitor health and maintain real-time data for further check-up and take necessary action in real-time. IoHT based biosensing systems combine a variety of tiny physiological sensors, transmission modules and also sustain high-processing capabilities like processing the data through machine learning and artificial intelligence techniques over the Cloud to give us advanced ratio through the day-to-day monitoring basis and also the whole system is pocket-friendly, unobtrusive health monitoring solutions. While using a wide range of sensors protocols the IoHT-based healthcare system delivers the data collected from cancer patients and monitors them in real-time, it becomes easy for patients and oncopathologists, to screen the OC patients, and differentiate between the stages of cancer for early diagnosis. IoHt-based systems reduce the workload demanded by the conventional biopsy [9].

In this paper, the canvased device detects inflammation and progressive fibrosis of the submucosal tissue by using the sensor MQ135. It examines the whole surface of the mouth in real-time and collects data from every fragmented section of the region using a low-power Wi-Fi chip named ESP 8266 Microcontroller, and sends it to ThingSpeak which is a web-based service as like as an IoT platform that supports REST API protocol. ThingSpeak is a free and open-source IoT application and API that uses the HTTP protocol to store and retrieve data from sensors via the Internet. the data collected and processed is represented as part of an IoT analytics web-server in the form of a graphical visualization system and is accessible by users as a virtual server, and objects communicate with the cloud via "wireless Internet connections" available to users, with the majority of objects relying on sensors to provide environmental analog data. Scripts, such as JSON, XML, and CSV, may display the measurements that were obtained in this manner. the data collected and processed is represented as part of an IoT analytics web-server in the form of a graphical visualization system and is accessible by users as a virtual server, and objects communicate with the cloud via "wireless Internet connections" available to users, with the majority of objects relying on sensors to provide environmental analog data. Scripts such as JSON, XML, and CSV may display the measurements that were obtained in this manner. the data collected and processed is represented as part of an IoT analytics web-server in the form of a graphical visualization system and is accessible by users as a virtual server, and objects communicate with the cloud via "wireless Internet connections" available to users, with the majority of objects relying on sensors to provide environmental analog data. Scripts such as JSON, XML, and CSV may display the measurements that were obtained in this manner. The data collected and processed is represented as part of an IoT analytics web-server in the form of a graphical visualization system and is accessible by users as a virtual system, and objects communicate with the cloud via "wireless Internet connections" available to users, with the vast majority of items relying on sensors to provide conservational analog data. Scripts, such as JSON, XML, and CSV, may display the measurements that were obtained in this manner.

1.2   Literature Survey

1.2.1   Oral Cancer

Oral cancer [OC] among various types of cancer is the imminent problem nowadays in the Indian population, it is the sixth most cancer reported worldwide in population and is found in both sexes. 200,000 new cases are reported annually worldwide, two-thirds of which occur in developing countries including India with a high mortality rate [11]. OC is increasing rapidly in India due to lack of hygiene, alcohol consumption, tobacco chewing, betyl quid, smoking. OC completely can be defined as a malignant neoplasm in the oral cavity, most frequently occurring oral cancer in India occur with its premalignant conditions like oral squamous cell carcinoma (OSCC), oral submucous fibrosis (OSF), erythoplakia (OE), leukoplakia (OLK), lichen planus (OLP) [12].

OC can be defined as uncontrolled cell growth along with lesions in the oral cavity basically it starts from any tissue of the mouth and invades any other neighboring areas in the mouth. The most common presenting features are prolonged ulceration, which does not heal, referred pain, to the ear, difficulty with speaking, and opening the mouth or chewing and ultimately it leads to death. Most people are diagnosed with premalignant lesions like OLK and OE white and red patches covering the oral cavity [13]. These lesions are further subdivided according to their types, homogenous (flat, thin), nonhomogenous (speckled). According to literature surveys, OLK and OSF are the most common occurring lesions in patients with frequent duration of chewing of betylquid, tobacoo, and it contains arecadine, arecoline, tanin, a harmful substrate when it comes in contact with the oral cavity it leads to activation of T cells, macrophages, IL6, TNF-α and other metabolites under its influence fibroblast differentiate and leads to accumulation and formation of collagen in oral mucousa [14].

According to the World Health Organization [WHO], OLK is defined as a white patch or plaque that cannot be characterized clinically or pathologically as any other disease. Erythroplakia is a condition in which bright red, velvety patches, or plaques are seen in the mouth floor, soft palate, ventral tongue, and tonsillar fauces and its malignant transformation rate is 20% to 68% [15]. OLP lesions are a condition in which white papules or white plaques with painful blisters and fine wavy keratotic lines which indicate lichen planus are seen in the buccal mucosa, tongue, and gingiva [16]. The malignant transformation rate is about 2% to 8%. The malignant potential of OLP is an ongoing controversial matter 25. Malignancy determination is very much difficult because oral lichenoid lesions (OLLs) are the same as OLP, and sometimes, premalignant lesions exhibit lichenoid characteristics [17].

OSF is a condition in which the mouth appears rigid and becomes difficult to open (i.e., trismus). It is mostly seen in buccal mucosa and the oral cavity and pharynx may also be affected. Inflammation and progressive fibrosis of the submucosal tissue is the hallmark of the disease. It has the highest malignant transformation rate in comparison to other precancerous stages [18]. There are various clinical symptoms that the patients show at the primary stage of the disease like halitosis also known as oral malodor is the most commonly notice with a patient suffering from any oral disease. Due to pathological or nonpathological reasons, halitosis is formed by volatile molecules. It is very commonly reported in more than 50% population has halitosis [19]. These volatile compounds are composed of alcohols or phenyl compounds, sulphur compounds, aromatic compounds, nitrogen-containing compounds, and ketones [20]. OC is a disease diagnosis is followed by the old conventional methods of diagnosis based on experts' clinical observation, cytological analysis, and histological observations are still followed, which is time-consuming and less sensitive and accurate [18].

1.3   Primary Concepts

1.3.1   Transmission Efficiency

Most current IoT systems send data to the cloud via hypertext transfer protocol (HTTP) and use the message queuing telemetry transport (MQTT) conventional transport protocols [21, 22]. A unique payload in the HTTP method is sent by every device that delivers data to the cloud. Like a normal web server, the IoT platform gets these data and saves it in a database. As a consequence of this method of communication, IoT devices are constrained by bandwidth, latency, and battery consumption. Consequently, the establishment of a new cloud connection and an HTTP request with various headers, and it is necessary to provide a payload for each identified location, which is usually in XML or JSON format. Using this method, which relies on conventional HTTP requests, entails a significant cost for delivering tiny and frequent payloads, such as sensor readings, which are often only a few bytes long. Firewire, cloud-based infrastructure for IoT platforms sponsored by the European Union and the European Commission, has used this approach in several iterations [23, 24]. Other open and standard solutions will benefit greatly from this approach. Other options include Xively [25], ThingSpeak [26], and Temboo [27], all of which began by providing just HTTP interfaces. MQTT [28] is an old telemetry system that enables a publish-subscribe–based messaging system that allows bidirectional communication between servers and devices. HTTP-based solutions, as described in Yasumoto *et al.* [21], are considerably less efficient since they need more bandwidth and have higher latency. AmazonWeb Services, for example, is using this protocol as the foundation for its Internet of Things offerings [21]. The aforementioned companies, as well as others like Kaa, Carriots, and Ubidots [29], have been integrating MQTT into their products in recent years.

For a related strategy, ThinkSpeak suggests raw binary connecting networks instead of HTTP pattern overhead or publishing-subscription protocols. In addition to transparent HTTP compatibility, it also defines the payload encoding for better transmission efficiency, something MQTT does not supply (as opposed to MQTT). PSON (https://github. com/thinger-io/Protoson) is an effective encoding method that uses few resources. For strategies with limited resources, for instance, memory or computational efficiency, Protoson was built from the ground up just for them. This approach makes it possible to encode unstructured data in a compact binary format, similar to JSON. To illustrate this point, Figure 1.1 shows the encoding sizes of numerous prominent platform formats, including BSON (Binary JSON), JSON, and MessagePack, as well as the recommended PSON and XML, which surpasses MessagePack in the IoT sector by a little margin. By using well-organized protocols and an encoding method, the proposed system decreases latency when data is directed to the cloud, conserves bandwidth, conserves battery power, and minimizes memory footprint.

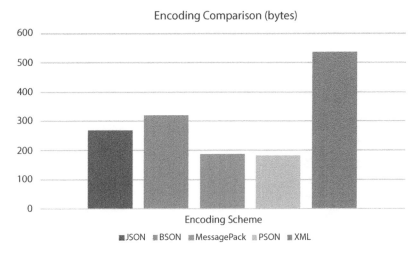

Figure 1.1 A comparison of the coding sizes of several formats. With Thinger.io, memory footprint is reduced, bandwidth is saved, and power consumption is reduced by using a PSON coding technique.

1.4 Propose Model

1.4.1 Platform Configuration

This section demonstrates how to model and set up a device on the ThinkSpeak platform. Registration on the ThinkSpeak platform requires the addition of two resources in the admin panel. Since the GasLevelMonitoring is connected to the platform, we must register the device that provides sensor information (in this instance, it is the GasLevelMonitoring), moreover, there is a data bucket for archiving the collected data. However, the fundamental procedures required for the creation of the case study are given here, in greater detail at https://thingspeak.com/channels/new For this task, we will utilize the devices part of the platform's side menu, which gives us access to our user account's devices. As soon as we are in this area, we'll have to add the device by clicking the add device button in the list of devices, which will open a section for recording basic information about the device, such as its identification and credentials. It is critical to save the identification and password information since you will need them later in the code you write for the device. The device's identification is GasLevelMonitoring, and its API Key is SKP9YQY2CFVNK919.

Figure 1.2 Harvard architectural based wireless communication board.

1.4.2   Harvard Architectural Microcontroller Base Wireless Communication Board

We constructed the Harvard Micro-Controller board to construct the strategic model. Transfer the sensed data to the server through the channel port. The proposed model board is shown in Figure 1.2. The major components of the board are:

1. NodeMCU ESP8266 Microcontroller
2. MQ135 Gas Sensor

1.4.2.1   NodeMCU ESP8266 Microcontroller

The ESP8266 Wi-Fi System on Chip (SoC) is used by NodeMCU's software, while the ESP12E module is used by the device's hardware. The ESP8266 is a low-cost WiFi module with an integrated WiFi module that utilizes ultra-low power technology. The low power consumption is due to the device's 32-bit TenSilica L 106 microprocessor. Table 1.1 shows the NodeMCU ESP8266 Microcontroller's basic specs.

In the ESP 8266, the power-saving design functions in three modes. Active mode, sleep mode, and deep-sleep mode with the RTC clock still operating are the three options. It has a built-in Wi-Fi network that can host an app even if the device does not have one. It also functions as a WiFi adaptor. The ESP8266 WiFi unit supports the 802.11 b/g/n protocol and WiFi direct (P2P), which allows devices from various manufacturers

Table 1.1 NodeMCU ESP8266 Specifications.

Specifications	Value
CPU	Tensilica L106 32-bit processor
RAM	36Kb
Clock Speed	80MHz/160MHz
Operating Voltage	3.0V 3.6V
Operating Current	80mA (Average)
Available GPIO Pins	10
Frequency range	2.4 GHz ~ 2.5 GHz
Protocols	802.11 b/g/n (HT20)
Security	WPA/ WPA2
Network Protocol	IPv4, TCP/UDP/HTTP

to connect and interact without the need for a wireless access point. Figure 1.3 depicts the NodeMCU ESP8266 Microcontroller integration. Furthermore, owing to its simple interoperability with application-specific devices and sensors, the ESP 8266 offers a wide range of applications in the Internet of Things deployments like the new generation home automation systems. By using the GPIO pins provided on the ESP 8266 module,

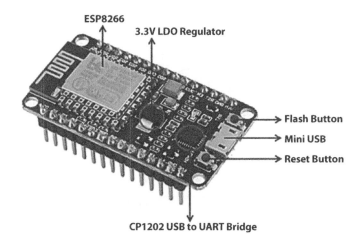

Figure 1.3 NodeMCU microcontroller.

devices or sensors may be readily integrated, and data from sensors can be quickly accessed by the ESP 8266 and processed to make choices based on the circumstance and demand.

1.4.2.2   Gas Sensor

The MQ135 gas sensor's sensitive substance is SnO2, which in pure air has a lower conductivity. When the target polluting gas is present, the conductivity of the sensor increases in lockstep with the gas concentration. Through a simple circuit, users may transform the change in conductivity to the corresponding output signal of gas concentration. MQ135 gas sensor has a high sensitivity to ammonia gas, hydrogen sulphide, benzene series steam, and smoke, among other harmful gases. It can detect kinds of toxic gases and is a kind of low-cost sensor for kinds of applications. The illustration is immediately above. The MQ135's fundamental test circuit is shown in Figure 1.4. Two voltage inputs are required for the sensor: one for the heater (VH) and another for the circuit voltage (VC). VH is used to power the sensor at its typical operating temperature and may be either DC or AC, while VRL is the voltage across the load resistance RL in series with the sensor. VC delivers detectable voltage to the load resistance RL and should operate on direct current.

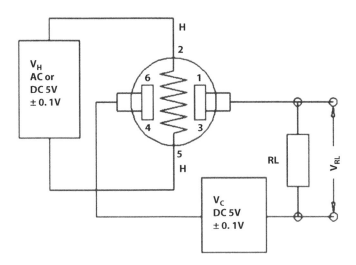

Figure 1.4 Basic circuit of gas sensor.

1.4.3   Experimental Setup

We deployed the sensor node to the micro-controller and the node is itself connected with the Cloud Server through Bi-directional communication the working mechanism is shown through the Flowchart of the model in Figure 1.5. When the sensor is in into the mouth and examines the whole surface, then the sensor node detects the Gas and sends the data in real time

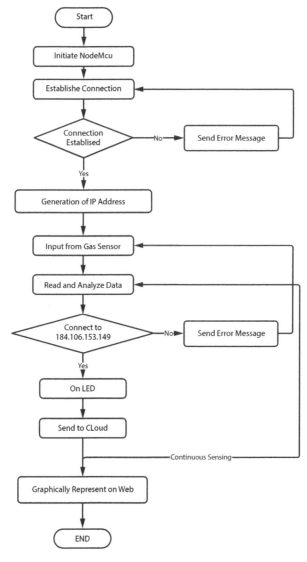

Figure 1.5 Flowchart of noninvasive detection of oral submucous detection device.

and constructs a datasheet which helps to identify which part is affected by oral cancer at the end onboard LED confirms the sensor properly detects or not. Continuing this process till the whole surface is examined.

1.4.4   Process to Connect to Sever and Analyzing Data on Cloud

In this part, we will demonstrate how to simulate physical device behavior such that data are sent to the appropriate data bucket. The device must be programmed so that it can connect to the platform, read sensor information, and write to the data bucket once it has been set up to allow device connections and a data bucket has been established for data storage. When it comes to programming the device, it will utilize the Arduino environment and the GasLevelMonitoring libraries, both of which need some tweaking to work with the ESP8266 microcontroller on which it is built. When you first add the GasLevelMonitoring to the Arduino environment, to add a new board to the Arduino environment, follow the instructions found at http://docs.Thinger.io/hardware/climaStick. The technique is documented in great depth at that location. All that is left is to model the GasLevelMonitoring gadget and then transmit the data to the destination folder on the Thinger.io platform. ThinkSpeak's basic programming language has been presented in the preceding section as a method to represent.

The following arguments are specified for Connection:

- USERNAME It is the username we selected throughout the registration procedure.
- DEVICE ID It is the device's identification, in this case, GasLevelMonitoring, that we utilize in the registration procedure.
- DEVICE CREDENTIAL In our case, SKP9YQY2CFVNK919. It is the device's credential that we utilize in the registration procedure.
- SSID With this method, the device will be connected to this Wi-Fi network, which is called "Meeble."
- SSID PASSWORD is the password for the wireless network interface device which identifies for connection to the Internet for communication, this is what we have here. "MeebleLabs."

A variable named thing of type GasLevelMonitoring is initialized with the USERNAME, DEVICE ID, and DEVICE API KEY parameters, which symbolizes our module and allows us to connect to the sensor through Wi-Fi and get data from it. Following that, inside the setup method (which is only called once at the start of the application), it is done:

- Using the device's SSID settings and SSID PASSWORD to set up the device's Wi-Fi connection. The add Wi-Fi function is used to connect to a wireless network.
- Open the serial monitor after uploading the code to test whether Wi-Fi is working. Ascertain that the baud rate is 115200. In this case, the gas level will be shown as a percentage and relayed to ThingSpeak if Wi-Fi is available. As shown in Figure 1.6, the Arduino software's serial monitor is in use.

In Figure 1.7, the console of Think Speak is shown with the values in the graph, which define the level of gases in every sort of area of the mouth area.

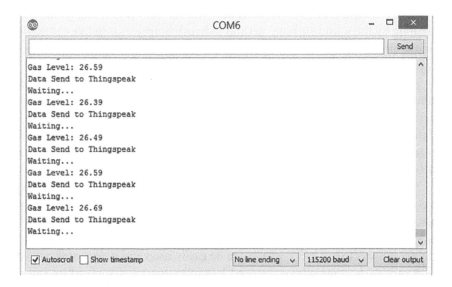

Figure 1.6 Serial monitor.

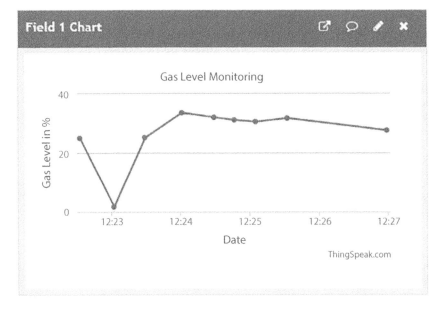

Figure 1.7 Think Speak Console.

1.5   Comparative Study

There are several methods for detection of Oral Cancer starting from vital staining by the toluidine blue method to brush biopsy, exfoliative cytology, liquid biopsy, CT Scan, MRI, PET CT, HPLC, different types of spectroscopy, and advanced diagnostic tools like molecular markers [30].

Among all these sophisticated methods incisional biopsy is the gold standard for detection and final diagnosis of oral cancer. Biopsy not only determines the disease but also grades the level of cancer (well-differentiated, moderately differentiated, or poorly differentiated squamous cell carcinoma), depth of malignancy, muscular or perineural invasion also be detected.

A biopsy is an invasive procedure and needs experienced surgical hands, a good amount of armamentarium and infrastructural supports and biopsy also facilitate the distant metastasis procedure. The term biopsy still causes anxiety and apprehension to the patient. Here we discuss and formulate digital sensors using IoHT which can be easily used and detect oral cancer in a very early stage where we need less infrastructural support and in a noninvasive way. And using advanced web-based API is a very effective way to identify the stage of oral cancer and it is the solution that is not so much complicated to use and comprehend the result.

1.6   Conclusion

This study also includes an implementation architecture for the proposed system, as well as a prototype design for a patient side unit (PSU). The suggested method has the potential to be used as a means of eliminating costly and tiresome hospital trips while maintaining a comparable level of medical care while at home.

There is no close-to-home device available today that can be used to monitor dental health at home. The purpose of the proposed model is to design a sophisticated, multimodal, personalized oral detection device that collects data in a real-time environment and provides intelligent advice regarding oral illness and periodontal disease. The plots give a visualization of the affected area within the mouth. Identifying the more affected zone makes the ease of treatment and increases the rate of curability.

The present diagnosis includes a gold standard method of histological slide evaluation, which is an invasive method and a time-consuming process. It will also help in reducing subjective errors in diagnosis.

References

1. Schoder, D. and Hassan, Q.F., Introduction to the Internet of Things, in: *Internet of Things A to Z: Technologies and Applications*, pp. 1–50, John Wiley & Sons, Inc., Hoboken, NJ, USA, 2018.
2. Mehrotra, R. and Gupta, D.K., Exciting new advances in oral cancer diagnosis: Avenues to early detection. *Head Neck Oncol.*, 3, 1, 1–9, 2011.
3. Rai, V., Mukherjee, R., Ghosh, A.K., Routray, A., Chakraborty, C., "Omics" in oral cancer: New approaches for biomarker discovery. *Arch. Oral Biol.*, 87, 15–34, 2018.
4. Rai, V., Bose, S., Saha, S., Kumar, V., Chakraborty, C., Delineating metabolic dysfunction in cellular metabolism of oral submucous fibrosis using 1H nuclear magnetic resonance spectroscopy. *Arch. Oral Biol.*, 97, 102–108, Jan 2019.
5. Rai, V., Bose, S., Saha, S., Chakraborty, C., Evaluation of oxidative stress and the microenvironment in oral submucous fibrosis. *Heliyon*, 5, 4, 1–14, Apr 12 2019.
6. Rai, V., Mukherjee, R., Routray, A., Ghosh, A.K., Roy, S., Ghosh, B.P., Mandal, P.B., Bose, S., Chakraborty, C., Serum-based diagnostic prediction of oral submucous fibrosis using FTIR spectrometry. *Spectrochim. Acta A Mol. Biomol. Spectrosc.*, 189, 322–329, Jan 15 2018.

7. Kruger, E. and Tennant, M., Socioeconomic disadvantage and oral-health-related hospital admissions: A 10-year analysis. *BDJ Open*, 2, 1, 1–7, 2016.

8. Hassani, H., Andi, P.A., Ghodsi, A., Norouzi, K., Komendantova, N., Unger, S., Shaping the future of smart dentistry: From Artificial Intelligence (AI) to Intelligence Augmentation (IA). *IoT*, 2, 510–523, 2021. https://doi.org/10.3390/iot2030026.

9. Jung, S.-K. and Kim, T.-W., New approach for the diagnosis of extractions with neural network machine learning. *Am. J. Orthod. Dentofacial Orthop.*, 149, 1, 127–133, 2016.

10. Speight, P.M., Elliott, A.E., Jullien, J.A., Downer, M.C., Zakzrewska, J.M., The use of artificial intelligence to identify people at risk of oral cancer and pre-cancer. *Br. Dent. J.*, 179, 10, 382–7, Nov 25 1995.

11. Bianco, R., Melisi, D., Ciardiello, F., Tortora, G., Key cancer cell signal transduction pathways as therapeutic targets. *Eur. J. Cancer*, 42, 3, 290–4, Feb 2006.

12. Mathon, N.F. and Lloyd, A.C., Cell senescence and cancer. *Nat. Rev. Cancer*, 1, 3, 203–213, 2001.

13. Diaz-Ruiz, R., Uribe-Carvajal, S., Devin, A., Rigoulet, M., Tumor cell energy metabolism and its common features with yeast metabolism. *Biochim. Biophys. Acta*, 1796, 2, 252–65, Dec 2009.

14. Gupta, M., Mhaske, S., Ragavendra, R., Oral submucous fibrosis: Current concepts in etiopathogenesis *People's Journal of Scientific Research (PJSR)*, 1, 39–44, July 08 2008.

15. Christofk, H.R., Vander Heiden, M.G., Harris, M.H., Ramanathan, A., Gerszten, R.E., Wei, R., Fleming, M.D., Schreiber, S.L., Cantley, L.C., The M2 splice isoform of pyruvate kinase is important for cancer metabolism and tumour growth. *Nature*, 452, 7184, 230–3, Mar 13 2008.

16. Blekherman, G., Laubenbacher, R., Cortes, D.F., Mendes, P., Torti, F.M., Akman, S., Torti, S.V., Shulaev, V., Bioinformatics tools for cancer metabolomics. *Metabolomics*, 7, 3, 329–343, Sep 2011.

17. González-Moles, M.Á., Warnakulasuriya, S., González-Ruiz, I., González-Ruiz, L., Ayén, Á., Lenouvel, D., Ruiz-Ávila, I., Ramos-García, P., Worldwide prevalence of oral lichen planus: A systematic review and meta-analysis. *Oral. Dis.*, 27, 4, 813–828, May 2021.

18. Wang, L. and Tang, Z., Immunopathogenesis of oral submucous fibrosis by chewing the areca nut. *J. Leukoc. Biol.*, 111, 2, 469–476, 2021.

19. Aylıkcı, B.U. and Çolak, H., Halitosis: From diagnosis to management. *J. Nat. Sci. Biol. Med.*, 4, 1, 14, 2013.

20. Izidoro, C. *et al.*, Periodontitis, Halitosis and oral-health-related quality of life—A cross-sectional study. *J. Clin. Med.*, 10, 19, 4415, 2021.

21. Yasumoto, K., Yamaguchi, H., Shigeno, H., Survey of real-time processing technologies of IoT data streams. *J. Inf. Process.*, 24, 195–202, 2016. [CrossRef].

22. Guth, J., Breitenbücher, U., Falkenthal, M., Leymann, F., Reinfurt, L., Comparison of IoT platform architectures: A field study based on a reference

architecture, in: *Proceedings of the IEEE Cloudification of the Internet of Things (CIoT)*, Paris, France, pp. 1–6, November 23–25 2016.

23. Fernández, P., Santana, J.M., Ortega, S., Trujillo, A., Suárez, J.P., Domínguez, C., Santana, J., Sánchez, A., SmartPort: A platform for sensor data monitoring in a seaport based on FIWARE. *Sensors*, 16, 417, 2016. [CrossRef] [PubMed].

24. López-Riquelme, J., Pavón-Pulido, N., Navarro-Hellín, H., Soto-Valles, F., Torres-Sánchez, R., A software architecture based on FIWARE cloud for Precision Agriculture. *Agric. Water Manag.*, 183, 123–135, 2017. [CrossRef].

25. Sinha, N., Pujitha, K.E., Alex, J.S.R., Xively based sensing and monitoring system for IoT, in: *Proceedings of the IEEE International Conference on Computer Communication and Informatics (ICCCI)*, Coimbatore, India, pp. 1–6, January 8–10 2015.

26. Pasha, S., ThingSpeak based sensing and monitoring system for IoT with Matlab Analysis. *Int. J. New Technol. Res.*, 2, 19–23, 2016.

27. Ray, P.P., A survey of IoT cloud platforms. *Future Comput. Inf. J.*, 1, 35–46, 2016. [CrossRef].

28. Hunkeler, U., Truong, H.L., Stanford-Clark, A., MQTT-S—A publish/subscribe protocol for wireless sensor networks, in: *Proceedings of the IEEE 3rd International Conference on Communication Systems Software and Middleware and Workshops (COMSWARE 2008)*, Bangalore, India, pp. 791–798, January 6–10 2008.

29. Singh, K.J. and Kapoor, D.S., Create your own Internet of Things: A survey of IoT platforms. *IEEE Consum. Electron. Mag.*, 6, 57–68, 2017. [CrossRef].

30. Borse, V., Konwar, A.N., Buragohain, P., Oral cancer diagnosis and perspectives in India. *Sens. Int.*, 1, 1–12, 2020.

Performance Evaluation of Machine Learning and Deep Learning Techniques: A Comparative Analysis for House Price Prediction

Sajeev Ram Arumugam[1]*, Sheela Gowr[2], Abimala[3], Balakrishna[2] and Oswalt Manoj[4]

[1]Department of AI&DS, Sri Krishna College of Engineering and Technology, Coimbatore, India
[2]Department of CSE, Vels Institute of Science, Technology & Advanced Studies, Chennai, India
[3]Department of ICE, St Joseph's College of Engineering, Chennai, India
[4]Department of CSBS, Sri Krishna College of Engineering and Technology, Coimbatore, India

Abstract

Prediction is the act of forecasting what will happen in the future. The field of prediction is gaining more importance in almost all the fields. Machine learning techniques have been used widely for predictions also in recent time deep learning algorithms gain more importance. In this paper, we will be performing prediction over a dataset using both machine learning and deep learning techniques, and the performance of each method will be identified and compared with each other. We have used the house price dataset, which consists of 80 features, which will help to explore data visualization methods, data splitting, data normalization techniques. We have implemented five regression-based machine learning models including Simple Linear Regression, Random Forest Regression, Ada Boosting Regression, Gradient Boosting Regression, Support Vector Regression were used. Deep learning models, including artificial neural network, multi output regression, regression using Tensorflow-Keras were also used for regression.

*Corresponding author: imsajeev@gmail.com

Rajdeep Chakraborty, Anupam Ghosh, Jyotsna Kumar Mandal and S. Balamurugan (eds.) Convergence of Deep Learning In Cyber-IoT Systems and Security, (21–66) © 2023 Scrivener Publishing LLC

The study was further extended to compare the performance of the classification models and hence six machine learning models and three deep learning models including logistic regression classifier, decision tree classifier, random forest classifier, Naïve Bayes classifier, k-nearest neighbor classifier, support vector machine classifier, feed forward neural network, recurrent neural network, LSTM recurrent neural networks were used. The models were also fine-tuned and results were also compared using performance metrics. We have split our dataset in to 70:30 ration for training and testing. In regression models random forest algorithms were performing better with MAE score 0.12, MSE score 0.55, RMSE score 0.230 and R2 score of 0.85 and in deep learning Tensorflow-Keras–based regression model was performing well with MAE score 0.12, MSE score 0.54, RMSE score 0.210 and R2-Score of 0.87, while in the other side, the classification model, random forest model, was performing good with accuracy of 89.21%, and in deep learning classification technique, feed forward neural network model, was performing good with accuracy of 89.52%. Other performance metrics including Cohen kappa score, Matthews correlation coefficient, average precision, average recall, and F1 score were also calculated to compare the performance.

Keywords: Machine learning, deep learning, KNN, SVM, CNN, RNN, prediction system, tensorflow

2.1   Introduction

Making predictions from an existing data are always typically the toughest job, as the predictions play a major role in making decisions. With the advancement in technology, we have bunches of algorithms with us, which helps us to do the prediction easier. Machine learning algorithms gathered huge attention in doing these kinds of predictions due to its higher accuracy rates. In recent days, deep learning algorithms (a part of machine learning algorithm) are used in almost all applications for carrying out the prediction tasks.

Predictions are majorly classified into regression-based and classification-based. In regression-based algorithms, we get with a single valued output, and in classification based, we come up with 2 or more than two outputs based on the labels available in the dataset. In this work, as we try to predict the selling price of the house, these experiment falls under regression problem and hence mostly used regression algorithms are being built and their performance are measured.

The work's main goal is to figure out how well machine and deep learning algorithms function, and hence, we have to check with the classification-based algorithms, and hence, the existing database is labeled based on the selling price, and with the modified dataset, classification algorithms are also build.

The rest of the chapter is organized as section 2.2 discuss the related works, we have done two related researches, survey about articles which compares the performance of different ML and DL algorithms and articles that discuss about prediction of price of the house. Section 2.3 will be the research methodology that gives a detail of how the research work was carried on from data collection till calculating the performance of the algorithms. Section 2.4 describes about how the experimentation is taken place. Section 2.5 discussion on results, section 2.6 is the suggestions, and section 2.7 concludes the research work.

2.2 Related Research

By forecasting the price of a house based on features provided, we hope to evaluate the performance of ML and DL methods. Our primary goal is to analyze and compare the performance of the prediction system, hence the related work is narrated as two sections. In the first section of related research, we discuss about few works in which the authors tried to compare the performance of the ML and DL algorithms and in the second section we discuss about some of the works carried out for predicting the house price. Section 2.1 various related works using ML and DL algorithms are discussed and in section 2.2 works in the field of house price prediction is discussed.

2.2.1 Literature Review on Comparing the Performance of the ML/DL Algorithms

Sewak *et al.* [1] presented the work of comparing the performance of machine learning algorithms for detection of malware in a system based on few features. Authors have used necessary dataset for training the system. As the dataset used had issues with data unbalancing, they have used Adaptive Synthetic (ADASYN) and have built models using machine learning-based random forest (RF) algorithm and deep learning–based deep neural network (DNN) algorithms. Various performance metrics were used for evaluating the performance and finally came up with 99.78%, 99.21% accuracy for RF and DNN methods.

Doleck *et al.* [2] gave a comparative analysis report of effectiveness of online education. They have used classification-based machine and deep learning methods over online education dataset and compared their performances. The authors have handled two dataset from MOOC and the other one from CEGEP Academic Performance. Neural networks are built using the predefined API from Keras and Tensorflow. They have also used few ML algorithms namely k-nearest neighbors (KNN), logistic regression (LR), Naive Bayes (NB), and support vector machine (SVM). In this method, they have tested the model with different optimizers, such as adadelta, adagrad, adam, adamax, nadam, and the accuracy of the models were presented using visual graphs. The accuracy using the MOOC dataset was identified to be 58.29% to 69.19% and while using CEGEP Academic Performance dataset the accuracy was identified to be 62.20% to 90.32%

Dong and Wang [3] came up with a comparative study for predicting the network intrusion. They compared deep learning approaches, such as the restricted Boltzmann machine (RBM), and back propagation (BP) with some of the traditional methods Native Bayes, random forests, decision tree, and SVM. They have used KDD-99 data set for training and testing the models which consists of data with four different classes. The dataset was holding unbalancing issue and hence synthetic minority oversampling technique (SMOTE) oversampling technique was used. Performance measures, including precision and recall, were used and concluded hybrid method combining SVM and RBM was performing better.

Liu *et al.* [4] presented a comparative analysis of three deep learning methods, namely region-based convolutional neural networks (R-CNN) and expanded convolutional neural network (U-NET) in identification of birds from aerial images. Authors used Little Birds in Aerial Imagery (LBAI) dataset which consists of 34,442 photos of birds captured in a farm. The system was evaluated using some of the performance metrics including precision, recall, F1 score, and mean absolute error (MAE). U-Net model, managed to give good performance with precision of 0.861, F1 score of 0.819 and MAE of 38.5.

Chen and McKeeverSarah [5] proposed a comparative analysis for analyzing text in social media and identify the abusive contents. Authors have collected and used datasets from social media pages like Twitter, YouTube, Myspace, forum spring, Kongregate and slash dot. The goal of the research was to compare deep learning algorithms to classic machine learning algorithms, namely decision tree, logistic regression, SVM, Naïve Bayes, CNN, and RNN. For comparing the performance of the systems, they have used the metric recall. Authors concludes that SVM was performing better than other ML and DL models.

Alakus *et al.* [6] considered the need of the time and proposed a model, which compares the different deep learning methods for predicting

COVID-19 infections. In the work, the authors have used 18 laboratory data consisting details of 600 patients by which the models are trained. They developed different deep learning models including artificial neural network (ANN), recurrent neural networks (RNN), long short-term memory (LSTM) and convolutional neural networks (CNN). Performance measuring metrics including precision, F1-score, recall, AUC, and accuracy score was used. They concluded the work with LSTM was performing better than other models with F1-score of 91.89%, accuracy of 86.66%, AUC of 62.50%, precision of 86.75%, and recall of 99.42%.

2.2.2 Literature Review on House Price Prediction

Ghosalkar and Dhage [7] proposed a house price prediction method using traditional linear regression model. To train and validate the model, authors have collected data for Mumbai home prices from zillo.com and magicbricks.com. Various performance parameters, such as mean absolute error (MAE), root mean squared error (RMSE), and mean squared error (MSE), were calculated and the model had a minimum prediction error of 0.3713.

Phan [8], for forecasting the price of properties in Melbourne, Australia, employed a variety of machine and deep learning approaches, such as polynomial regression, regression trees, and feed forward neural networks. Authors have used Melbourne Housing Market dataset for training and validating the models. Principal component analysis (PCA) was also used which handles the feature selection part. Finally, the mean square error (MSE) is determined to assess the system's performance, and it was identified that linear regression performed better in terms of MSE score and execution time.

Nahib *et al.* [9] presented a model on predicting the real estate value of King County region in Seattle. Different prediction models like linear regression, multivariate regression models, polynomial regression were used. After evaluating the models' performance using the root mean square score, the authors came to the conclusion that none of the approaches generated appropriate models. For improving the performance of the system, authors further suggested to use a bigger dataset and also to involve a more complex model.

Varma [10] tried to predict the house price in Mumbai, they used linear regression, forest regression, boosted regression, neural networks models for predicting the price. The data analysis part and feature selection and the prediction were represented in an easily understandable manner. But the authors did not evaluate the performance and compared with other prediction models.

Madhuri *et al.* [11] used datasets from Vijayawada, Andrapradesh to predict the price of homes in the city. In the study, they have implemented Ridge, Multiple linear, LASSO, gradient boosting elastic net, and Ada Boost Regression models for making the prediction. For evaluating the performance of the models, when compared to the other models employed, the authors determined that the gradient boosting approach had the best accuracy.

Panda *et al.* [12] performed two predictions: to predict the salary of employees a specific number of years and predicting the real estate values. The authors have used datasets from Kaggle for training and validation. The models Simple Linear Regression (SLR) and Multiple Linear Regression (MLR) algorithms were implemented for predictions. The performance of the system was measured using R-squared value, MAE, MSE, RMSE, MDAE, and Variance Score. Finally, the authors concluded that the Multiple Linear Regression model was performing better for both the predictions when compared with other models.

Rawool *et al.* [13] presented a house prediction model using linear regression, decision tree regression, K-means regression, and random forest regression. The dataset was obtained from online real estate websites and repository and have used median values to fill the empty faces in it. The root mean square error (RMSE) was used to assess the model's performance, and it was discovered that random forest models outperformed the others.

2.3   Research Methodology

The basic process of the work involves the following seven steps,

     I.   Data Collection
    II. Data Visualization
   III. Data Preparation
   IV. Regression Models
    V. Classification Models
   VI. Performance Metrics for Regression Models
  VII. Performance Metrics for Classification Models

Although house prediction falls on the regression problem, to explore about the deep learning models, we have used both regression and classification models and made predictions. the rest of the section is organized as section 2.3.1 describes about data collection methods, section 2.3.2 describes about the different data visualization techniques, Section 2.3.3

describes the data preparation methodology, section 2.3.4 describes the working of different regression models, section 2.3.5 describes different classification models, section 2.3.6 describes different performance metrics for regression model, and finally, section 2.3.7 describes about different performance metrics used for evaluating the classification models.

2.3.1   Data Collection

For training and testing a machine learning or deep learning method, it is more important we hold a good dataset with all the necessary information available in it, after going through many datasets finally we end up with a public available dataset in Kaggle for house price detection [14]. The dataset holds 79 features with 2919 records in total which is split in to two csv files train and test, which holds 1460 and 1459 records, respectively. The house price of the records in the test dataset is available as a separate csv file named sample submissions.

The dataset which we collected can be used for regression methods directly as it holds the price of the house in it, but to use for classification models a categorial output is required, and hence, we have converted the price in to categorical data. The minimum price of the home is 34,900 and the max price was listed as 75500, hence we separated the price field into four classes. Class 0: houses holding the price less than 100,000, Class 1: homes priced between 100 and 200 thousand, Class 2: houses priced between 200,000 and 300,000, and Class 3: Houses which are priced more than 300,000. None of the features in the dataset was modified other than the house price. After converting the house price to class categories, we have proceeded with classification models.

2.3.2   Data Visualization

Data visualization provides us with a clear information on what is the data about and make us understand about the pattern of data available in it. Before passing the dataset to machine learning or deep learning models, it is good to have only the necessary features and remove the features, which could not help us in predictions. Data visualizations also have the following advantages, identifying patterns, better analysis, finding errors, quick action, exploring business insights, understanding the story, grasping the latest trends [15].

Visualizations, such as infographics, heatmap, fever charts, area chart, and histogram, could be used [16] and in our work we have implemented histogram, box plot, quantile plot, scatter plot, and count plot.

Histogram: a graphical bar chart that shows data on the horizontal axis and counts on the vertical axis [17].

Box Plot: also termed as whisker plot used to represent the spread and the center of the data, this helps us to identify the min, max, mean, median, and average of the data [18].

Quantile Plot: Graphical method of identifying if two of the data are of the same distribution. It plots the again two data and explore the common distributions [19].

Scatter Plot: a sort of chart that depicts the relationship between variables by using dots to represent each variable [20].

Count Plot: a similar plot to histogram which could be used not only for numeric data, but also for categorial data [21].

2.3.3   Data Preparation

Data preparation is often referred as data preprocessing, it is the process of making modifications in the raw data before proceeding to machine and deep learning techniques. It includes handling missing records, improperly formatted, anomalies, inconsistent values, and limited attributes [22].

In our work the following data pre-processing steps are performed

   a. Merging the train and test csv files
   b. Identifying the null values available with the dataset and the features have more null values have to be identified and removed (using drop command)
   c. Separate the dataset into numeric and categorical data
   d. Identify the most prominent features in numeric data and could be converted to categorial data by converting the type from integer to string.
   e. For the numeric data, we have to perform two operations (i) filling the missing values, (ii) scaling the data.
       a. kNN Imputation: a method of finding a new sample and imputing it in the place of missed values. identifies the nearest samples and takes an average of it and impute the new values [23].
       b. Standard Scalar: Scaling is a process of fitting the data in a particular scale, for which we have used standard scalar function. It scales the data to have a mean of 0 (zero) and a standard deviation of 1 (one) [24].

    f.   Converting the categorial value to numeric value using ordinal encoder. Ordinal encoding assign a unique value for every category [25].

Finally, splitting the modified data set to training and testing data set in ratio 80:20.

2.3.4   Regression Models

In our work, for estimating the price of the house, we utilized five machine learning and three deep learning models, as mentioned below.

- Simple Linear Regression
- Random Forest Regression
- Ada Boosting Regression
- Gradient Boosting Regression
- Support Vector Regression
- Artificial Neural Network
- Multi Output Regression
- Regression using Tensorflow-Keras

2.3.4.1   *Simple Linear Regression*

The optimum link between the input characteristics and the output parameter is determined using linear regression. (to be predicted value) in which both of them are founded to be continues [26]. The model of linear regression looks more similar to that of slope of a line and it is shown in Equation 2.1.

$$y = \alpha + \beta x \qquad (2.1)$$

Where,
    y represents the y- coordinates
    α represents the y intercepts
    β represents the slope of the line
    x represents the x- coordinates

Implementation of linear regression

    i.   Analyze the dataset
    ii. Get the training model to build the model

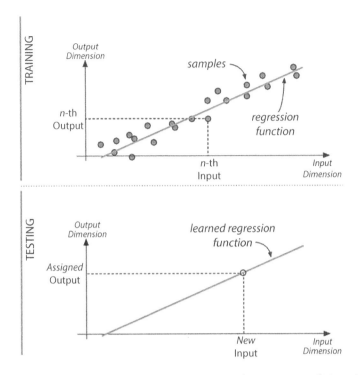

Figure 2.1 Linear Regression Classification. (Source: Machine Learning of Musical Gestures [27]).

    iii.   Using Equation 2.1 the model is built
    iv.   Using the developed model, the new predictions are made

Once the model is developed, all the necessary input parameters are fed to the model and required predictions are made, provided both the parameters and the predictors must be of continues variables, and the prediction can be clearly understood from Figure 2.1.

2.3.4.2   Random Forest Regression

Random forest method is an ensemble-based technique that can do both regression and classification problems (by creating several models and then combining all of the results). It creates multiple decision tree and make prediction for every tree and the results are finally combined for the best results [28].

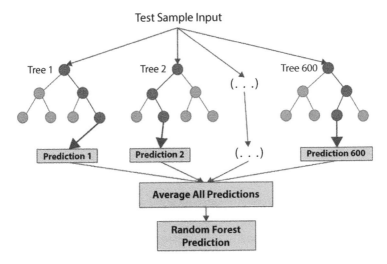

Figure 2.2 Random forest regression model. (Source: A Research Paper on Loan Delinquency Prediction [29]).

Implementation of forest regression

I.   Get the training data from the dataset
II. Build a decision tree based in the training dataset
III. The number of trees that have to be built is decided
IV. The average of the tree's individual forecasts is used to get the final prediction

Figure 2.2 shows the working of random forest algorithm in detail.

2.3.4.3   Ada Boosting Regression

Boosting is a method of converting the weaker model into a stronger model, Ada boosting is also a type of ensemble model, it is also known as adaptive model. In this model for every instance, the weight of the model is re assigned. As it reduces the bias and the variance by boosting, it is termed as Ada Boosting. The major difference between Ada and random forest is, in random forest n number of leaves can be created from a stem, but in case of Ada only two leaves are allowed for a stem. For every stem, the performance is calculated and the performance is increased by modifying by adjusting the weights of the model [30]. The model is demonstrated in Figure 2.3.

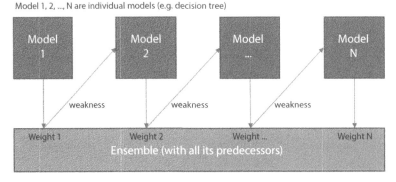

Figure 2.3 Ada boosting regression. (Source: towardsdatascience.com [31]).

Implementation of Ada Boosting Regression

    I.   Assign equal weights to all the observations
    II.   Classify random samples using stumps
    III. Calculate Total Error of the model
    IV. Calculate Performance of the Stump
    V.   Update Weights in the observation
    VI. Update weights in iteration
    VII. Final Predictions

2.3.4.4 Gradient Boosting Regression

Gradient boosting algorithm are one of the most popular regression models, also it is identified to be more effective than random forest and adaptive boosting algorithms. As like random forest and adaptive boosting, gradient boosting is also an ensemble-based model. The main ideology behind the model is to boost to the new model [32]. It continuously creates tree with boosting the previous model, and hence the new model is identified to be more superior than the previous tree as shown in Figure 2.4.

Implementation of Gradient Boosting Regression

    I. From the raw datasets split the train dataset
    II. Create a decision tree and fit the model using the training data
    III. Calculate the error and fit the next tree by boosting the previous tree
    IV. Repeat step I – III till we get the required results.

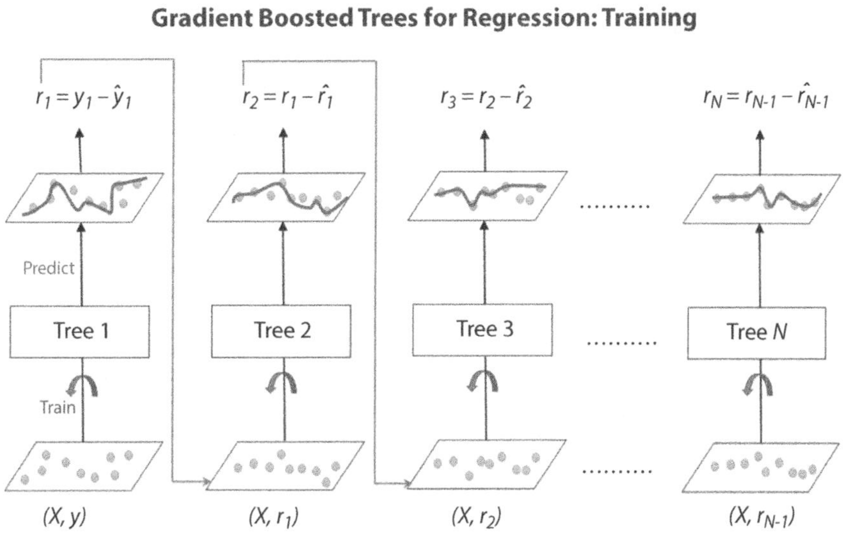

Gradient Boosted Trees for Regression: Training

$r_1 = y_1 - \hat{y}_1$ $r_2 = r_1 - \hat{r}_1$ $r_3 = r_2 - \hat{r}_2$ $r_N = r_{N-1} - \hat{r}_{N-1}$

Predict

| Tree 1 | Tree 2 | Tree 3 | .... | Tree N |

Train

(X, y) (X, r_1) (X, r_2) (X, r_{N-1})

Figure 2.4 Gradient boosting regression. (Source: deepnote.me [33]).

2.3.4.5 *Support Vector Regression*

Support vector regression (SVM), which are considered to be more famous and most used classification-based machine learning algorithms, mostly researchers use SVM machines in classification and it is being used very rarely in Regression platforms. SVM classifier creates a hyperplane and tries to classify the data accordingly but in SVM regressor we create a decision boundary from the hyperplane on both sides termed as positive and negative hyperplane [34]. Only the points which are available inside the plane are considered and they are mapped to the hyperplane and the error rate is considered. The new predictions are made by plotting the point using the hyperplane. Figure 2.5 gives more clarity on how the hyperplane, positive and negative hyperplane are drawn and predictions are made.

The equation of the hyperplane can be written as shown in Equation 2.2

$$Y = ix + j \qquad (2.2)$$

where represents the y coordinates
    j represents the y intercepts
    i represents the slope of the line
    x represents the x coordinates

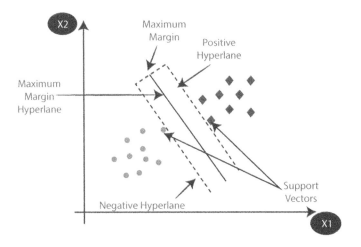

Figure 2.5 Support vector regression. (Source: medium.com [35]).

The equation of the positive and negative hyperplane becomes as in Equation 2.3 and Equation 2.4

$$ix + j = + m \qquad (2.3)$$

$$ix + j = - m \qquad (2.4)$$

And hence the hyperplane must satisfy the Equation 2.5

$$-m < Y - ix + j < + m \qquad (2.5)$$

Implementation of Support Vector Regression

    I.   From the raw datasets split the train dataset
    II. Plot the data in a spatial field
    III. Identify the hyperplane
    IV. Using hyperplane draw the positive and negative hyperplane

Using the hyperplane, the new coordinates are predicted.

2.3.4.6 *Artificial Neural Network*

Artificial neural network (ANN) will be the very first model every researcher uses to perform both regression and classification model under deep learning methodology [36]. The basic implementation strategy of ANN is as follows

   i.   Reading the input data
   ii.   Preparing the mathematical-based prediction model
   iii. Measure the error and performance of the model
   iv. Making necessary changes in the model to optimise the output
   v.   Using the model to make predictions

Artificial neural networks have layers connected with one another; layers hold neurons which are responsible for the predictions. The neurons and layers are arranged as in Figure 2.6.

Input Layer: accepts input from the user
Hidden Layer: Performs necessary calculations for identification of the features
Output Layer: Output is presented to the user

Apart from the layers other two important factors to consider is bias and weights. The input is multiplied with weights and bias is added to it.

Every neuron except which are available with input layer produces an output based on a function called as activation function. As we are dealing

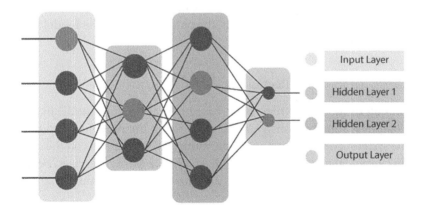

Figure 2.6 Neural network structure. (Source: www.javatpoint.com [37]).

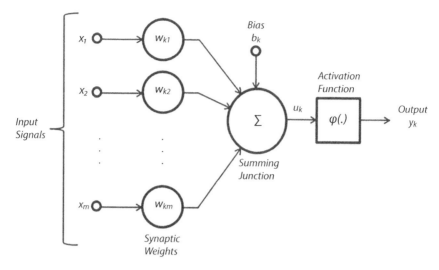

Figure 2.7 Regression function for ANN. (Source: Comparison of linear regression and artificial neural network model of a diesel engine fueled with biodiesel-alcohol mixtures [38]).

with regression problem simple linear regression function will be used as shown in Equation 2.6

$$Y = B + W_1 x_1 + W_2 x_2 + W_3 x_3 + \cdots W_n x_n \qquad (2.6)$$

where, Y is the variable to be predicted, B is the bias, W_1, W_2, W_3.... W_n are the weights of the attributes x_1, x_2, x_3.... x_n are the attributes.

   As we are handling with regression, we need only one output, and hence, we will be having only one neuron in the output layer and the model will be looking as in Figure 2.7.

2.3.4.7   Multioutput Regression

Multi output model is a regression-based neural network model in which the output is simultaneously predicted by using the previous output back to the system. The performance of the model always depends on the quality of the output label which is predicted. And hence extra care has to be taken in labelling the output [39]. Figure 2.8 shows how the output is named in the model.

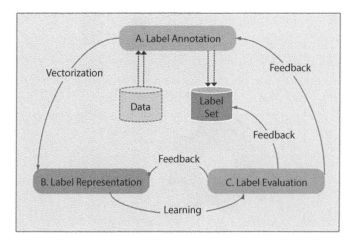

Figure 2.8 Life cycle of multioutput regression model. (Source: Survey on multi-output learning [39]).

Multioutput regression model is capable of handling multiple labels during regression process, which makes it unique from the other regression models beside the output model might be any type like image, text, audio or video. The multi output regression model working is displayed in Figure 2.9.

2.3.4.8 Regression Using Tensorflow—Keras

Tensorflow has an API, which is capable of performing the regression function in just three steps

    i.   Create the network model using Keras API belongs to Tensorflow
    ii.   Train the model
    iii. Test the model

During training the model, it first assigns random weights to each neuron of the model, and based on the model backpropagation is applied to modify the weights to get the desired outputs. The training is done for certain iteration until we get the desired output, also we should take care such that the model does not under train or over train [41]. Once the training and testing are done, predictions can be made.

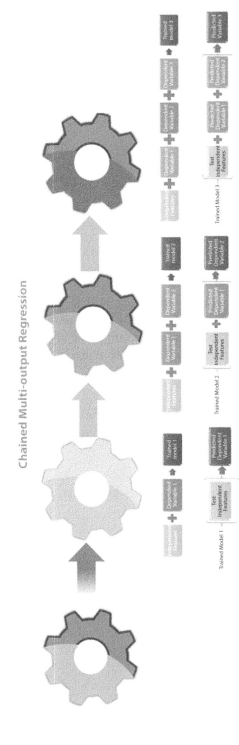

Figure 2.9 Working of multioutput regression. (Source: towardsdatascience.com [40]).

2.3.5 Classification Models

We have similarly carried out classification of house prices too, for that we have used six machine learning and three deep learning classification models as follows

- Logistic Regression Classifier
- Decision Tree Classifier
- Random forest Classifier
- Naïve Bayes Classifier
- k-Nearest Neighbor Classifier
- Support Vector Machine Classifier
- Feed Forward Neural Network
- Recurrent neural network
- LSTM Recurrent Neural Networks

2.3.5.1 *Logistic Regression Classifier*

Logistic regression is a machine learning algorithm for performing classification tasks, this algorithm is meant specially for binary classification but could be used for multi classification also. Logistic regression and logistic classification are more similar to each other, Linear regression deals with the regression problems and the other deals with the classification tasks. Among different classification algorithms, it is considered as one of the significant models as it can handle both continues as well as discrete datasets [42].

Logistic regression has an S-shaped curve between 0 and 1, for predicting a value the number is mapped in the curve and if the point lies in the above region over threshold, it is marked as positive and if on the lower side it marked as negative as shown in Figure 2.10. Logistic regression is of three types, namely binomial, multinominal, and ordinal classification.

2.3.5.2 *Decision Tree Classifier*

Decision tree algorithms is a machine learning algorithm which deals both the regression and classification problems. Decision tree creates a tree structure and have three types of nodes with it, namely root node, decision node, and termination node. Root node are the parent nodes and further divided to further nodes [44]. The decision nodes are nodes which are not a root node but further divides to separable nodes and termination nodes

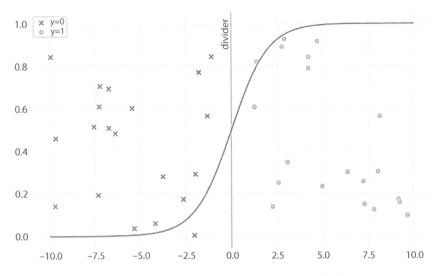

Figure 2.10 Logistic regression. (Source: towardsdatascience.com [43]).

does not have any other branches and it is the last node in the branch as shown in Figure 2.11.

Decision tree uses multiple algorithms to create a split in the node and creating the next nodes which could be terminal or decision node. Identifying the root node is a complex task in decision tree, one possible way for identifying the root node might be random selection but the results might not be as expected and reduces the accuracy of the system,

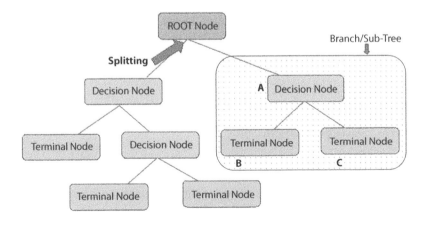

Figure 2.11 Decision tree classifier. (Source: kdnuggets.com [45]).

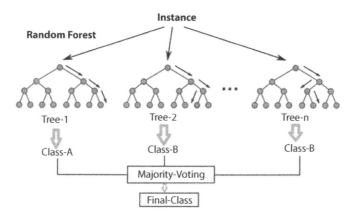

Figure 2.12 Structure of random forest classification. (Source: medium.com [47]).

hence some of the criteria like Gini Index, Gain Ratio, or Chi Square could be used for deciding the Root node.

2.3.5.3   Random Forest Classifier

Random forest classification task is already described in section 2.3.4.2, the model described in 2.3.4.2 was a regression algorithm which takes the average of the score and predict the values [46]. In the case of classification task and voting is done for all the trees and the output, which have the highest vote is chosen as the final output of the model as shown in Figure 2.12.

2.3.5.4   Naïve Bayes Classifier

Naïve bayes classifier is one of the Bayes theorem-based classification algorithm, which makes prediction on the basis of probabilities, and is applied in most of the classification applications including, sentiment analysis, spam detection in mails, etc [48]. Bayes theorem is mathematically described as shown in Equation 2.7

$$P(A \mid B) = \frac{P(B|A)P(A)}{P(B)} \tag{2.7}$$

where P(A|B) chance of A occurring in event B; P(B|A) change of B being true; P(A) chances of A occurring; P(B) chances of B occurring.

Implementing Naïve Bayes

    i.   Calculate the prior probabilities
   ii.   identify the likelihood probabilities
  iii.   substitute all the detected values in the bayes equation and predict the class.

2.3.5.5   K-Nearest Neighbors Classifier

Because of its benefits, such as prediction power and classification speed, the K-nearest neighbour method is one of the most widely used machine learning algorithms in classification tasks. It can also be used for regression problems but not frequently used because of its adaptiveness toward the regression problems. Basically K-nn finds the similarity of new cases and the existing cases and put in a class which have maximum matches. Unlike other algorithms it does not get trained completely using the dataset, instead it stores the dataset and when new variables approach, it performs calculation on the dataset and make predictions [49]. The most important factor that has to considered in K-nn is the identifying the nearest points in the algorithm. The classification is carried out as shown in Figure 2.13.

Implementing K-nn Algorithm

    i.   Identifying the number of neighbours (K value)
   ii.   Calculate the distance between the new variable and the K-points using Euclidean distance
  iii.   Count the number of classes in the k-points
  iv.   Assign the new variable to the class which holds maximum k-points

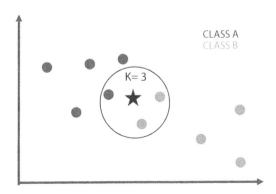

Figure 2.13 Classification based on K-nn algorithm. (Source: edureka.co [50]).

2.3.5.6 Support Vector Machine Classifier (SVM)

Support vector machine (SVM) algorithm which is often used in both regression and classification tasks. The algorithm is already described in section 2.3.4.5. The major difference is as it's a regression the score was calculated and if used for classification the class is identified using the hyper plane.

2.3.5.7 Feed Forward Neural Network

Feed forward neural network is a supervised learning deep learning machine. In this type of network, the information travels only in forward direction, i.e., from the input layer to the hidden layers, and then from the hidden layer to the output layer as shown in Figure 2.14.

A pattern is displayed in the input layer of a feed forward neural network during the learning process, and it is transmitted through the network's subsequent levels until it reaches the output layers. The output layer's neuron count is equal to the number of class labels [52]. The model's output is compared to the real output, and if there is a significant difference, the model is retrained by changing the weight of the neurons. During the classification phase the weights will be fixed and they are not adjusted, the output class is decided by the pattern mapping with the existing patterns.

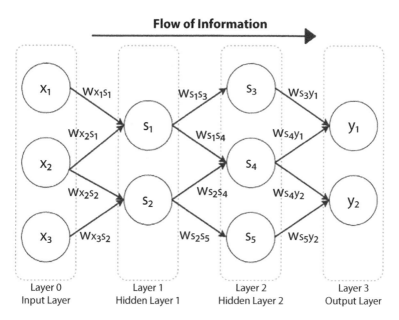

Figure 2.14 Feed forward network. (Source: brilliant.org [51]).

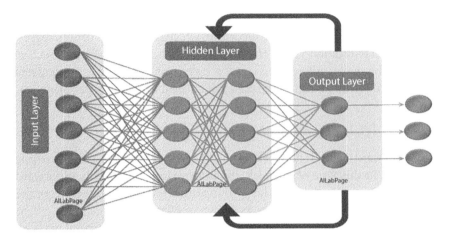

Figure 2.15 Recurrent neural network architecture. (Source: medium.com [54]).

2.3.5.8   Recurrent Neural Networks

Recurrent neural network (RNN) are network-based models used commonly for sequential data. It holds an input memory which helps us to save the previous outputs, which helps in classification of the sequential data [53]. In feed forward network, the information passes from input to output and never comes back, whereas in recurrent neural network the information cycles through a loop as in Figure 2.15.

RNN varies from other networks in that it contains two inputs: as other networks, the current input and the recent variable's output. This model uses backpropagation for optimising the output. It also uses gradient descent which reduces the function.

2.3.5.9   LSTM Recurrent Neural Networks

LSTM neural networks, are specialised network to solve pattern-based predictions. This LSTM model, like the Feed forward model, has input, hidden, and output layers. LSTM layer consists of self-connected recurrent blocks, called as memory blocks. Each block consists of one or more recurrent networks connected to it as shown in Figure 2.16.

The three gates of LSTM are input, forget and output gate, all these gates are fully dependent on the previous hidden layer. The output of the network is decided by the current cell state. These cell states are transferred from one cell to another by the tanh functions.

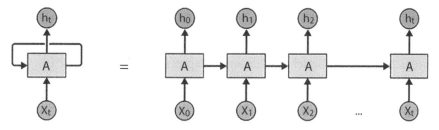

Figure 2.16 Architecture of LSTM network model. (Source: pydeeplearning.weebly.com [55]).

2.3.6   Performance Metrics for Regression Models

Performance metrics are used to identify how efficient our model is prediction. There are many performance measures in which we are using few of the metrics, namely mean absolute error (MAE), mean square error (MSE), root mean square error (RMSE), and R-Squared value (R2 score) is used in this work.

Mean Absolute Error (MAE)
It is used to calculate the average magnitude of prediction mistakes. The MAE is defined in Equation 2.8. A perfect model is it have an MAE score of 0.0.

$$MAE = \frac{\sum_{i=1}^{n} |y_i - x_i|}{n} \tag{2.8}$$

where y_i is the predicted values, x_i is the true value, n is the data count

Mean Square Error (MSE)
The mean of the square difference between the real and forecasted values is calculated using MSE as shown in Equation 2.9. A good model will be holding a MSE value of 0.0

$$MSE = \frac{1}{n} \sum_{i=1}^{n} \left(y_i - \hat{y}_i \right)^2 \tag{2.9}$$

where $\left(y_i - \hat{y}_i \right)$ is the difference between the expected and real values, n is the data count.

Root Mean Square Error

Root mean square error (RMSE) square root of the mean square error value, it tells us how efficiently the data is fit in the model and also how close the predictions of the model is made and is expressed as in Equation 2.10.

$$\text{RMSE} = \sqrt{\frac{\sum_{i=1}^{n}(y_i - \hat{y}_i)^2}{2}} \qquad (2.10)$$

R-Squared value

R-Squared value (R2 score) is closely related to MSE but not the same. It denotes the variance of dependent variable (target variable) from the independent variable (features). It is calculated using Equation 2.11. The model is identified to be more efficient when the score is 1.0

$$R^2 = 1 - \frac{\text{Unexplained Variation}}{\text{Total Variation}} \qquad (2.11)$$

2.3.7   Performance Metrics for Classification Models

The dataset which is used here has four classes in the target variable and hence multiclassification models will be used and the performance metrics including Accuracy, Cohen kappa Score, Matthews correlation coefficient, Precision, Recall, and F1-Score are used.

Accuracy

The ratio of correct predictions to the total number of values in the dataset is called accuracy. Accuracy score will be also depending on the distribution of classes in the dataset. If the distribution of the class is not even, it might result in drop in accuracy.

Cohen Kappa Score

It measures how closely the prediction is made. It can be calculated using two scores total accuracy and random accuracy and is calculated using the Equation 2.12

$$kappa = \frac{(Total\ Accuracy - Random\ Accuracy)}{(1 - Random\ Accuracy)} \qquad (2.12)$$

Matthew Correlation Coefficient (MCC)
Matthew Correlation Coefficient is the measure of quality of classification system. MCC can be calculated Equation 2.13

$$MCC = \sqrt{PPV * TPR * TNR * NPV} - \sqrt{FDR * FNR * FPR * FOR}$$

$$(2.13)$$

where PPV: Positive Predictive Value, TPR: True Positive Rate, TNR: True Negative Rate, NPV: Negative Predictive Value, FDR: False Discovery Rate, FNR: False Negative Rate, FPR: False Positive Rate, and FOR: False Omission Rate.

Precision and Recall
Precision is defined as the proportion of true positives to all positives, while recall is defined as the model's ability to accurately identify true positives. As the model is multi classification the precision and recall are calculated for each class and averaged to get the precision and recall score.

F1 Score
F1 is the measure of test accuracy and using precision and recall are calculated by applying those values in Equation 2.14

$$F1\ score = 2\frac{(Precision * Recall)}{(Precision + Recall}$$

$$(2.14)$$

2.4 Experimentation

The entire implementation was carried over in Google colab platform using python language.
The experimentation process is as follows

- Download the required dataset and upload to the colab platform or google drive for using it
- Necessary library files are installed/imported to the environment
- Data visualization is performed and data is pre-processed
- For regression and classification, the appropriate machine learning and deep learning models are created, trained, and evaluated.

- Necessary validation metrics are calculated and results are tabulated and compares using graphs.

2.5   Results and Discussion

The first step of the work will be exploring the dataset. Table 2.1 describes the dataset and its variables. The dataset consists of 79 variables, every variable is not necessarily required for the predictions however for training purpose all the variables have been included. Most of the variables are numerical and few are categorial data types.

The dataset holds 80 features and have to verify the missed data percentage and identified that five variables hold highest missing percentage: PoolQC-99.52%, MiscFeature-96.30%, Alley-93.76%, Fence-80.75%, FireplaceQu-47.26%. these variables holding highest missing values will be deleted in the data pre-processing step. Few other data variables also holds some missing values but as those variables could be important in predicting the target variables, we are not neglecting it. One of such variables is LotFrontage which holds 17% missing values, but as it could be important variable in detection of price of the house we are not including it in the remove list.

The target value for the dataset is house sale price, and hence we try to visualize the variable before and after logarithm transferred. For this box plot and histogram plots from matplot library is used and shown in Figure 2.17. From the plots its clear that the price of the house is distributed widely between 34,900 and 755,000 USD. Histogram plots the amount of data in the price range and box plot shows the lower and highest value also the mid value of the variable also could be identified.

The dataset holds both the numeric and categoric data, as on numeric data it can be directly fed for training but considering categorial data it is not the case, hence the categorial variables are visualized to identify the distribution of the data, to have an understanding of how to visualize the categorial data, we have done few visualizations for the variables SaleCondition, and OverallQual. In which the first two are plotted using Histogram which is shown in Figure 2.18.

From the histogram few things will be clear, the number of homes is too high if the sale condition is normal and also the number of homes sold is high for the overall quality being 5 to 8. Such interpretations can be made by visualizing these variables. Similarly, box plot also could be used to visualize the variables, one such is visualizing the variable neighbourhood which holds 25 categories in it and shown in Figure 2.19. We could

Table 2.1 Data description in the Dataset.

Variable name	Description	Variable name	Description
MSSubClass	Type of property involved in sale.	BsmtCond	Basement condition score
MSZoning	Tells the zone of the house	BsmtExposure	Basement Exposure (type of wall)
LotFrontage	Property front facing street type	BsmtFinType1	finished area in the basement
LotArea	Size of the house in square feet	BsmtFinSF1	square feet of the home after completion
Street	The street which takes us to the property	BsmtFinType2	finished area in the basement (if multiple types)
Alley	property access from the alley	BsmtFinSF2	finished area of property in sq. feet—type 2
LotShape	Shape of the saleable property	BsmtUnfSF	Unfinished area of basement measured in sq.feet
LandContour	Flat portion available in the property	TotalBsmtSF	Total available area in the basement.
Utilities	Utilities available if any	Heating	Available heaters
LotConfig	Configuration of Lot	HeatingQC	QC of the heater
LandSlope	Slope of the property if available	CentralAir	Is air conditioning available?
Neighborhood	Nearest landmarks	Electrical	Electrical system available in the home
Condition1	Proximity conditions	1stFlrSF	Area of first floor in Sq.feet

(Continued)

Table 2.1 Data description in the Dataset. (*Continued*)

Variable name	Description	Variable name	Description
Condition2	Proximity conditions available incase of more floor	2ndFlrSF	Area of second floor in Sq.feet
BldgType	Type of the Dwelling	LowQualFinSF	Finished square feet
HouseStyle	Style of the Dwelling	GrLivArea	Sq. feet of living area
OverallQual	Overall Quality of house	BsmtFullBath	No of bathrooms in basement (full)
OverallCond	Overall Condition of house	BsmtHalfBath	No of bathrooms in basement (half)
YearBuilt	Year of construction	FullBath	No of bathrooms (full)
YearRemodAdd	Year of remodel (if any)	HalfBath	No of bathrooms (half)
RoofStyle	Roof Type	Bedroom	No of bedrooms above grade
RoofMatl	Material used for Roof	Kitchen	No of kitchens above grade
Exterior1st	Exterior covering	KitchenQual	Quality of kitchen
Exterior2nd	Second Exterior covering if available	TotRmsAbvGrd	No of rooms over grade point
MasVnrType	Type of Masory vener	Functional	Home functionality
MasVnrArea	Masonry veneer area in sq. feet	Fireplaces	Availability of fireplaces

(*Continued*)

Table 2.1 Data description in the Dataset. (*Continued*)

Variable name	Description	Variable name	Description
ExterQual	Exterior quality of the house	FireplaceQu	Fireplace quality of the house
ExterCond	Exterior condition	PavedDrive	Paved driveway
Foundation	Type of the Foundation	WoodDeckSF	Wood deck area
BsmtQual	Basement Height		
GarageType	Location of the Garage	GarageCars	No of car parking avilable
GarageYrBlt	Year of the Garage construction	GarageArea	Area of garage
GarageFinish	Interior structure of the garage	GarageQual	Garage quality point
OpenPorchSF	Open porch available area	GarageCond	Present condition of Garage
EnclosedPorch	Enclosed area	PoolArea	If pool available, size of the pool
3SsnPorch	porch area of the seasons	PoolQC	Quality of the pool in the house
ScreenPorch	Screen size of the porch	Fence	Quality of the fense in the house
YrSold	Year Sold (YYYY)	MiscFeature	Miscellaneous features
SaleType	Type of sales	MiscVal	Net worth of miscellaneous feature available in the house
SaleCondition	Condition of sale	MoSold	Month of the house being sold

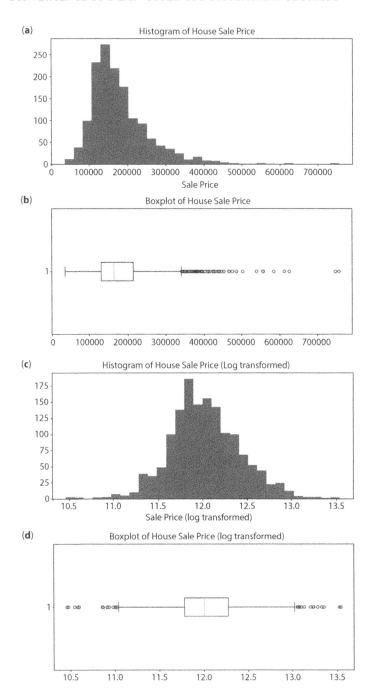

Figure 2.17 Histogram plot (a)(c) and Box plot (b)(d) of the target variable.

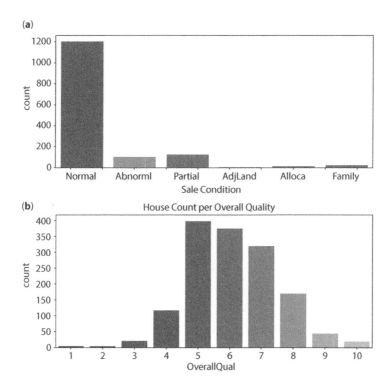

Figure 2.18 Histogram plot for the categoric variable (a) Sale condition and (b) OverallQual.

identify the distribution of the category on sale of the home and categories NridgHt and StoneBr are having high count and this variable could be a strong predicted due to its distribution.

The next step will be data preparation, we have already listed the top 5 features which have more missing variables and hence the variables PoolQC, MiscFeature, Alley, Fence, and FireplaceQu is removed from the dataset. After removing the 5 variables we will be holding 75 variables with us, in which 39 is categorial and 36 numerical variables.

Few of the variables, including MSSubClass, OverallQual, OverallCond, YearBuilt, YearRemodAdd, GarageYrBlt, MoSold, YrSold, are strong predictors with numeric data in it, hence we change these eight variables into categorical data by converting the type of the variable from integer to text making the number of categorial data to 47 and numeric data to 28.

The most important task with the categorial data is to converting it to numeric data for which one hot encoder is used. The data before and after applying one hot encoder is shown in Figure 2.20.

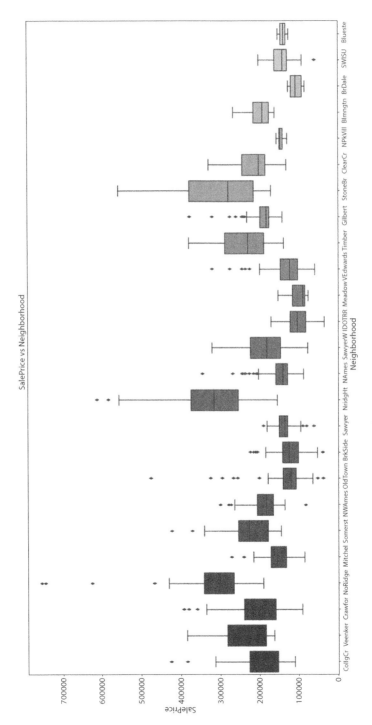

Figure 2.19 Distribution of categories in neighborhood variable.

MSSubClass	MSZoning	Street	LotShape	LandContour	Utilities	LotConfig
120	RL	Pave	Reg	Lvl	AllPub	Inside
60	RL	Pave	Reg	Lvl	AllPub	Inside
20	RL	Pave	Reg	Lvl	AllPub	Inside
75	RM	Pave	IR1	Bnk	AllPub	Corner
120	RL	Pave	Reg	Lvl	AllPub	Inside

(**a**)   Before One hot encoder

MSSubClass	MSZoning	Street	LotShape	LandContour	Utilities	LotConfig	L
0.0	3.0	1.0	3.0	3.0	0.0	4.0	
9.0	3.0	1.0	3.0	3.0	0.0	4.0	
4.0	3.0	1.0	3.0	3.0	0.0	4.0	
11.0	4.0	1.0	0.0	0.0	0.0	0.0	
0.0	3.0	1.0	3.0	3.0	0.0	4.0	

(**b**)   After One hot encoder

Figure 2.20 Categorial variables before and after one hot encoder.

After applying one hot encoder and converting into numeric, still we have few missing variables and hence KNN Impuser is used. The categorial data is now ready, on the other side the numerical data have to be prepared for which the data are applied to KNN Impuser and standard scalar for filling the missing values and scale the data. Finally, the numeric and categorial data are combined together.

With the processed data, all regression models were built, trained, and tested, and the performance metrics for machine learning systems were tallied in Table 2.2 and could be identified that random forest regression performs good than other models with R2score of 0.85.

The deep learning methods were also implemented, and the first model used was artificial neural network-based regression model, and the summary of the model is shown in Figure 2.21. In the ANN based model, we have used input layers with 90 neurons and capable of getting 75 features as input and activation function was Relu. Following the input layer, two hidden layers with 90 neurons each were added and the Relu activation function was employed, followed by the output layer with one neuron and the linear activation function. The loss function is mean squared logarithmic error, the optimizer is ADAM, and the performance metrics are MSE.

The ANN-based model was trained for 100 Epochs with validation split of 20% and batch size of 50. The results of the model were compromising with lower MSE value of 0.36. In multi output regression the layer count was similar to the previous model with one input, two hidden and

Table 2.2 Performance metrics for regression-based machine learning models.

	MAE	MSE	RMSE	R2-score
Linear Regression	0.30	0.18	0.043	0.50
Random Forest Regression	0.12	0.55	0.230	0.85
Gradient Boosting Regressor	0.14	0.6	0.240	0.83
Ada Boost Regressor	0.28	0.14	0.037	0.62
Support Vector Regressor	0.37	0.37	0.061	0.57

one output, he_uniform initializer is used. SGD optimizer, mean squared logarithmic error, loss function, and MSE metrics are utilised to build the model. The model is trained with 100 Epochs with validation split of 20% and batch size of 50.

The final model in regression to be implemented is Tensorflow-Keras–based regression model. The loss function curve for the three deep learning models is shown in Figure 2.22, and the performance metrics for the models are tabulated in Table 2.3.

On the other side the Classification tasks are being carried out using both the machine and deep learning methods, the performance metrics Accuracy, Matthews Correlation coefficient, Cohen kappa Score, Average Recall, Average Precision and average F1 score are computed. For precision, recall and f1score we are considering the average as we will have values for every class individually. The precision and recall for the machine learning techniques is shown in Figure 2.23.

```
Model: "sequential_6"
_____
Layer (type)                 Output Shape              Param #
=================================================================
dense_18 (Dense)             (None, 90)                6840
_____
dense_19 (Dense)             (None, 90)                8190
_____
dense_20 (Dense)             (None, 90)                8190
_____
dense_21 (Dense)             (None, 1)                 91
=================================================================
Total params: 23,311
Trainable params: 23,311
Non-trainable params: 0
_____
```

Figure 2.21 Artificial neural network model for regression.

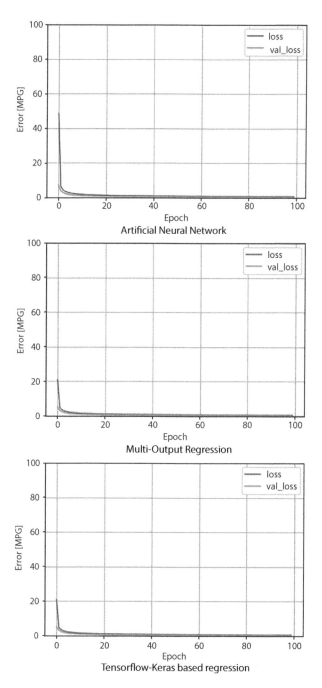

Figure 2.22 Mean_squared_logarithmic_error loss for deep learning models.

Table 2.3 Performance metrics for regression-based deep learning models.

	MAE	MSE	RMSE	R2-score
Artificial Neural Network	0.16	0.7	0.340	0.86
Multi-Output	0.19	0.6	0.230	0.84
Tensorflow-Keras	0.12	0.54	0.210	0.87

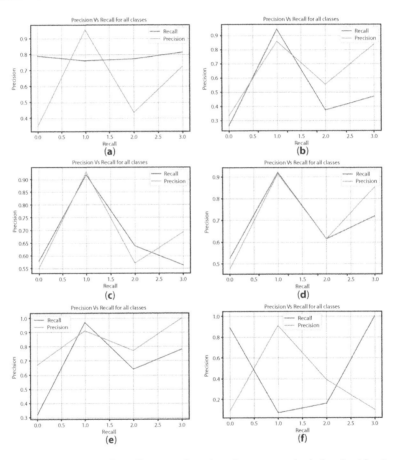

Figure 2.23 Precision and recall scores of machine learning methods for classification task. (a) Logistic regression. (b) K-nearest neighbours. (c) Decision tree. (d) Support vector classification. (e) Random forest. (f) Naïve bayes.

From Figure 2.23, when compared to other classes, accuracy and recall are shown to be greater for Class 1. This might be due to the fact that class 1 has more samples than the other classes. The other performance parameters are listed out in Table 2.4.

Table 2.4 Performance parameters of machine learning models for classification.

	Accuracy	Cohen kappa score	Matthews corrcoef	Average precision	Average recall	F1-score
Logistic regression	76.54	51.74	54.78	61.54	78.32	68.92
K-Nearest Neighbours	81.33	43.56	44.80	64.42	51.19	57.04
Decision Tree	84.76	60.58	60.62	68.50	67.44	67.97
Support Vector Classification	85.27	61.08	61.09	71.41	69.48	70.43
Random Forest	89.21	68.79	69.61	83.75	67.75	74.90
Naïve Bayes	74.82	50.68	52.64	59.44	78.12	67.81

From the performance measures listed in Table 2.4, When comparing the performance parameters of the mentioned machine learning models, it is obvious that the random forest method outperforms the others. Three deep learning networks were employed in this study: feed forward, LSTM, and CNN-based models. The sparse categorical cross entropy loss, SGD optimizer, and accuracy metrics are utilised in all three models.

All the three models are trained for 200epocs and the performance metrics of the three models are listed in Table 2.5 and it is observed that Feed Forward Neural Network is performing well while compared with other classification-based models.

2.6   Suggestions

The article will be helpful for the readers to understand about machine and deep learning algorithms, for the convenience of readers the same dataset is used for both the regression and classification task. However, we suggest the readers to use a dataset, which is prominent for classification to perform the classification task and regression for performing regression tasks. Also, in our dataset, there was no missing data and imbalance in the classes was not identified and hence the results might be difference if we have a dataset with missing values or imbalanced classes.

2.7   Conclusion

Using a home price dataset, we attempted to evaluate the performance of machine learning and deep learning models. The primary objective of this work includes Evaluating the performances of the models using various performance metrics and hence the models were not optimized much to get better results which might lead our system to overfit or underfit and mislead the comparison studies. While evaluating the performance measures, such as MAE, MSE, RMSE, and R2 score, it was identified that Random forest algorithm performs better among Machine learning models and Tensorflow-Keras–based model performs better in Deep Learning Models. On the classification-based models, six performance parameters including Accuracy, Cohen Kappa Score, Matthews Correlation Coefficient, average precision and average recall were calculated and identified random forest classification and feed forward–based neural network was performing good among machine learning (ML) and deep learning (DL) models.

Table 2.5 Performance parameters of deep learning models for classification.

	Accuracy	Cohen kappa score	Matthews corrcoef	Average precision	Average recall	F1-score
Feed Forward Neural Network	89.52	69.54	70.68	83.89	68.64	75.23
LSTM	82.02	44.64	46.20	68.75	48.50	56.87
CNN	84.76	60.58	60.62	68.50	67.44	67.97

It was also discovered that deep learning models outperformed machine learning models in both regression and classification tests.

References

1. Sewak, M., Sahay, S.K., Rathore, H., Comparison of deep learning and the classical machine learning algorithm for the malware detection, in: *19th IEEE/ACIS International Conference on Software Engineering, Artificial Intelligence, Networking and Parallel/Distributed Computing (SNPD)*, pp. 293–296, 2018.

2. Doleck, T., Lemay, D.J., Basnet, R.B., Bazelais, P., Predictive analytics in education: A comparison of deep learning frameworks. *Educ. Inf. Technol.*, 25, 3, 1951–1963, 2020.

3. Dong, B. and Wang, X., Comparison deep learning method to traditional methods using for network intrusion detection, in: *8th IEEE International Conference on Communication Softw are and Networks Comparison*, pp. 581–585, 2016.

4. Liu, Y. *et al.*, Performance comparison of deep learning techniques for recognizing birds in aerial images, in: *Proceedings - 2018 IEEE 3rd International Conference on Data Science in Cyberspace, DSC 2018*, pp. 317–324, 2018.

5. Delany, S.J., Chen, H., McKeever, S., A comparison of classical versus deep learning techniques for abusive content detection on social media sites, in: *Social Informatics*, pp. 117–133, 2018.

6. Turkoglu, I. and Alakus, T.B., Comparison of deep learning approaches to predict COVID-19 infection. *Chaos Solitons Fractals*, 140, 1–8, November 2020.

7. Ghosalkar, N.N. and Dhage, S.N., Real estate value prediction using linear regression, in: *Proceedings - 2018 4th International Conference on Computing, Communication Control and Automation, ICCUBEA 2018*, pp. 1–5, 2018.

8. Phan, T.D., Housing price prediction using machine learning algorithms: The case of Melbourne city, Australia, in: *Proceedings - International Conference on Machine Learning and Data Engineering, iCMLDE 2018*, pp. 8–13, 2019.

9. Nahib, I., Suryanta, J., Analysis, R., Daoud, J., II, Real estate value prediction using multivariate regression models Real estate value prediction using multivariate regression models. *IOP Conf. Ser. Mater. Sci. Eng.*, 4, 1–7, 2017. .

10. Varma, A., House price prediction using machine learning and neural networks, in: *Second International Conference on Inventive Communication and Computational Technologies (ICICCT)*, pp. 1936–1939, 2020.

11. Madhuri, C.H.R., Anuradha, G., Pujitha, M.V., House price prediction using regression techniques: A comparative study, in: *IEEE 6th International Conference on smart structures and systems ICSSS 2019. House*, pp. 1–5, 2019.

12. Kashyap, I., Panda, S.P., Bansal, U., Narang, A., Sachdeva, A., Empirical analysis of regression techniques by house price and salary prediction Empirical

analysis of regression techniques by house price and salary prediction. *IOP Conf. Ser. Mater. Sci. Eng.*, 1022, 43, 1–13, 2021.

13. Rawool, A.G., Rogye, D.V., Rane, S.G., Vinayk, A., House price prediction using machine learning. *IRE Journals*, 4, 11, 29–33, 2021.

14. Kaggle, House prices - Advanced regression techniques. https://www.kaggle. com/c/house-prices-advanced-regression-techniques/data (accessed Jun. 10, 2021).

15. Bold BI, Data visualization: Importance and benefits. https://www.boldbi.com/ blog/data-visualization-importance-and-benefits (accessed Jun. 10, 2021).

16. Analytiks, Why data visualization is important. https://analytiks.co/impor tance-of-data-visualization/ (accessed Jun. 10, 2021).

17. Histogram Definition. https://www.investopedia.com/terms/h/histogram. asp (accessed Jun. 10, 2021).

18. Statistics How To, Box Plot (Box and Whiskers): How to read one & how to make one in excel, TI-83, SPSS. https://www.statisticshowto.com/probability- and-statistics/descriptive-statistics/box-plot/ (accessed Jun. 10, 2021).

19. Quantile-Quantile Plot, https://www.itl.nist.gov/div898/handbook/eda/sec- tion3/qqplot.htm (accessed Jun. 10, 2021).

20. Scatter Plot - Overview. https://corporatefinanceinstitute.com/resources/ knowledge/other/scatter-plot/ (accessed Jun. 10, 2021).

21. Countplot. https://seaborn.pydata.org/generated/seaborn.countplot.html (accessed Jun. 10, 2021).

22. Data Preparation for Machine Learning. https://www.datarobot.com/wiki/ data-preparation/ (accessed Jun. 10, 2021).

23. Al-Helali, B., Chen, Q., Xue, B., Zhang, M., A hybrid GP-KNN imputation for symbolic regression with missing values, in: *AI 2018: Advances in Artificial Intelligence*, pp. 345–357, 2018.

24. Santurkar, S., Tsipras, D., Ilyas, A., Madry, A., How does batch normaliza- tion help optimization? in *32nd Conference on Neural Information Processing Systems (NeurIPS 2018)*, May 2018, 43, pp. 1–26, Accessed: May 17, 2022. [Online]. Available: http://arxiv.org/abs/1805.11604.

25. Potdar, K., Pardawala, T.S., Pai, C.D., A comparative study of categorical vari- able encoding techniques for neural network classifiers. *Int. J. Comput. Appl.*, 175, 4, 7–9, 2017.

26. Vining, G., Montgomery, D.C., Peck, E.A., *Introduction to Linear Regression Analysis*, John Wiley & Sons, United States, 2012.

27. Caramiaux, B. and Tanaka, A., Machine learning of musical gestures. *Proc. Int. Conf. New Interfaces Music. Expr. 2013 (NIME 2013*, pp. 513–518, 2013, [Online]. Available: http://nime2013.kaist.ac.kr/.

28. Li, L., Chen, S., Yang, C., Meng, F., Sigrimis, N., Prediction of plant transpi- ration from environmental parameters and relative leaf area index using the random forest regression algorithm. *J. Clean. Prod.*, 261, 44, 1–13, 2020. doi: https://doi.org/10.1016/j.jclepro.2020.121136.

29. Sarkar, A., Sai, K.K., Prakash, A., Veera, G., Sai, V., Kaur, M., A research paper on loan delinquency prediction. *Int. Res. J. Eng. Technol.*, 8, 4, 715–722, 2021.

30. Taherkhani, A., Cosma, G., McGinnity, T.M., AdaBoost-CNN: An adaptive boosting algorithm for convolutional neural networks to classify multi-class imbalanced datasets using transfer learning. *Neurocomputing*, 404, 351–366, 2020.

31. Boosting Algorithms Explained. https://towardsdatascience.com/boosting-algorithms-explained-d38f56ef3f30 (accessed Jun. 10, 2021).

32. Cai, J., Xu, K., Zhu, Y., Hu, F., Li, L., Prediction and analysis of net ecosystem carbon exchange based on gradient boosting regression and random forest. *Appl. Energy*, 262, 114566, 2020.

33. Gradient Boosting Regression. http://deepnote.me/2019/08/25/datascience-18-machine-learning-with-tree-based-models-in-python/ (accessed Jun. 11, 2021).

34. Jerrita, S., Sajeev Ram, S., Haribaabu, V., Arun, S., Analysis of filters in ECG signal for emotion prediction. *J. Adv. Res. Dyn. Control Syst.*, 12, 04, 896–902, 2020.

35. medium.com, Support Vector Regression. https://medium.com/essence-of-learning/intuition-behind-support-vector-regression-3601f670a2ef (accessed Jun. 11, 2021).

36. Pujari, S., Ramakrishna, A., Padal, K.T.B., Comparison of ANN and regression analysis for predicting the water absorption behaviour of jute and banana fiber reinforcedepoxy composites. *Mater. Today Proc.*, 4, 2, Part A, 1626–1633, 2017. doi: https://doi.org/10.1016/j.matpr.2017.02.001.

37. Artificial Neural Network. https://www.javatpoint.com/artificial-neural-network (accessed Jun. 11, 2021).

38. Bilgili, M., Tosun, E., Aydin, K., Comparison of linear regression and artificial neural network model of a diesel engine fueled with biodiesel-alcohol mixtures. *Alex. Eng. J.*, 5, 4, 3081–3089, 2016.

39. Xu, D., Shi, Y., Tsang, I.W., Ong, Y.S., Gong, C., Shen, X., Survey on multi-output learning. *IEEE Trans. Neural Netw. Learn. Syst.*, 31, 7, 2409–2429, 2020.

40. Multi-output Regression. https://towardsdatascience.com/chained-multi-output-regression-solution-with-scikit-learn-4f44bf9c8c5b (accessed Jun. 12, 2021).

41. Géron, A., *Hands-on machine learning with Scikit-Learn, Keras, and TensorFlow: Concepts, Tools, and Techniques to Build Intelligent Systems*, O'Reilly Media, United States, 2019.

42. Basis, R., Classifier, F., Mapping, S., A comparative study of kernel logistic regression, radial basis function classifier, multinomial naïve bayes, and logistic model tree for flash flood susceptibility mapping. *Water*, 12, 1, 239–260, 2020.

43. Logistic Regression. https://towardsdatascience.com/binary-classification-with-logistic-regression-31b5a25693c4 (accessed Jun. 12, 2021).

44. Rau, C.S. *et al.*, Prediction of mortality in patients with isolated traumatic subarachnoid hemorrhage using a decision tree classifier: A retrospective analysis based on a trauma registry system. *Int. J. Environ. Res. Public Health*, 14, 11, 1–10, 2017.

45. Decision Tree Algorithm. https://www.kdnuggets.com/2020/01/decision-tree-algorithm-explained.html (accessed Jun. 12, 2021).

46. Mursalin, M., Zhang, Y., Chen, Y., Chawla, N.V., Automated epileptic seizure detection using improved correlation-based feature selection with random forest classifier. *Neurocomputing*, 241, 204–214, 2017.

47. Random Forest Classification. https://medium.com/swlh/random-forest-classification-and-its-implementation-d5d840dbead0 (accessed Jun. 12, 2021).

48. Feng, X., Li, S., Yuan, C., Zeng, P., Sun, Y., Prediction of slope stability using naive bayes classifier. *KSCE J. Civ. Eng.*, 22, 3, 941–950, 2018.

49. Singh, A., Halgamuge, M.N., Lakshmiganthan, R., Impact of Different data types on classifier performance of random forest, naïve bayes, and K-nearest neighbors algorithms. *Int. J. Adv. Comput. Sci. Appl.*, 8, 12, 1–11, 2017.

50. Edureka, KNN algorithm. https://www.edureka.co/blog/k-nearest-neighbors-algorithm/ (accessed Jun. 13, 2021).

51. Brilliant.org., Feedforward Neural Networks. https://brilliant.org/wiki/feed-forward-neural-networks/ (accessed Jun. 13, 2021).

52. Chen, X.-Y. and Chau, K.-W., Uncertainty Analysis on hybrid double feed-forward neural network model for sediment load estimation with LUBE method. *Water Resour. Manag.*, 33, 10, 3563–3577, 2019.

53. Raj, J.S. and Ananthi, J.V., Recurrent neural networks and LSTM explained. *J. Soft Comput. Paradig.*, 01, 01, 33–40, 2019.

54. Boufeloussen, O. and Medium, Recurrent Neural Network (RNN). https://medium.com/swlh/simple-explanation-of-recurrent-neural-network-rnn-1285749cc363 (accessed Jun. 13, 2021).

55. Pydeeplearning, Architecture of LSTM. https://pydeeplearning.weebly.com/blog/basic-architecture-of-rnn-and-lstm (accessed Jun. 13, 2021).

3

Cyber Physical Systems, Machine Learning & Deep Learning—Emergence as an Academic Program and Field for Developing Digital Society

P. K. Paul

Department of CIS, Raiganj University, Raiganj, WB, India

Abstract

Cyber-physical systems or CPS is dedicated in integrating, sensing, controlling, as well as computation activities into the physical objects, and infrastructure. Furthermore, it is dedicated in proper connection to the internet systems. Cyber-physical systems (CPS) combined with the software, as well as hardware components, which are integrated toward performing well-defined tasks; and all these are highly automated with multiple agents such as artificial intelligence (AI), as well as ML, i.e., machine learning functionalities. It is important to note that there are many subjects in computing and IT and among these few emerging are machine learning, which is one of the important type in artificial intelligence (AI), this is particularly focused on the use of data and algorithms, whereas deep learning is abbreviated as DL and it is the subfield of machine learning (ML), which is normally do with the algorithms. Deep learning is dedicated in creating artificial neural networks regarding how the human brain is works. Deep learning may be treated as a technique of machine learning. In the IT and computing domain all these cyber-physical systems, machine learning, deep learning are emerging in the industries and organizations, therefore different universities in the world are moving toward launching of emerging degrees and programs for solving the manpower-related aspects. There are shortages of the manpower in such fields and this chapter is deals with the aspects, feature, applications regarding cyber physical

Email: pkpaul.infotech@gmail.com

Rajdeep Chakraborty, Anupam Ghosh, Jyotsna Kumar Mandal and S. Balamurugan (eds.) *Convergence of Deep Learning In Cyber-IoT Systems and Security*, (67–84) © 2023 Scrivener Publishing LLC

systems (CPS), Machine Learning and Deep Learning including academic program available and having potentialities to offer.

Keywords: Cyber physical systems, machine learning, deep learning, academic degrees, emerging programs, university programs

3.1   Introduction

In the year 2006, cyber physical systems was coined by the then program manager Dr Helen Gill, of United States National Science Foundations. Cyber-physical systems is a prime example of integrating networking, computation systems, embedded computing systems etc. Here, it is worthy to note that embedded computers is monitor and control with the physical process with the feedback or similar loop. The cyber-physical systems has greater impact in economic and social development; directly and indirectly [1, 7]. Cyber-physical systems is associated with the traditional embedded systems, computers, software systems practically in such systems in which principle mission is not computation. It is important and applicable in the cars, toys, medical devices, engineering systems, etc. The biggest advantage of cyber-physical systems is it merges and combines with the physical process with computational systems *viz.* software, network, modeling, designing, and analysis techniques. However, cyber-physical systems can be defined and marked its progress during the beginning of cybernetics. Machine learning in short called as ML, and it is part of artificial intelligence. The ML is applicable in allowing software to be more accurate with proper predicting outcomes without explicitly programming. Machine learning algorithms   predict new output values based on previous data. Machine learning is important because it has many abilities *viz.* identification of the trends in customer behavior, in identification of proper development of new products. Some of the companies, such as Facebook, Google, Uber, etc, are actively using machine learning in their operations and activities. Machine learning is the competitive differentiator in many organizations and fall under the AI or artificial intelligence it is required when machines typically depends on human intelligence [14, 30]. In the machine learning system, the machines are able in learning by experience and that is without required or proper human involvement and whereas the subset is deep learning; and here artificial neural networks, algorithms are basically inspired by the human brain. Deep learning can be called as deep structured learning, and deep learning can be three types, such as supervised, semisupervised, or unsupervised.

3.2   Objective of the Work

The chapter entitled "Cyber Physical Systems, Machine Learning & Deep Learning—*Emergence as an Academic Program and Field for Developing Digital Society*" is planned to undertake with the mentioned agenda, and objective.

- To gather about the fundamentals of the cyber physical systems including its features, nature, and characteristics.
- To know regarding basics or overview of ML and DL, such as its features and characteristics.
- To learn about the foundation, historical overview of the cyber physical systems, machine learning, deep learning, etc.
- To digout the educational programs specially masters level on cyber physical systems, machine learning (ML) as well as deep learning (DL) in international academic markets and educational institutions.
- To find out the available and emerging program on the areas of machine learning and deep learning in Indian context at masters level.
- To dig out the potential program in the areas of the cyber physical systems, machine learning, deep learning etc. in Indian context keeping in mind job potentialities.

3.3   Methods

As far as the work "Cyber Physical Systems, Machine Learning & Deep Learning—*Emergence as an Academic Program and Field for Developing Digital Society*" is concerned the methods are include basic secondary sources, including primary sources etc. Web review also been conducted for doing this research work and to find out latest academic program in the fields *viz.* cyber physical systems, machine learning & deep learning. Here Google is considered as major search engine to find out the latest of emerging program and here keyword/search engine are used *viz.* 'Master/MSc Cyber Physical Systems', 'Master/MSc Machine Learning' 'Master/MSc Deep Learning' Here the result of up to 10 pages considered important. For studying Machine Learning and Deep Learning programs in India the search strategy used as 'Master/MSc Machine and Deep Learning in India' and considered up to 10 pages and picked the appropriate data and results.

3.4   Cyber Physical Systems: Overview with Emerging Academic Potentiality

Cyber-physical systems as a nomenclature coined in 2006 by Ellen Gill. Cyber-physical systems is important embedded systems may be considered as next-generation computing system equipped with the computational techniques. Here, computation, communication, and controls may be considered as most valuable [5, 26]. Regarding cyber-physical systems here Internet of Things treated as important in connections with the computational and physical units with advancement in implementations of proper communication systems. Cyber-physical systems is simply the merger of "digital controls" and also "physical environment," therefore, it is referred as cyber-physical systems that lies on information processing system and may be integrated to different places *viz.* car, plane or any kind of other device. cyber-physical systems is kind of intelligent systems and may be deals with the following attributes:

- Intelligence, adaptive and robustness—may be considered as worthy in the CPS or Cyber-Physical Systems
- Network is important within Cyber-Physical Systems (CPS) for the activities in communication, cooperation, cloud solutions.
- The CPS is depends on various Functionalities and here User friendliness play a leading role.

Therefore, Cyber-Physical Systems is integrated by the computation as well as physical processes. Further it may works on proper wireless sensor networks [3, 27].

Due to the importance of the Cyber-Physical Systems in the organizations, institutions, and industries many universities internationally has started academic programs leading to the MS/Masters in the areas of Cyber-Physical Systems, as depicted in Table 3.1.

Cyber-physical systems is gaining rapidly as far as its utilizations is concerned therefore many universities and higher learning institutions are offering educational, research, skill and training concentrated program in cyber-physical systems or in the allied or merged areas [6, 19]. According to the study it has noticed that most of the cyber-physical systems are offered in the developed/ western countries however it is the high time to introduce this subject in India with fully on the areas of cyber-physical

Table 3.1 Available masters program internationally started in CPS (Cyber Physical Systems).

Sl. no.	Degrees offered	Universities	Remarks	Country
1	MSc-Cyber Physical Systems & Embedded Systems	Advanced Learning and Research Institute	120 ECTS Open to Engineering, Computing, and Pure Science Students	Switzerland
2	MSc-Cyber Physical Systems (Specialization: IoT)	North Eastern University	Offered as Full Time & Part Time basis with multiple locations	USA
3	M.Engg-Mechatronic & Cyber Physical Systems	Deggendorf Institute of Technology	Offered in multiple locations. 3 Semester Program	Germany
4	MSc Cyber Physical Systems	The Polytechnic Institute of Paris	60 Credit, 2 Semester	France
5	MSc Cyber Physical Systems	The University of Nottingham	2 Years (Graduates with Program or Interest in)	UK

systems or allied areas. Furthermore the programs can be offered as the specializations in the existing programs such as—

- BSc/MSc- IT (Information Technology)
- BSc/MSc-CS (Computer Science)
- BTech/ MTech-IT (Information Technology)
- BTech/MTech-Computer Science & Engineering
- BCA/MCA

However there is also requirement of offering Cyber-Physical Systems as training or short term non degree program such as Certificate, Diploma, Advanced Diploma etc.

3.5   ML and DL Basics with Educational Potentialities

Machine learning (ML) and deep learning (DL) together are imperative aspects and subfields within artificial intelligence and emergently in the computer science. Due to its wider and rapid applications machine learning and deep learning, both are required in intelligent solutions throughout the world [8, 11].

3.5.1   Machine Learning (ML)

As far as machine learning is concerned, it is considered as important part of artificial intelligence, and it is a kind of method of data analysis which helps in automation of analytical model development. Machine Learning is important in identification of patterns and decision making furthermore ML is lies on minimal human intervention [2, 9, 10]. Machine learning is changing day by day, and in recent past, it has changed radically. The concept of ML was emerged from the pattern recognition and theories that can learn without being programmed. The models of machine learning are important as such models are exposed to get new data and lies on healthy computation dedicated in reliable, repeatable decision making. There was many algorithm employed previously but the recent association with the data analytics and big data changes the scenario of machine learning. There are many areas and recent examples of machine learning applications *viz.*

- In self-driving car and automated car and similar mechanism.
- Getting consumers behavior on purchasing any items (such as in Amazon, Flipcart, etc.)
- Users search pattern in the search engines or twitter or Facebook.
- In fraud detection and management [12, 15].

The machine learning applications sector wise are tremendous and emerging *viz.* business industries, healthcare, transportations, marketing, hospital management, education and training, government, administration, etc [4, 21]. The merger of data mining with Bayesian analysis becomes popular these days. Since today, data are emerged with variety of types, computational processing therefore Machine learning applications are also changing. The machine learning support leads quick, automatic models, complex data management, accurate result, and transparencies. Machine learning is also allied with the computational statistics, which will be suitable for the making prediction by the computer. Here, mathematical optimizations play a leading role in preparing the systems, theory and applications [13, 17, 29]. Machine learning furthermore developed into three major categories *viz.*:

- Supervised learning (SL)
- Unsupervised learning (UL)
- Reinforcement learning (RL)

Nowadays similar to other departments and sections human resource departments can also find the right candidates, in managing the tasks and assessments, in predict attrition and candidate success, etc. using machine learning [16, 18, 37].

3.5.2   Deep Learning

Deep learning or DL is a subset within the machine learning means indirectly it is also a section or part of artificial intelligence. And we are already aware that artificial intelligence is the that mechanism and systems that acts like a human being using automated systems. Here, proper algorithms play an important role for further automatic system development [20, 23, 36].

Deep learning, therefore, inspired by the structure of a human brain to attempt to draw similar conclusions as humans with a given logical structure and it does the activities by the neural networks, i.e., multilayered structure of algorithms. Therefore, sometimes, it is also called multiple neural networks. Deep learning is engaged in developing expert knowledge with the ability in designing machine learning systems, deep neural systems, proper architecture, and sophisticated architecture, software engineering principles, etc. Owing its structure deep learning also known as deep structured learning under the family of machine learning methods represented by the learning *viz.* supervised, semisupervised, or unsupervised. The role and structures of each of these AI, ML, and DL can be identified by Figure 3.1.

Deep learning depends on deep neural networks, deep belief networks, deep reinforcement learning, recurrent neural network, convolutional neural networks, etc [22, 26]. Furthermore, all these are healthy and important in the following:

- In computer vision
- In speech recognition

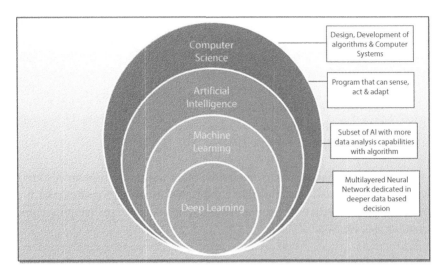

Figure 3.1 Deep learning with allied stakeholders and their attributes.

- In NLP or natural language processing
- In Machine translation
- In bioinformatics
- In drug development
- In automobiles, etc [10, 25].

In deep learning artificial neural networks (ANNs) is lies on information processing, and ANNs are static, symbolic, etc. Deep learning is healthy and fruitful in developing the automated systems and makes easier life living and enriching digital society system. Since worldwide data is generating numerously and adding the existing system daily therefore structuring data systematically deep learning is important and required. Here, deep learning uses the growing volume and availability of data into proper management [19, 31, 32].

3.6   Manpower and Developing Scenario in Machine Learning and Deep Learning

Machine learning (ML) and deep learning (DL) are being popular and used worldwide in different kind of organizations, institutions and research centers [3, 34]. Here, important and required technologies are being used to keep the system advanced and worthy. The term and concept of the artificial intelligence, neural network was popular during the late of 1990s and in recent past deep learning and machine learning become popular and valuable [28, 33]. Today, educational and degree programs are even available focuses on state-of-the-art technologies for machine learning and deep neural network systems with the degrees *viz.* MSc, MS, MTech etc. Here, the programs are normally focused on architectures, algorithms and implementation automated systems. However, according to the proposed study, here it is noted that majority of the program are available with the degrees with the nomenclature *viz.* deep learning, machine learning, or integrated ML & DL. Table 3.2 depicted such available programs.

According to the study, it has been noted that deep learning/machine learning programs are available in the developed countries *viz.*, USA, UK, Australia, etc. The syllabus of the program may vary university to university but commonly all are related to the deep learning, machine learning, AI, advanced computing, intelligent systems, sensing systems, graphical methods, robot vision and navigation, probabilistic methods, etc. Here in Table 3.3, one of the sample MSc program nomenclature on "Machine Learning and Deep Learning" is depicted.

Based on the universities, programs, degrees and territories, and applications of the deep learning/machine learning, the additional courses may be proposed and some of the program are depicted in Figure 3.2 herewith.

Here, it is worthy to note that there are different reasons to do the educational, training and research program in the field of deep learning (DL)/ machine learning (ML) *viz.*:

- To gain knowledge and basics of the fundamental aspects in deep learning/machine learning and how to implement this into the solving the problems.
- To gain deep knowledge regarding the machine learning, language processing, computer vision, up-to-date technologies, etc [9, 35].
- To prepare the skilled manpower in the areas of deep learning/machine learning, artificial intelligence with presentation skilled.
- To enhance the ability of critical analysis of the AI, computing skills, deep learning/machine learning.

Table 3.2 Available Masters Program internationally in the areas of Machine Learning and Deep Learning based on methodology adopted.

Sl. no.	Degrees offered	Universities	Remarks	Country
1	MSc Machine Learning & Deep Learning	University of Strathclyde	1-Year full time program. Open to bachelors in computer or physical sciences	UK
2	MSc Machine Learning	University College London	1-Year full time program. Open to 180 credit, bachelors in computer or physical sciences	UK
3	MSc Machine Learning	Carnegie Mellon University	2-Year full time program. Open to bachelor degree in any discipline but with focus on computing contents	USA
4	MSc Computing (Artificial Intelligence & Machine Learning)	Imperial College London	1-Year full time program. Bachelor degree in any discipline but with focus on computing contents	UK
5	MSc AI & Machine Learning	The University of Birmingham	1-Year full time program. Bachelor degree with focus on physical science/computing/mathematics contents or economics	UK

(Continued)

Table 3.2 Available Masters Program internationally in the areas of Machine Learning and Deep Learning based on methodology adopted. (*Continued*)

Sl. no.	Degrees offered	Universities	Remarks	Country
6	MSc AI & Machine Learning	University of Limerick	1-Year full time program. Bachelor degree with focus on physical science/computing/ mathematics contents	Ireland
7	MS Machine Learning & AI	Drexel University	2-Year full time program. Minimum 4 years bachelor degree with computing/ software engineering/ mathematics contents	USA
8	Master of Machine Learning	The University of Adelaide	2-Year full time. Open to 3 years bachelor's degree with mathematical sciences	Australia
9	MSc Computer Vision, Robotics & Machine Learning	University of Surrey	1 Year FT & 2 years PT. Bachelor degree with focus on physical Science/computing/ mathematics contents	UK
10	MSc Machine Learning	Mohamed Bin Zayed University of Artificial Intelligence	35 Credit course, open to computing/ mathematical science bachelors	UAE

Table 3.3 The example of MSc program in ML & DL.

University of Strathclyde of MSc Machine Learning & Deep Learning
Autonomous Sensing, Reasoning & Deep Learning
Digital Signal Processing Principles
Big Data Technologies
Machine Learning for Data Analytics
Assignment and Professional Studies

Some of the Possible Courses in Machine and Deep Learning Programs	
Advanced Topics in Machine Learning	Statistical Natural Language Processing
Applied Machine Learning	Affective Computing and Human-Robot
Approximate Inference and Learning in	Interaction
Probabilistic Models	Computational Modeling for Biomedical
Bioinformatics	Imaging
Graphical Models	Information Retrieval and Data Mining
Introduction to Deep Learning	Inverse Problems in Imaging
Machine Learning Seminar	Multi-agent Artificial Intelligence
Machine Vision	Numerical Optimization
Probabilistic and Unsupervised Learning	Robot Vision and Navigation
Reinforcement Learning	Robotic Control Theory and Systems

Figure 3.2 Possible courses related to the ML & DL programs.

- To create manpower who are able in marketable products related to the deep learning/machine learning, etc.
- To create the skilled computing professionals having abilities in research projects, products, etc. that can be applicable in diverse areas and sectors to enhance the living of the common people.

Due to the growing importance of deep learning/machine learning in contemporary scenario in the organizations and institutions various job positions are emerged in recent past and among these few important are depicted in Figure 3.3.

Moreover, additional designations and job opportunities are coming day by day, and industries and organizations are moving toward the development the separate units in order to excel ML- and DL-related areas.

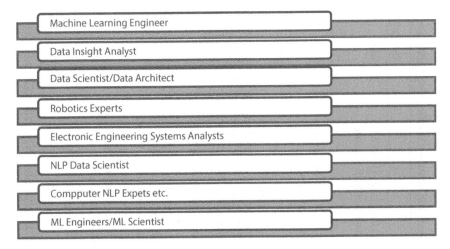

Machine Learning Engineer

Data Insight Analyst

Data Scientist/Data Architect

Robotics Experts

Electronic Engineering Systems Analysts

NLP Data Scientist

Compputer NLP Expets etc.

ML Engineers/ML Scientist

Figure 3.3 Possible job titles and designation from the ML & DL programs.

3.7   DL & ML in Indian Context

Deep learning/machine learning applications and utilizations in various sectors and areas as a result developed many academic courses and programs In India especially at Masters level with MSc, MTech degree. Furthermore, it is noted that the subjects are available, such as deep learning, machine learning or integrated deep learning & machine learning, or in it also noted the merging of deep learning with AI or Data Science. For this study, a total of 10 results of the Google Search Engine page considered as most vital to get the data and analysis. Here, during the study, the term "deep learning/machine learning" or "deep learning" or "machine learning" or combination of deep learning/machine learning with AI or Data Science or Communication Systems. etc. Table 3.4 here depicted available program on AI, machine learning & deep learning in Indian context.

Deep learning/machine learning as a part of AI (and AI as a part of computer science) can be offered with other nomenclatures as well as far as Indian context is concerned. Here, Table 3.5 depicted some of the possible deep learning/machine learning-related program at MCA level, which is one of the popular in India.

Deep learning/machine learning are research-related aspects therefore, these may be offered in research-based masters degrees as shown in Table 3.6.

Therefore, such programs in the field of deep learning/machine learning may be offered at masters level with research context.

Table 3.4 Available masters program in India in the areas of machine learning and deep learning based on methodology adopted.

Sl. no.	Degrees offered	Universities	Remarks	Country
1	MSc Deep Learning and Artificial Intelligence	Reva University, Bangalore	2 Years Weekend Program, Open to Computing/Mathematical Science Bachelors	India
2	MSc Artificial Intelligence & Machine Learning	NMIMS Deemed University, Pune	2 Years Program for BTech or Masters in Computing/Mathematics etc.	India
3	MTech Machine Learning and Computing	IIST, Thiruvananthapuram	2 Years Program for BTech or Masters in Computing/Mathematics etc.	India
4	MTech Data Science & Machine Learning	PES University, Bangalore	2 Years Weekend Program, for BTech or Masters in Computing/Mathematics etc.	India
5	MTech Machine Learning and Artificial Intelligence	Lovely Professional University	2 Years Full Time Program, for BTech	India
6	MTech Communication Systems & Machine Learning	Dhirubhai Ambani Institute of Information and Communication Technology (DAIICT)	2 Years Full Time specially for the BTech. It is run in association with C.R.Rao Advanced Institute of Mathematics, Statistics and Computer Science (C. R. Rao AIMSCS), Hyderabad	India
7	MTech CSE (Artificial Intelligence & Machine Learning)	Galgotias University	2 Years Full Time Program, for BTech or MCA	

Table 3.5 Possible MCA in machine learning and deep learning and allied areas.

Proposed Cyber Physical Systems Program potentiality with MTech/ME Program level
MCA- Deep Learning (DL) MCA- Machine Learning (ML) MCA- Deep Learning & Machine Learning MCA- AI with Deep Learning & Machine Learning MCA- Computational Intelligence with DL

Table 3.6 Possible MCA in machine learning and deep learning and allied areas in research degrees context.

Proposed Cyber Physical Systems Program potentiality with MTech/ME Program level
MSc CS (by research) Deep Learning & Machine Learning MCA (by research) in AI & Deep Learning MS (by research) ML & DL MTech (by research) AI with Deep Learning/Machine Learning

3.8 Conclusion

Cyber physical systems, deep learning, machine learning—all three technologies become important in contemporary research and IT arena. Almost all the organizations, institutions, industries these days are using such technologies for better results, efficiencies, and productivity. The world is becoming more and more digitalized and automated toward a real and healthy digital society and knowledge economy therefore such technological implications and applications are worthy and timely requirement. As far as educational institutions, colleges and universities are concerned the role in designing, developing courses on Cyber Physical Systems, Deep Learning, Machine Learning already considered as valuable for the Computing and IT and allied students. Though the recent development of academic degrees and training program in cyber physical systems (CPS) and other emerging areas *viz.* deep learning, machine learning significant in developing proper manpower as per the industrial need and requirements. Some of the proper strategies, planning is essential to start the programs where such are not yet implemented in order to run with the contemporary world.

References

1. Aasheim, C.L., Williams, S., Rutner, P., Gardiner, A., Data analytics vs. data science: A study of similarities and differences in undergraduate programs based on course descriptions. *J. Inf. Syst. Educ.*, 26, 103, 2015.

2. Agarwal, P., Higher education in India: Growth, concerns and change agenda. *High. Educ. Q.*, 61, 197, 2007.

3. Alguliyev, R., Imamverdiyev, Y., Sukhostat, L., Cyber-physical systems and their security issues. *Comput. Ind.*, 100, 212, 2018.

4. Altbach, P.G., The dilemma of change in Indian higher education. *High. Educ.*, 26, 3, 1993.

5. Ashibani, Y. and Mahmoud, Q.H., Cyber physical systems security: Analysis, challenges and solutions. *Comput. Secur.*, 68, 81, 2017.

6. Baheti, R. and Gill, H., Cyber-physical systems, in: *The Impact of Control Technology*, vol. 12, p. 161, 2021.

7. Chen, G., Xu, B., Lu, M., Chen, N.S., Exploring blockchain technology and its potential applications for education. *Smart Learn. Environ.*, 5, 1, 2018.

8. Deng, L. and Yu, D., Deep learning: methods and applications. *Found. Trends Signal Process.*, 7, 197, 2014.

9. Ghahramani, Z., Probabilistic machine learning and artificial intelligence. *Nature*, 521, 452, 2015.

10. Goldstein, I. and Papert, S., Artificial intelligence, language, and the study of knowledge. *Cogn. Sci.*, 1, 84, 1997.

11. Guo, Y., Hu, X., Hu, B., Cheng, J., Zhou, M., Kwok, R.Y., Mobile cyber physical systems: Current challenges and future networking applications. *IEEE Access*, 6, 12360, 2017.

12. Iqbal, R., Doctor, F., More, B., Mahmud, S., Yousuf, U., Big data analytics and computational intelligence for cyber–physical systems: Recent trends and state of the art applications. *Future Gener. Comp. Sy.*, 105, 766, 2020.

13. Hehenberger, P., Vogel-Heuser, B., Bradley, D., Eynard, B., Tomiyama, T., Achiche, S., Design, modelling, simulation and integration of cyber physical systems: Methods and applications. *Comput. Ind.*, 82, 273, 2016.

14. Huang, M.H. and Rust, R.T., Artificial intelligence in service. *J. Serv. Res.*, 21, 155, 2018.

15. Humayed, A., Lin, J., Li, F., Luo, B., Cyber-physical systems security—A survey. *IEEE Internet Things J.*, 4, 1802, 2017.

16. Khaitan, S.K. and McCalley, J.D., Design techniques and applications of cyberphysical systems: A survey. *IEEE Syst. J.*, 9, 350, 2014.

17. Jordan, M., II and Mitchell, T.M., Machine learning: Trends, perspectives, and prospects. *Science*, 349, 255, 2015.

18. Ker, J., Wang, L., Rao, J., Lim, T., Deep learning applications in medical image analysis. *IEEE Access*, 6, 9375, 2017.

19. Kim, K.D. and Kumar, P.R., An overview and some challenges in cyber-physical systems. *J. Indian Inst. Sci.*, 93, 341, 2013.

20. Krämer, B.J., Evolution of cyber-physical systems: A brief review, in: *Applied Cyber-Physical Systems*, p. 1, 2014.
21. Lee, I., Sokolsky, O., Chen, S., Hatcliff, J., Jee, E., Kim, B., Venkatasubramanian, K.K., Challenges and research directions in medical cyber–physical systems. *Proc. IEEE*, 100, 75, 2011.
22. Tran, T.B.L., Törngren, M., Nguyen, H.D., Paulen, R., Gleason, N.W., Duong, T.H., Trends in preparing cyber-physical systems engineers. *Cyber-Phys. Syst.*, 5, 65, 2019.
23. Lu, T., Lin, J., Zhao, L., Li, Y., Peng, Y., A security architecture in cyber-physical systems: Security theories, analysis, simulation and application fields. *Int. J. Secur. Its Appl.*, 9, 1, 2015.
24. Marwedel, P., Mitra, T., Grimheden, M.E., Andrade, H.A., Survey on education for cyber-physical systems. *IEEE Des. Test*, 37, 56, 2020.
25. Najafabadi, M.M., Villanustre, F., Khoshgoftaar, T.M., Seliya, N., Wald, R., Muharemagic, E., Deep learning applications and challenges in big data analytics. *J. Big Data*, 2, 1, 2015.
26. Obermeyer, Z. and Emanuel, E.J., Predicting the future—Big data, machine learning, and clinical medicine. *N. Engl. J. Med.*, 375, 1216, 2016.
27. Paul, P., Bhuimali, A., Aithal, P.S., Indian higher education: With slant to information technology—A fundamental overview. *IJRRSET*, 5, 31, 2017.
28. Paul, P., Aithal, P.S., Bhuimali, A., Kumar, K., Emerging degrees and collaboration: The context of engineering sciences in computing & IT—An analysis for enhanced policy formulation in India. *IJRRSET*, 5, 13, 2017.
29. Rocher, G., Tigli, J.Y., Lavirotte, S., Le Thanh, N., Effectiveness assessment of cyber-physical systems. *Int. J. Approx. Reason.*, 118, 112, 2020.
30. Sadiku, M.N., Wang, Y., Cui, S., Musa, S.M., Cyber-physical systems: A literature review. *Eur. Sci. J.*, 13, 52, 2017.
31. Sanislav, T. and Miclea, L., Cyber-physical systems-concept, challenges and research areas. *J. Control Eng. Appl. Inform.*, 14, 28, 2012.
32. Sedjelmaci, H., Guenab, F., Senouci, S.M., Moustafa, H., Liu, J., Han, S., Cyber security based on artificial intelligence for cyber-physical systems. *IEEE Netw.*, 34, 6, 2020.
33. Serpanos, D., The cyber-physical systems revolution. *Computer*, 51, 70, 2018.
34. Törngren, M., Grimheden, M.E., Gustafsson, J., Birk, W., Strategies and considerations in shaping cyber-physical systems education. *ACM SIGBED Rev.*, 14, 53, 2017.
35. Wang, J., Ma, Y., Zhang, L., Gao, R.X., Wu, D., Deep learning for smart manufacturing: Methods and applications. *J. Manuf. Syst.*, 48, 144, 2018.
36. Xu, L.D. and Duan, L., Big data for cyber physical systems in industry 4.0: A survey. *Enterp. Inf. Syst.*, 13, 148, 2019.
37. Zanero, S., Cyber-physical systems. *Computer*, 50, 14, 2007.

4

Detection of Fake News and Rumors in Social Media Using Machine Learning Techniques With Semantic Attributes

Diganta Saha*, Arijit Das, Tanmay Chandra Nath, Soumyadip Saha and Ratul Das

Department of Computer Science and Engineering, Faculty of Engineering and Technology, Jadavpur University, Kolkata, West Bengal, India

Abstract

Spreading rumors and fake news over popular social media like Facebook, Twitter, WhatsApp, etc creates serious social problems. It is observed that the administration had to stop Internet service in a large area to control the spreading of such rumors or fake news. Bar in the internet service creates another serious problem for the citizens as we are heavily dependent on the internet nowadays. To detect fake news, this work suggests a machine learning method using the Naïve Bayes classifier. The system can be plugged in with any social media, as it predicts the probability of news to be fake or rumor the same can be stopped from spreading farther with the software control in the social media. This model was trained and tested in three datasets (two of the English language and one of Bengali language). We have successfully achieved a high accuracy, which is 81% for the English language and 93% for the Bengali language. This is an acceptable result comparing the same with the recent works. Using deep learning or a combination of classifiers, the result may be improved further.

Keywords: Fake news, machine learning, Naive Bayes, rumors, semantic attributes, NLP, natural language processing

*Corresponding author: ds.cse.ju@gmail.com

Rajdeep Chakraborty, Anupam Ghosh, Jyotsna Kumar Mandal and S. Balamurugan (eds.) Convergence of Deep Learning In Cyber-IoT Systems and Security, (85–98) © 2023 Scrivener Publishing LLC

4.1   Introduction

What is fake news? "fake news" is a term that can, in a broader sense, classify news which are either false or rumour or click-bait or hate news. It is a kind of news consisting of disinformation and can spread via traditional newsprint media or digital media. With the advent of social networking sites, common people have become more susceptible to this kind of news and knowingly or unknowingly have become an agent to spread this news. Fake news is avoidable as it can refer to a diverse range of disinformation covering topics such as health, environment and economics across all platforms and genres. However, the term is new. Fake news started to roll out since 2016, and it was named in Collins dictionary as official word of the year for 2017. Clickbait, misleading headlines, sloppy journalism, biased news targeted toward a person or a community are the causes of creating fake news around people.

Nowadays, social media is playing an important role in spreading news whether it is real or fake and people are ready to imbibe it. News in social media uses interesting text, images and videos which attract the readers even more. It is cheap to access and circulated quickly. News through social media has got more popularity than the traditional news of the newspaper. So news reports made with purposely false information are easy to spread. It is considered harmful for the news ecosystem and changes people's mind towards real news. In a nutshell, fake news and rumours create a negative effect on individuals and as well as in society. To alleviate the effect of this, the detection of fake news or rumours now becomes an alluring topic to research.

For the current research, three datasets have been used. Two of them were in English where one dataset called Liar has only small statements and the other dataset called fake news corpus has headlines as well as body parts. The Bengali dataset which is called BanFakeNews has headlines and body parts too.

Supervised Machine Learning methods have been used on the datasets. The objective of this work is to recognize fake or false news by considering different attributes of the news corpus in the classification process.

This work is one of the very first works on Fake News Detection in the Bengali Language. As this work achieved an accuracy of 93%, we can say it's a very good first step towards the future.

The contributions and novelties of this chapter are 1) Application of machine learning techniques to detect fake news and rumours, 2) Proposing an algorithm which can work on the dataset having sentences of short length using NLP technique like semantic analysis whereas all other proposed algorithms either have not used NLP methods or have used long sentences, 3) To the best of our knowledge this is the first work for detecting Bengali fake news and rumours, 4) The proposed technique can be used for any language including low resource languages and other regional languages as the method is language independent, 5) Our proposed approach has the highest impact for the suspicious text spreading over social media like FB, Twitter, WhatsApp etc. where sentence length of fake news or rumours is small and often the origin, trace of routing are unknown leaving no other way but NLP for detection of accuracy, 6) The result of the proposed method has been compared in Table 4.6, 7) The proposed method has been tested in three different dataset which are publicly available.

4.2   Literature Survey

The authors have proposed a method by using HAN to detect fake news in Okano et al. [1]. This model has been evaluated in Brazilian and Portuguese fake news corpus, which is named as Fake.Br. Removing or keeping stop words and varying the word embeddings' size showed slightly less accuracy. The authors have proposed a modern approach to detect fake news, which achieves high accuracy in Zhang et al. [2]. To group news articles in clusters, it has a topic-based classifying mechanism and to extract events it has event extraction mechanism. It compares their events with legitimate events to find the credibility of news. H. Karimi, P. Roy, S. Saba-Sadiya, & J. Tang have introduced a framework called MMFD which combines extracted features, multisource fusion and degrees of the fakeness of articles into a single understandable model in Karimi et al. [3] and in Wang et al. [4] the authors have proposed a new framework named EANN. This framework is made of three elements, a feature extractor which extracts textual and visual features from posts, a detector which learns the differentiable representations and event discriminator to distinguish between fake and not fake news.

In Yang et al. [5], the authors have proposed a network which is named as TI-CNN. The method projects the latent and explicit features to a single space. This model can be trained and tested with both the image and text data at the same time. H. Ahmed, I. Traore, & S. Saad have proposed a method which uses an analysis technique called N-Gram with some techniques of artificial intelligence in Ahmed et al. [6]. After experimenting with many of feature extraction techniques and classification techniques they have found that TF-IDF feature extraction technique and LSVM classification technique gives the best performance. The authors have used an automated detector which is based on the Artificial Intelligence technique deep learning and a 3HAN to achieve speed and accuracy in Singhania *et al.* [7]. The network consists of three tiers, one tier for words, one tier for sentences made of those words and one tier for news vector. This method provides an easy to understand outcome using the values given to components of the used article.

In Ruchansky *et al.* [8], the authors have proposed a method called CSI, which consists of three models, for capturing, for scoring and for integrating. The first module uses RNN to capture the user activity, the second module learns the characteristics of the source. Then, by integrating both the modules with the integrate module, the model can classify whether the article is not fake or fake. W. Y. Wang has proposed a benchmark dataset consists of manually labeled and decade-long short statements of various contexts, 'LIAR' [9]. The dataset yielded an improved result of the deep learning model. In M. Granik, and V. Mesyura [10] have proposed an elementary approach for fake news detection using the Naive Bayes technique. The software system was tested against a dataset created using Facebook posts and achieved a decent result. The authors have introduced a model that uses a hybrid approach, which is a combination of ML techniques and linguistic cue with behavioural data in [11].

4.3   Proposed Work

We have tried and tested many classification techniques like Logistic Regression, K-Nearest Neighbours, Naive Bayes and many more. Naive Bayes classifier stands out in the list in terms of accuracy and simplicity of the approach.

Mathematical Explanation of Naive Bayes Classifier:
We can consider a given news report fake or not in the basis of calculating the conditional probability of that report which contains some certain word in it.
The formula is stated in equation 4.1.

$$P(F \mid W) = \frac{P(W \mid F).P(F)}{P(W \mid F).P(F) + P(W \mid T).P(T)} \tag{4.1}$$

where :
$\quad$ P(F|W): conditional probability of a report is fake given that the
$\quad\quad$ word W occurs in the report

P(W|F): conditional probability of searching the W word in news reports which are fake

P(F): probability of the news report is fake

P(W|T): conditional probability of searching the W word in non-fake reports

P(T): probability of the news report is non-fake

(This expression is obtained from Bayes' Theorem)

First, we consider that P(F|W) values for all the words of the news report are available to us. Second, we combine the probability to get probability of the certainty that the news report is fake.

The expressions are presented in equations 4.2, 4.3, and 4.4.

$$a1 = P(F|W_1).P(F|W_2). \ldots .P(F|W_n) \tag{4.2}$$

$$a2 = (1-P(F|W_1)). (1-P(F|W_2)). \ldots .(1-P(F|W_n)) \tag{4.3}$$

$$a = a_1/(a_1 + a_2) \tag{4.4}$$

where:

n: Count of words in the report

a1: Product value of the probability that a news report is fake which contains a certain word for every word in the report

a2: Same as a1 but using complement probability

$P(F|W_n)$: Conditional probability that a report is fake given the word W_n occurs in it

a: The overall probability of the news report to be fake.

Now assuming there is a train set which contains many news reports marked as real or fake. So, calculate the conditional probability of searching a certain word in that training set. Now we can describe the probability of searching a certain word in fake reports as a ratio of the fake article which consists of this word to the total no. of fake articles. Similarly, we can describe the probability of searching certain words in true articles.

4.3.1   Algorithm

<u>Input:</u> Set of labeled news articles, which has been divided into training dataset (80%) and test dataset (20%).

<u>Output:</u> The percentage of news articles which have been labeled successfully comparing with its original label.

Step 1. Load all the articles.

Step 2. Use stemming on all words and remove stop words from each article.

Step 3. Convert the articles into its feature vector (using the bag of words method).

Step 4. Separate the data into training and testing dataset

Step 5. Train the Naïve Bayes Classifier

Step 6. Test and evaluate the accuracy.

4.3.2   Flowchart

The detailed flowchart of the method is given in Figure 4.1.

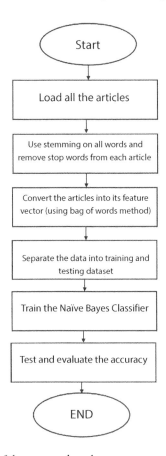

Figure 4.1 The flowchart of the proposed work.

4.3.3   Explanation of Approach

We have used the News Headline and News Body attributes to train our current model. Those articles where the type of article was not mentioned clearly are ignored. Also, the articles, which are broken or not complete, are also ignored.

At first, we have stemmed every word of the articles and ignored all the stop words. Stemming is a process to get the root form of the derived words. This technique is necessary to handle similar words (like 'sleep' and 'sleeping') as same words and this may increase accuracy. For finding the stemma of the English words we have used the NLTK [15] stemma methods and for Bangla words, we have used Bangla_stemmer [16] tool. Function words, like articles and prepositions, which do not contribute to the meaning of the sentences, are called Stop Words. These words hardly affect the performance of the classifier hence have been removed. Then, we have prepared the global vector using the bag-of-words [17] method.

The bag-of-words is a simple technique used in NLP and IR. In this technique, a text (sentence or document) is represented as the bag of its words ignoring the grammar and the word order. The bag-of-words technique is used mostly in document classification methods where the number of occurrences of each and every word is considered as a feature value to train a classifier. But here we are only concerned about whether a word is present or not in the article. So, every feature value must be in (0, 1).

Suppose there are two sentences -

1. Tanmay likes to play PUBG and Soumya likes FIFA too.
2. Soumya also likes to watch PUBG games.

So, the bag-of-words for these two sentences is given in Figure 4.2.

Using this bag-of-words method, we have created the global feature vector which is a binary one-hot vector which is presented in Table 4.1.

After that, we split the dataset into two parts as Train dataset and Test dataset. Then we have evaluated the accuracy of our proposed approach in the datasets. In most of the cases, 80% of train dataset has given us more accuracy. Training and testing percentages of three datasets is presented in Table 4.2.

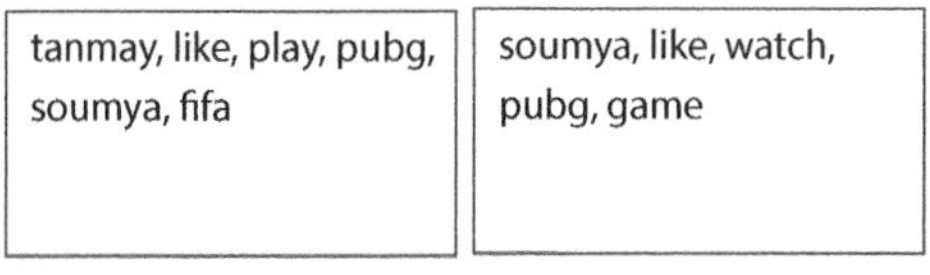

tanmay, like, play, pubg, soumya, fifa	soumya, like, watch, pubg, game

Figure 4.2 Bag-of-Words of the two sentences.

Table 4.1 One hot vector constructed by the two sentences.

No.	tanmay	like	play	pubg	soumya	fifa	watch	game
1.	1	1	1	1	1	1	0	0
2.	0	1	0	1	1	0	1	1

Table 4.2 Training and testing percentage of datasets.

Name of dataset	Training percentage	Testing percentage
LIAR	66	34
Fake News Corpus	80	20
BanFakeNews	80	20

4.4   Results and Analysis

4.4.1   Datasets

We have used a total of three datasets to extensively test our proposed model.

a) Liar Dataset [9]—Liar is a benchmark dataset which is publicly available to detect fake news. The makers created a collection of more than 10K manually classified short statements from the website POLITIFACT.COM. There are a total of six labels which are half-true, mostly-true, true, false, barely-true, pants-fire. Half-true, true and mostly-true labels have been considered as non-fake and the other labels have been considered as fake. The size of the dataset is near about 3 MB.

b) Fake News Corpus [13]—Fake News Corpus is a dataset composed of more than million of news articles mostly taken from domains from "www.opensources.com" and the dataset is open source. There are near about 1L articles in the version that we have used. There are many labels such as some corresponds to fake and some corresponds to not fake. The news articles have been labeled using these labels, fake news, satire, extreme bias, conspiracy theory, junk science, hate news, clickbait. fake news, satire, hate news and click-bait have been considered as fake and others have been considered as non-fake. The size of the dataset is near about 28 GB.

c) BanFakeNews [14]—BanFakeNews is a labeled dataset of approximately 50K news articles that can be helpful in building a model to automatically detect fake news for a language like Bangla which has very few resources. There are basically four labels, such as Authentic, Clickbait, Satire, and Fake. The first one is considered as non-fake and others have been treated as fake news. The total size of the corpus is near about 300 MB.

4.4.2   Evaluation

We are considering that when the model labels a news report as a fake then the result is positive. Then:

Number of originally fake news, correctly recognized as fake (tp)
Number of originally not fake news, incorrectly recognized as fake (fp)
Number of originally fake news, incorrectly recognized as not fakes (fn)
Number of originally not fake news, correctly recognized as not fakes (tn)

Then, the formula of precision is given in equation 4.5.

$$Precision\ (Pr) = \frac{tp}{tp + fp} \tag{4.5}$$

And the formula of recall is given in equation 4.6.

$$Recall\ (Rc) = \frac{tp}{fn + tp} \tag{4.6}$$

4.4.2.1   Result of 1st Dataset

Results of LIAR dataset is presented in Table 4.3 with the following values for the parameters of confusion matrix

tp=1092, fp=651, tn=655, fn=602
Precision = 1092/ (1092 + 651) = 0.63
Recall = 1092 / (1092 + 602) = 0.64

Table 4.3 Result of liar dataset.

News type	Count of news	Count of correctly recognized news	Correctness
Fake News	1694	1092	64.46%
Non-Fake news	1306	655	50.15%
Total	3000	1747	58.23%

Table 4.4 Result of fake news corpus dataset.

News type	Count of news	Count of correctly recognized news	Correctness
Fake News	285	205	71.93%
Non-Fake news	394	347	88.07%
Total	679	552	81.29%

4.4.2.2 Result of 2nd Dataset

Results of "fake news corpus: dataset is presented in Table 4.4 with the following values for the parameters of confusion matrix

tp=205, fp=47, tn=347, fn=80
Precision = 205/ (205 + 47) = 0.81
Recall = 205 / (205 + 80) = 0.72

4.4.2.3 Result of 3rd Dataset

Results of 'BanFakeNews' dataset is presented in Table 4.5 with the following values for the parameters of confusion matrix

Table 4.5 Result of BanFakeNews dataset.

News type	Count of news	Count of correctly recognized news	Correctness
Fake News	46	40	86.95%
Non-Fake news	54	53	98.14%
Total	100	93	93.00%

Table 4.6 Relative performances.

Method	Proposed method	[4]	[5]	[6]	[7]	[10]
Accuracy	93%	84%	92%	92%	94%	75%

tp=40, fp=1, tn=53, fn=6
Precision =40 / (40 + 1) = 0.97
Recall = 40 / (40 + 6) = 0.87

An accuracy of 58% has been achieved for the Liar dataset which is least of all. The accuracy for the Fake News Corpus dataset is 81% and for BanFakeNews dataset it is 93%. So, BanFakeNews dataset outperforms the other two datasets.

Usually, fake news contains similar word sets that typically indicate the chances of news to be fake or non-fake. But it should be kept in mind that it is inappropriate to mention a report is fake since some word sets arise in it; however, these word sets hit the prospects of this certainty. The principal goal is to handle every single word of the news report separately.

4.4.3 Relative Comparison of Performance

A relative comparison of performance of our proposed method in 'BanFakeNews' dataset with the other established method is given in Table 4.6.

4.5 Conclusion

Fake news is becoming a threat to the community and affecting the lives of common people. There are many good approaches in fake news detection in English language but the researches in Bengali language and most other regional languages is in a very nascent stage. In this study, we are using the Naïve Bayes to be the classifier, which can distinguish between fake and non-fake news. This elementary AI algorithm has shown this much great result on such a significant problem as the detection of fake news. The outcomes of this experiment suggest that AI techniques and algorithms may take a crucial role in tackling this kind of problems, which are driving the world insane.

Deep learning using neural networks are proven to increase accuracy and efficiency in such kinds of experiments. In this work, machine learning techniques are used. An accuracy of 82% in English language and 93% in Bengali language are achieved. We wish to apply deep learning method in the future.

The experiment has been done on two languages which are English and Bengali and has achieved a significant result. The same work can be done in other languages specially Indian languages like Hindi, Tamil, Marathi, etc. As this experiment is independent of languages and independent of grammatical syntaxes it should work in other languages. So, the experiment of applying this algorithm in fake news detection in other languages is our next target in the future.

Detecting fake image, video and stopping them before spreading over internet through social media, is another possible enhancement of this work.

References

1. Okano, E.Y., Liu, Z., Ji, D., Ruiz, E.E.S., Fake News Detection on Fake. Br Using Hierarchical Attention Networks, in: *International Conference on Computational Processing of the Portuguese Language*, Springer, Cham, pp. 143–152, March 2020.
2. Zhang, C., Gupta, A., Kauten, C., Deokar, A.V., Qin, X., Detecting fake news for reducing misinformation risks using analytics approaches. *Eur. J. Oper. Res.*, 279, 3, 1036–1052, 2019.
3. Karimi, H., Roy, P., Saba-Sadiya, S., Tang, J., MuWlti-source multi-class fake news detection, in: *Proceedings of the 27th International Conference on Computational Linguistics*, pp. 1546–1557, August 2018.
4. Wang, Y., Ma, F., Jin, Z., Yuan, Y., Xun, G., Jha, K., Gao, J., Eann: Event adversarial neural networks for multi-modal fake news detection, in: *Proceedings of the 24th ACM Sigkdd International Conference on Knowledge Discovery & Data Mining*, pp. 849–857, July 2018.
5. Yang, Y., Zheng, L., Zhang, J., Cui, Q., Li, Z., Yu, P.S., TI-CNN: Convolutional neural networks for fake news detection, 2018, arXiv preprint arXiv:1806.00749.
6. Ahmed, H., Traore, I., Saad, S., Detection of online fake news using N-gram analysis and machine learning techniques, in: *International Conference on Intelligent, Secure, and Dependable Systems in Distributed and Cloud Environments*, pp. 127–138, Springer International Publisher, Vancouver Canada, October 2017.
7. Singhania, S., Fernandez, N., Rao, S., 3han: A deep neural network for fake news detection, in: *International Conference on Neural Information Processing*, Springer, Cham, pp. 572–581, November 2017.

8. Ruchansky, N., Seo, S., Liu, Y., Csi: A hybrid deep model for fake news detection, in: *Proceedings of the 2017 ACM on Conference on Information and Knowledge Management*, pp. 797–806, November 2017.

9. Wang, W.Y., "Liar, liar pants on fire": A new benchmark dataset for fake news detection, 2017, arXiv preprint arXiv:1705.00648.

10. Granik, M. and Mesyura, V., Fake news detection using naive Bayes classifier, in: *2017 IEEE First Ukraine Conference on Electrical and Computer Engineering (UKRCON)*, pp. 900–903, IEEE, Vinnytsia National Technical University, Vinnytsia, Ukraine, May 2017.

11. Conroy, N.J., Rubin, V.L., Chen, Y., Automatic deception detection: Methods for finding fake news. *Proc. Assoc. Inf. Sci. Technol.*, 52, 1, 1–4, 2015.

12. https://en.wikipedia.org/wiki/Naive_Bayes_classifier accessed on 26-03-2020,7.30 p.m.

13. https://github.com/several27/FakeNewsCorpus accessed on 28-03-2020, 6.00 pm

14. https://arxiv.org/abs/2004.08789 accessed on 29-03-2020, 7.00 pm

15. https://www.nltk.org/howto/stem.html accessed on 27-03-2020, 2.00 pm

16. https://pypi.org/project/bangla-stemmer/ accessed on 30-03-2020, 3.00 pm

17. https://en.wikipedia.org/wiki/Bag-of-words_model accessed on 26-03-2020, 7.00 pm

Part II

INNOVATIVE SOLUTIONS BASED ON DEEP LEARNING

5

Online Assessment System Using Natural Language Processing Techniques

S. Suriya[1*], K. Nagalakshmi[2] and Nivetha S.[1]

[1]Department of Computer Science and Engineering, PSG College of Technology, Coimbatore, India
[2]Department of Computer Science and Engineering, Sethu Institute of Technology, Tamil Nadu, India

Abstract

Recently, online mode–based education is having more demand. Major reason behind this that the learners can easily gain insight of the concepts sitting at any geographically location. Also this has paved way for conducting exams in online mode. The knowledge gained by the students through online study has to be assessed. Hence, online assessment system helps to assess knowledge level gained by a learner and highlight the weaker portions of those concepts in the course of study. Need of the hour during any crisis is that education system of a country has to improved, which can be enriched through online assessment kind of system. Conducting examination and answer evaluation are hectic. Testing tools for assessing academic performance, integration of ideas are highly required but might have challenges from the perspective of resource availability and time constraints in order to generate question and evaluate responses automatically. Also, security concerns is one of the other important challenges to conquer. Hence, this chapter proposes an automated assessment system using supervised machine learning algorithm. The proposed system automatically generate questions with its respective answers and assess user responses. It then corrects the responses given by the learner based on the answers generated and records the results.

Keywords: Online assessment system, automation system, machine learning, supervised machine learning algorithm

Corresponding author: suriyas84@gmail.com; ss.cse@psgtech.ac.in

Rajdeep Chakraborty, Anupam Ghosh, Jyotsna Kumar Mandal and S. Balamurugan (eds.) Convergence of Deep Learning In Cyber-IoT Systems and Security, (101–122) © 2023 Scrivener Publishing LLC

5.1   Introduction

Online assessment also referred to as e-assessment, enables examiners to conduct examinations through internet for remote candidates. The goal of these systems is to offer the candidates an easy way to write the examinations and to provide the results at the earliest with the help of answer processing modules, without any manual evaluation. There are two types of online assessment system: multiple-choice question–based examination system (as shown in Figure 5.1) and descriptive question–based examination system (as shown in Figure 5.2). Descriptive question–based examination systems have lots of complexities, which include different ways of answering the same question, some questions require diagram or equation, some questions require answers more than a word and the length of the answers varies from individual to individual. Hence, evaluation of descriptive question–based answers is difficult. A manual question paper usually have several categories of question, such as describe, explain, define, and discuss.

The current examination systems are painstaking. Hence, online assessment system with automatic evaluation module is the need of the day.

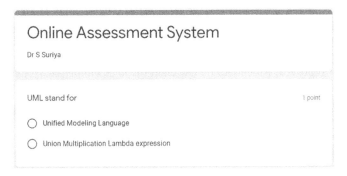

Figure 5.1 Multiple Choice Question based examination system.

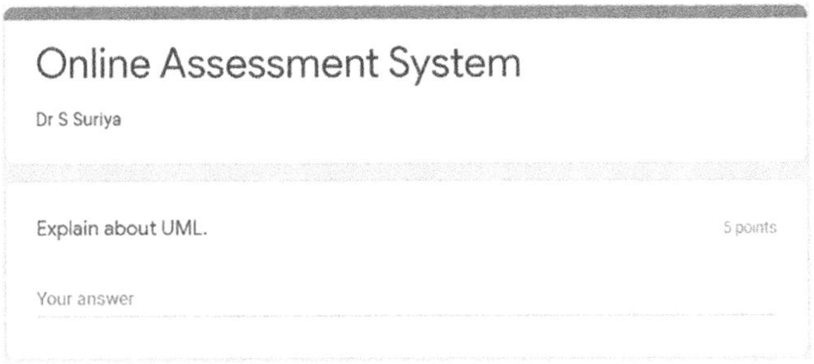

Figure 5.2 Descriptive question based examination system.

Considering the various hurdles like resource availability, timing constraints, proctoring, evaluation of answers and development of effective assessment system as a competitor to physical mode of exams. Manual evaluating of answer sheet takes up a significant amount of time and effort. The main motive of this online assessment system is to reduce the effort and time spent by the faculty on setting up the physical question paper, conducting offline examinations and evaluating the papers manually. The goal of the system is to train a system to understand the questions and the corresponding answers from the text so that the system could conduct online examinations with the generated questions and evaluate the answers by learners with the generated answers. Considering the pandemic situation of COVID where the entire education process has been transmuted into online means, the task of faulty team has become an onerous one. Hence, the best supervised algorithm, which has the highest accuracy will be taken by this online assessment system and then it will be coded in such a way to generate question and answers from the dataset efficiently. This system is designed by focusing on educational institutions like schools, colleges and private institutes to conduct online assessment for their employees on regular basis. As this system also involves question generation and answer evaluation modules, it reduces the effort of faculty team. The faculty have to give the lecture topic, for which the test is conducted as input to this system. The system generates questions and its corresponding answers and then conduct the online assessment. Once the learner completes the test and submits, the system evaluates the questions and grades the learner.

5.2   Literature Survey

Das *et al.* [1] proposed an approach for descriptive online examination system. Multiple choice questions are easy to deal with, but this is not the case in descriptive questions. Natural language processing concept is adopted for evaluating the answers. Answers are usually in the form of words technically called as strings, which is taken for evaluation against the answers, technically called as keywords given by the examiner. A list of preposition and articles are usually preprocessed, as they are treated as stop words, from the strings before evaluating it. A sparse matrix is generated based on the occurrence of each keyword in the preprocessed string and evaluation done based on NLP algorithms. Accuracy rate of the system was around 95%.

Tashu *et al.* [2] present a system for online descriptive exam, evaluation of the learner's answers and its scoring. The proposed system automatically scores descriptive responses in a semantic way using a suitable pair-wise approach with neural word embedding technique. Adding to it, faculty can also give textual feedback to the learners. Semantic similarity plays a vital role in evaluating the descriptive responses of a learner against the reference answer submitted by the faculty. Automatic essay evaluation (AEE) algorithm enriches this evaluation procedure. The scores are computing using Word Mover's distance (WMD) algorithm, which is based on cosine similarity of descriptive responses of a learner and reference answer submitted by the faculty. Accuracy rate of the system was about 80%.

Patil *et al.* [3] proposed automatic way of assessing the descriptive answers of an online exam using semantic analysis. The modules of the system are as follows:

1. Question answering module: admin uploads the question-answer dataset which is technically verified according to specific subject.
2. User authentication and validation module: the admin creates multiple users and set the authorization process, followed by validation of the answers.
3. Subjective examination module: manages the exam time and scheduling.
4. Feature extraction module: It is implemented using NLP which involves data preprocessing, data normalization, stop word removal, porter stemmer algorithm, features extraction and features selection. Answers of candidates are ranked based on measures of distance between keywords, numbers of keywords matched and other similar heuristic metrics.
5. Semantic analysis module: classifies all answers based on similarity weights.
6. Using Artificial Neural Networks (ANN) evaluation of the marks is done automatically according to the current weights. Finally, Classification results where the final results are displayed with accuracy.

Yanghoon Kim *et al.* [4] proposed an answer-separated seq2seq. It utilizes the information of the descriptive part and the answer given by the faculty. The proposed approach trains itself to identify interrogative words. Adding to it, a module called keyword-net is used to generate questions using the information available in the stored answers. This techniques helps in reducing the count of improper questions.

Riza, L.S *et al.* [5] suggested a way to take sentence completion question using NLP and K-Nearest Neighbor. They have gathered data from foreign newspaper and the data is preprocessed, tokenized and Part of Speech (POS) Tagging by Stanford Core NLP is done. Then they have calculated feature value and the blank space is decided by using KNN Classifier and at last the other options are determined. This system provides accuracy of 81.25%.

Xinyuan Lu *et al.* [6] proposed an approach to better handle and manage the difficulty of question generation from given input. It involves bidirectional LSTM architecture to generate questions from the input. Stanford Question Answering Dataset (SQuAD) was the dataset taken for experimenting the proposed approach.

Vrindavan Harrison *et al.* [7] presented an attentional encode-decode recurrent neural network model for question generation. It incorporated linguistic features and sentence embedding to capture meanings. Their model maps a source sequence to a target sequence. The encoder is a multilayer bidirectional LSTM and decoder is a unidirectional LSTM that uses global attention with input-feeding. The baseline model contains 4 different token level supervision features to the input, a sentence encoder and a copy mechanism. The experiments were performed using the SQuAD dataset and the model was evaluated using both automatic evaluation metrics and a human evaluation using crowd sourced workers.

Xiaozheng Dong *et al.* [8] has focused on an approach that focuses on semantics of a question. It is implemented with the help of Convolutional Neural Network (CNN) for prediction of semantics of any question. A question generating skeleton is built using Bidirectional Long Short-Term Memory (Bi-LSTM). Stanford Question Answering Dataset (SQuAD) is taken foe testing the proposed approach.

Upadhyay *et al.* [9] attempts to grade descriptive answers so that theoretical exams can be conducted online and hence proposed the system 'Checkpoint – An Online Descriptive Answers Grading Tool'. This proposed technique makes use of NLP for evaluating and grading the descriptive questions. The four basic operations of this technique are grammar check, removal of stop words, stemming, grading. The proposed technique was able to exhibit an accuracy of 98%.

Sandeep Subramanian *et al.* [10] has addressed the generation of questions based on a two-stage neural model. Questions are generated based on key phrases using sequence to sequence model. SQuAD and NewsQA datasets were used for experimenting the proposed technique.

Pranali Nikam *et al.* [11] suggested a pattern matching algorithm-based method. Here student's answer and true answer in the form of a graph and pattern is matched between two graphs. If the words do not match properly then synonym of the word is matched with true answer and similarity is found. The issue with above approach is when ordering of the word is changed with respect to true answer then their proposed system gets confused and thus provides wrong score.

Kaiche *et al.* [12] proposed a system with a flexible interface that tackles the requirements of a test. This proposed approach targets at conducting online assessment for objective type of questions with automatic grading. Pattern Matching Technique algorithm was addressed to solve the descriptive type of questions. This system provides an accuracy of about 70%.

Paul *et al.* [13] has tried using concept of Syntactic Similarity for grading the descriptive answers. Vector-based similarity matrix is used for automatic evaluation of descriptive answer. The system was able to give an accuracy of 70%.

Meena *et al.* [14] aims at usage of Hyperspace Analog to language (HAL) for grading descriptive answers. HAL performs computations on the input text to generate vectors. These vectors hold information about meaning and translates the text into vector. Kohonen Self-Organizing Map (SOM) takes input of HAL vectors. It results in formation of a document map.

Kudi *et al.* [15] proposed an automated system capable of evaluating descriptive answers. Automatic assessment tools are used for evaluation of answers against a predefined set of answers. The process of text mining is preprocessing the text from various sources. The clustering, summarization, classification algorithms can be used to preprocess text.

Kaur *et al.* [16] has proposed an approach for grading descriptive answers. Predefined answers and answers submitted by the students are represented in graphical format. Later similarity matching them is performed using various matching features to calculate the similarity score.

Agarwal *et al.* [17] suggested a way to take fill in the blanks and multiple-choice questions. There are three stages in their system which includes sentence selection, key selection and distractor selection. In each stage proper candidates are chosen and features are extracted and corresponding score is assigned to each feature by weighted sum of extracted feature and it is given by

$$\text{score} = \sum_{i=0}^{n} \text{wi} * \text{fi}$$

Their system selected most informative sentences of the chapters and generates gap-fill questions on them. Syntactic features helped in quality of gap-fill questions.

Hoshino, A. *et al.* [18] suggested a way to take multiple choice question along with options. The proposed system extracts features to explore the answers, blank spaces and wrong choices. KNN and a Naive Bayes classifier algorithm are used for training the dataset.

Dubey *et al.* [19] have performed a computer-assisted evaluation using builtin classification algorithms with the support of WEKA tool. It involves the following stages namely Tokenization, Vectorization, Training, Filtering and Classification. Tokenization involves dividing the answer text into tokens. Vectorization involves transformation of tokens into column vector. Random Forest classifier, J48 classifier, FT classifier, naïve bayes classifier, random tree classifier, reptree classifier are used for training the dataset. Filtering addresses the problem of unequal column vectors by equalizing the training and testing samples. The efficiency of the system is around 60%.

Ghavat *et al.* [20] proposed AI based symmetric answer evaluation system for descriptive answering. It is an automatic system which checks the descriptive type of answers based on given input Keywords. The actual evaluation is performed by using Hyperspace Analog to Language (HAL) and Self Organizing Map (SOM) methods. The modules of the system are as follows:

1. Exam System Admin which is for the admin, the person or a team under whom the entire control will be. Registering the subjects and registering the staff members and creating user ID and passwords for the staffs, allotting subjects to staffs are all controlled by the admin.
2. Staff are those who are engaged on conducting exams for the students and sets question papers.
3. Students will be registered by the staffs; they are provided with username and password with which they could login and write the test.
4. Online descriptive exam portal where all these activities take place. The evaluation process will have both the teacher's answer students' answers.

The model answer will be stored in the database. When the student submits its test, those answers will be compared with the model answer. The system will read both the model and student answer and then extract the keywords using keyword extraction algorithm such TF/IDF (text frequency/ inverse document frequency). Then the text will be tokenized and stemmed and the stop words will be removed. Latent Semantic Analysis will be applied and then Self Organizing Map Clustering will be applied on the text. Marks will be allotted using Cosine Similarity.

5.3   Existing Algorithms

Natural Language Processing (NLP). NLP is a divisional portion of artificial intelligence that enables computers understand, interpret and manipulate human language. NLP combined with Machine Learning (ML), creates systems that learn to perform tasks on their own and gets better by gaining experience. NLP takes its roots from many disciplines to bridge the gap between human communication and computer understanding.

Kohonen Self Organizing Maps (Kohonen SOM). The objective of this algorithm is transformation of arbitrary dimensions of input patterns into a two-dimensional feature map. It is done using topological ordering. Architecture of SOM involves a feed-Forward structure with a single computational layer of neurons arranged in rows and columns. Initialization, Competition, Cooperation and Adaptation are the four basic processes required to build Kohonen SOM maps.

Vector Based Similarity. The similarity between two vectors are evaluated using a function called s Vector based similarity. Cosine similarity is the most popularly used similarity measure for real-Valued vectors. It is helpful in retrieval of information to score the similarity of documents.

K-Nearest Neighbor (KNN) classifier. KNN classifier is the simplest Machine Learning algorithm that assumes the similarity between the input case and available cases. This algorithm stores all the available data and classifies a new data point based on similarity. This algorithm is mostly used for classification problem rather than regression.

Naive Bayes classifier. Naive Bayes classifiers are a collection of classification algorithms based on Bayes' theorem with an assumption of independence among predictors. It assumes that the presence of a particular feature in a class is unrelated to the presence of any other feature.

Convolutional Neural Network (CNN). Convolutional Neural Network is a multilayered neural network which can detect complex features in data. It is a deep learning algorithm which can take an input image, assign importance to various objects in the image and be able to differentiate one from the other.

Recurrent Neural Network (RNN). Recurrent Neural Network is a class of ANN where connections between nodes form a directed graph along a sequence. It is a sequence of neural network blocks that are linked to each other like a chain. It is trained to recognize patterns.

Random Forest. Random forests are an ensemble learning method for classification, regression construction of decision tress.

As conclusion to survey, the working of existing algorithms are shown in Figure 5.3. The advantages and disadvantages of existing algorithms are shown in Table 5.1.

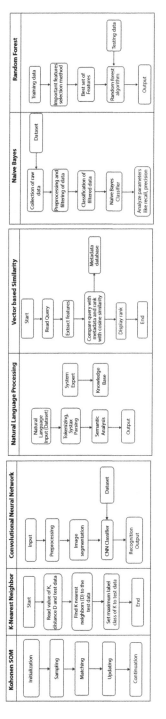

Figure 5.3 Algorithms used in existing systems.

Table 5.1 Advantages and disadvantages of supervised algorithms.

Algorithm	NLP	KOHONEN SOM	Vector Based Similarity	KNN Classifier	Naïve Bayes	CNN	RNN	Random Forest
Advantages	+ Provides high accuracy of about 98% + supports the largest number of languages. + Supports image captioning, machine translation, language understanding, paraphrasing, questions answering	+ Data mapping + Capable of organizing complex data sets	+ Query language is simple. + Ranking - reduces to a dot product. + Provides an accuracy of about 80%	+ No assumptions about data + Simple algorithm + Multi-class problems can be solved	+ Ease of predicting test class of dataset. + Multi class prediction. + Scalable for large datasets.	+ Great for short texts. + Learns the filters automatically without mentioning it explicitly. + Follow the concept of parameter sharing.	+ Process inputs of any length is flexible. + Utilization of internal memory for processing of the arbitrary inputs.	+ Relatively simple to implement. + Can judge the importance of the features. + For unbalanced datasets, it balances the error. + Training speed is faster.
Disadvantages	– Difficult to learn and use. – Slow comparatively. – Lack of semantic analysis while splitting text by sentences. – Lack of neural network models	– Difficult to determine what input weights used. – Mapping leads to clusters – Requires similarity between nearby points.	– Text VSM can't deal with lexical ambiguity and variability.	– High memory requirement – Slow for large datasets. – Sensitive to outliers – Prediction stage might be slow – Can't deal with missing values	– Independence of features does not hold. – A bad estimator. – Training data should represent population well.	– High computational cost. – Difficult for long texts when a large vocabulary is needed. – Takes more time to train a model. – Need a lot of training data.	– Training the models is difficult. – Leads to problems like exploding and gradient vanishing.	– Over fits certain noisy classification or regression problems. – Random forest is a black box approach, hence we have little control on what the model does. – Doesn't predict beyond the range in training data, in case of regression.

5.4   Proposed System Design

Block Diagram (Student)
Once the students get registered to the system, they could now access the resources available in the system. After logging onto the system, the students are enabled to choose the type of test and the subject for which they are going to attempt the test. After selecting the test type and the subject, they are now allowed to answer the questions generated by the system for the type chosen by them. After completing the test, the students can submit their answers and can log out of the system as shown in Figure 5.4.

Block Diagram (Faculty)
The faculty members after been registered to the system, they could login the system to conduct a test. They should provide the lecture chapters as

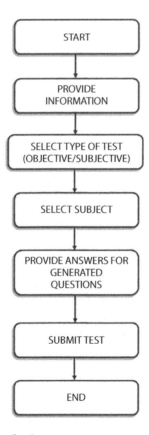

Figure 5.4 Block Diagram (Student).

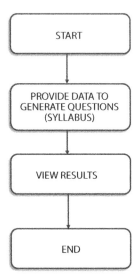

Figure 5.5 Block Diagram (Faculty).

inputs to the system for which the test is conducted. The online examination system now generates questions and answers from these topics as the student selects the type of test. After the test has been completed, the answer evaluation takes place and the results are stored. The faculty members are now able to view the grades of the students as shown in Figure 5.5.

Block Diagram (Online Assessment System)
The online examination system acts as a master for the entire working of the system. It stores all the details about the students and the faculty members. It authenticates the students and the faculty members, each time they log onto the system. It receives the chapter inputs from the faculty member and the test type and subject from the students and generates necessary question and answers for those generated questions. The test is now open for the students to attempt. Once the student completes the test and submits it. The answers given by the students are extracted by the system and evaluates those answers by comparing with those answers that were generated by the system and using similarity measures to compute the score. These grades are then stored in a sheet from where the faculty could view the results of the students as shown in Figure 5.6.

UML Usecase Diagram
Use case diagram represents the dynamic behavior of a system. It encapsulates the system's functionality by incorporating use cases, actors, and

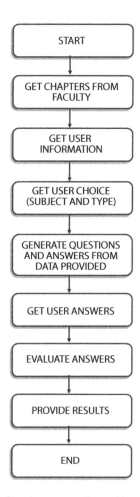

Figure 5.6 Block Diagram (Online Assessment System).

their relationships. It models the tasks, services, and functions required by a system of an application. It depicts the high-level functionality of a system and also tells how the user handles a system as shown in Figure 5.7.

Actor Specification
Student
Description: This actor plays the role of a student who can register into the website and select the type of test he or she wishes to attempt. The actor then attempts the test and after completing the test, the test is submitted so that results can be evaluated.

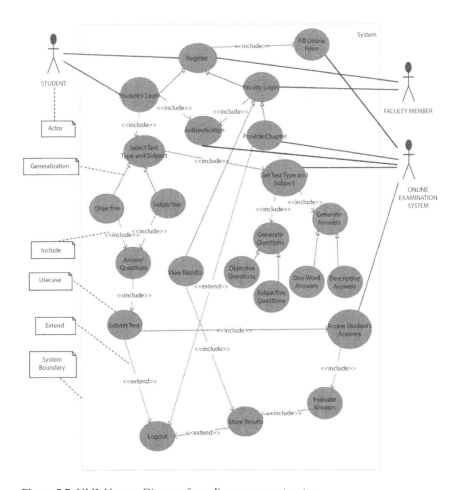

Figure 5.7 UML Usecase Diagram for online assessment system.

Faculty Member

Description: This actor plays the role of a faculty member who can register onto the website and then provide those chapters for which the system must generate questions and answers and conducts the test for the students. This actor could also view the grades of the students.

Online Examination System

Description: This acts as the master of this website which provides certain services. This maintains the details of the students and the faculty members who have registered to the website. This system takes the chapters provided by the faculty and generate objective and subjective questions and its corresponding answers. These questions, thus generated, are out to students to attempt the test. Once the students attempt the test and submit their responses, the students' responses are compared with the answer key generated by the system and based on some similarity measure these answers are graded. The system then stores the results of the students for the faculty to view.

5.5   System Implementation

The five basic stages of natural language processing, shown in Figure 5.8, are

> Stage I: Lexical Analysis—this first stage of natural language processing aims in analyzing the words once after identifying them. Lexicon is a terminology that refers to words or phrases of a language under consideration. Lexical analysis process of splitting of input into words.
>
> Stage II: Syntactic Analysis—the second stage of natural language processing that focuses on analysis of words. Later, the relationship between the words is analyzed and transformed into structural format.

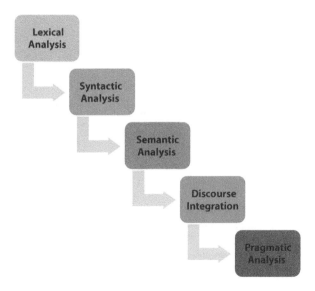

Figure 5.8 Stages in natural language processing.

Stage III: Semantic Analysis—the third stage of natural language processing targets at extraction of meaning of the words. It is implemented by mapping of syntactic structures.

Stage IV: Discourse Integration—the fourth stage of Natural Language processing focuses on integration of words based the meaning of their preceding words.

Stage V: Pragmatic Analysis—the fourth stage of Natural Language processing enhances the necessity of real world knowledge.

Modules of the Proposed System

The following are the modules of the Online Assessment System are shown in Figure 5.9.

Module 1—Creation of Dataset

A dataset is a set or a collection of data records for computer processing. Dataset type is distinguished on the basis of data storage and structure. The type of dataset that suits best for this system is a file-based dataset. The dataset for the online assessment system (as shown in Figure 5.10) consists of the portions covered by the faculty for the respective examination. This has to be prepared by the faculty prior to the date of the examination in

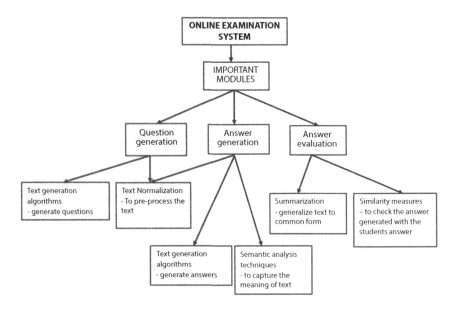

Figure 5.9 NLP algorithms used in online examination system.

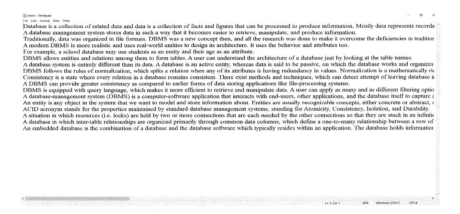

Figure 5.10 Dataset.

the required format. The dataset must be in the form of a collection of sentences with each sentence representing a piece of information, which is stored in a text file (.txt). This dataset remains the same for both the objective and subjective tests. The dataset differs from one subject to another.

Module 2—Authentication

This module deals with the login and authentication part of the proposed idea. Each student is provided with a unique user name and password through which they can access the tests. Upon startup, the students are required to enter the username and password. Only if the credentials match with the credentials present in the system in the form of a database, the student is allowed to proceed to the next module. If the credentials do not match, then an error message is displayed and the student is again asked to provide the correct credentials.

Module 3—Objective Question Generation

This module deals with the generation of questions for objective type questions. Not all sentences can be used for an objective type question. The following steps are followed to check if a sentence has the potential to be an objective type question and to generate that particular question. The first step is to identify the sentence which has potential to create objective questions. We use sentence tokenization for this process. The sent_tokenize() function is used to split the paragraphs into single sentences. Each sentence is then evaluated to check if it has the potential to generate an objective question. If the length of the sentence is less than four words and the sentence starts with an adverb, then the sentence is probably not the best fit to generate a question. A grammar is defined to extract noun phrases from the sentence. A regular expression parser is created with the defined grammar. The sentence is then tokenized and the syntax tree is generated as shown in Figure 5.11.

The noun phrases are then selected from the Syntax Tree. These noun phrases are the most possible answers that can be given for a particular question as shown in Figure 5.12. In the next step, these noun phrases are check for certain conditions. The noun phrases that does not satisfy these conditions are removed. If no noun phrases remain, then the question cannot be generated from this sentence. If noun phrases remain, a dictionary is generated with the noun phrase, which can be the answer, a key that contains a value and a list of similar options, which can be substituted for that particular noun phrase. The similar words are found by using WordNet. The noun phrase to be replaced is generated and the black spaces with respect to the noun phrase is generated. The regular expression for the noun phrase is generated and is used in replacing the noun phrase by the blank phrase which are generated.

Module 4—Subjective Question Generation

This module seals with the generation of question for subjective question generation. In order to generate a subjective question, more than one sentence must be considered. A question pattern, such as "EXPLAIN

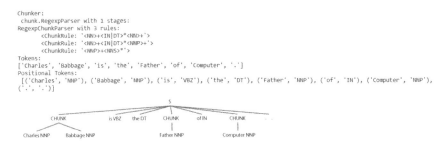

```
Chunker:
  chunk.RegexpParser with 1 stages:
RegexpChunkParser with 3 rules:
      <ChunkRule: '<NN>+<IN|DT>*<NN>+'>
      <ChunkRule: '<NN>+<IN|DT>*<NNP>+'>
      <ChunkRule: '<NNP>+<NNS>*'>
Tokens:
['Charles', 'Babbage', 'is', 'the', 'Father', 'of', 'Computer', '.']
Positional Tokens:
  [('Charles', 'NNP'), ('Babbage', 'NNP'), ('is', 'VBZ'), ('the', 'DT'), ('Father', 'NNP'), ('of', 'IN'), ('Computer', 'NNP'),
('.', '.')]
```

Figure 5.11 Generated syntax tree.

```
Replace Nouns -> ['Charles', 'Babbage']

Replace Phrase -> Charles Babbage

Blank Phrase -> _____

Regular Expression -> re.compile('Charles\\ Babbage', re.IGNORECASE)

Sentence -> _____ is the Father of Computer.

Final Format of the Question :
  {'Answer': 'Charles Babbage', 'Key': 7, 'Similar': [], 'Question': '_____ is the Father of Computer.'}
```

Figure 5.12 Objective question formation.

IN DETAIL," "DEFINE," etc. are predefined by the faculty. The following steps are performed in order to generate a question. The paragraph is first divided into separate sentences. The grammar is defined and a regular expression parser is trained on the grammar. The next step deals with the identifying important sentences to generate questions based on them. For each sentence in the given paragraph, we create a syntax tree by tagging each word in a sentence with its respective positional tokens. We traverse each and every node in the Syntax Tree till we reach the required keywords. The keywords are then added to a dictionary along with the sentence in which they are present in. Since the answer must be in descriptive form, the answer must be a bit elaborate. If the current sentence is greater than 20 characters long, the current sentence can be used for answer evaluation. If not, the next sentence in which the keyword is present is added along with the current sentence. The questions and answers are currently in a list format and must be reformatted into a dictionary type. Each keyword in searched in a random manner, and the respective answer is then searched and appended into a dictionary with the question being created by using one of the predefined question patterns along with the keyword. The answer is then created with the already selected sentences. The final dictionary contains a dictionary of questions along with the answers.

Module 5—Answer Evaluation
The evaluation of answers varies along with the mode of the test. The answer evaluation for the two modes of the test are listed below:

Objective Answer Evaluation
The answer for the objective type question is generated along with the process of question generation. A variable "SCORE" is used to keep track of user's makes. For every correct answer given by the user, the score is increased by 100. For every wrong answer given by the user, the score remains the same. The final score is divided by the number of questions to get the final result. If the final result if greater than 33.33, then the user is declared as "PASS" else the user is declared as "FAIL."

Subjective Answer Evaluation
The answer for the subjective type question is generated along with the process of question generation. The evaluation technique uses both the answer given by the user and the answer generated during the question generation. The user answer is then divided into tokens and the generated answer is generated into tokens. Both the tokens are combined and a list containing all tokens is created. A vector is created for both the user answer

Figure 5.13 Result generation and storing result.

and the generated answer. The sentence is tokenized on word level. A one-hot encoded vector is then created by creating a vector with 0s and 1s with 1 representing a word present in user answer as well as generated answer and 0 representing a word not present in user answer but is present in generated answer and vice versa. The final score is calculated by using the resulting two vectors using cosine similarity score with Euclidian distance. The final score is then displayed and if the score is greater than 50, then the user is declared as "PASS" else the user is declared as "FAIL."

Module 6—Result Generation
The final result is then stored in a database which is created as shown in Figure 5.13. The data logged into the database includes the date and time at which the test was taken, the username, the subject name, the subject code, the test type, score, and result.

5.6 Conclusion

A lot of research works exist in the survey for question and answer evaluation but there is only very limited system, which has both objective questions and descriptive question along with answer evaluation without any bias to any user. Using the proposed system, it reduces laborious manual work and automates the above task. Hence, the proposed system covering the stated functionality with optimal accuracy. Various NLP techniques and methods have been used in each phase in this system. Challenges still prevail in the system like taking up challenging question from given document and evaluating the answer if the user has referred from another document rather than the given document. In this chapter, various aspects of each phase of the question and answer evaluation process were discussed. Understanding the given context conceptually by the system and taking up analytical question based on the concept is the hardest task of NLP and will focused into further research on this perspective. The proposed system has shown enhanced performance in taking the question and answer evaluation.

This chapter can be further enhanced by mooting the number of hard, medium and easy questions desired in the test. Answer evaluation scheme can even be fine-tuned for better accuracy by working more on word lemmatization part. The format of questions varies from domain to domain say, GRE exams focuses on grammatical part whereas other exams in college level focuses on question, which has some concepts as keyword, hence the preprocessing and other method slightly vary. It can extend as the next level of research.

References

1. Das, I., Sharma, B., Rautaray, S.S., Pandey, M., An Examination System Automation Using Natural Language Processing. *IEEE International Conference on Communication and Electronics Systems (ICCES)*, pp. 1064–1069, 2019.
2. Tashu, T.M., Esclamado, J.P., Horvath, T., Intelligent on-line exam management and evaluation system. *International Conference on Intelligent Tutoring Systems*, Springer, pp. 105–111, 2019.
3. Patil, T., Automatic Assessment of Descriptive Answers for Online Examination using Semantic Analysis. *J. Gujarat Res. Soc.*, 21, 5, 413–419, 2019.
4. Kim, Y., Lee, H., Shin, J., Jung, K., Improving neural question generation using answer separation. *AAAI Conference on Artificial Intelligence*, vol. 33, pp. 6602–6609, 2019.
5. Riza, L.S., Pertiwi, A.D., Rahman, E.F., Munir, M., Abdullah, C.U., Question Generator System of Sentence Completion in TOEFL Using NLP and K-Nearest Neighbor. *Indones. J. Sci. Technol.*, 4, 2, 294–311, 2019.
6. Lu, X., Learning to generate questions with adaptive copying neural networks. *International Conference on Management of Data*, pp. 1838–1840, 2019.
7. Harrison, V. and Walker, M., *Neural generation of diverse questions using answer focus, contextual and linguistic features*, 2018.
8. Dong, X., Hong, Y., Chen, X., Li, W., Zhang, M., Zhu, Q., Neural question generation with semantics of question type. *CCF International Conference on Natural Language Processing and Chinese Computing*, Springer, pp. 213–223, 2018.
9. Upadhyay, S., Nehete, C., Powar, V., Wadhwani, J., Checkpoint-An Online Descriptive Answers Grading Tool. *IJARCS*, 8, 3, 637–640, 2017.
10. Subramanian, S., Wang, T., Yuan, X., Zhang, S., Bengio, Y., Trischler, A., *Neural models for key phrase detection and question generation*, 2017.
11. Nikam, P., Shinde, M., Mahajan, R., Kadam, S., Automatic Evaluation of Descriptive Answer Using Pattern Matching Algorithm. *Int. J. Comput. Sci. Eng.*, 3, 1, 69–70, 2015.

12. Kaiche, B., Kalan, S., More, S., Shelukar, L., Online descriptive examination and assessment system. *Int. J. Emerg. Technol. Adv. Eng.*, 4, 3, 660–664, 2014.
13. Paul, D.V. and Pawar, J.D., Use of Syntactic Similarity Based Similarity Matrix for Evaluating Descriptive Answer. *IEEE Sixth International Conference on Technology for Education*, 2014.
14. Meena, K. and Raj, L., Evaluation of the Descriptive type answers using Hyperspace Analog to Language and Self-organizing Map. *IEEE International Conference on Computational Intelligence and Computing Research*, pp. 1–5, 2014.
15. Kudi, P., Manekar, A., Daware, K., Dhatrak, T., Online Examination with short text matching. *IEEE Global Conference on Wireless Computing & Networking (GCWCN)*, pp. 56–60, 2014.
16. Kaur, A., Sasikumar, M., Nema, S., Pawar, S., Algorithm for Automatic evaluation of single sentence descriptive answer. *IJIES*, 19, 112–121, 2013.
17. Agarwal, M. and Mannem, P., Automatic gap-fill question generation from text books. *Sixth Workshop on Innovative Use of NLP for Building Educational Applications*, pp. 56–64, 2011.
18. Hoshino, A. and Nakagawa, H., A real-time multiple-choice question generation for language testing: a preliminary study. *Second Workshop on Building Educational Applications Using NLP*, pp. 17–20, 2005.
19. Dubey, R. and Makwana, R.R.S., Computer-Assisted Valuation of Descriptive Answers Using Weka with RandomForest Classification. *Second International Conference on Microelectronics, Computing & Communication Systems (MCCS 2017)*, pp. 359–366, 2017.
20. Ghavat, A.K., Tekade, B.G., Bhute, V.S., Chikhalkar, M.D., Vijaykar, P., AI Based Symmetric Answer Evaluation System for Descriptive Answering. *Int. Res. J. Mod. Eng. Technol. Sci.*, 3, 3, 449–455, 2020.

6

On a Reference Architecture to Build Deep-Q Learning-Based Intelligent IoT Edge Solutions

Amit Chakraborty[1], Ankit Kumar Shaw[1]* and Sucharita Samanta[2]

[1]M.Tech, Swami Vivekananda University, Kolkata, India
[2]M.Tech, Techno India University, Kolkata, India

Abstract

Reinforcement learning involves the learning by an agent, which is essentially a mathematical function in an interactive environment. It learns through trial and error in which it receives a positive or negative reward for each action taken against the environment. The agent takes actions via policies, which are the decision-making functions and maps the various environment states to actions. The goal of RL is to find a set of suitable actions that would maximize the total cumulative reward of the agent. Q learning and its neural network, i.e., counterpart has been significant in solving reinforcement learning problems. For IoT-based solutions, usage of reinforcement learning helps in better decision making where the volume of known data is less to be used effectively in a supervised algorithm. It also helps in distinctive identification of states and experiment with the reward mechanism to simulate various real-world scenarios. One roadblock in using deep reinforcement learning algorithm in IoT-based solutions is to frame an architecture that would support the learning, as well as be scalable enough to support increasing IoT workload and improve the agent performance. In this chapter, we would like to propose a public cloud-based IoT solution architecture that can host a deep reinforcement learning network, implement learning patterns for the same and use the network on IoT edge devices. The architecture will provide a reference to deploy Deep Q Learning based workloads to run on IoT edge devices with the help of containers. This will help in building solutions that spend less time to sync with cloud and rather focus on to react more quickly to localized changes and improve agent response to events.

**Corresponding author*: aankitsshaw@gmail.com

Rajdeep Chakraborty, Anupam Ghosh, Jyotsna Kumar Mandal and S. Balamurugan (eds.) *Convergence of Deep Learning In Cyber-IoT Systems and Security*, (123–146) © 2023 Scrivener Publishing LLC

Keywords: Q learning, deep learning, Azure, IoT solutions, cloud, cloud architecture

6.1   Introduction

Q learning that is essentially derived from Bellman's equation and its deep learning counterpart called deep Q learning are some of the popular algorithms that dominate the applicable field of reinforcement learning. In this book chapter, we will build up from machine learning and introduce Q and Deep Q learning. On building a solid foundation, we will approach a case study of optimizing a business problem with the help of Q learning and thereby build and deploy a model. The model deployment will be based on a reference architecture based on cloud based IOT to use the model in an edge device. The deployment architecture will also consist of containerization using docker and deployed in cloud. We have used Microsoft Azure as our cloud platform due to its support of IOT and edge services.

6.1.1   A Brief Primer on Machine Learning

Machine learning is a subfield of artificial intelligence which explores the development of algorithms which allow a computer to learn from the data and past experiences on their own. It allows a machine to automatically learn from the previous data, upgrade working performance by using their previous experiences and then make the result. With the help of sample previous data, which is known as training data, machine learning algorithms basically make a mathematical model which helps in making predictions or decisions without being explicitly programmed. Machine learning constructs or uses the algorithms that learn from any previous data. If we can provide huge number of data to train the model the result will be much accurate.

6.1.1.1   Types of Machine Learning

6.1.1.1.1   Supervised Learning
It is defined by the use of labeled datasets to train the algorithms so that they can easily trained and classify data or predict the outcomes accurately. Cross validation process is used here to ensure that the model avoids overfitting or underfitting. Supervised learning helps to solve huge number of real-world problems, such as it can classify the spam and separate this from

your inbox folder. Some popular methods used in supervised learning include logistic regression, linear regression, k-nearest neighbors, decision trees support, vector machine (SVM), and more.

6.1.1.1.2   Unsupervised Learning

In unsupervised machine learning technique, the users do not need to train the model. Basically, it allows the model to work on its own experience to achieve the accuracy. There is no dataset to train the model and it mainly deals with the unlabeled data. Unsupervised Learning Algorithms allow users to perform more complex processing tasks compared to supervised learning. Although, unsupervised learning can be more unpredictable compared with other natural learning methods. Unsupervised learning algorithms include clustering, anomaly detection, neural networks, etc.

- Unsupervised machine learning finds all kind of unknown patterns in data.
- Unsupervised methods help you to find features which can be useful for categorization.
- It is taken place in real time, so all the input data to be analysed and labeled in the presence of learners.
- It is easier to get unlabelled data from a computer than labelled data, which needs manual intervention.

6.1.1.1.3   Reinforcement Learning

It is a type of machine learning precedent [1] in which the algorithm is based on a feedback system rather than trained on some data. It is basically a method to train the machine learning models based on some sequence of performance by the agent. This trial and error–based learning method is based on giving rewards for the desired behaviors or punishing for the undesired ones. There are some building blocks for this algorithm:

a) State—It is fostered by the agents to know the environment
b) Reward—It is a function to teach the right behavior.
c) Environment—There are some different conditions may arise and the agent has to deal with it.
d) Action—It is taken by the agent depending on the environment.
e) Agent—It has to perform all the functions and that decision will train the model.

As we can see this is not based on dataset, we can consider this as the advanced version of machine learning because there is no expenditure for collecting and cleaning the data.

6.1.1.1.4 Types of Reinforcement Learning Algorithm

Positive: In this approach a specific behavior occurs so that the performance should get increased [2]. This approach of reinforcement helps the user to get the maximize result of each action.

Negative: In this approach, we just take away the positive response making behavior [3].

6.1.1.1.5 Learning Models of Reinforcement Algorithm

6.1.1.1.5.1 MARKOV DECISION PROCESS

This is basically a reinforcement learning model where an agent is supposed to decide the best action to select based on his current state. When this step is repeated, this problem is known as a **Markov Decision Process.**

A Markov Decision Process (MDP) model contains:

- A set of possible world states S.
- A set of Models.
- A set of possible actions A.
- A real valued reward function R(s,a).
- A policy the solution of Markov decision process [6].

In the Markov decision process, each environment's response at time t+1 depends only on the state and action presented at time t. Previous experience and their result do not affect the current scenario at all [7].

6.1.1.1.5.2 Q LEARNING

Q learning algorithm is a form of reinforcement learning algorithm which depends on some value which is used as the action value to simultaneous increase of the good behavior and reward of the learning agent. So this is basically an off-policy learning algorithm where learning functions learns from some random actions and no such existing policy is needed.

- In this algorithm, Q is basically defined for states and actions. Q(S,A) is approximate evaluation to measure the action A which is taken by the agent at state S. This calculation of Q(S,A) will be continuously computed using the TD–Update rule.

- During the whole process of the learning algorithm, an agent starts from a starting state and then go through a number of transitions from its present state to next state depends on its choice of action and the environment.
- We can represent the TD - Update rule as follows-

$$Q(S,A) \leftarrow Q(S,A) + \alpha(R + \gamma Q(S',A') - Q(S,A))$$

- This TD—update rule is used to estimate the value of Q is applied throughout the each and every process of the algorithm. The terms are described below:
- S: Present state of the agent.
- A: Present action by the agent.
- S': Next state of the agent.
- A: Next best action to be taken by using the present Q-value estimation.
- R: Present reward gained from the environment with respect to the present action.
- γ (>0 and ≤1): This is the discounting factor for future rewards. This factor is needed because the future rewards are less important than present rewards.
- α: This is the length of the step to update the estimation of Q(S,A).

Let us take an example of Q-learning. A robot is used to cross a puzzle and come to the end point. But obstacle is the mines which are present over the puzzle and the robot can move one tile at a particular time. If any robot steps onto a mine, it will be finished. The robot has to come to the end point with taking minimum time.

The reward system consists some of the following rules:

i) After taking each step, the robot losses 1 point. This is a reminder for the robot to select the shortest way and come to the target point in minimum time.

ii) After taking steps on a mine, the robot will loss 100 point and the game ends.

iii) After getting power the robot gains 1 point.

iv) After arriving the target position, the robot will get 100 points.

But the problem is how we can train the robot to get the target position with the shortest path without stride on a mine. In that case, we take the help of Q-table. By taking the help of this table, we can calculate the maximum expected rewards for every action at each particular state.

Four numbers of actions will be present at each nonedge tile. From a particular position, a robot can move up or down or right or left.

6.2   Dynamic Programming

Dynamic programming is an algorithmic technique to solve an optimization problem that supports to break the problem into different subproblems and utilizing the concept that the optimal solution to the total problem depends on the optimal solution to its subproblems. Individual subproblems are considered often as stages of decisions because this technique has been used to optimize the discrete time dynamic process which can be shown as a sequence of decisions in time. This is basically the reason of using the word "dynamic." Firstly, any optimization problem has some objectives. The objective function is a mathematical equation which explain the production result corresponds to maximize profits or minimize losses based on a set of alternative values or variables. The variables can be referred as resources, availability, capacity, technology, etc. and try to reduce the restrictions of the environment in which the business works. Any optimization problem must have some objectives like minimizing travel time, minimizing cost, maximizing profits, maximizing utility.

Bellman equation basically used to solve Markov decision process by helping us in finding the best optimal policy and value function. As we know in deterministic environment, we are always aware about the present state and the next state after performing some actions. Bellman showed that a dynamic optimization problem in discrete time can be stated in a recursive which follow a step-by-step form known as backward induction by noticing relationships between the value function in a single time period and the value function in another time period. Basically, this relation is called "Bellman Equation." In this technique, the optimal strategy in the last time period is described previously as a function of the given variable's value at a particular time and the optimal value of the objective function is represented as the value of the state variable. Then, the intermediate period's optimization includes maximizing the sum of the period's specified objective function and the optimal value of the objective function in future, showing the particular period's optimal policy depend upon the value of the mentioned variable as of the intermediate decision. Some important factors of Bellman Equation are –

State—A mathematical representation of what the agent is
noticing at some particular time in the environment.

Action—This is the input which the agent provides to the environment and calculated by doing an application policy to the
present state.

Reward—A responsive signal from the environment reflecting
the agent's good performance to the goals of the game.

The Bellman Equation is given by:

$$V(s) = max_a \{R(s, a) + \gamma V (s')$$

$V(s)$—this is the value for being in a particular state

$V(s')$—this is the value of being in the next state after taking an
action

γ—this is the discount factor

max_a—this is the value where we want the maximum of action
(which maximizes the value) so that the agent is in the optimal solution.

6.3   Deep Q-Learning

Deep Q-Learning algorithm is one of the most important concepts in
Reinforcement Learning [4]. Basically, in deep Q Learning, we take the
help of a neural network to guess the Q-value function. The state is considered as the input and the Q-value of every possible action is generated as
the output [5]. The comparison between Q-Learning & deep Q-Learning
is explained properly in the diagram below-

So, there are some steps involved in reinforcement learning using
Q-Learning networks-

i) The user stores the past experience in memory.

ii) The maximum output of the Q-Network decides the next
action.

iii) The loss function is the mean squared error of (the predicted
Q-value and the target Q-value) – Q*. Actually, it is a regression problem.

$$Q(S_t, A_t) \leftarrow Q(S_t, A_t) + \infty [S_{t+1} + \gamma \, max_a \, Q(S_{t+1}, a) - Q(S_t, A_t)]$$

6.4   IoT

It is basically an approach, which helps you to collect data and makes the devices smarter. We all are social being. So, we meet people and during communication we exchange our thoughts. In this way, actually, we are exchanging information or data. Devices also stores data that might be useful but how do we can collect this type of data. There are some smart devices that collect data for us and they will do a lot of things what we want them to do. Internet enables us to these devices to connect each other and that actually simplifies the data collecting process and also make them interactive.

6.4.1   Azure

It is a cloud [9] platform that provides us various services that concern computing and software development. We should use IOT on Azure because Azure [10] is basically one of the leading cloud service providers. It provides integration, security and services that will help us to implement IOT services on top of it.

6.4.1.1   IoT on Azure

Azure has various services like data visualization, machine learning, data warehousing, application creation, instance and virtual machine creation, storage [8] security, etc., are taken care by Azure. So basically, we have application on Microsoft azure, and we can apply it on IOT and make them more smarter. And if we do not have any application in azure, we can create them and then use IOT on top of it.

6.4.1.1.1   Azure IOT Components
6.4.1.1.1.1   Azure IOT Central
It is basically a SAAS kind of a service. It provides us similar services that basically lets us create similar software as a service kind of application For IOT platforms.

6.4.1.1.1.2   Azure IOT Solution Accelerators
It is a PAAS kind of a service that lets us create templatized IOT applications which can be used to create ready to use IOT services. It requires more effort than Azure IOT central but it is more flexible also. As this provides a platform, we can customize our applications.

6.4.1.1.1.3   Azure IOT Hub

It basically lets us connect other services and applications, So it creates a central point of communication for all the applications. Azure IOT hub is a complete independent service.

6.4.1.1.1.4   Azure Digital Twins

It basically helps to create models.

6.4.1.1.1.5   Azure Time series Insights

A series of information that varies time to time is called as time series analysis of data. Azure TSI gives us insights or helps us to create applications to collect real time data and generates insights out of it.

6.4.1.1.1.6   Azure Sphere

It has a set of devices/classifications that lets us do a lot of IOT things. It has a sets of micro controlling unit that can helps us to get better IOT services.

6.4.1.1.1.7   Azure Maps

It is used for finding locations, tracking cars etc.

6.4.1.1.2   Architecture

6.4.1.1.2.1   Devices

A device or a thing is any object that has networking capability, can securely registered with cloud, can send data and receive instructions from cloud, e.g., ESP32 Thing.

6.4.1.1.2.2   Cloud Gateway Service/Hub

It is a junction point which securely accepts the data, provide device management, and it also has the control and storage capabilities which property is helpful to store meta data [11].

6.4.1.1.2.3   Azure IOT Hub

It acts as a centralized message hub for communicating in both directions between any IOT application and the other devices attached with it. There is no limit of devices we can connect, and the Azure IOT Hub is extremely secure.

6.4.1.1.2.4   Azure Stream Analytics
It is a properly organized and real-time analytics service designed to analyze and process the fast-moving data streams, which can be used to get the insight. Depending on the insight, the action is generated.

6.4.1.1.2.5   Case Study
As an example, to highlight the architecture discussed in this chapter let us consider a use case that can be implemented in a simulated environment. We have considered a business process use case because we could use simulation and value stream mapping to test the same in an environment of choice and deploy that in the cloud.

6.4.1.1.2.5.1   Case Study Description
Optimizing the Flows in an E-Commerce Warehouse. We will study the flow of goods in an e-commerce warehouse with a special focus on optimization of the business process via the usage of reinforcement learning. We will use Q learning which we explained in the earlier sections to try to optimize the business process.

6.4.1.1.2.5.2   Business Process Description
Let us assume that the warehouse belongs to an e-commerce business to consumer company. It sells a variety of products to a heterogeneous set of customers but underlying business process for the it remains the same. The warehouse E-Commerce system integral part of the business process. It is the central location where different sellers stores the inventory and maintains its inventory. the business process associated with an inventory comprises of receiving, put away, storage, [12] picking, packing, and shipping. there should always be a technique for research to optimize the above six processes.

Let us define an environment in the following manner (Figure 6.1):

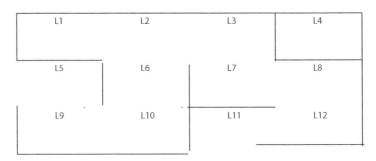

Figure 6.1 A schematic representation of e-commerce business process having heterogeneous sources.

These locations denoted by L1, L2, ... L12 are autonomous locations in which we have different categories of goods placed. Let us consider a business process where an autonomous agent must collect these products from these locations. These locations in turn have a priority ranking. That is the warehouse system ranks the locations in terms of priority of items stored. This priority may be decided as per item demand, easy of availability, price, popularity, etc. The ranking is as follows:

At a time, this priority ranking influences the autonomous robot movement in the warehouse. Let us consider the problem of making the autonomous agent learn the shortest route from any location-to-location L7 as this is the location with the highest priority. We will also train the AI agent to go to L7 via the second priority location that is L11. After training the AI agent we will deploy it in an edge using cloud based IoT architecture so that it can be used by any other devices for agent training.

Let us first define the environment in which the AI agent would work. An environment would fundamentally consist of three elements (Table 6.1):

- State definition
- Action definition
- Reward definition

Table 6.1 Priority wise business process schematic representation.

Priority	Location
1	L7
2	L11
3	L12
4	L10
5	L1
6	L9
7	L8
8	L3
9	L2
10	L4
11	L6
12	L5

6.4.1.1.2.5.3   State Definition

State is the physical space among the 12 locations where the autonomous AI agent will be at any time "t." (Table 6.2).

Table 6.2 State wise business process schematic representation.

State	Location
0	L1
1	L2
2	L3
3	L4
4	L5
5	L6
6	L7
7	L8
8	L9
9	L10
10	L11
11	L12

We have defined the locations as states to justify the usage of metrics in Q Learning.

6.4.1.1.2.5.4   Action Definition

Next let us define the action to be played. To represent the action in terms of data structure expression, we can represent it in terms of an array as:

$$\text{Actions} = [0,1,2,3,4,5,6,7,8,9,10,11]$$

According to the experiment zone the autonomous AI agent cannot take some actions due to restriction in barriers.

6.4.1.1.2.5.5   Rewards

Let us now define the rewards that the agent would get. In the terminology of reinforcement learning we must define a function R, such that given the two parameters, an input state S and an action a, R will return a numerical reward by acting as in state S (Table 6.3):

$$R \text{ --}>$$

Table 6.3 Rewards representation based on business process matrix.

	L1	L2	L3	L4	L5	L6	L7	L8	L9	L10	L11	L12
L1	0	1	0	0	0	0	0	0	0	0	0	0
L2	1	0	1	0	0	1	0	0	0	0	0	0
L3	0	1	0	0	0	0	1	0	0	0	0	0
L4	0	0	0	0	0	0	0	1	0	0	0	0
L5	0	0	0	0	0	0	0	0	1	0	0	0
L6	0	1	0	0	0	0	0	0	0	1	0	0
L7	0	0	1	0	0	0	1000	1	0	0	0	0
L8	0	0	0	1	0	0	1	0	0	0	0	1
L9	0	0	0	0	1	0	0	0	0	1	0	0
L10	0	0	0	0	0	1	0	0	1	0	1	0
L11	0	0	0	0	0	0	0	0	0	1	0	1
L12	0	0	0	0	0	0	0	1	0	0	1	0

We have given the highest reward to L7.

6.4.1.1.2.5.6   Implementation of the Q Learning Algorithm—Module and Interaction Map

Step 1: Initializing the Q Learning parameters - $\gamma = 0.75$ and $\alpha = 0.9$

Step 2: Define location_to_state = {'L1': 0, 'L2': 1, 'L3': 2, 'L4': 3, 'L5': 4, 'L6': 5, 'L7': 6, 'L8': 7, 'L9': 8, 'L10': 9, 'L11': 10, 'L12': 11}

Define actions = {01,2,3,4,5,6,7,8,9,10,11}

Define rewards = [

```
0   1   0   0   0   0   0     0   0   0   0   0
1   0   1   0   0   1   0     0   0   0   0   0
0   1   0   0   0   0   1     0   0   0   0   0
```

0	0	0	0	0	0	0	1	0	0	0	0
0	0	0	0	0	0	0	0	1	0	0	0
0	1	0	0	0	0	0	0	0	1	0	0
0	0	1	0	0	0	1000	1	0	0	0	0
0	0	0	1	0	0	1	0	0	0	0	1
0	0	0	0	1	0	0	0	0	1	0	0
0	0	0	0	0	1	0	0	1	0	1	0
0	0	0	0	0	0	0	0	0	1	0	1
0	0	0	0	0	0	0	1	0	0	1	0

]

Step 3: Initialize the Q-Values with zeroes [0,0,0,0,0,0,0,0,0,0,0,0]
Step 4: Iterate temporary variable "j" for "n" times:
Randomize the current state
Playable actions:
 If (reward (Currentstate, j)) > 0
 Playableaction.append (j)
Nextstate = Randomize (playableactions)
Step 5: Calculate the temporal difference:

TD = R[current_state, next_state] + gamma*Q[next_state, np.argmax(Q[next_state,])] - Q[current_state, next_state]

Q[current_state, next_state] = Q[current_state, next_state] + alpha*TD

```
Q-Values:
[[   0 1661    0    0    0    0    0    0    0    0    0    0]
 [1246    0 2213    0    0 1246    0    0    0    0    0    0]
 [   0 1661    0    0    0    0 2970    0    0    0    0    0]
 [   0    0    0    0    0    0    0 2225    0    0    0    0]
 [   0    0    0    0    0    0    0    0  703    0    0    0]
 [   0 1661    0    0    0    0    0    0    0  931    0    0]
 [   0    0 2213    0    0    0 3968 2225    0    0    0    0]
 [   0    0    0 1661    0    0 2968    0    0    0    0 1670]
 [   0    0    0    0  528    0    0    0    0  936    0    0]
 [   0    0    0    0    0 1246    0    0  703    0 1246    0]
 [   0    0    0    0    0    0    0    0    0  936    0 1661]
 [   0    0    0    0    0    0    0 2225    0    0 1246    0]]
```

Step 6: state_to_location = {state: location for location, state in location_
to_state.items()}
   Step 7: Final route example: route (L5 --> L7)
      Output: ['L5', 'L9', 'L10', 'L6', 'L2', 'L3', 'G7']

Deployment
We ran the code with several combinations and once the output converged serialized the trained agent and deployed as per below architecture in cloud-based system. The details of which is discussed generally below.

6.4.1.1.2.5.7   Reference Architecture Explanation
The Internet of Things defines the physical object network that are integrated with software, sensors, and other technical components, which is meant to exchange and connect data from different systems and devices on the Internet. The IoT module in Azure is a collection of cloud services managed by Microsoft that monitors, connects, and controls multiple IoT assets. In other words, within a cloud-hosted environment, several IoT devices are connected to generate a KPI which can help the business to grow.

IoT devices are mainly a combination of circuit board and sensors connected through =internet. There are several IoT devices what we see around us daily. Few of the examples are:

1. Air Conditioning System—Humidity and Temperature Sensor
2. Elevator—Accelerometer
3. Electrical Devices—Smart Bulb, Smart Fans etc.

Generally, the IoT devices used to send a measuring data collected from the sensor to the cloud back-end components. Typically, the flow is to send the telemetries from device to cloud and device to cloud. There are several components in Azure which helps to setup the communication between IoT device and cloud back-end services. Let's take an example of an industrial use case where conational monitoring needs to be done. Let's look at the block diagram shown below (Figure 6.2):

The block diagram explains how Azure components are combined to do conditional monitoring on Industrial use case. Here, first Industrial devices are getting connected through Azure IOT Edge Platform which has the container to run the Azure Services, custom codes, or third-party services. The main purpose of having IoT edge is to enable and manage service deployed on the specific devices. The next step is to involve Kubernetes, Event Hub, Stream Analytics together to get the service converted to microservices

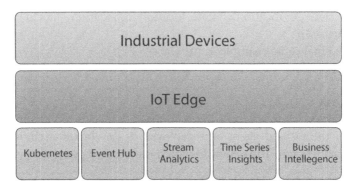

Figure 6.2 A detailed architecture showing how IoT components are connected with several analytical and deployment services.

and expose the streaming data to event hub. Azure Event Hub is platform that handles the large streaming data. The next step is to involve the analytics service and get the forecasted insight which will show there in Power BI for an end user as an UI [13].

6.4.1.1.2.5.7.1   Azure IoT ML Edge Analytics

The Internet of Things world has increased business demands to respond instantly to any kind of fraud, disaster, or anomalies. Most of the time, the response needs to be a mandate output based on device type, if the domain is related to some critical activity or application with life-saving impact etc. This kind of situation requires real-time responses based on the predictive analysis done on historical data or sensor data. Analytics related to IoT helps to accomplish the ongoing gadget demand with numerous different advantages.

Typically, unified information investigation frameworks can break down and decide the issues causing potential downtime, but it is not possible to respond instantly, i.e., real time. Numerous IoT devices produce enormous measures of information ceaselessly. Sending this huge information to data analytics framework and getting handled in cloud prompts an inactivity in reacting to the issues.

In specific circumstances and IoT-related devices, cannot depend on organization availability. Irregular network or the gadget going disconnected can be perilous.

The transfer speed needed to communicate with the information gathered by sensors additionally develops with the increment in device quantity. However optional in contrast with the basic issues portrayed above, enormous information moves to cloud with tremendous, distributed computing cycles could likewise bring significant expenses.

6.4.1.1.2.5.7.2   EDGE ANALYTICS WITH IOT

Organizations can react to difficulties handling edge analytics with IoT—the assortment, handling, and information investigation at edge of an organization or near to a sensor, an organizational switch, or an associated device.

Considering the quick response in respective devices, associations around enterprises like assembling, and transportation, are producing enormous amount of information for the organization. Compute examination empowers information investigation progressively and on location where information assortment is happening. It may be unmistakable or symptomatic or prescient or prescriptive analytical investigation [18].

6.4.1.1.2.5.7.3   ML WITH IOT

Supplementing edge analytics with IoT is similar to machine learning with IoT, which empowers systems to gain knowledge from information and encounters, and act accordingly. It can be handled by utilizing incredible calculations which finds design in information to build strong numerical concepts utilizing the examples.

Arranging and preparing a ML framework requires gigantic registering assets, so it can be a fit to the cloud. In any case, derivation takes significantly less figuring power and is commonly done continuously with new information being free. Eventually, getting induction data with extremely poor inertness guarantees that applications can react rapidly toward neighborhood occasions.

6.4.1.1.2.5.7.4   INTEGRATION AZURE IOT HUB WITH AZURE IOT EDGE DEVICE—DEVICE CONTROL STREAMING DATA (REAL TIME) USE CASE

Combining ML and edge analytics with IoT can handle the issue related to associate device controlling in real time. The concept is to focus to business experiences an oppose to enormous information gathered through sensors. Figure 6.3 gives significant view of such arrangements.

We should mainly give importance on edge device associated with IoT to investigate how precisely ML and edge analytics with IoT complete one another in controlling device progressively.

Let's discuss a bit about the figure which shows how Azure IoT hub and IoT edge devices are integrated together to handle real time device control

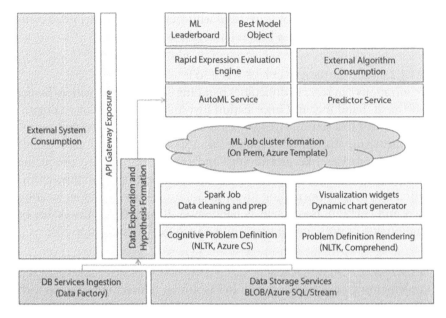

Figure 6.3 Implementation of the Q learning algorithm—module and interaction map.

use cases. Continuous real time data feed is shared from the industry to Azure IoT setup, which further gets processed with the help of several components like

- Reinforcement learning
- Insights
- Azure functions
- Stream analytics
- Hub
- Other Azure services

Investigating quality of water in supply related to drinking water frameworks, and so forth, progressively can possibly stay away from genuine medical problems for buyers. Privately introduced IoT edge device with processing capacities can empower continuous quality maintenance [8] and prescient support. It can handle filtration boundaries, blending proportion to value control added substances or in any event, siphoning and insemination increased by utilizing ML and edge analytics calculations dependent on the supply quality water boundaries, buyer use with ecological elements (Figure 6.4).

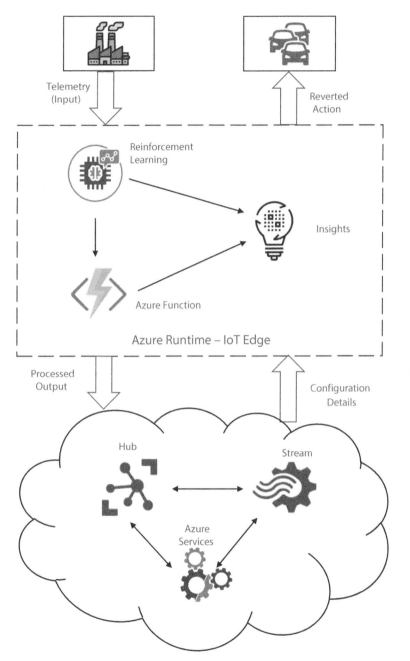

Figure 6.4 Azure IoT edge real time data transmission.

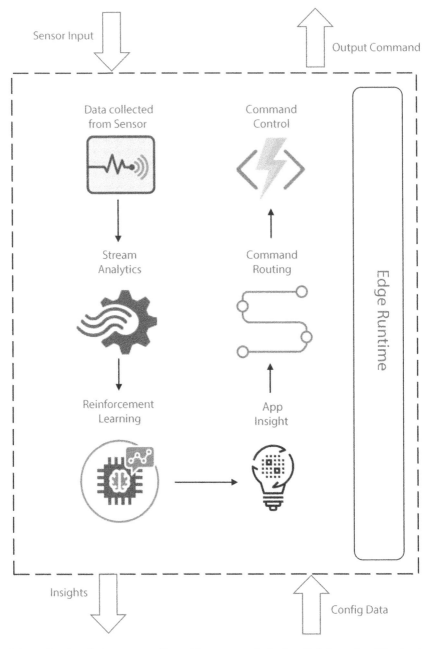

Figure 6.5 A real time message flow with stream analytics handled through public cloud edge.

Reinforcement learning and IoT edge analytics can convey quantifiable business advantages and benefits by decreasing the dormancy of choices. This is accomplished by preparing crude information close to the actual device and by scaling out logical hubs conquering the data transmission issue [16] (Figure 6.5).

Advantages:

- Locally gather the information without missing anything because of irregular network channels
- Reduce latency by incorporating more refined AI programming/machine learning/reinforcement learning modules
- Diminish transfer speed costs through sending just business experiences needed, handling devices conduct with cloud IoT setup.
- Upgrade/redesign the ML/Edge Analytics modules through simple arrangement and by means of compartments.
- Specific preparing – the colossal amount of information which is gathered at Edge sources which are not important.
- Edge Analytics streams in rapidly confining fascinating information for rich examination.

6.4.1.1.2.5.8   Azure Containerize Docker Service

A container is a standard bundle of programming packages, an application's code along with the connected arrangement documents and libraries, and with the conditions needed for the application to run. This permits engineers and IT stars to send applications consistently across conditions.

A Docker container image is a lightweight, independent, executable bundle of programming that incorporates all that expected to run an application: code, runtime, framework devices, framework libraries and settings [15].

A few Cloud Providers have the likelihood to run your Docker Images on their framework, Microsoft Azure is one of them. It saves cost by lifting and moving your current applications to containers and assemble microservices applications to convey worth to your clients. Utilize end-to-end designer and CI/CD devices to create, refresh and send your containerized applications. Scale container with a completely managed Kubernetes arrangement that incorporates with Azure Active Directory. Any place in your application modernization application, speed up your containerized application advancement while meeting your security necessities [14] (Figure 6.6).

Figure 6.6 Deployment using Azure Docker container service.

6.5 Conclusion

In this book chapter, we have taken the case of Q learning and its counterpart deep Q learning. These are two very popular algorithm of reinforcement learning algorithm. We have included a case study for optimizing path of an autonomous agent in a warehouse to collect goods so that the entire process of sales and delivery became optimized for the end customers. We have developed this case study using Q learning and have tried to show that Q learning can be used in a very efficient way to determine the shortest path and also determine the maximum rewards for a particular agent. We have shown a reference architecture to deploy this agent as a serializable machine learning algorithm in any of the edge devices. We have taken the case of Azure cloud computing platform to deploy the agent in Azure IOT edge which in turn provides reusability for the agent to be used in any of the autonomous device in a warehouse. In this particular chapter, we have also shown that how this cloud computing module can be made available and durable along with securing the same using various Azure cloud services. The deployment was containerized using docker.

6.6 Future Work

i) We will extend this work to deep Q learning using TensorFlow 2.0 and Terrace Framework. We will also experiment with Pytorch as a deployment platform for deep Q learning for this particular case study.

ii) We will use this case study in an actual simulated environment using the concept of digital twin. We will explore this concept using the Azure platform.

iii) We will use various other deep reinforcement learning techniques to simulate this environment.

iv) We will also explore the possibility of the reference architecture using hybrid and permit cloud in future.

References

1. van Hasselt, H., Guez, A., Silver, D., Deep Reinforcement Learning with Double Q-Learning. *Thirtieth AAAI Conference on Artificial Intelligence*, vol. 30, 2016.

2. Dzeroski, S., De Raedt, L., Driessens, K., Relational Reinforcement Learning. *Mach. Learn.*, 43, 1-2, 7–52, April 2001-May 2001.

3. Sutton, R.S., Introduction: The Challenge of Reinforcement Learning, in: *Machine Learning*, vol. 8, pp. 225–227, Kluwer Academic Publishers, Boston, 1992.

4. Smith, T.W. and Colby, S.A., Teaching for Deep Learning. *Clearing House*, 80, 5, 205–210, May-Jun. 2007.

5. Schmidhuber, J., Deep learning in neural networks: An overview. 61, 95–117, January 2015.

6. White, D.J., A Survey of Applications of Markov Decision Processes, *J. Oper. Res. Soc.*, 44, 11, 1073–1096, 1993. http://www.jstor.org/stable/2583870.

7. Kapuruge, M., Colman, A., Han, J., Bouguettaya, A., Hauswirth, M., Liu, L., *Achieving Multi-tenanted Business Processes in SaaS Applications*, pp. 143–157, Springer-Verlag, Berlin Heidelberg, 2011.

8. Reddy, G. and Subashini, N., Secure Storage Services and Erasure Code Implementation in Cloud Servers. *Int. J. Eng. Res. Technol. (IJERT)*, 3, 1, 1810–1814, 2014.

9. Schubert, P. and Adisa, F., Cloud Computing for Standard ERP Systems: Reference Framework and Research Agenda, in: *Arbeitsberichte aus dem Fachbereich Informatik*, vol. 4, p. 29, 2011.

10. Na, S., Kim, K., Huh, E., A Methodology for Evaluating Cloud Computing Security Service-Level Agreements. *IJACT*, 5, 13, 140–142, 2013.

11. Müller, J., Krüger, J., Enderlein, S., Helmich, M., Zeier, A., Customizing enterprise software as a service applications: Back-end extension in a multi-tenancy environment, in: *Enterprise Information Systems*, pp. 66–77, Springer, Berlin Heidelberg, 2009.

12. Mushtaque, M.A. and Sindhu, R., A New Innovation On User'S Level Security For Storage Data In Cloud Computing. *Int. J. Grid Distrib. Comput.*, 7, 3, 213–220, 2014.

13. Lenart, A., ERP in the Cloud–Benefits and Challenges, in: *Research in Systems Analysis and Design: Models and Methods*, pp. 39–50, Springer, Berlin Heidelberg, 2011.

14. Takabi, H., Joshi, J.B.D., Ahn, G.-J., Secure, Cloud: Towards a Comprehensive Security Framework for Cloud Computing Environments, in: *2010 34th Annual IEEE Computer Software and Applications Conference Workshops.*
15. Esteves, R.M. and Rong, C., Social Impact of Privacy in Cloud Computing, in: *2010 IEEE Second International Conference on Cloud Computing Technology and Science (CloudCom)*, Nov. 30-Dec. 3 2010, pp. 593–596, 2010.
16. Ruiter, J. and Warnier, M., Chapter 17 Privacy regulations for cloud computing, compliance and implementation in theory and practice, in: *Computers, Privacy and Data Protection: an Element of Choice*, S. Gutwirth, Y. Poullet, P. de Hert, R. Leenes, (Eds.), pp. 293–314, Springer, The Netherlands, 2011.
17. Sultan, N., Cloud computing for education: A new dawn? *Int. J. Inf. Manage.*, 30, 2, 109–116, April 2010.
18. Esteves, R.M. and Rong, C., Social Impact of Privacy in Cloud Computing, in: *2010 IEEE Second International Conference on Cloud Computing Technology and Science (CloudCom)*, Nov. 30-Dec. 3 ,2010, pp. 593–596, 2010.

Fuzzy Logic-Based Air Conditioner System

Suparna Biswas*, Sayan Roy Chaudhuri, Ayusha Biswas and Arpan Bhawal

Faculty of Electronics & Communication Engineering Department,
Guru Nanak Institute of Technology, Kolkata, India

Abstract

With the exponential increase in population, thus increasing the temperature of earth day by day air-conditioner has become an indispensable part of our life. In this situation, energy saving should be our key role. In this paper, we have presented a fuzzy control based mechanism for air-condition system. By considering the input variables or parameters we can lower the use of electricity by adjusting the function of ac. For better application we consider the climatic conditions of rural and urban area separately. This research paper work will increase the scope of fuzzy logic control systems in large prospective with potential benefits. This Fuzzy logic based algorithm for Air Condition controlling system is simulated by using MATLAB.

Keywords: Transitional, prosaic, FIS, antecedent, Fuzzification, Defuzzification, mamdani, gradient

7.1 Introduction

In real world, sometimes, we face a situation when we cannot define whether the state is true or false, in this situation, fuzzy logic provides a very suitable flexibility for reasoning. This Fuzzy Logic was commenced in 1965 [1]. Fuzzy logic is a logic that consists of many values that permits transitional values to be defined within prosaic such as true or false, yes or no, high or low, etc [8]. Zadeh also composed the idea of fuzzy control that allows small set innate values to be used in order to command the functioning of electronic devices. We can consider the inaccuracies and

---

**Corresponding author*: suparna.biswas@gnit.ac.in

Rajdeep Chakraborty, Anupam Ghosh, Jyotsna Kumar Mandal and S. Balamurugan (eds.) Convergence of Deep Learning In Cyber-IoT Systems and Security, (147–164) © 2023 Scrivener Publishing LLC

uncertainties of any situation. Boolean system represent only two states, 1.0 (truth) and 0.0 (false). But in fuzzy logic, there is intermediate state between true and false. Figure 7.1 shows the block diagram of fuzzy logic and boolean logic.

The main aim of applying fuzzy logic is to fabricate the thinking of a computer like a human. With the help of fuzzy logic algorithm, we can allow the electronic devices to recognize and counter to human language such as very large, very small, hot, cold, etc. One of the advantages of fuzzy logic is that it can be simply carried out on an ordinary computer. There are various uses of fuzzy logic in the field of artificial intelligence, natural language processing as well as in modern control systems. There is many countries in the world like Japan who are using fuzzy logic in micro oven, video camera, air conditioner, vacuum cleaner, etc. [1].

Fuzzy logic has numerous applications in different fields [2]. Like management of thermal energy [3] in residential buildings, microcontroller based smart home temperature system [4], reduction of energy consumption system [5], fuzzy proportional-integral-derivative (PID) controller-based home temperature control system [6], Intelligent air conditioner [7] by integrating temperature sensors, smartphones, human motion sensor, fuzzy logic–based power consumption forecasting system for air conditioner [8], etc.

In this paper, we have designed a plan for using fuzzy logic in air-conditioning system which will enhance the working of the device more efficiently. This logic will help the air conditioner to judge the aspects, such as user temperature, humidity, and improves the working of the system and, therefore, provides pleasant environment to the user. Organization of the paper is as follows:

Section 7.2 describes the fuzzy logic based control system, proposed system is discussed in section 7.3, and simulated results are discussed in section 7.4. Finally, section 7.5 concludes the paper.

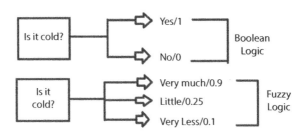

Figure 7.1 Difference between boolean logic and fuzzy logic.

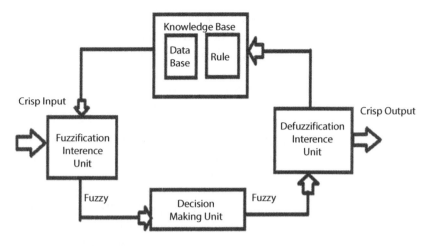

Figure 7.2 Block diagram of FIS [9].

7.2 Fuzzy Logic-Based Control System

This section describes the basic concept of fuzzy logic based control system. Fuzzy inference system (FIS) forms the base of the fuzzy control system. The block diagram of FIS [9] is given in Figure 7.2. Here, rule base consists of IF-THEN rules of fuzzy logic, database describes the membership functions of fuzzy sets, Decision-making unit, as per rules, it performs operations, fuzzification-interface unit transforms the crisp quantities into fuzzy quantities and defuzzification interface unit transforms the fuzzy quantities into crisp quantities.

7.3 Proposed System

In this section, we have explained our proposed method. The different Fuzzy variables are explained in section 7.3.1, section 7.3.2 explains fuzzy bases class, all the fuzzy rules of our proposed system explained in section 7.3.3, section 7.3.4 describes fuzzy rule viewer.

7.3.1 Fuzzy Variables

There are two types of fuzzy variables: a) input variable and b) output variable. On the basis of input variable, we determine the output variable. In this plan, we have taken user temperature and humidity as the input variable. Here user temperature is the temperature, which is given by the user, with respect to the room temperature through the remote of air conditioner. The temperature range for membership function is given in Table 7.1, and membership function graph for user temperature is depicted in Figure 7.3.

Another input variable humidity is the presence of water vapors in the air. The suitable indoor humidity depends on the room temperature. The amount of water vapor required to meet saturation increases as the temperature increases. Humidity signifies the possibility of precipitation, dew, or fog to be present in the atmosphere. Table 7.2 shows the ranges of membership function for humidity and depicted in Figure 7.4.

In this plan, we have taken heat fan speed, cool fan speed of the motor controlling the fan and humidifier as output variables. The heat fan speed will be either in ON condition or OFF condition depending on the user temperature given. The speed is measured in revolutions per meter (rpm).

Table 7.1 User temperature reference function.

Range (%)	Membership function
16–20	Very low
20–23	Low
23–27	Medium
27–30	High
30–33	Very high

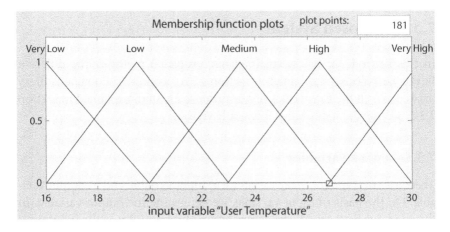

Figure 7.3 User temperature membership function.

Table 7.2 Categorizing of humidity.

Range (%)	Membership function
0–15	Dry
16–28	Not too dry
29–45	Moderately suitable
46–65	Suitable
66–80	Not too wet
81–100	Wet

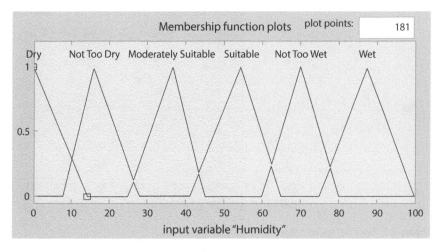

Figure 7.4 Humidity reference membership function.

The table for categorizing heat fan speed is given in Table 7.3 and depicted in Figure 7.5.

The cool fan speed will be either in ON or OFF condition depending on the user temperature given. The speed is measured in revolutions per meter (rpm). The temperature ranges for membership function of cool fan speed is given in Table 7.4 and shown in Figure 7.6.

Here, humidifier is another output variable. A humidifier is a device that increases the amount of moisture in air. Humidifier helps to recover from symptoms like dry skin, strained vocal chords, headaches, etc. The humidifier ranges of membership function is given in Table 7.5 and depicted in Figure 7.7.

Table 7.3 Categorizing of heat fan speed.

Range (%)	Membership function
0–20	Minimum
10–43	Slow
30–60	Medium
50–80	Fast
70–100	Very Fast

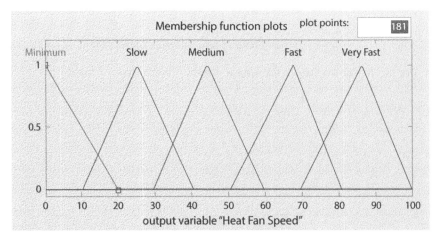

Figure 7.5 Heat fan speed reference membership function.

Table 7.4 Categorizing of cool fan speed.

Range (%)	Membership function
0–20	Minimum
10–40	Slow
26–66	Medium
50–80	Fast
70–100	Very fast

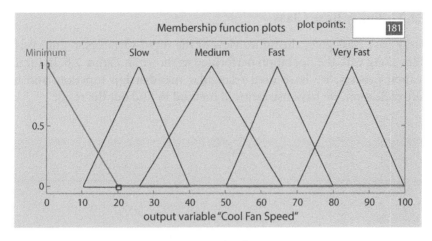

Figure 7.6 Cool fan speed reference membership function.

Table 7.5 Categorizing of humidifier.

Range (%)	Membership function
0–10	Dry
5–17	Slow
12–25	Medium
19–33	Fast
28–40	Very fast

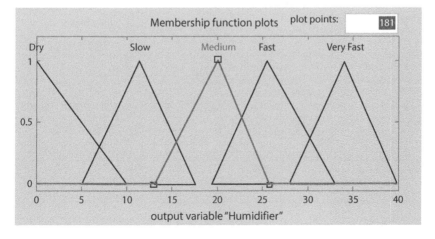

Figure 7.7 Humidifier reference membership function.

7.3.2   Fuzzy Base Class

Fuzzy base class gives the entire view of the input variables, output variables along with the operation performed as shown in Figure 7.8. In fuzzification process, we have used triangular membership function, and in defuzzification, we have use centroid method to find out the result.

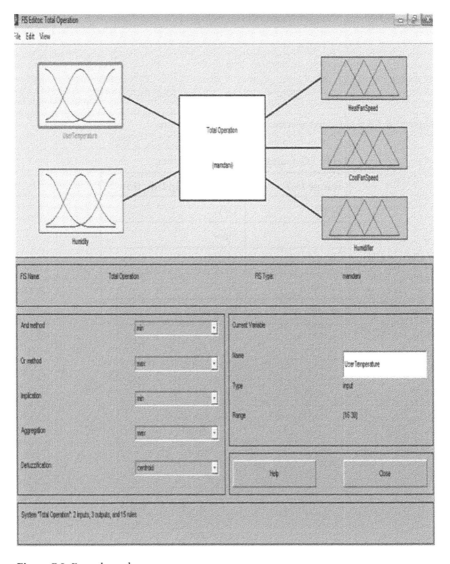

Figure 7.8 Fuzzy base class.

7.3.3   Fuzzy Rule Base

The system under consideration has a simple rule base consisting of 15 fuzzy rules. It is in a (IF, AND)–THEN rule base form. The IF part of a rule is a proposition known as the rule antecedent, The THEN part is called rule consequent (Conclusion) [9].

> IF < antecedent 1 >
> AND < antecedent 2 >
> . THEN < consequent >

The antecedent of a rule incorporates to parts: a feature/attribute (linguistic) and its value. The feature and its value are linked by operators, such as are, is, not [9]. Input, output distribution as per Mamdani Fuzzy interface system described in Figure 7.9. The rules can be combined in a table called rule base as given in Table 7.6. Fuzzy Base Rule is shown in Figure 7.10.

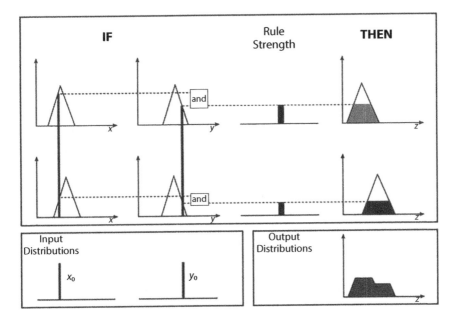

Figure 7.9 Mamdani fuzzy interface system.

Table 7.6 Rule base.

Temperature	Humidity	Heat fan speed	Cool fan speed	Humidifier
Very low	Dry	Stop	Very fast	Very fast
Low	Not too dry	Minimum	Fast	Fast
Medium	Moderately suitable	Medium	Medium	Medium
High	Suitable	Fast	Slow	Slow
Very high	Not too wet	Very fast	Minim um	Dry
Very low	Wet	Minimum	Very fast	Dry
Low	Not too wet	Slow	Fast	Slow
High	Suitable	Fast	Fast	Slow
Very high	Dry	Very fast	Minimum	Very fast
Medium	Not too dry	Medium	Medium	Fast
Very high	Dry	Very fast	Minimum	Very fast
Medium	Not too wet	Medium	Medium	Slow
High	Wet	Fast	Slow	Slow
Very low	Moderately suitable	Minimum	Very fast	Medium
Low	Moderately suitable	Slow	Fast	Medium

7.3.4   Fuzzy Rule Viewer

The rule viewer is used to view the inference and application process for the fuzzy system as shown in Figure 7.11. Input values can be adjusted every time and parallel output values, the overall fuzzy set and the value after defuzzification can be viewed.

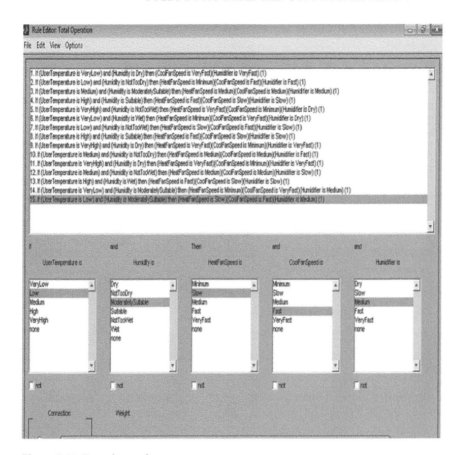

Figure 7.10 Fuzzy base rule.

7.4   Simulated Result

The following graphs are result of surface viewer of the fuzzy logic toolbox. To view the output surface we must declare the input and output variables of our fuzzy inference system and the fuzzy rules for our system. Surface graphs can only be formed by taking minimum two inputs in the input variable or else only a 2-D graph will be formed with only x and y axes. Figure 7.12 shows the gradient graph of user temperature vs humidity vs heat fan speed. Figure 7.13 depicted the gradient graph of user temperature vs. humidity vs. cool fan speed. Figure 7.14 shows the gradient graph of user temperature vs. humidity vs humidifier.

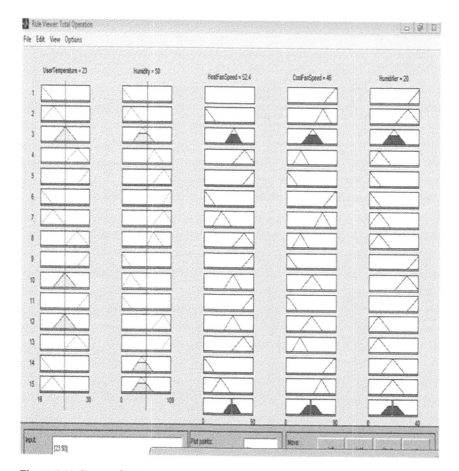

Figure 7.11 Fuzzy rule viewer.

Figure 7.15 shows the user temperature vs. heat fan speed curve. In this graph, user temperature is in the x-axis and heat fan speed is in the y-axis. The graph shows an increase in temperature with an increase in Heat Fan Speed. It becomes constant for a while when the temperature ranges from 22.5 to 26 degree Celsius and then again decreases; then again at 27°C, it becomes sustained at 45 rpm of the heat fan.

Figure 7.16 depicts user temperature vs cool fan speed graph. In the graph, user temperature is in the x-axis and cool fan speed is in the y-axis. Graph shows a decrease in temperature with an increase in cool fan speed. At 45 rpm, the temperature becomes almost saturated and decreases by very small amount, that is at very low temperature cool fan speed should be very fast to make the room cool.

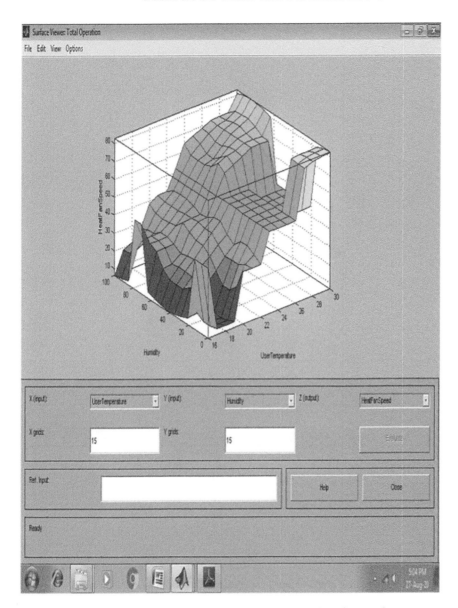

Figure 7.12 Gradient graph of user temperature vs humidity vs heat fan speed.

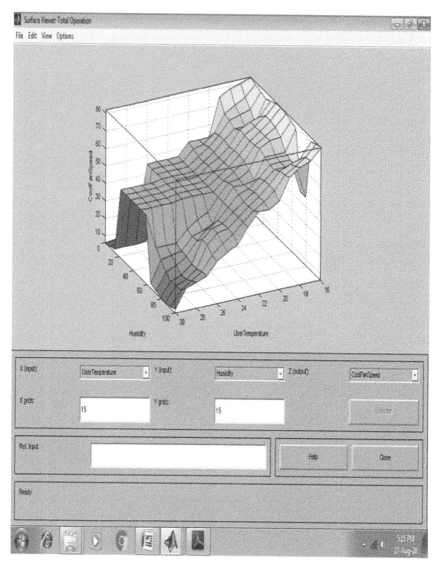

Figure 7.13 Gradient graph of user temperature vs. humidity vs. cool fan speed.

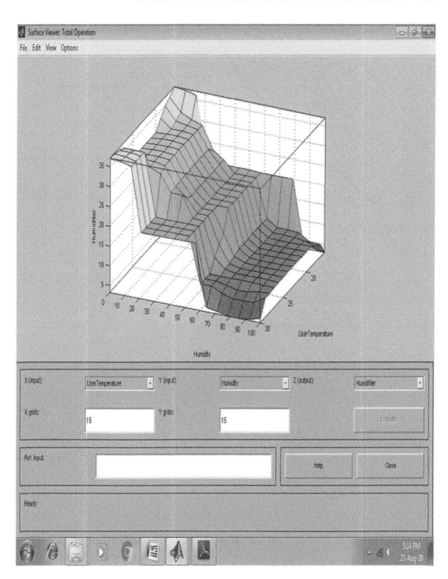

Figure 7.14 Gradient graph of user temperature vs. humidity vs humidifier.

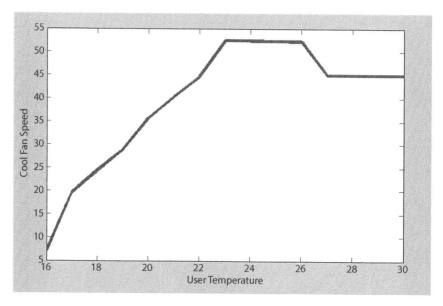

Figure 7.15 Graph of user temperature vs. heat fan speed.

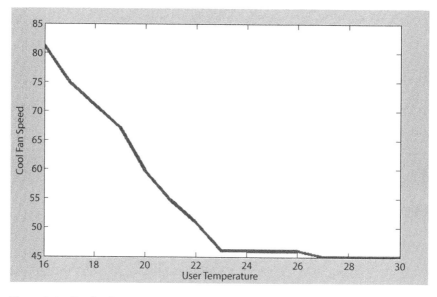

Figure 7.16 Graph of user temperature vs cool fan speed.

7.5   Conclusion and Future Work

With the advancement of technology and to ensure high performance soft computing techniques are being used to overcome the lack due to conventional controlling systems. The brief algorithms under fuzzy logic have been discussed in the paper. Soft computing techniques are used to control a nonlinear motor [10]. Fuzzy logic is the most powerful and structured approach for controlling the process. This saves a lot of electricity and also machines can be made fully automatic which are more user-friendly to customers. The logic easily solves difficult problems in its own without the interference of the user much. This saves the machine from wrong use which would have been the case if the machine was semiautomatic where there is no fuzzy logic applied. The aim of this work is to bring out good results in soft computing systems and bridge the space between software engineer and computational intelligence. Its application spread from washing machine, vacuum cleaners, facial pattern recognition, car logic, age detector, traffic control, handwriting recognition, analysis of human behavior, traffic light control, etc.

References

1. Dash, S.K., Mohanty, G., Mohanty, A., Intelligent air conditioning system using fuzzy logic. *Int. J. Sci. Eng. Res.*, 3, 12, 1–6, 2012.
2. Lewis, A.P., *Optimal Fuzzy Logic Control Technique*, Whitecap Publishing Co., Lagos, Nigeria, 2009.
3. Elmoudi, A., Asad, O., Erol-Kantarci, M., Mouftah, H.T., Energy consumption control of an air conditioner using web services. *Smart Grid Renew. Energy*, 02, 03, 255–260, 2011. http://dx.doi.org/10.4236/sgre.2011.23028.
4. Mowad, M., Fathy, A., Hafez, A., Smart home automated control system using android application and microcontroller. *Int. J. Sci. Eng. Res.*, 5, 5, 935–939, 2014.
5. Graditi, G. *et al.*, Innovative control logics for a rational utilization of electric loads and air-conditioning systems in a residential building. *Energy Build.*, 102, 1–17, 2015. https://doi.org/10.1016/j.enbuild.2015.05.027.
6. Shein, W.W., Tan, Y., Lim, A.O., PID controller for temperature control with multiple actuators in cyber-physical home system, in: *Proceedings of the 2012 15th International Conference on Network-Based Information Systems, NBIS 2012*, pp. 423–428, 2012, https://doi.org/10.1109/NBiS.2012.118.
7. Cheng, C.C. and Lee, D., Smart sensors enable smart air conditioning control. *Sensors*, 14, 6, 11179–11203, 1. https://doi.org/10.3390/s140611179.

8. Fukazawa, T., Iwata, Y., Morikawa, J., Ninagawa, C., Stabilization of neural network by combination with AR model in FastADR control of building air-conditioner facilities. *IEEJ Trans. Electr. Electron. Eng.*, 11, 1, 124–125, 2016. https://doi.org/10.1002/tee.22196.

9. Ross, T.J., *Fuzzy logic with engineering applications*, 2nd edition, John Willey & Sons, Ltd, New Delhi, 2010.

10. http://shodhganga.inflibnet.ac.in/bitstream/10603/10311/11/11_chapter%206.pdf.

8

An Efficient Masked-Face Recognition Technique to Combat with COVID-19

Suparna Biswas

Faculty of Electronics & Communication Engineering Department, Guru Nanak Institute of Technology, Kolkata, India

Abstract

Since the major COVID-19 pandemic hit the world, using face masks has become an important part of our daily lives. Not wearing masks for a moment when outside can be a life-threatening mistake. But the mask covers the lower portion of the face region. So we were not able to extract important features from the lower region. That is why in this paper, an efficient face recognition scheme has been presented by integrating discrete curvelet transform (DCT), compressive sensing (CS), and principal component analysis (PCA) to improve the face recognition rate of masked faces. The use of discrete curvelet transform (DCT) provides an enhancement of edge information of face images by applying an image fusion technique. To extract the feature vector in lower dimensional feature space, PCA has been applied on the fused images. Finally, the performance of this proposed technique is tested by using compressive sensing–based classifier. Extensive experiments are simulated on masked and unmasked faces, and our method performs better than the conventional PCA.

Keywords: Face mask, discrete curvelet transform, compressive sensing, principal component analysis, masked face recognition, coronavirus, COVID-19

8.1 Introduction

The coronavirus (COVID-19) has created a pandemic situation all over the world from the last 2 years. This virus can be transmitted through direct

---

*Corresponding author: suparna.biswas@gnit.ac.in

Rajdeep Chakraborty, Anupam Ghosh, Jyotsna Kumar Mandal and S. Balamurugan (eds.) Convergence of Deep Learning In Cyber-IoT Systems and Security, (165–182) © 2023 Scrivener Publishing LLC

contact. That is why we have to avoid conventional biometric systems like passwords and fingerprints. In this situation face recognition (FR) is one of the safer recognition techniques. To reduce the spreading of this virus, wearing a mask is mandatory for all. But it covers a large region of faces and reduces the recognition rate. It is a challenge for the FR researchers to deal with masked faces.

FR is a technique of identification and verification of a person from digital face images or from videos. It is basically a challenging task in the research field of biometrics. Different researchers are dealing with different challenges of FR like pose variations, illumination variations, variations in facial expressions, blurring effect and occlusions etc. Sometimes preprocessing schemes are a very essential or important task to remove or to reduce the different types of noise from the images and indirectly to increase the recognition rate. But the most important part of any recognition technique is extraction of important features and dimension of extracted features. Due to the very large dimension of input feature vectors most of the FR methods are expensive computationally or time consuming.

Feature dimension and feature types are other important issues of FR [1]. It is also studied in Yang and Zhang [1] to solve the difficulties of high dimensionality and for the selection of feature types. To resolve the abovementioned problem, this paper explores a novel FR framework by integrating CS, digital curvelet transform (DCT) [2], and fusion-based PCA for masked faces. Here CS, DCT, and PCA are integrated for constructing a novel FR method, where the foremost aim is lower feature dimension and of course recognition accuracy of masked faces.

The objective of this proposed method is to improve the FR rate in the presence of a mask. In this work, DCT, PCA, and CS are integrated to increase the accuracy of masked face images. Here, DCT has been used to get the better edge information from the unmasked face region and a PCA-based feature level fusion technique has been used to extract important features of low dimension. At the last step, to improve the recognition rate a CS-based classification technique has been utilized.

This paper is structured as: Section 8.2 presents literature review of unmasked and masked face recognition technique, Section 8.3 provides the description of digital curvelet transform and compressive sensing-based classification. Section 8.4 presents the concept of proposed FR method, Section 8.5 analyzes the result applied on ORL and AR database for masked and unmasked face images. Finally, the paper is concluded in Section 8.6 followed by future scope.

8.2   Related Works

This section provides a brief review of FR for unmasked and masked face images. In section 8.2.1 recent FR techniques are reviewed, mainly based on CS, modified LBP, CNN, and deep learning for unmasked face images. Section 8.2.2 presents the literature review of FR techniques of last two years for masked faces.

8.2.1   Review of Face Recognition for Unmasked Faces

Recently compressive sensing (CS)–based technique is used widely in different recognition problems. The CS theory–based sparse representation–based classification (SRC) technique for FR was first implemented in Wright et al. [3]. In Wright et al. [3], test images are represented as a sparse linear combination of the training images and feature extraction steps are based on eigenface and Laplacianface images. Their experiment shows that for the large dimension of feature vectors this technique is insensitive to types of features. Nagesh et al. [4] proposed an expression-invariant FR technique based on CS theory. Here different images of same subjects are considered as an ensemble of intercorrelated signals. It is also assumed that the changes of face due to expression variations are sparse in nature with respect to the whole face images. Here training images of any individual person is represented by only two types of feature images, first one is the holistic features and another which captures the various expressions of all training images. Fang et al. [5] presented an infrared FR method by integrating the CS theory and Principal Component Analysis [6]. Their experiment shows that this method is robust under the variation of illumination, shadow and facial expression, and provides higher recognition rate.

In the last 5 years, many FR-based automated attendance systems have been presented [7–12] ,and implemented successfully. In some cases, existing techniques have been modified or combined with another technique to improve the accuracy in presence of different challenges [13–16]. Different challenges for efficient FR systems are pose variation, illumination differences, scaling, occlusion, and expression variation [17, 18]. Krishna et al. [19] presented an automated FR system to cope up with the illumination variation. To overcome the drawback of pose variation Yogesh et al. [20] proposed an efficient FR technique by integrating local binary pattern(LBP), dual cross pattern (DCP), and support vector machine (SVM).

Deep learning network (DNN) is now widely used in different fields of pattern recognition. In 2014, Wolf et al. [21] proposed a DNN-based FR system. The DNN method gives a very high recognition rate. From literature review, it has been noticed that deep learning-based convolutional neural network (CNN) is more fruitful for image classification. A detailed review of CNN-based FR approaches are explained in Taigman *et al.* [21], Taskiran *et al.* [22], Tolba *et al.* [23]. In Pranav *et al.* [24], the authors proposed a CNN-based real-time FR technique to increase the recognition rate of the system. In 2018, Sun *et al.* [25] presented a CNN-based FR approach to cope up with the occlusion variation.

8.2.2 Review of Face Recognition for Masked Faces

For the last 2 years, many researchers have been working with masked faces. Like in Ge *et al.* [26], they presented an LLE-CNN–based masked FR technique. In 2020, Walid Hariri proposed a deep CNN model to recognize the masked faces [27]. At first, they have removed the masked face region as shown in Figure 8.1 and then CNN has been applied on the unmasked region (cropped face as in Figure 8.1) to extract the important features as shown in Figure 8.2.

Here, VGG-16 face CNN descriptor [29] has been used for feature extraction. At the last step multilayer perceptron model has been applied for the classification. They have worked with real-world masked FR dataset (RMFRD) [28] and provide the maximum recognition rate of 91.3%.

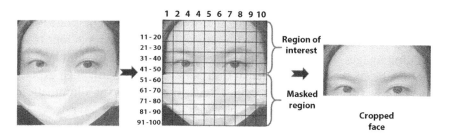

Figure 8.1 Masked face is divided into 100 blocks of same size and then extracted unmasked region (cropped face) [27].

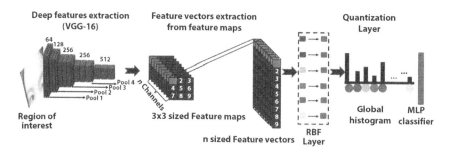

Figure 8.2 Feature extraction method using CNN [27].

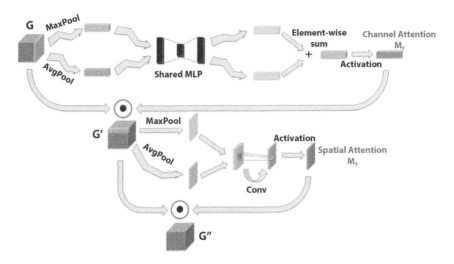

Figure 8.3 Diagram of convolutional block attention module [30].

Liu *et al.* [30] presented a masked FR technique by integrating cropping and convolutional block attention module (CBAM). They have used
the CBAM module as shown in Figure 8.3 to extract the important features around the eyes. They performed the experiments on AR, SMFRD,
Extended Yale B and CASIA-Webface databases and showed a good recognition rate for masked faces.

8.3 Mathematical Preliminaries

This section provides the brief introduction of transform domain and classification technique used in this paper. The objective of this discussion is to
make the paper self-explanatory. Section 8.3.1 describes DCT and Section
8.3.2 briefly explains the CS-based classification algorithm.

8.3.1 Digital Curvelet Transform (DCT)

Curvelet is a multidirectional transform that represents edges and other
singularities concisely than the other transforms. For the implementation
of digital curvelet transform (DCT), the first step is application of two-
dimensional Fast Fourier transform (FFT) on face images and after that
two-dimensional frequency plane is partitioned into parabolic segment. In
the next step inverse FFT is taken on each wedge for each value of scale j

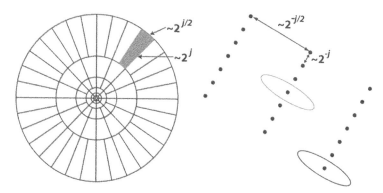

Figure 8.4 Curvelet tiling of space and frequency.

and angle. Figure 8.4 shows the division of each segment. A detail implementation step of DCT via wrapping has been explained in Candes *et al.* [2].

8.3.2 Compressive Sensing–Based Classification

Recently, CS theory-based classifier named as sparse representation-based classification (SRC) technique has received high attention in recognition problems [31]. But SRC is a very slow process and time consuming since it requires optimizing an objective function with L1-Norm. SRC basically consists of two important steps: first step is collaborative representation and second step is L1-norm constraint. To increase the speed of classification, a collaborative representation-based classification with regularized least square (CRC_RLS) is presented [32]. While the SRC is based on the solution of l1-regularized least square decomposition, CR starts from l2-regularized least square formulation. In the paper, to increase the speed and accuracy of classification, a CRC_RLS classifier [32] is used. The algorithm of CRC_RLS is discussed in Algorithm 1.

Algorithm 1: CRC_RLS Algorithm1

Input: Matrix A of training samples.
1: Normalize the columns of A matrix to have unit l_2 norm
2: Code the test samples y_{test} over A by $\hat{p} = p y_{test}$,
Where $p = (A^T A + \lambda I)^{-1} A^T$ (using Least square solution)
3: Compute the residuals $R_i = \left. \left\| y_{test} - A_i \widehat{p_i} \right\| \middle/ \left\| \widehat{p_i} \right\| \right.$
4: Compute the identity of test sample as *identity* $(y_{test}) = argmin_i\, R_i$
Output: Identity the test sample.

8.4   Proposed Method

In the work, a FR scheme has been proposed based on fusion of features in curvelet domain. The flow chart of the proposed method for FR is depicted in Figure 8.5. To increase the recognition rate of masked and unmasked faces, DCT, PCA, and CS technique has been exploited.

The first step of this proposed face recognition technique is preprocessing as shown in Figure 8.6. The importance of this step is face mask recognition. Here PCA has been applied on resized test images. Then, CS-based classifier [32] is used to detect mask. If the test image is with mask, then we extract the lower portion of face image, which is covered by mask and upper portion (uncovered region) of the face image or cropped face is applied for next step. For unmasked faces, the whole resized face images is passed to next step.

In the next step, DCT has been applied on cropped face image (for masked faces) to extract detail and coarse subbands. For DCT, we choose scale of 3 and angle 8. After curvelet decomposition, we get coarse subband and eight detail subbands. Then PCA has been applied on all the detail subbands and coarse subband. For the reduction of feature dimension or to select the important feature, which has more discriminative power a fusion rule is applied. The detail of fused rule is described in Figure 8.7.

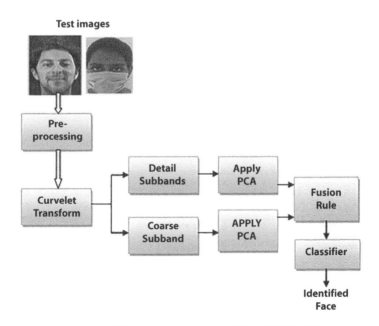

Figure 8.5 Block diagram of face recognition using DCT and CS classifier.

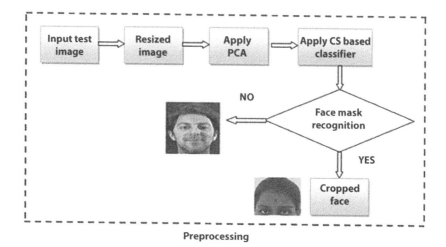

Preprocessing

Figure 8.6 Block diagram of pre-processing step.

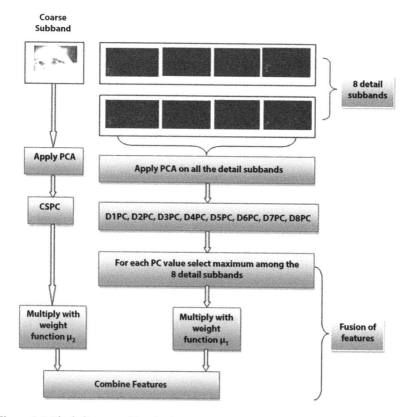

Figure 8.7 Block diagram of fused rule.

Applying the feature extraction step, we get the principal component (PC) from the detail subbands D1PC, D2PC, D3PC, D4PC, D5PC, D6PC, D7PC, and D8PC. Then the maximum value for each PC is chosen out of eight detail subbands and multiplied with a weight. On the other hand, extracted PC, CSPC from coarse subband is also multiplied with weight considering linear combination rule. So finally, the fused features are:

Fused feature $= \mu_1 \times$ CSPC$+\mu_2 \times$ Max (D1PC, D2PC, D3PC, D4PC, D5PC, D6PC, D7PC, D8PC), where $\mu_1 = 0.7$ and $\mu_2 = 0.3$ is used. Numerical values of μ_1 and μ_2 are obtained from running the algorithm over a large set of images. After fusion of features classifier is used for identification of the test images. Here, CS theory-based CRC_RLS classifier is used for the recognition.

8.5   Experimental Results

The proposed framework is applied on: ORL and AR databases. ORL and AR are both of unmasked face databases. So to create the database of masked faces at first mask is of type of Figure 8.8 (a) is superimposed on the original face image Figure 8.8(b) and then Figure 8.8(c) masked faces are generated. Here, cropped faces are generated by using the method [27].

8.5.1   Database

The ORL [33] database consists of 400 frontal and nearly frontal face images of 40 different persons with 10 different poses. From 400 images some samples are shown in Figure 8.9. For the pose variation, a maximum of 20 degree rotation of the face images is allowed. In this database, all

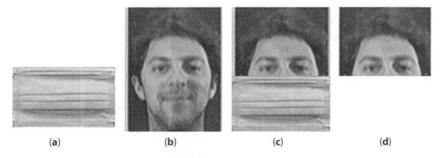

(a)   (b)   (c)   (d)

Figure 8.8 (a) Used mask, (b) sample face image, (c) generated masked face, (d) cropped face.

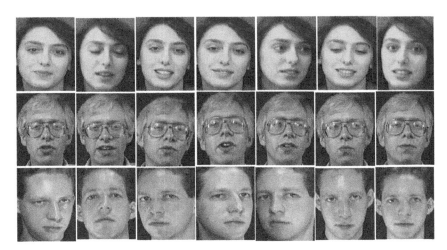

Figure 8.9 Sample images of ORL face database.

gray scale images are resized to 92×112, and variations in the scaling up to 10% are considered. During experiment for each person, five images are randomly chosen for training and remaining five are selected for testing.

The AR [34] face database consists of 4,000 images of 126 individuals among which 70 male and 56 female candidate's face images with expression and illumination variation. In this present work, we choose 1,399 face images. The images are resized to 60×43, as shown in Figure 8.10. During the experiment for each person, seven images are randomly chosen for training and remaining seven are selected for testing.

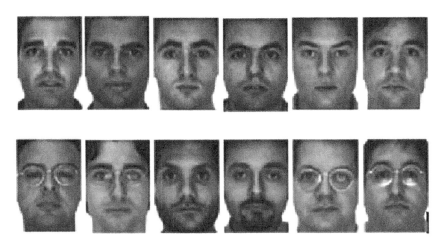

Figure 8.10 Sample images of AR face database.

8.5.2   Result

Recognition rate of the proposed technique for ORL and AR database is shown in Table 8.1 and Table 8.2. For ORL database, principal component (PC) is increased up to 100, and for AR database, it is increased up to 300. From Table 8.1 and Table 8.2, it is noticed that the proposed method provides the maximum recognition rate 91.5% for ORL database and 94.95% for AR database for unmasked face images. In case of masked faces, the proposed method provides the maximum accuracy of 90.35% for ORL database and 91.70% for AR database.

Performance of the proposed technique is also compared with conventional PCA as shown in Figure 8.11 and Figure 8.12 for masked and unmasked faces. From Figure 8.11 and Figure 8.12, it has been observed that the proposed method is better than the conventional PCA-based method for both the databases and for both the cases (masked and unmasked).

Figure 8.13 and Figure 8.14 show the comparison curve of proposed method for AR database. In Figure 8.13, the recognition rate of proposed technique is compared with conventional PCA for unmasked faces, and in Figure 8.14, for masked faces. For both the cases, the

Table 8.1 Recognition rate of ORL dataset.

PC	Recognition rate(%) for unmasked faces	Recognition rate(%) for masked faces
10	67.00%	63.57%
20	81.50%	80.50%
30	87.50%	85.71%
40	90.50%	87.50%
50	90.00%	87.00%
60	91.50%	90.35%
70	91.00%	89.50%
80	89.50%	88.21%
90	89.00%	87.85%
100	89.00%	87.50%

Table 8.2 Recognition rate of AR database.

PC	Recognition rate for unmasked faces (%)	Recognition rate (%) for masked faces
30	67.71%	64.37%
60	84.12%	80.11%
90	88.21%	83.83%
120	90.97%	85.55%
150	92.13%	88.84%
180	92.87%	89.12%
210	92.96%	89.69%
240	94.29%	91.13%
270	94.95%	91.70%
300	94.01%	91.41%

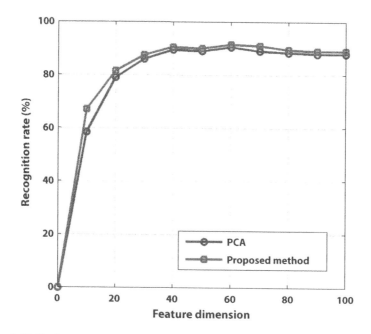

Figure 8.11 Performance comparison of recognition rate vs. feature dimension of ORL database for unmasked faces.

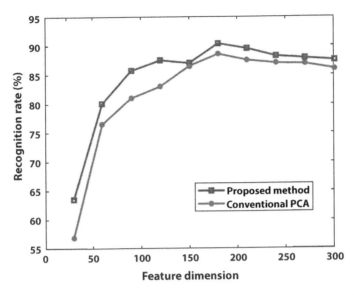

Figure 8.12 Performance comparison of recognition rate vs. feature dimension of ORL database for masked faces.

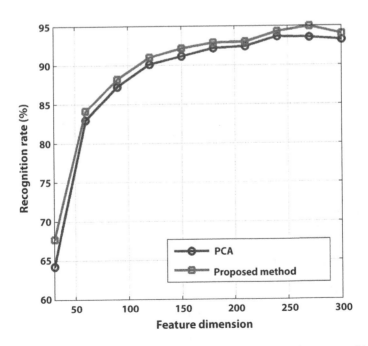

Figure 8.13 Performance comparison of recognition rate vs. feature dimension of AR database for unmasked faces.

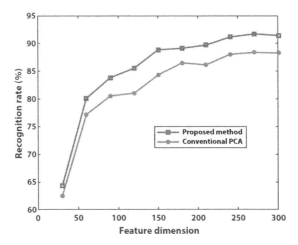

Figure 8.14 Performance comparison of recognition rate vs. feature dimension of AR database (masked faces).

proposed technique provides better accuracy compared to conventional PCA.

Comparisons with the existing methods are depicted in Table 8.3 and Table 8.4, showing the improved performance of the proposed technique compared to the other methods.

Table 8.3 Comparisons with other FR methods on AR database.

Method	Recognition rate (%)
PCA+CRC RLS [32]	90.00%
SRC [35]	90.10%
Proposed Method	94.95% (For unmasked faces) 91.70% (For masked faces)

Table 8.4 Comparisons with other FR methods on ORL database.

Method	Recognition rate (%)
PCA+SRC-MP [36]	89.00%
PCA+SR [37]	90.70%
PPCA [38]	90.5%
Proposed Method	91.50% (For unmasked faces 90.35% (For masked faces)

8.6   Conclusion

In this paper, an efficient FR method is presented utilizing a new technique of feature level fusion approach which improves the recognition rate of masked and unmasked faces. This technique integrates the discrete curvelet transform, PCA, and compressive sensing. This method is also applicable for real time problems due to the low dimension of fused features. The simulated results on ORL and AR databases clearly show that the proposed technique is more preferable compared with other techniques and provide the maximum recognition rate 91.5% on ORL database and 94.95% on AR database for unmasked face images. For masked faces, this technique also performs well and provides 90.35% maximum recognition rate for ORL database and 91.70% maximum recognition rate for AR database. Results show that the proposed technique provides better recognition rate compared to conventional PCA for both the cases of masked and unmasked faces. The proposed technique can be extended in the future as follows:

(i)   Other fusion rules can be used for the selection of features to get better recognition rate under the different constraint of FR.

(ii) The importance of other features in the transform domain may be used to improve the recognition rate.

(iii) Deep learning technique can be applied to improve the recognition rate.

References

1. Yang, M. and Zhang, L., Gabor feature based sparse representation for face recognition with gabor occlusion dictionary, in: *Proc. 11th European Conference on Computer Vision*, pp. 448–461, p. 6316, 2010.
2. Candes, E., Demanet, L., Donoho, D., Ying, L., Fast discrete curvelet transforms. *Multiscale Model. Sim.*, 5, 3, 861–899, 2006.
3. Wright, J., Yang, A.Y., Ganesh, A., Sastry, S.S., Ma, Y., Robust face recognition via sparse representation. *IEEE Trans. Pattern Anal. Mach. Intell.*, 31, 2, 210–227, 2009.
4. Nagesh, P. and Li, B., A compressive sensing approach for expression-invariant face recognition, in: *Proc. IEEE Conference on Computer Vision and Pattern Recognition*, pp. 1518–1525, 2009.
5. Lin, Z., Wenrui, Z., Li, S., Fang, Z., Infrared face recognition based on compressive sensing and pca, in: *Proc. IEEE International Conference on Computer Science and Automation Engineering*, vol. 2, pp. 51–54, 2011.

6. Sirovich, L. and Kirby, M., Low-dimensional procedure for the characterization of human faces. *J. Opt. Soc Am. A*, 4, 3, 519–524, 1987.

7. Jadhav, A., Jadhav, A., Ladhe, T., Yeolekar, K., Automated attendance system using face recognition. *Int. Res. J. Eng. Technol. (IRJET)*, 04, 01, 1467–1471, 2017.

8. Punjani, A.A., Obaid, C., Yasir, C., Automated attendance management system using face recognition. *Int. J. Adv. Res. Comput. Eng. Technol. (IJARCET)*, 6, 8, 1–5, 2017.

9. Kutty, N.M. and Mathai, S., Face recognition-a tool for automated attendance system. *Int. J. Adv. Res. Comput. Sci. Software Eng.*, 07, 06, 334–336, 2017.

10. Chaudhari, C., Raj, R., Shirnath, S., Sali, T., Automatic attendance monitoring system using face recognition techniques. *Int. J. Innov. Eng. Technol. (IJIET)*, 10, 01, 103–106, 2018.

11. Kowsalya, P., Pavithra, J., Sowmiya, G., Shankar, C.K., Attendance monitoring system using face detection & face recognition. *Int. Res. J. Eng. Technol. (IRJET)*, 06, 03, 6629–6632, 2019.

12. Bah, S.M. and Ming, F., An improved face recognition algorithm and its application in attendance management system. *Array*, 5, 1–7, 2020.

13. Mallikarjuna Reddy, A., Venkata Krishna, V., Sumalatha, L., Face recognition based on Cross diagonal complete motif matrix. *Int. J. Image Graph. Signal Process.*, 3, 59–66, 2018.

14. Kamencay, P., Benco, M., Mizdos, T., Radil, R., A new method for face recognition using convolutional neural network. *Digital Image Process. Comput. Graphics*, 15, 4, 663–672, 2017.

15. Kambi Beli, I.L. and Chunsheng, G., Enhancing face identification using local binary patterns and K-nearest neighbors. *J. Imaging*, 3, 37, 1–12, 2017.

16. Gaikwad, A.T., LBP and PCA based on face recognition system. *Glob. J. Eng. Sci. Res.*, 5, 11, 368–373, 2018.

17. Lal, M., Kumar, K., Arain, R.H., Maitlo, A., Ruk, S.A., Shaikh, H., Study of face recognition techniques: a survey. *Int. J. Adv. Comput. Sci. Appl.*, 9, 6, 42–49, 2018.

18. Sharif, M., Naz, F., Yasmin, M., Shahid, M.A., Rehman, A., Face recognition: A survey. *J. Eng. Sci. Technol. Rev.*, 10, 2, 166–177, March 2017.

19. Ramaiah, N.P., Ijjina, E.P., Mohan, C.K., Illumination invariant face recognition using convolutional neural networks. *IEEE International Conference on Signal Processing, Informatics, Communication and Energy Systems (SPICES)*, pp. 1–4, 2015.

20. Bhangale Kishor, B., Jadhav Kamal, M., Shirke Yogesh, R., Robust pose invariant face recognition using DCP and LB. *IJMTE*, 8, 1026–1034, 2018.

21. Taigman, Y., Yanga, M., Ranzato, M., Wolf, L., Deep Face: closing the gap to human-level performance in face verification, in: *IEEE Conference on Computer Vision and Pattern Recognition*, pp. 1701–1708, 2014.

22. Taskiran, M., Kahraman, N., Erdem, C.E., Face recognition: Past, present and future (a review). *Digit. Signal Process.*, 106, 1–27, 2020.

23. Tolba, A.S., El-Baz, A.H., El-Harby, A.A., Face recognition: A literature review. *Int. J. Computer Electrical Automation Control Inf. Eng.*, 2, 7, 2556–2571, 2008.

24. Pranav, K.B. and Manikandan, J., Design and evaluation of a real-time face recognition system using convolutional neural networks. *Procedia Comput. Sci.*, 171, 1651–1659, 2020.

25. He, L., Li, H., Zhang, Q., Sun, Z., Dynamic feature matching for partial face recognition. *IEEE Trans. Image Process.*, 28, 2, 791–802, 2018.

26. Ge, S., Li, J., Ye, Q., Luo, Z., Detecting masked faces in the wild with lle-cnns, in: *Proceedings of the IEEE Conference on Computer Vision and Pattern Recognition*, pp. 2682–2690, 2017.

27. Hariri, W., Efficient masked face recognition method during the COVID-19 pandemic. *Signal Image Video Process.*, 16, 1–8, Nov. 15 2021.

28. Wang, Z., Wang, G., Huang, B., Xiong, Z., Hong, Q., Wu, H., Yi, P., Jiang, K., Wang, N., Pei, Y., Masked face recognition dataset and application. *CoRR*, 1, 1–3, 2020.

29. Simonyan, K. and Zisserman, A., Very deep convolutional networks for large-scale image recognition, in: *Proceedings of ICLR*, pp. 1–14, 2015.

30. Li, Y., Guo, K., Lu, Y., Liu, L., Cropping and attention based approach for masked face recognition. *Appl. Intell.*, 51, 3012–3025, 2021.

31. Zhang, S., Zhao, X., Lei, B., Robust facial expression recognition via compressive sensing. *Sensors*, 12, 3, 3747–3761, 2012.

32. Zhang, L., Yang, M., Feng, X., Sparse representation or collaborative representation: Which helps face recognition?, in: *Proc. International Conference on Computer Vision*, pp. 471–478, 2011.

33. http://www.cl.cam.ac.uk/Research/DTG/attarchive.

34. http://www2.ece.ohio-state.edu/leix/ARdatabase.html.

35. Yang, M., Zhang, L., Yang, J., Zhang, D., Robust sparse coding for face recognition, in: *CVPR*, pp. 625–632, 2011.

36. Shiau, Y.H. and Chen, C.C., A sparse representation method with maximum probability of partial ranking for face recognition, in: *Proc. 19th IEEE International Conference on Image Processing*, pp. 1445–1448, 2012.

37. Wang, C., Wang, Y., Liang, L., Sparse representation theory and its application for face recognition. *Int. J. Smart Sens. Intell. Syst.*, 8, 1, 107–124, 2015.

38. Jiang, T.-X., Huang, T.-Z., Zhao, X.-L., Ma, T.-H., Patch-based principal component analysis for face recognition. *Comput. Intell. Neurosci.*, 2017, 1–9, 2017.

9

Deep Learning: An Approach to Encounter Pandemic Effect of Novel Corona Virus (COVID-19)

**Santanu Koley[1]*, Pinaki Pratim Acharjya[1], Rajesh Mukherjee[1], Soumitra Roy[1]
and Somdeep Das[2]**

*[1]Department of Computational Science and Engineering, Haldia Institute of
Technology, Haldia (WB), India
[2]Department of Computer Science, Brainware University, Kolkata (WB), India*

Abstract

Researchers around the world are struggling to discover ground-breaking equipment aimed at building a great healthcare structure to fight the novel corona virus for the duration of this global epidemic. How deep learning (DL) encountered the COVID-19 epidemic and what are the current guidelines for exploring the potential in COVID-19 are the subject to walk around. Over time, genetic material of novel corona viruses mutates itself and changed its characteristics to create different variants of viruses. These distinctive variants can trigger different waves of destructive infection in different parts of world. The substantiation of DL pertinences on the precedent pandemic motivates the professionals by giving an innovative trend to organize this outburst to make it least effective. The main target of this article is to study the utility of deep learning–based approaches on COVID-19 and also their credibility in terms of containment of the pandemic based on recent works around the globe. The study has listed down recent works within DL approaches regarding marking out of virus-affected people, investigation of its protein formation, vaccine & medicine finding, virus relentlessness, and contamination to direct the enduring eruption. DL is endowed with a suitable contrivance intended for rapid selection COVID-19 along with pronouncement possible high-risk patients, which possibly will be cooperative for medical resource optimization and early prevention prior to patients suffering rigorous indication. In this study, the wide-ranging consequence of DL on several magnitudes to be in command of novel coronavirus (COVID-19)

**Corresponding author*: santanukoley@yahoo.com

Rajdeep Chakraborty, Anupam Ghosh, Jyotsna Kumar Mandal and S. Balamurugan (eds.) Convergence
of Deep Learning In Cyber-IoT Systems and Security, (183–206) © 2023 Scrivener Publishing LLC

is discussed, and attempts are made to investigate it. Despite rich studies being conducted through DL algorithms, there are still many limitations and contradictions in the area of COVID research. The continuous evolution of DL on coronavirus handles contamination and is costly to create the right resolution task. Apart from this, in this work, a DL-based pandemic analysis has been done using the received dataset from about 55 hospitals in West Bengal, India. According to some research scientists, we may enter the third and fourth waves too, thus this work will be helpful for further research activity in the years to come. Finally, it is expected this work will help many researchers throughout the world get some opportunity to find out the final remedy to get rid of this deadly virus.

Keywords: Deep learning (DL), corona virus (COVID-19), pandemic, algorithms

9.1 Introduction

The COVID-19 pandemic is continuing, establishing new records for infection and mortality. The virus's variations are anticipated, but their consequences are unclear. For fighting the forthcoming variants, the second wave has already demonstrated the necessity for early action and model development. The researchers investigate all the potential steps through simple demographic data, which would help in combating the anticipated third wave of COVID-19 pandemic. The researchers explore all possible methods that might aid in preventing the predicted third wave of COVID-19 pandemic.

The pandemic continues to challenge a wide range of medical systems around the world in many aspects, including the strong increase in demand from many medical devices and the significant scarcity of medical devices. Many medical institutions workers are infected. Therefore, the effective use of urgent clinical determination and the effective use of medical resources is very important. The most verified diagnostic test of COVID-19 with reverse transcriptase polymerase chain reaction (RTPCR) is lacking for a long time in developing countries. This contributes to the improvement of the rate of infection and differences the important precautionary measures. Effective detection allows a rapid and efficient diagnosis of COVID-19 and reduces the loading of medical systems.

This research looked at COVID-19 patients who were hospitalized from May 4, 2020, and died or were released from quarantine on January 18, 2021. The data consisting of simple demographic data points were collected from around 55.

In both the derivation and validation groups, descriptive statistics were run on all variables. For categorical variables, counts with proportions were used, while for continuous variables, median with interquartile range was used. The variables which were used are age, sex, confirmed cured, active, home isolation, etc.

9.2   Interpretation With Medical Imaging

In this fierce era of the COVID-19 pandemic, worldwide scientists are trying to find a systematic but fast approach to identify the infectivity of the virus. The unconventional DL approaches are emerging as the leading choice of scientists to aid the rapid identification of the infection. In this unconventional/traditional DL process, researchers examine the medical image for better interpretation of the respective virus during this medical crisis period.

In [1], An Xception architecture-based pretrained end-to-end CNN model is proposed to recognize COVID-19 infection from chest X-ray images. The authors have considered 1300 COVID-19 x-ray images from two open databases and use random undersampling to balance the considered data. The transfer learning technique has been employed in the proposed to initialize the initial model parameters, and this also has helped to overcome the overfitting problem due to insufficient training data.

A multiview fusion-based DL model has been waged on chest CT images to aid the screening process of COVID-19 patients in [2]. Three views of CT images—axial, coronal, and sagittal of the lungs have been considered to train the DL network. CT images of 495 patients have been used to train the typical ResNet50 architecture, and it was noticed that the multiview fusion model produces better results with respect to the single view. The multiview fusion employed in the proposed model also addresses over fitting due to insufficient data [2]. Figure 9.1 shows the CT images of four patients in axial, coronal, and sagittal view with pneumonia diagnosis presented in Wu *et al.* [2].

Wang and Wong [3] presented a lightweight residual projection-expansion-projection-extension design pattern-based model for COVID-19 infection detection long with a CXR dataset of 13,870 patients. The proposed architecture presides over the selective long-range connection to reduce the noticeable computational complexity and memory overhead.

Pathogenic laboratory testing is a standard way to detect COVID-19 infection that comes with the cost of false negativity. An InceptionV3-based predefined DL model has been presented in Wang *et al.* [4] as an alternative diagnostic method. The proposed model [4] exhibits good performance to differentiate COVID-19 and seasonal viral pneumonia.

Axial   Coronal   Saggital

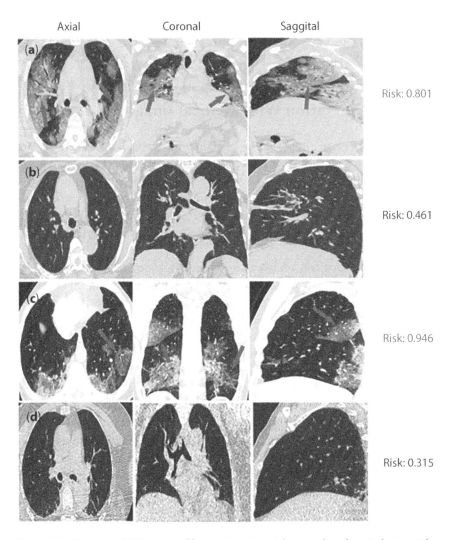

Figure 9.1 Example of CT images of four patients in axial, coronal, and sagittal view with pneumonia diagnosis [2].

In parallel with RT-PCR test, radiographic features of CT images are also exhibiting promising sensitivity in COVID-19 detection. It is observed that the focus of infection near the pleura is most likely to be diagnostic as COVID-19–positive. To capture this propitious phenomenon, in Butt *et al.* [5], relative distance from the edges has been considered as extra weight to diverge the appearance and structures of different infections. Figure 9.2 shows CT scan images of a COVID-19 patient presented in Butt *et al.* [5], which demonstrate the evolvement of lungs opacities over time.

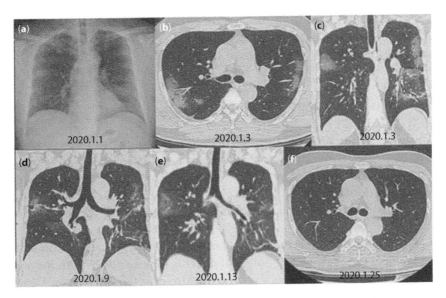

Figure 9.2 Chest images of COVID-19 patients presented in [5].

The relative performance of CT and CXR in COVID-19 detection has been studied, and the diagnostic ability of AI-based systems with human skill is compared in Cheng *et al.* [6]. The developed AI-based work in Cheng *et al.* [6] on clinically representative large-scale datasets outperforms five experienced radiologists in terms of diagnostic efficacy. Guided Grad Cam has been taken into consideration in the work to select the ROI to extract features. It is also noted that only extraction of the considered regions through Guided Grad-CAM limits the feature analysis.

A neural network-based fully automated lung CT diagnosis system was developed by Ying, Y. *et al.* [7] to detect COVID-19 infections. The model is based on ResNet50 architecture where feature pyramid Network (FPN) is employed for top-level feature extraction. In the proposed model, mean pooling is used for the integration of image-level results. The authors also have incorporated an attention module in the proposed system to elucidate the output of the neural network. The provided outcomes reflect that the proposed model exhibits high accuracy in pneumonia and COVID-19 detection. In Takahashi *et al.* [8], pulmonary involvement of COVID-19 is estimated by a DL approach to detect the infection.

Islam *et al.* [9] introduced an amalgamation of an artificial recurrent neural network (RNN) LSTM and CNN to identify the COVID-19 infection from X-rays images. In the study, LSTM is employed for classification based on features extracted by CNN and authors notice the high performance of LSTM in the separation of COVID-19 cases from others. Total 6000 x-ray images, including 1525 number of confirmed COVID-19 cases are considered in the proposed system.

9.3   Corona Virus Variants Tracing

Tracking the corona virus-infected people and finding the different variants of viruses is an immense challenge for scientists and administrators globally. In this perspective, DL is also establishing itself as an eminent technique. Most of the recently proposed systems are successfully tracing the pandemic-affected global citizens globally with the aid of DL methods.

Based on the respiratory pattern, a real-time system has been proposed by Wang *et al.* [10] to detect potential patients in public areas with the aid of a depth camera. The heterogeneous nature of respiratory pattern and unavailability of suitable data set makes this application inappropriate for transfer learning. Thus, the researcher has proposed a respiratory simulation model for generating training data. In the proposed work, authors consider bidirectional recurrent neural network and attentional neural network mechanisms with the GRU model to be trained by the simulated data which was later validated with actually acquired data. The manual selection of ROI does not fit with the real-time system as it does necessitate the selection before each use and also does not guarantee to be figurative the effective areas when people move. And so, automatic selection of ROI has been considered with the help of Microsoft Azure Kinect API has been considered in the proposed work. In the proposed work, researchers have selected three ROI—chest, abdomen, and shoulder and extracted repository signals from selected ROIs by calculating average value of depth data. Figure 9.3, presented in Wang *et al.* [10], demonstrate measurement of Central-Apnea waveforms of a specific subject to three ROIs.

Medical laboratory test for COVID-19 detection is costly and time-consuming, which is not very suitable for detection of pandemic infectious disease where the larger mass of the population is at risk. In Maghdid *et al.* [11], a low-cost, Smartphone sensor-based, a quick responsive, artificial intelligence-based framework has been proposed for preliminary COVID-19 diagnosis. The proposed framework comprises four layer—input/reading layer, measurement layer, sensor layer and computation layer. Consideration of multiple readings from multiple sensors provides the ground for the reliability of the framework. Further improvement of the proposed model is also possible with the aid of transfer learning and cloud.

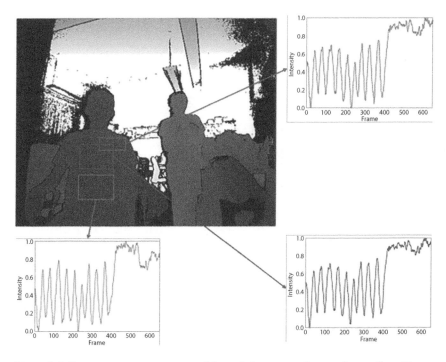

Figure 9.3 Demonstrate measurement of Central-Apnea waveforms of a specific subject to three ROIs [10].

To slow down the community mitigation of this contagious disease, people must be aware of risk factors associated with day-to-day actions with minimal daily life disruptions. A work on COVID-19 risk estimation has been done through empirical studies in Ye *et al.* [12] and has been corroborated through a large real-world dataset. Developed system alpha-satellite in the proposed work automatically produced risk indices in hierarchy fashion to guide people's action to provide protection from the pandemic infection ensuing minimal disruption to the day-to-day life. Developed system alpha-satellite (Figure 9.4) in the proposed work automatically produced risk indices in a hierarchy fashion to guide people's action to provide protection from the pandemic infection ensuring minimal disruption to the day-to-day life.

Reddy *et al.* [13] have presented a long short-term memory-based DL model to forecast the trend and probable stop time of the COVID-19. Augmented Dickey Fuller Test [25] has been performed in the considered data to identify the impact of trends in the data. The interpretation of the obtained results also has justified the use of social distancing in this pandemic era.

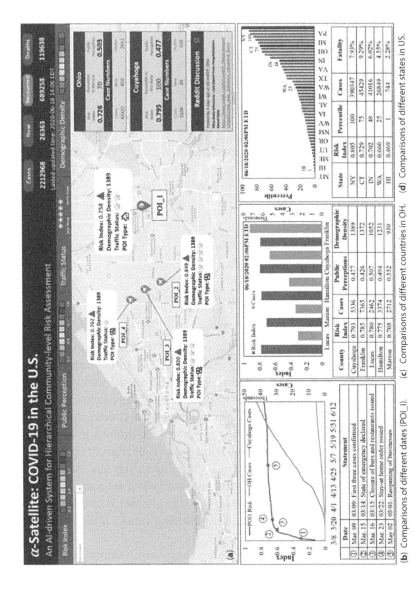

Figure 9.4 Glimpse of alpha satellite which estimates risk factor over different parameters [12].

Beck, B.R., *et al.* [25] have proposed three RNN-based DL models—gated recurrent unit (GRU)—RNN, LSTM-RNN, and GRU-LSTM-RNN model for COVID-19–confirmed, negative cases, recovered cases, and death cases prognostication. A comparative study of all the proposed models has been done, and obtained results are also validated through certified medical practitioners. Based on obtained results, the authors claim the performance of GRU-LSTM-RNN presides over the other two models.

9.4 Spreading Capability and Destructiveness of Virus

One of the common phenomena of viruses is that they evolve at an extremely fast rate. And the primary concern about it is that they do not only evolve faster but they tend to evolve faster than the host. Two different kinds of viruses in a particular host can exchange genetic material and give birth to new viruses with unique characteristics. As a consequence, it can also increase its power of infectivity, which multiplied the destructive capability of the viruses' multiple times. This mandates the requirement of a trustworthy process for viral host foreboding to conserve biosecurity and biosafety.

In Bartoszewicz *et al.* [14], a neural network-based work has been done where authors claim the improvement over viral host predictions from next-generation sequencing read. The proposed method for convolution filter visualization uses partial Shapley values, which discriminate between simple nucleotide information content and benefaction of each sequence position to the classification score. In the proposed work, LSTM and CNN-based architectures with average pooling has been taken into consideration. and a comparative study also has been performed with existing benchmark models. Although the necessity of high-quality labels and sequences limits the performance of the proposed model. The authors have demanded supremacy of the CNN-based model over LSTM-based model but also have suggested LSTM for shorter reads, which do not necessitate retraining.

Guo, Q., *et al.* [15], have proposed a DL-based algorithm virus host prediction (VHP) for potential host prediction for viruses. Based on their model prediction, authors have claimed bat corona viruses and mink viruses have more similar infectivity patterns to COVID-19. They also have predicted that COVID-19 also has close transmissibility with other different corona viruses, mainly the severe acute respiratory syndrome corona virus (SARS-CoV), bat SARS-like corona viruses, and the Middle East respiratory syndrome corona virus (MERS-CoV). The analysis made upon the outcome of the proposed model in Zhu *et al.* [15] of similarity on COVID-19 infectivity pattern, exhibits bat and mink as the most probable reservoirs of COVID-19.

9.5   Deduction of Biological Protein Structure

Joynt and Wu [16] have empathized that the affinity between viral RNA load kinetics and disease severity among COVID-19–infected persons remains crumbled. In their article, they have expressed their interest to know whether viral RNA load in lung tissue or in a surrogate sample like tracheal aspirate, mirrors the downfall in nasopharyngeal aberration. With their inspection, they concluded the late, severe manifestations might as immunologically mediated and have agreed on the evident implications of the potential use of immune-modulatory therapies for these late manifestation patients.

Knowledge in protein structures benefits the diagnosis and treatment process of the underlying disease. But the existing procedure to know protein structure may take months or more. Thus, Scientists are looking for a trustworthy computational procedure to know the protein structure from amino acid sequence. DL methods are also playing an promising role in this journey. Senior *et al.* [17] have elaborated their vast genomic data-fed neural-based hypothesis model AlphaFold for predicting protein structure. They have claimed their work significant progress in one of biology's core challenges based on the obtained accuracy in 3D models of proteins that AlphaFold generates. The predictions of protein structure aid in understanding the roles of these protein structures within the body and thus it is believed to help in diagnosing and treating diseases. The proposed model also has been employed in multiple COVID-19 protein [18]. The proposed model has accurately predicted the protein structures in the scenario where similar kinds of experimentally determined protein structures exist. The proposed AlphaFold is still under development and focusing on predicting protein structures for the scenario where no similar protein structures exist [18].

9.6   Pandemic Model Structuring and Recommended Drugs

Now, the top priority for global public health is a trustworthy blueprint to minimize the severity of the corona pandemic. In Ferguson *et al.* [19], the authors have concluded through their investigation that border restriction or internal restriction delays the spread of corona pandemic at most 2 to 3 weeks, unless it is more than 99% effective. The study [19] strengthens the case isolation or household quarantine strategy by concluding the fact based on analysis that the impact of case isolation or home quarantine is much more fruitful over school closure strategy during the peak of the pandemic. Further, it is also noticed by authors that school closure during the peak of a pandemic declines the attack rate at a max of 40%, whereas its impact on the overall attack is negligible. Findings direct that immediate treatment with antiviral upon the start of symptoms can reduce the transmission. It is expected that a combination of home quarantine, reactive school closure, and medication for 50% population could reduce clinical attack rates by 50%. It is also stated that even vaccines having minimum efficiency can also decline the attack if applied in sufficient quantity.

Halloran *et al.* [20] have used three different models to introspect the targeted layered containment approach on social distancing, rapid case establishment, and targeted prevention. Generally, these targeted preventive measures are very useful to reduce the transmission of pandemic circumstances. It is also true that timely intervention declines the ultimate number of pandemics diseases.

Ferguson *et al.* [21] have shown that the use of social distancing and antiviral protection make possible the confinement and eradication of an incipient pandemic. The work also concludes that even the incipient virus has the transmissibility near to past pandemic virus then also simple socially targeted preventive measures are not sufficient, multiple approaches are required for the eradication and confinement of the virus. Further, it is also noted that geographically targeted policies are very much required for obtaining higher degree containment along with area quarantine to boost policy effectiveness. Socially targeted measures are adequate when the transmissibility unfolds incrementally.

Ferguson *et al.* [22], in their hypothesis, propose two fundamental policies—mitigation and suppression (Figure 9.5) to alleviate the pandemic situation. Proposed mitigation slows down the pandemic aiding the peak healthcare need and suppression to reverse the pandemic widening and decreasing case numbers to a low level. The major challenges of both the policies have also been noted and which necessitates the layer of multiple interventions even if suppression or mitigation is the overarching policy goal. Proposed suppression needed more intensive and socially disruptive measures in comparison to mitigation (Figure 9.6). Lastly, the authors are agreed that the feasibility and effectiveness in the social context of a country ultimately determine the choice of interventions.

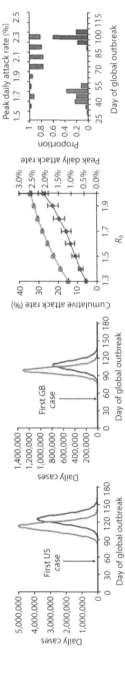

Figure 9.5 The expected pattern of pandemic presented in Ferguson *et al.* [19].

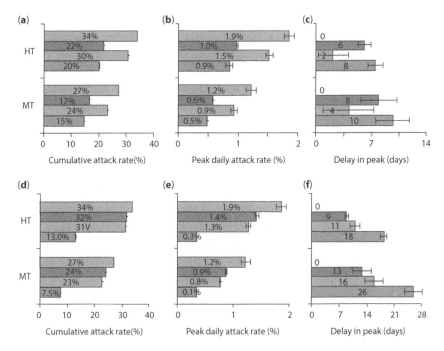

Figure 9.6 Impact of household and socially targeted policies presented in Ferguson *et al.* [19].

9.7 Selection of Medicine

As of now, there is no fully systematic and effective antiviral plan/system after the economic and societal impact of the COVID-19 pandemic. To prevent this infection the necessary process is to find the right drugs for the betterment of world public health.

In absence of fully proven treatment for COVID-19, Zhavoronkov *et al.* [23] have used their proprietary generative chemistry pipeline based on the knowledge of the crystal structure and homology model of the target protein to assert the novel drug-like compound.

After the failed attempt of SARS-CoV-2 infected patient's treatment with approved drugs like lopinavir/ritonavir, Tang *et al.* [24] generated new chemical entities against this virus. It is also notified by the authors that a key enzyme in the life-cycle of corona virus is the most attractive for antiviral drug design. A novel advanced deep Q-learning network with the fragment-based drug design (ADQN-FBDD) based on a newly solved structure (PDB ID: 6LU7), is developed in the work for generating potential lead compounds targeting SARS-CoV-2 3CLpro.

Beck *et al.* [25] have used a deep learning network to predict fruitful drugs on coronavirus from existing commercial medicines. The proposed deep learning-based target interaction model is named molecule transformer-drug target interaction (MT-DTI). The authors based on their model results analysis claimed that atazanavir, which is an antiretroviral medication used to treat and prevent the human immunodeficiency virus (HIV), is the most effective compound for corona virus. Upon identification of various effective antiviral agents like Kaletra by the proposed model, authors also have proposed a list of drugs for ascertain effective treatment strategies for SARS-CoV-2.

In Patankar [26], deep learning-based models for the drug solution of COVID-19 viruses have been proposed. A predictive LSTM model has been used in the proposed models in which the proposed models screen 310k drugs from the ZINC database for the identification of effective compounds. All the predicted drugs predicted by the proposed model claimed to have shown better binding properties in docking simulations relative to the existing medically approved drugs for the COVID-19 like remdesivir, favipiravir, and galidesivir. Additionally, the 310k ZINC database molecules with their predicted IC50s were used to train a generative SemiSupervised Variational Auto Encoder (SSVAE) model. Their proposed model was used to generate 10 new molecules by sampling from the latent space to demonstrate its utility. Among the 10 new molecules generated by the SSVAE model, the most stable new molecule had binding energy lower than the comparison group of prior drugs. These molecules could potentially be good drug candidates for the SARS CoV and COVID-19. Their experimental results conclude that deep learning-based models could be useful in screening existing compound and generating new molecules to find drugs for COVID-19.

In Zhang *et al.* [27], the neural network-based framework is presented for COVID-19. As a dense fully convolution neural network is capable to extract more features from data that aid in more accurate prediction, it become the most effective method for drug discovery in the post-genomics era. In addition to being effective, it is also the cheapest and faster method. One of the burning examples of this technique is the discovery of pyrimethamine—an anti-malarial drug against the dihydrofolatereductase (DHFR) enzyme and also BPM31510 is another example that is under phase II trial related to advanced pancreatic cancer [28–30]. Hence, authors advocate the deep learning model's immense usefulness in therapeutic drug targeting. The proposed data-driven DFCNN model educates itself 3C-like protease–ligand interaction from known binding and non-binder data. Authors claim their proposed model is fast and accurate in respect to all other molecular docking procedures as the proposed model uses the binding pocket of 3C-like protease–ligand conformation instead of whole conformation of the complex. The authors suggested that the identified potential 3C-like protease-ligand pairs by the proposed model can be considered to MD simulation for inspection to narrow down the candidate list. In accordance with this, in the proposed work a deep learning-based drug screening has been done for COVID-19 and potential compound and tripeptide lists like protease have been provided.

9.8   Result Analysis

Figure 9.7 and Figure 9.8 plotted below demonstrate the distributions of some of the patient information. The data states that a significantly large number of COVID-19 patients reported at hospitals have been home isolated and rest are being admitted to the hospitals, which are lesser in count.

It was also noted that the female patient is relatively less than the male in admission to hospital, as well as home isolation.

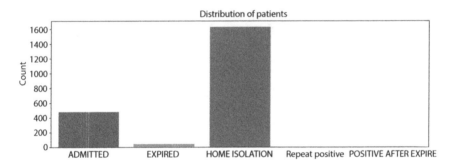

Figure 9.7 Distributions of patients in the dataset.

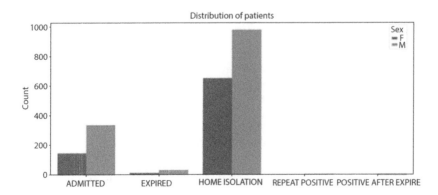

Figure 9.8 Gender wise distributions of patients in the dataset.

The gender wise distributions of patients in the dataset are described in the category of admitted, expired, home isolated, repeat positive in COVID-19 for several times and positive found after expiring.

Figure 9.9 and Figure 9.10 plotted below demonstrate the distributions of patient tested asymptomatic or symptomatic. The asymptomatic cases are more that the symptomatic cases. Here also, female patients are relatively less than their male patients.

Figure 9.11 shows that patients ranging in age from 10 months to 90 years completed their containment zone and cured, the majority of the patients being between the ages of 30 to 39 years.

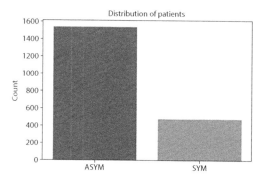

Figure 9.9 Distributions of patients tested asymptomatic or symptomatic.

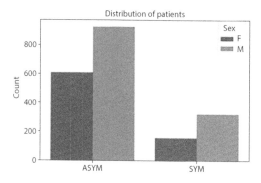

Figure 9.10 Gender wise distributions of patients tested asymptomatic or symptomatic.

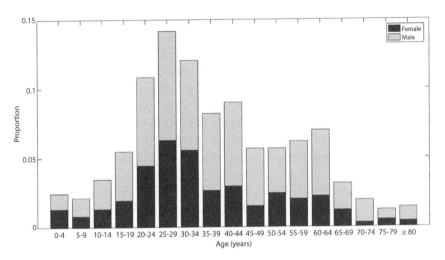

Figure 9.11 Age wise distribution of patients completing containment.

Figure 9.12 below describes the number of patients confirmed positive with COVID-19 and either admitted or home isolated. The patients' ages range from 10 months to 90 years. A number of female patients is in the age group of 1 to 85 years. The most affected age group among female patients is 20-49 years.

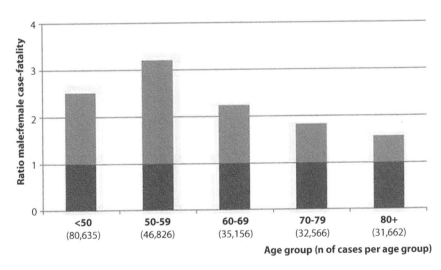

Figure 9.12 Gender and age wise distribution of patients.

Figure 9.13 below demonstrates the status/condition of patients distributed according to their age group. The age group confirmed with COVID-19–positive ranges from 10 months to 90 years including the admitted patients as well as the home isolated patients. Mortality rate is higher in the age group of 50 to 79 years. Mortality in female is higher in the age group of 60 to 69 years and in male, it is in 50 to 79 years age group. Figure 9.14 above shows that the active cases are 2.13% of the confirmed cases, cured cases are 97.86%, and mortality is 2.41%. Using a dataset from about 55 hospitals in West Bengal, India, this research aimed to use machine

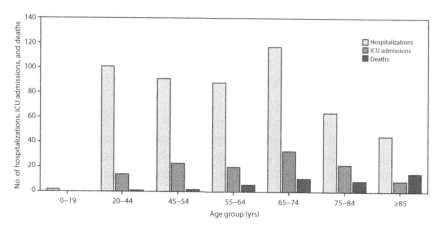

Figure 9.13 Age wise condition of patients.

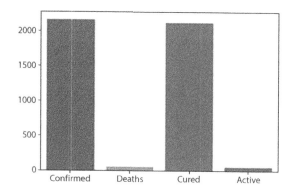

Figure 9.14 Status of cases.

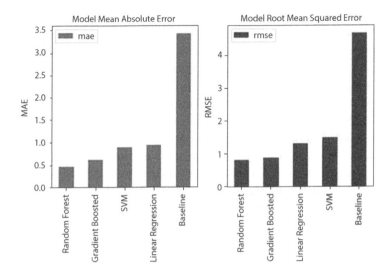

Figure 9.15 Model mean absolute and squared error.

learning algorithm for pandemic analysis. The correlation matrix indicated that people were most likely to die from COVID-19 if they are in the age group over 50 years. Finally, when it came to predicting the COVID-19 transmission, the Random Forest (RF) technique produced the smallest root mean square error (RMSE) and mean absolute error (MAE) compared to other methods (as shown in Figure 9.15).

9.9 Conclusion

DL-based algorithms data are the important input to structure the model. But during the study of COVID-19, all the researchers face some general problems: (i) COVID-19 appeared recently throughout the globe; (ii) collected data for COVID-19 should be accurate and reliable, as well as represent the central tendency of the data, but the availability of data aiding the study of the pandemic in the public domain is not enough. (iii) According to the different reports, the features of COVID-19 can be different for different parts of the globe due to different variants of the corona virus. Thus, data collected from specific geographical regions may restrict the study. Recent studies reveal that the myth that COVID-19 comes from animal resources has no significant base. Also, from the community transmission rate of COVID-19 between people, no conclusion can be drawn about the acceptability of this narrative as global inhabitants are not sure how or from where they are affected by this novel virus. The survey upon various deep learning-based works on COVID-19 explored in this study acknowledges that deep learning-based approaches are paving the way to encounter this pandemic in every possible facet. However, from the above discussion, it can be concluded that experimented data in different manuscript are not synchronized as they are taken from different region of this globe. For our research, COVID-19 dataset is collected from about 55 hospitals in West Bengal during the period of May 4, 2020, to January 18, 2021. Based on collected data, we have performed a comparative study upon the performance of various DL-based approaches upon the prediction of COVID transmission. Final outcome of the comparison reflects that the random forest–based approach presides over other considered approaches in terms of prediction of COVID transmission as it provides the smallest root mean square error (RMSE) and mean absolute error (MAE).

References

1. Khan, A.I., Shah, J.L., Bhat, M.M., CoroNet: A deep neural network for detection and diagnosis of COVID-19 from chest X-ray images. *Comput. Methods Programs Biomed.*, 196, 105581, 2020.
2. Wu, X., Hui, H., Niu, M., Liang, L., Wang, L., He, B., Yang, X., Li, L., Li, H., Tian, J., Zha, Y., DL-based multi-view fusion model for screening 2019 novel coronavirus pneumonia: A multi centre study. *Eur. J. Radiol.*, 128, 109041, 2020.
3. Wang, L. and Wong, A., COVID-Net: A tailored deep convolutional neural network design for detection of COVID-19 cases from chest X-ray images. *Sci. Rep.*, 10, 1, 19549, 2020.
4. Wang, S., Kang, B., Ma, J., Zeng, X., Xiao, M., Guo, J., Cai, M., Yang, J., Li, Y., Meng, X., Xu, B., A deep learning algorithm using CT images to screen for corona virus disease (COVID-19). *Eur. Radiol.*, 31, 8, 6096–6104, 2021.
5. Butt, C., Gill, J., Chun, D., Babu, B.A., Deep learning system to screen corona virus disease pneumonia. *Appl. Intell. JCT*, 2019.

6. Cheng, J., Feng, J., Chen, W., Cao, Y., Zhanwei, X., Zhang, X., Deng, L., Zheng, C., Zhou, J., Shi, H., Development and evaluation of an AI system for COVID-19 diagnosis. preprint, 11, 5088, 2020.
7. Ying, Y., Zheng, S., Li, S., Zhang, L., Zhang, X., Huang, X., Chen, Z., Zhao, J., Jie, H., Wang, Y., Chong, R., Shen, Y., Zha, J., Yang, Y., Deep learning enables accurate diagnosis of novel coronavirus (COVID-19) with CT images. *IEEE/ACM Trans. Comput. Biol. Bioinform.*, 18, 6, 2775–2780, 2021.
8. Takahashi, M.S., de Mendonça, M.R.F., Pan, I., Pinetti, R.Z., Kitamura, F.C., Regarding serial quantitative chest CT assessment of COVID-19: Deeplearning approach. *Radiology Cardiothoracic Imaging*, 2, 2, e200075, Mar 30, 2020.
9. Islam, M.Z., Islam, M.M., Asraf., A., A combined deep CNN-LSTM network for the detection of novel coronavirus (COVID-19) using X-ray images. *Inform. Med. Unlocked*, 20, 100412, 2020.
10. Wang, Y., Hu, M., Li, Q., Zhang, X.-P., Zhai, G., Yao, N., Abnormal respiratory patterns classifier may contribute to large-scale screening of people infected with COVID-19 in an accurate and unobtrusive manner, 2020, arXiv preprint arXiv: 2002.05534. https://doi.org/10.48550/arXiv.2002.05534
11. Maghdid, H.S., Ghafoor, K.Z., Sadiq, A.S., Curran, K., Rabie, K., A novel AI-enabled framework to diagnose coronavirus COVID 19 using smartphone embedded sensors: Design study. *2020 IEEE 21st International Conference on Information Reuse and Integration for Data Science (IRI)*, pp. 180–187, 2020.
12. Ye, Y., Hou, S., Fan, Y., Zhang, Y., Qian, Y., Sun, S., Peng., Q., Ju, M., Song, W., Laparo, K., α-Satellite: An AI-driven system and benchmark datasets for hierarchical community-level risk assessment to help combat COVID-19, *IEEE J. Biomed. Health Inform.*, 24, 2755–2764, 2020.
13. Chimmula, V.K.R. and Zhang, L., Time series forecasting of COVID-19 transmission in Canadausing LSTM networks. *Chaos Solitons Fractals*, 135, 109864, 2020.
14. Bartoszewicz, J.M., Seidel, A., Renard, B.Y., Interpretable detection of novel human viruses from genome sequencing data. *NAR Genom. Bioinform.*, 3, 1, 1qab004, 2021.
15. Guo, Q., Li, M., Wang, C., Fang, Z., Wang, P., Tan, J., Wu, S., Xiao, Y., Host and infectivity prediction of Wuhan 2019 novel coronavirus using deep learning algorithm, BioRxiv, 2020. https://doi.org/10.1101/2020.01.21.914044
16. Joynt, G.M. and Wu, W.K., Understanding COVID-19: What does viral RNA load really mean? *Lancet Infect. Dis.*, 20, 635, 2020.
17. AlphaFold: Using AI for scientific discovery, 2020. https://deepmind.com/blog/article/alphafold-casp13.

18. Computational predictions of protein structures associated with COVID-19, 2020. https://deepmind.com/research/open-source/computational-predictions-of-protein-structures-associated-with-COVID-19.

19. Ferguson, N.M., Cummings, D.A.T., Fraser, C., Cajka, J.C., Cooley, P.C., Burke, D.S., Strategies for mitigating an influenza pandemic. *Nature*, 442, 448, 2006.

20. Halloran, M.E., Ferguson, N.M., Eubank, S., Longini, I.M., Jr, Cummings, D.A.T., Lewis, B., Xu, X., Fraser, C., Vullikanti, A., Germann, T.C., Wagener, D., Beckman, R., Kadau, K., Barrett, C., Macken, C.A., Burke, D., Cooley, P. *et al.*, Modeling targeted layered containment of an influenza pandemic in the United States. *Proc. Natl. Acad. Sci. U. S. A.*, 105, 4639, 2008.

21. Ferguson, N.M., Cummings, D.A.T., Cauchemez, S., Fraser, C., Riley, S., Meeyai, S., Iamsirithaworn, S., Burke, D.S., Strategies for containing an emerging influenza pandemic in Southeast Asia. *Nature*, 437, 209, 2020.

22. Ferguson, N., Laydon, D., Nedjati-Gilani, G., Imai, N., Ainslie, K., Baguelin, M., Bhatia, S., Boonyasiri, A., Cucunubá, Z., Cuomo-Dannenburg, G., Dighe, A., Report 9—Impact of non-pharmaceutical interventions (NPIs) to reduce COVID-19 mortality and healthcare demand, Imperial College COVID-19 Response Team, 2020. https://doi.org/10.1101/2020.01.21.914044

23. Zhavoronkov, A., Aladinskiy, V., Zhebrak, A., Zagribelnyy, B., Terentiev, V., Bezrukov, D.S., Polykovskiy, D., Shayakhmetov, R., Filimonov, A., Orekhov, P., Yan, Y., Popova, O., Vanhaelen, Q., Aliper, A., Ivanenkov, Y., Potential 2019-nCoV 3C-like protease inhibitors designed using generative deep learning approaches, ChemRxiv. Cambridge: Cambridge Open Engage, 2020.

24. Fu, Z., Huang, B., Tang, J., Liu, S., Liu, M., Ye, Y., Liu, Z., Xiong, Y., Zhu, W., Cao, D., Li, J., Niu, X., Zhou, H., Zhao, Y.J., Zhang, G., Huang, H., The complex structure of GRL0617 and SARS-CoV-2 PLpro reveals a hot spot for antiviral drug discovery. *Nat. Commun.*, 12, 1, pp. 488, 2021.

25. Beck, B.R., Shin, B., Choi, Y., Park, S., Kang, K., Predicting commercially available antiviral drugs that may act on the novel coronavirus (2019-nCoV), through a drug-target interaction deep learning model. *Comput. Struct. Biotechnol. J.*, 18, 784, 2020.

26. Patankar, S., Deep learning-based computational drug discovery to inhibit the RNA Dependent RNA Polymerase: Application to SARS-CoV and COVID-19, OSF Preprints, 2020. https://doi.org/10.31219/osf.io/6kpbg

27. Zhang, H., Mani Saravanan, K., Yang, Y., Hossain, M.T., Li, J., Ren, X., Pan, Y., Wei, Y., Deep learning based drug screening for novel coronavirus 2019-nCov. *Interdiscip. Sci.*, 12, 368, 2020.

28. Fleming, N., How artificial intelligence is changing drug discovery. *Nature*, 557, 555, 2018.

29. Liu, Z., Du, J., Fang, J., Yin, Y., Xu, G., Xie, L., Deep screening: A deep learning-based screening web server for accelerating drug discovery. *Database*, 2019: baz104. Published online 2019.
30. Chen, H., Engkvist, O., Wang, Y., Olivecrona, M., Blaschke, T., The rise of deep learning in drug discovery. *Drug Discov. Today*, 23, 1241, 2018.

10

Question Answering System Using Deep Learning in the Low Resource Language Bengali

Arijit Das*† and Diganta Saha

Department of Computer Science and Engineering, Faculty of Engineering and Technology, Jadavpur University, Kolkata, West Bengal, India

Abstract

Question answering (QA) in natural language based on text corpus needs human intelligence. In this work, a system is proposed for automatic QA in natural language based on the large unstructured text corpus repository. Conventionally, computer system is more proficient in retrieving from a large data set or repository by matching keywords. Web search runs on the basic principle of keyword matching and the popular search engines improve the ranking of list of URLs collected by the crawler using page-rank algorithm, user's web cache, location, preference, etc. The principle of the QA system is different from those syntactic search algorithms. Here, actual answer is expected irrespective of number of matching terms in between question and answer. QA system built in English and other resourceful languages handles the challenge with machine readable dictionary, WordNet, ontology etc. Absence of annotated text, incomplete WordNet and ontology are the main challenges toward building QA system in the low resource language like Bengali. In the present work, supervised methods of learning algorithms are used to build Bengali QA system. Bengali literature in the form of text corpus, which was created in Technology Development of Indian Languages (TDIL) project, works as the repository of the proposed system. Four classification algorithms, ANN, SVM, Naïve Bayes, and decision tree, are used as supervised learning methods for question classification. Word2Vec algorithm is used for measuring similarity during answer retrieval. The system has achieved 95.88% accuracy in questions classification. Coarse-grain accuracy in retrieval of the answer is 98.77%. Fine-grain accuracy in retrieval of the answer is 93.25%. If the answer returned by the

Corresponding author: arijit.das@ieee.org
†Arijit Das, the first author of this chapter received a UGC UPE fellowship.

Rajdeep Chakraborty, Anupam Ghosh, Jyotsna Kumar Mandal and S. Balamurugan (eds.) Convergence of Deep Learning In Cyber-IoT Systems and Security, (207–230) © 2023 Scrivener Publishing LLC

system is the accurate exact answer, then the result is treated as fine grain accurate; whereas if the answer returned by the system contains the exact answer, then the result is treated as coarse grain accurate. Majority of the QA system, which are built in English or other popular languages, work with a structured relational database as repository and give answer of multiple-choice type questions. Novelty of this work is in building the complete natural language-based QA system with high accuracy in low resource language, with a flat file system as repository.

Keywords: QA system, Word2Vec, deep learning, chatbot, neural network, machine learning, NLP, natural language processing

10.1   Introduction

QA system is the backbone of chatbots, virtual assistants. With the increased use of service-based IT applications, the pressure is increasing on the customer care, and it is the demand of the industry to automate the answering of the customers' query. Robot for chatting or chatbot is being used by the industries, like banking, hospital, hospitality, automobile where the authority needs to attend huge queries from a large number of customers. Banking industries like State Bank of India, City Bank, Standard Chartered Bank; food Delivery industries like Zomato, Swiggy; transportation industries like Uber, Ola, Indian Rail all are implementing their chatbot system or automatic query response system to reduce the pressure on the employees working in the customer care department.

Popular manufacturers of the operating systems have started using QA system in the form of virtual assistants to enhance the user satisfaction and user experience. Siri from Apple, Cortana from Microsoft, Google assistant by Google android, Alexa from Amazon are the most popular virtual assistants nowadays. QA system may be communicated either by voice or text. In case of voice-based QA system generally voice to text software is used to convert the user's voice query into text and output is converted to audio by text to voice software.

QA system works with the principles—first processing the question or query and extract the context or meaning of the question then to return the answer by processing its backend repository. Generally, web or some special company database is used as repository. Researchers, scientists and engineers have worked to build QA systems for various purpose time to time. Most of them are in English or other popular languages. Amazon has started to train Alexa in Hindi in India. Unavailability of resources to make the system understand the language, is the main challenge to develop

QA in regional languages but the QA system should be available in the mother tongue for major portions of citizens who can communicate in their mother tongue only.

In this work, we have explored research-based solutions to build the QA system in one such low resource language Bengali. Bengali literature is considered to be one of the richest in the world. Collection of novels, dramas, prose from the ancient time to modern age written by the renowned authors are used as the repository. The same was digitized in the TDIL (Technology Development of Indian Languages) project by the IT ministry of Government of India. Broadly the repository has eighty-six categories of domains covering almost 11,300 A4 pages.

The training set is formed with the sentences from this repository and the system is trained with the training set. Then, test set—a set of questions, is formed and get tested with the system for determining category among eighty-six domains. Some examples of test set are-

Q1. আনন্দমঠ কার লেখা?
('Ananda Math Kar Lekha?' or 'Who is the author of the Anandamath?')

Q2. কবে বঙ্কিমচন্দ্রকে হাওড়ায় বদলি করা হয়?
('Kobe Bankimchandrake Howrahte Badli Kora Hoy?' or 'When Bankimchandra was transferred to Howrah?')

Q3. সগররাজার পৌত্র কে ছিলেন?
('Sagar Rajar Poutra Ke Chhilen?' or 'Who was the grandson of king Sagar?')

Q4. স্যার রিচার্ড হ্যাডলি কোন দেশের খেলোয়াড়?
('Sir Richard Hadley Kon Desher Kheloar?' or 'Sir Richard Hadley played for which country?')

Q5. রক্তাল্পতা নিবারণের শ্রেষ্ঠ উপায় কি?
('Roktalpota NibaronerS restho Upay Ki?' or 'What is the best way to avoid anemia?')

Q6. " বাজল তোমার আলোর বেণু.." –গানের সুরকার কে?
('"Bajlo Tomar Alor Benu.."—Gaaner Surkar Ke?' or 'Who is the composer of the song "Bajlo tomar Alor Benu.."?')

Classification techniques are used as supervised method to determine the class of the question and therefore reduce the search domain. Then, Word2Vec and WordNet similarity are used to retrieve the answer of the question. Though there are some work in Bengali, but scope of them are very much limited. Some have only proposed the evaluation framework and some have only tried to classify the questions.

In such a context, the novelty of the work is in designing an algorithm using various machine learning techniques in different phases and developing an end to end solution for Bengali QA. Novelty lies in addressing all the sentences in natural language, in using flat file system for the repository whereas major QA systems are designed against relational database repository. Part of SQuAD [9] is translated into Bengali using Google transliterate and the performance of the proposed system is tested on that translated SQuAD dataset. Last but not the least the performance of our system has been compared with existing work in the state-of-the-art SQuAD dataset and also with the available result set of Bengali QA system.

10.2   Related Work

In this section, we have discussed the recent relevant and state-of the-art work in QA system is discussed. The existing research work toward Bengali QA system is discussed first.

Statistical approach is used to develop factoid QA system in Bengali by Monisha and her group [1]. 90.6% accuracy is achieved in question classification. In case of answer retrieval, fine grain accuracy is 56.8% and coarse grain accuracy is 66.2%.

Banerjee and his group [2] have achieved 87.79% accuracy in Bengali question classification using supervised methods.

A Das and his group [3] have used combination of statistical method to rank the answers in their developed Bengali QA system. The system has achieved 82.3% accuracy in predicting the actual answer as the 1st rank and 95.38% accuracy in predicting the actual answer with in 1st to 15th rank.

Stochastic Gradient Decent (SGD) classifier is used for word-based answer classification for retrieving answer in Islam *et al.* [6] Bengali QA system. Fine grain accuracy is 87.64% and coarse grain accuracy is 95.56% for answer retrieval in this system.

Manna and Pal [7] have used keyword matching for domain selection. Domains are ranked in the descending order of number of match and answer of the question is searched in the top-ranked domain. The overall accuracy achieved is 80% in this work.

Naïve Bayes, decision tree, support vector machine (SVM) classifiers are used to classify the questions in Bengali [8]. The result is improved with SGD optimizer. 90.5% accuracy is achieved for five domains.

Demand of industry boosted the research in QA system from 2004. Since then, QA system started to address multidomains. Question classifier was introduced and answering agent started to work in the specific domain determined by the classifier. Corporate giants became interested to employ QA system in place as per industry requirement. IBM came up with a QA project "Watson" which is very successful now. Initially QA systems were built in English language. A group of scientists, academicians, engineers, students devoted themselves to find better algorithms to improve the performance of the automatic QA system. Stanford university built "Stanford Question Answering Dataset (SQUAD)" in English with the help of volunteers. SQUAD [9] which is open dataset available online, contains millions of questions, answers and answer-repository to give the researchers a readily available experimental setup to test the performance of their algorithms in English QA. It would be very contextual to mention two of the earliest static English QA system LUNAR [10] and BASEBALL [11] which were built in the decades of 1960s and 1970s and were dedicated to answer geological data of Apollo Moon Mission and famous baseball league of USA respectively. SQUAD eased the work of creating and collecting dataset for the researchers who are working in English language and many of them have tested and published the performance of their QA system. Recently, Albert [12] achieved significant performance with 92.215 F1 score. The retro-reader [13] built on top of Albert has achieved 92.978 F1 score.

As per article 344(1) and 355, the eighth schedule of the constitution of India has 22 scheduled languages which have been given status of official languages and are used by a considerably large population. They are Assamese, Bangla, Gujarati, Hindi, Kannada, Kashmiri, Konkani, Malayalam, Manipuri, Marathi, Nepali, Oriya, Punjabi, Sanskrit, Sindhi, Tamil, Telugu, Urdu, Bodo, Santhali, Maithili, and Dogri. In this section, recent research to develop QA systems in these scheduled languages, except Bengali or Bangla, are explored. Bengali QA systems are already discussed in the starting of this survey.

In Hindi, [17–29] are the current research on the QA system. Nanda and her group [17] used feature extraction and Naive Bayes classification to determine the category of the question. Knowledge base is used to retrieve the sentence containing the answer. Devi and Dua [18] applied KNN method for question classification and nine similarity functions to retrieve the answer. Smith Waterman similarity gave the best result and handled both misspelled words and multiphase words. Ray and his group [19] presented an explorative review question answering system in Hindi in their published book in 2018. In his master's thesis [20]

Srivastava developed an architecture for Hindi QA system using PurposeNet based ontology as the data resource. Bagde and her group [21] compared the performance of different similarity functions like "Jaro–Wrinkler," "Euclidean similarity measure," "Jaccard coefficient similarity," "N-gram approach," and "text similarity" in case of Hindi QA system. Schubotz and the group [22] developed a system to answer mathematical questions expressed in Hindi or English. Questions in natural language were processed and converted to the mathematical formula using the knowledge base of Wikidata. The values of the constants were also extracted from Wikidata. Singla and the group [23] compared the performance of different similarity functions in the bilingual QA system in Hindi and English. Bhagat, Prajapati, and Seth [24] developed an IVR based automatic Hindi QA system in the domain named SRHR (sexual and reproductive health and rights). Taking the Jaccard Similarity as baseline the authors applied BERT model in the stored questions and answers to generate QA pair and return as the response of Frequently Asked Questions (FAQ). Bhattacharyya and his group [25] developed multi domain multilingual QA system in Hindi and English. Hindi question is translated into English question, and then CNN and RNN were applied to classify the questions. Candidate answers were extracted from the retrieved passages which were retrieved by Lucene's text retrieval functionality and ranked using Boolean and BM25 vector space models. Finally, the prospective answers are ranked using different similarity functions. A good amount of accuracy is achieved in question classification. Gupta and his group [26] proposed a deep neural network-based model for generalized multilingual QA system and tested the same for English-Hindi. The model has layers like question sentence encoding, probable answer sentence encoding, snippet encoding, and answer extraction layer. 39.44% exact match and 44.97 F1 score are observed for standard collected dataset whereas 50.11% exact match and 53.77 F1 score are observed in the translated SQuAD dataset. Chandu et al. [27] crowd sourced questions and answers for multilingual code-mixed languages. This has 1694 Hinglish (Hindi + English) question answer pairs. Though directly not related, Chandra and Dwivedi [28] presented a good way of query expansion using Okapi BM25 document ranking for Hindi query in English document retrieval. Lewis et al. [29] presented a multilingual QA system for seven languages which includes only Hindi as Indian language. They presented benchmark dataset and benchmark results applying different ML and neural networking models for the evaluation of performance in multilingual forms in those seven languages.

In the Malayalam language, [30, 31] are the current research on the QA system. Archana and her group [30] developed QA system in Malayalam language using supervised or rule-based approach. The approach includes Vibhakthi and POS tag analysis. Seena and her group [31] developed Malayalam QA system which gives word level answer by question type detection. After getting the type of the question, the system finds prospective documents based on keyword matching using "TnT tagger." Finally, the answer word is extracted using the speculation and prediction from the question word. Overall, 70% accuracy is achieved by the system.

In Marathi language, [32, 33] are the current research on QA system. Lende and Raghuwanshi [32] developed QA system for the closed domain in education sector. Though the system is claimed to be generalized QA system, it is tested in Marathi QA system only. Kamble and Baskar [33] manually translated the questions and answers of famous television show "Kaun Banega Crorepati" or "KBC" into Marathi. Then, Marathi questions are classified using SVM. 73.5% accuracy is achieved in the best case.

In Punjabi language, [34–36] are the current research on QA system. Walia and the group [34] applied RNN and LSTM based neural network for scoring and ranking of answers and observed improvement of result than statistical methods like cosine similarity, Jaccard similarity etc. Dhanjal and the group [35] explored gravity-based approach to build QA system in Punjabi language and observed 91% accuracy and 91% precision. Agarwal and Kumar [36] used UNL or Universal Networking Language for developing QA system in Punjabi. The system achieved a 97.5 F1 score after UNLization of questions and answers in Punjabi.

In Sanskrit, Terdalkar and Bhattacharya [37] developed a QA system in Sanskrit using a knowledge graph. The system gives factoid answer on relationships based on the Ramayana, the Mahabharata and the BhāvaprakāśaNighantu (an Ayurveda text) with 50% accuracy.

In Tamil language, [38–45] are the current research on QA systems. Ravi and Artstein [38] explored translation mechanisms from English to Tamil for dialogue systems. Performance is compared and it is observed that accuracy of correct response in Tamil is 79% and in English is 89%. Machine translation from English to Tamil drops the accuracy 54%, whereas Tamil to English stands at 79%. In her postgraduate thesis Niveditha [39] proposed the "Agrisage" QA system in Tamil based on HMM and ontology. The system is tested against 100 Tamil questions and 68.33% precision is achieved. Sankaravelayuthan and the group [40] designed a parser for Tamil QA system. Basically, Stanford parser's POS tagging modules, chunking techniques, and the dependency sets are modified to make it suitable for Tamil QA system. Liu and the group [41] proposed a cross-lingual and multilingual QA system involving Tamil using BERT-based neural networking model. Thara *et al.* [42] explored code-mixed QA systems in Hindi, Telugu, and Tamil languages using RNN and Hierarchical Attention Network (HAN). On average, 80% accuracy is achieved in the best case. The work of Chandu *et al.* [43] is already mentioned for Hinglish (Hindi + English) language. The same system for code-mixed language works for Tamlish (Tamil + English) language as well. Selvarasa *et al.* [44] explored various techniques for similarity calculation of short Tamil sentences, which is useful for ranking the answers. Knowledge-based methods, and corpus specific techniques blended with string similarity measurement and graph alignment measurement gave 85% accuracy. Rajendran and the group [45] presented a beautiful resource—OST or Ontological Structure of Tamil. Based on Tamil WordNet and Tamil dictionary this work as UGC sponsored post-doctoral work will definitely help in the IR system and QA system in Tamil.

In Telugu language, [46–51] are the current research on QA system. Ravva and her group [46] presented AVADHAN—the QA system in Telugu using SVM, multi-layer perceptron, and logical regression. In case of partial match, SVM gave the highest 68.5% accuracy. Khanam and Subbareddy [47] proposed a system for Telugu question answering with structured databases using NLIDB (Natural Language Interface to Database). Query or question in Telugu natural language is transformed to SQL query and the answer is retrieved.

Duggenpudi [48] built a QA system in Telugu using deep learning for question classification and rule-based approach for processing the question. They got 99.326% accuracy in question classification applying LSTM and 90.769% accuracy for retrieving the right answer. Chandu *et al.* [49, 50] are mentioned for Hindi and Tamil previously; the work includes a factoid QA system for Telugu code-mixed (Telugu + English) language as well. Danda and the group [51] developed an end-to-end dialogue cum QA system in Telugu in the tourism domain. They have claimed an excellent accuracy of the system.

In Urdu, Singh *et al.* [52] proposed a cross-lingual QA system in fourteen languages including Urdu. BERT with a trained classification layer is used. A very good accuracy is achieved in four languages including Urdu.

10.3   Problem Statement

Receiving a natural language question or query Q our system should

    a) Categorize into one or more sets of domains among 86 categories of text. The text of these selected domains would be processed in the next phase.

    b) Retrieve the answer A from the selected categories of text. A may be the exact answer (EA) or EA may be the part of A.

10.4   Proposed Approach

Supervised learning methods are applied in the present approach to retrieve the answer of the question or query. Conventional preprocessing is required to make the fonts similar, to mark and collect the punctuation marks, to remove the uneven spaces and to tokenize the words of the question sentence as well as sentences of the repository. Thereafter, each word of the question is tagged with the Parts of Speech (POS) using service of the parser developed by IIT Bombay and hosted by IIIT Hyderabad. Applying grammatical rules, content words (CW), function words (FW), named entities, subjects, objects, and WH words are marked and their term frequencies (tf) are calculated in the question or query sentence with the help of POS. Person, number, tense of the subject of the question are extracted from the surface level verb(s) of the sentence and also the root form of the verb of the surface level verb is determined using the algorithm depicted in Das *et al.* [5]. These two step preprocessing methods are applied to repository-sentences also.

Next, four classification methods namely Artificial Neural Network (ANN), Support Vector Machine (SVM), Decision Tree (DT), and Naïve Bayes (NV) are used individually to categorize the question into one of the eighty-six categories like—novels, mass-media, physics, play and drama, political science, etc. If different categories are determined by different classifiers, all the categories are processed in the next phase of searching. Clearly, there can be minimum one class when all the four classifiers predict same and maximum four classes when four classifiers predict different about the class of the question. Use of classifier for the question is to reduce the search domain and processing time & cost. Reason to employ four classifiers is to remove any biasness from the system. The detailed of the question classification is presented in Das *et al.* [16].

After getting the class(es) of the question, search operation is carried out in those specific class(es) only. The sentences of the repository are also classified taking the grammatical derived attributes like FW, CW, subject, object, number, gender, person, tense etc. All the sentences with at least one match of the above-mentioned attributes, are collected in a file ANSWER_COLLECTION with sentence id, in the descending order of matches.

A pretrained Word2Vec module is available for Bengali in Grave *et al.* [14, 15]. Receiving any word, the module gives its vector with dimension size of 300 using Skip Gram and CBOW algorithm. The module is pretrained by the Bengali Wikipedia corpus. The words of the question sentence are passed and the vectors are collected in the matrix A. Out of vocabulary words are collected in a separate file and they are replaced by the synonyms from the WordNet (if available).

The words of the sentences from the ANSWER_COLLECTION are passed one by one to Word2Vec module and collected in the matrices B1, B2,...,Bn.

Dot product (cosine multiplication) of the matrix A and Bi is done and the value is recorded in the ANSWER_COLLECTION.

$$A.B1 = V1$$
$$A.B2 = V2$$
$$\cdot$$
$$\cdot$$
$$\cdot$$
$$A.Bn = Vn$$

The answers are arranged in the descending order of $|V|$. Rank is associated against the sentence id depending the value of $|V|$. The sentence id with the highest value of $|V|$ gets the first rank and the sentence id with the smallest value of $|V|$ gets the last rank.

10.5   Algorithm

Input: User's question or query.
Output: Answer returned to the user.

Step 1: Input question or query is gone through standard pre-processing technique, parsing and tokenization.

Step 2: Words of the question or query sentence are tagged with POS with the help of LTRC shallow parser developed by IIT Bombay and hosted by IIIT Hyderabad.

Step 3: Applying grammatical rules, Content Words (CW), Function Words (FW), Named Entities, subjects, objects and WH words are marked in the question or query sentence with the help of POS.

Step 4: Person, number, tense of the subject of the question are extracted from the surface level verb(s) of the sentence and also the root form of the verb of the surface level verb is determined using the algorithm depicted in Das *et al.* [5].

Step 5: Four classification methods namely Artificial Neural Network (ANN), Support Vector Machine (SVM), Decision Tree (DT), and Naïve Bayes (NV) are used individually to categorize the question into one of the eighty-six categories using feature vector containing tf of all the grammatical attributes extracted in Step 3 & 4 like FW, CW, subject, object, person, number, tense etc.

Step 6: Step 1 to step 5 is repeated for the sentences in the repository pertaining to the class(es) of the question to collect the sentences in the ANSWER_COLLECTION associated with sentence_id.

Step 7: Collect the vector in matrix A using Word2Vec algorithm [14].

Step 8: Collect the vector in matrix Bi using Word2Vec algorithm [14] for all the sentence i=1 to n in ANSWER_COLLECTION.

Step 9: Perform $A.Bi^T$ for i= 1 to n and write the value $|Vi|$ in the ANSWER_COLLECTION against the sentence_id i.

Step 10: Rank the answers in the descending order of $|V|$.

Step 11: Try to form the exact answer (EA) from the answer sentence with rank i (with the smallest rank) using rule-based knowledge base or return the selected sentence as A and record the feedback.

Step 12: For negative feedback repeat step 11 with rank i=2 and so on upto n. (n = number of sentences in the ANSWER_COLLECTION)

Step 13: END.

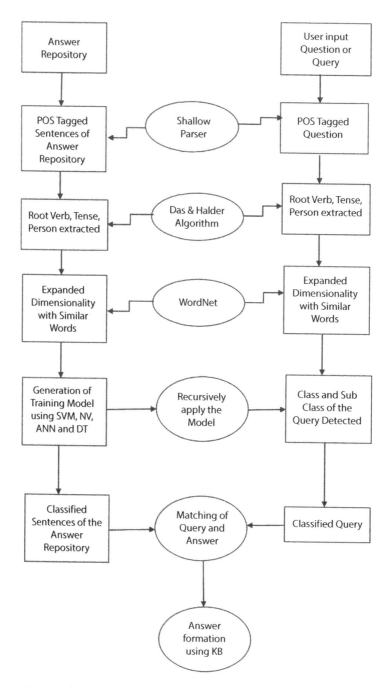

Figure 10.1 Detailed flowchart of the methodology used.

Flowchart for the algorithm is given in Figure 10.1. Root Verb Extraction and associated algorithms are available in the published paper [5]. Details of service used for POS tagging has been acknowledged at last. Training and test sets are prepared independently. Cross validation of 10 folds is used with shuffling for avoiding any biasness.

10.6   Results and Discussion

10.6.1   Result Summary for TDIL Dataset

A total number of 340 questions are fired to the system. Among 340 questions, 326 questions are classified correctly among eighty-six classes. So, the accuracy of the question classification is 95.88%.

Among these correctly classified 326 questions, for 322 questions the answer A returned by the system contains exact answer EA. So, the coarse-grain accuracy is 98.77% for answer prediction.

Among these correctly classified 326 questions, for 304 questions the answer A returned by the system is the exact answer EA. So, the fine-grain accuracy is 93.25% for answer prediction.

10.6.2   Result Summary for SQuAD Dataset

A total number of 952 questions are fired to the translated SQuAD. Among 952 questions, 916 questions are classified correctly among 86 classes. So, the accuracy of the question classification is 96.21%.

Among these correctly classified 916 questions, for 900 questions the answer A returned by the system contains exact answer EA. So, the coarse-grain accuracy is 98.25% for answer prediction.

Among these correctly classified 916 questions, for 850 questions the answer A returned by the system is the exact answer EA. So, the fine-grain accuracy is 92.79% for answer prediction.

Examples of the retrieved answers are given in the next section (Table 10.1).

10.6.3   Examples of Retrieved Answers

Table 10.1 Example questions and their retrieved answers.

Questions	Predicted class(es)	Answer retrieved
Q1. আনন্দমঠ কার লেখা? ('Ananda Math Kar Lekha?' or 'Who is the author of the Anandamath?')	Education, Mass media	1. বঙ্কিমচন্দ্র
Q2. কবে বঙ্কিমচন্দ্রকে হাওড়ায় বদলি করা হয়? ('Kobe Bankimchandrake Howrahte Badli Kora Hoy?' or 'When Bankimchandra was transferred to Howrah?')	Essay	1. ১৮৮৩ খ্রীষ্টাব্দে
Q3. সগররাজার পৌত্রর কে ছিলেন? ('Sagar RajarPoutraKeChhilen?' or 'Who was the grandson of king Sagar?')	Class not determined	No Answer Retrieved
Q4. স্যার রিচার্ড হ্যাডলি কোন দেশের খেলোয়াড়? ('Sir Richard Hadley Kon Desher Kheloar?' or 'Sir Richard Hadley played for which country?')	Games and Sports	1. নিউজিল্যাণ্ডের
Q5. রক্তাল্পতা নিবারণের শ্রেষ্ঠ উপায় কি? ('Roktalpota NibaronerS restho Upay Ki?' or 'What is the best way to avoid anemia?')	Home Science	1. দৈনিক আহারে রক্ত তৈরীর উপাদান
Q6. " বাজল তোমার আলোর বেণু.." –গানের সুরকার কে? ('"Bajlo Tomar Alor Benu.."—Gaaner Surkar Ke?' or 'Who is the composer of the song "Bajlo tomar Alor Benu.."?')	Music	1. পঙ্কজ কুমার মল্লিক 2. সুপ্রীতি ঘোষ

10.6.4   Calculation of TP, TN, FP, FN, Accuracy, Precision, Recall, and F1 score

TP = True Positive = The system predicts that the answer of the question is present in the repository and actually the repository has the answer (the answer is returned as part of output)

TN = True Negative = The system predicts that the answer of the question is not present in the repository and actually the repository does not contain the answer

FP = False Positive = The system predicts that the answer of the question is present in the repository but actually the repository does not contain the answer

FN = False Negative = The system predicts that the answer of the question is not present in the repository but actually the repository contains the answer

TP for TDIL dataset is TP_TDIL= 322

TN for TDIL dataset is TN_TDIL= 9

FP for TDIL dataset is FP_TDIL= 3

FN for TDIL dataset is FN_TDIL= 6

So, accuracy for TDIL dataset is Accuracy_TDIL = (TP+TN)/ (TP+TN+FP+FN)

= 97.35

So, precision for TDIL dataset is Precision_TDIL= TP/ (TP+FP)

= 99.07

So, recall for TDIL dataset is Recall_TDIL= TP/(TP+FN)

= 98.17

So, F1 score for TDIL dataset is F1 score_TDIL = 2*(Recall*Precision)/ (Recall + Precision)

= 19451.4/197.24 = 98.61

TP for translated SQuAD dataset is TP_SQuAD= 900

TN for translated SQuAD dataset is TN_SQuAD= 25

FP for translated SQuAD dataset is FP_SQuAD= 14

FN for translated SQuAD dataset is FN_SQuAD= 13

So, accuracy for translated SQuAD dataset is Accuracy_SQuAD = (TP+TN)/ (TP+TN+FP+FN) = 97.16

So, precision for translated SQuAD dataset is Precision_SQuAD = TP/ (TP+FP)

= 98.46

So, recall for translated SQuAD dataset is Recall_SQuAD = TP/(TP+FN)

= 98.57

So, F1 score for translated SQuAD dataset is F1 score_SQuAD = 2*(Recall*Precision)/(Recall + Precision)
= 19410.4/197.03 = 98.51

10.6.5 Comparison of Result with other Methods and Dataset

Performance of the question classification techniques of different research groups is presented in Table 10.2.

Table 10.3 represents the F1 score calculation of QA system working in SQuAD dataset.

Table 10.2 Comparison of accuracy for question classification with previous work.

Author	Language	Dataset	QC percentage
Banerjee and his group [2]	Bengali	Own created dataset [2]	87.79%
Sarkerand his group [8]	Bengali	SUST database	90.5%
Monisha *et al.* [1]	Bengali	SUST database	90.6%
M A Islam and his group [6]	Bengali	University database	95.6%
A Das and D Saha	**Bengali**	**TDIL**	**95.88%**
A Das and D Saha	**Bengali**	**Translated SQuAD**	**96.21%**

Table 10.3 Comparison of F1 score with previous work.

Author	Language	Dataset	F1 score
Z Lan *et al.* [12] (Albert system)	English	SQuAD	92.215
Z Zhang *et al.* [13]	English	SQuAD	93.11
A Das and D Saha	**Bengali**	**TDIL**	**98.61**
A Das and D Saha	**Bengali**	**Translated SQuAD**	**98.51**

10.7   Analysis of Error

From the confusion matrix, it is derived that classification is prevailing the worst-case complexity. Out of 322 questions which were classified correctly, the system was able to draw the correct answer or the sentence containing correct answer at some point of iterations.

Difference between fine-grain and coarse-grain accuracy for answer retrieval is due to majorly on the fact that whether the answer is contained in one sentence or multiple sentences. If direct answer is available in one sentence then system was able to return the exact answer. Otherwise the system returned the sentences containing the answer.

In case of classifiers, it is analyzed that different classifiers have predicted differently in case of the questions which may belong to two different categories like "Who is Navjyot Sing Sidhu?" Both "politics" and "sports" are probable outcome classes as Navjyot Sing Sidhu was a cricketer and is a politician now depending upon if both the sentences supporting his multiple identities are contained in the different classes of the training set.

10.8   Few Close Observations

a) Word2Vec helps in improving the performance a lot.
b) With Word2Vec the system learns and becomes able to give the correct answer of a question which was previously answered incorrectly.
c) Classification is taking a longer time for the first time as it includes all kind of preprocessing and all. Once the model is built, reclassification is taking much less time. So, system returns the answer much quickly for repeated question; though neither the question nor the answer is saved in the system.
d) The system performs ideally for factoid question. For the questions which demands descriptive answer the system performance degrades.
e) For the questions in code-mixed language or question having foreign words, the performance degrades. The reason is that neither Bengali Wikipedia trained Word2Vec nor Bengali WordNet contains the foreign word or code-mixed word. So, the system suffers.

10.9 Applications

Applications of the QA system are already discussed. From virtual assistant to chatbot, QA is the backbone. With increased market presence service-based organizations, pressure on the customer care is increasing. So, automation in replying to the customer query or question is becoming the natural choice for the large entrepreneurs.

Applications of the QA system in the low resource languages are seen both in government and private sector. Many remote users are proficient in their mother tongues only. Their questions or queries asked dynamically cannot be resolved with static translation of "Frequently Asked Questions" (FAQ) to the local languages. Even machine translation also cannot solve this if the answer is not available in the translated language of the question.

Nowadays digital contents like text and audio are available in regional languages, so QA system in local languages only can solve this challenge efficiently. This scenario is equally applicable for some Vojpuri buyer (who knows only Vojpuri language) over e-commerce platform like Flipkart as well as for some feedback collection program of Ministry of Micro Small and Medium scale Enterprise (MSME), Govt. of India from rural entrepreneurs.

10.10 Scope for Improvements

The system is tested for Bengali language. The acceptance of our developed system will become universal if it is tested in some other languages; preferably in some South Asian low resource languages.

10.11 Conclusions

The present work has been carried out in the supervised learning method. First, the questions are classified using four classification techniques and those classes or domains are introspected for searching of answers. WordNet and Word2Vec are used for retrieving the best answers semantically. Here machine learning (ML) is applied diligently to give an end-to-end solution to build QA system in the low resource language Bengali.

The specialty of this work is in handling the dynamic questions in natural language for the low resource language.

Though the current trend (as discussed for SQuAD dataset) is employing only deep learning (DL) method for this QA system. DL from scratch needs a high-end hardware facility and laboratory. So, our research, mixing ML (classification) and DL (Word2Vec), is prevalent in this time of pandemic due to COVID 19, when all the governments are going for cost-cutting. With reduced fund for academic, our work can show the way of achieving the same goal without any dedicated facility of DL. Though we need more human effort and time but in the country like India such a system in large scale can generate the employment and reach the rural people in the remotest corner of the country.

Acknowledgments

The authors cordially acknowledge the help of Professor N. S. Dash by providing the TDIL dataset. He is the professor of Language Research Unit of Indian Statistical Institute, Kolkata. As a famous linguist of Bengali, he contributed in evaluation of the result also. The dataset or repository is the product of TDIL project funded by MeiTY, Govt. of India. This is one of the largest repositories available in Bengali containing popular creations of Bengali literature. The repository may be shared for academic use and research purpose only.

We acknowledge the LTRC shallow parser developed by IIT Bombay and hosted by IIIT Hyderabad. The parser has been used for POS tagging in our research work.

References

1. Sarker, S., Monisha, S.T., Nahid, M.M., Bengali Question Answering System for Factoid Questions: A statistical approach, in: *International Conference on Bangla Speech and Language Processing (ICBSLP)*, vol. 27, p. 28, Sep 2019.
2. Banerjee, S., Naskar, S.K., Rosso, P., Bandyopadhyay, S., Classifier combination approach for question classification for Bengali question answering system. *Sādhanā*, 44, 12, 247, Dec 1 2019.

3. A. Das, J. Mandal, Z. Danial, A. R. Pal, D. Saha, An improvement of Bengali factoid question answering system using unsupervised statistical methods", Sadhana, *Journal of Indian Academy of Science*, Springer, 47, 2, 2022.

4. Das, A. and Saha, D., Improvement of electronic governance and mobile governance in multilingual countries with digital etymology using Sanskrit grammar, in: *2017 IEEE Region 10 Humanitarian Technology Conference (R10-HTC)*, IEEE, pp. 502–505, Dec 21 2017.

5. Das, A., Halder, T., Saha, D., Automatic extraction of Bengali root verbs using Paninian grammar, in: *2017 2nd IEEE International Conference on Recent Trends in Electronics, Information & Communication Technology (RTEICT)*, IEEE, pp. 953–956, May 19 2017.

6. Islam, M.A., Kabir, M.F., Abdullah-Al-Mamun, K., Huda, M.N., Word/phrase-based answer type classification for Bengali question answering system, in: *2016 5th International Conference on Informatics, Electronics and Vision (ICIEV)*, IEEE, pp. 445–448, May 13 2016.

7. Manna, P.P. and Pal, A.R., Question answering system in Bengali using semantic search, in: *2019 International Conference on Applied Machine Learning (ICAML)*, IEEE, pp. 175–179, May 25 2019.

8. Monisha, S.T., Sarker, S., Nahid, M.M., Classification of Bengali questions towards a factoid question answering system, in: *2019 1st International Conference on Advances in Science, Engineering and Robotics Technology (ICASERT)*, IEEE, pp. 1–5, May 3 2019.

9. Rajpurkar, P., Zhang, J., Lopyrev, K., Liang, P., Squad: 100,000+ questions for machine comprehension of text, Jun 16 2016, arXiv preprint arXiv:1606.05250 https://arxiv.org/abs/1606.05250.

10. Woods, W.A., Progress in natural language understanding: An application to lunar geology, in: *Proceedings of the June 4-8, 1973, National Computer Conference and Exposition*, pp. 441–450, Jun 4 1973.

11. Green, B.F., Jr, Wolf, A.K., Chomsky, C., Laughery, K., Baseball: An automatic question-answerer, in: *Papers presented at the May 9-11, 1961, Western Joint IRE-AIEE-ACM Computer Conference*, pp. 219–224, May 9 1961.

12. Lan, Z., Chen, M., Goodman, S., Gimpel, K., Sharma, P., Soricut, R., Albert: A lite bert for self-supervised learning of language representations, Sep 26 2019, arXiv preprint arXiv:1909.11942 https://arxiv.org/abs/1909.11942.

13. Zhang, Z., Yang, J., Zhao, H., Retrospective reader for machine reading comprehension, Jan 27 2020, arXiv preprint arXiv:2001.09694 https://arxiv.org/abs/2001.09694.

14. Grave, E., Bojanowski, P., Gupta, P., Joulin, A., Mikolov, T., Learning word vectors for 157 languages, Feb 19 2018, arXiv preprint arXiv:1802.06893 https://arxiv.org/abs/1802.06893.

15. https://fasttext.cc/docs/en/crawl-vectors.html on 05 17 2020.

16. A. Das, D. Saha, Enhancing the performance of semantic search in Bengali using neural net and other classification techniques", *International Journal of Engineering and Advanced Technology*, 9, 3, 4170-4180, February, 2020.

17. Nanda, G., Dua, M., Singla, K., A Hindi question answering system using machine learning approach, in: *2016 International Conference on Computational Techniques in Information and Communication Technologies (ICCTICT)*, IEEE, pp. 311–314, March 2016.

18. Devi, R. and Dua, M., Performance evaluation of different similarity functions and classification methods using web based hindi language question answering system. *Proc. Comput. Sci.*, 92, 520–525, 2016.

19. Ray, S.K., Ahmad, A., Shaalan, K., A review of the state of the art in Hindi question answering systems, in: *Intelligent Natural Language Processing: Trends and Applications*, pp. 265–292, Springer, Cham, 2018.

20. Srivastava, R., *PurposeNet Ontology based Question Answering (QA) System for Hindi*, Doctoral dissertation, International Institute of Information Technology Hyderabad, 2017.

21. Sneha, B., Mohit, D., Singh, V.Z., Comparison of different similarity functions on Hindi QA system, in: *Proceedings of International Conference on ICT for Sustainable Development*, Springer, Singapore, pp. 657–663, 2016.

22. Schubotz, M., Scharpf, P., Dudhat, K., Nagar, Y., Hamborg, F., Gipp, B., Introducing mathqa: A math-aware question answering system. *Inf. Discovery Deliv.*, 2018.

23. Singla, K., Dua, M., Nanda, G., A language based comparison of different similarity functions and classifiers using web based bilingual question answering system developed using machine learning approach, in: *Proceedings of the Second International Conference on Information and Communication Technology for Competitive Strategies*, pp. 1–4, March 2016.

24. Bhagat, P., Prajapati, S.K., Seth, A., Initial lessons from building an IVR-based automated question-answering system, in: *Proceedings of the 2020 International Conference on Information and Communication Technologies and Development*, pp. 1–5, June 2020.

25. Gupta, D., Kumari, S., Ekbal, A., Bhattacharyya, P., MMQA: A multi-domain multi-lingual question-answering framework for English and Hindi, in: *Proceedings of the Eleventh International Conference on Language Resources and Evaluation (LREC 2018)*, May 2018.

26. Gupta, D., Ekbal, A., Bhattacharyya, P., A deep neural network framework for english hindi question answering. *ACM Trans. Asian Low-Resour. Lang. Inf. Process. (TALLIP)*, 19, 2, 1–22, 2019.

27. Chandu, K., Loginova, E., Gupta, V., Genabith, J.V., Neumann, G., Chinnakotla, M., Nyberg, E., Black, A.W., Code-mixed question answering challenge: Crowd-sourcing data and techniques, in: *Third Workshop on Computational Approaches to Linguistic Code-Switching*, Association for Computational Linguistics (ACL, pp. 29–38, 2019.

28. Chandra, G. and Dwivedi, S.K., Query expansion for effective retrieval results of Hindi–English cross-lingual IR. *Appl. Artif. Intell.*, 33, 7, 567–593, 2019.

29. Lewis, P., Oğuz, B., Rinott, R., Riedel, S., Schwenk, H., MLQA: Evaluating cross-lingual extractive question answering, 2019, arXiv preprint arXiv: 1910.07475.

30. Archana, S.M., Vahab, N., Thankappan, R., Raseek, C., A rule-based question answering system in Malayalam corpus using vibhakthi and pos tag analysis. *Proc. Technol.*, 24, 1534–1541, 2016.

31. Seena, I.T., Sini, G.M., Binu, R., Malayalam question answering system. *Proc. Technol.*, 24, 1388–1392, 2016.

32. Lende, S.P. and Raghuwanshi, M.M., February. Question answering system on education acts using NLP techniques, in: *2016 world conference on futuristic trends in research and innovation for social welfare (Startup Conclave)*, IEEE, pp. 1–6, 2016.

33. Kamble, S. and Baskar, S., Learning to classify marathi questions and identify answer type using machine learning technique, in: *Advances in Machine Learning and Data Science*, pp. 33–41, Springer, Singapore, 2018.

34. Walia, T.S., Josan, G.S., Singh, A., An efficient automated answer scoring system for Punjabi language. *Egypt. Inform. J.*, 20, 2, 89–96, 2019.

35. Dhanjal, G.S., Sharma, S., Sarao, P.K., Gravity based Punjabi question answering system. *Int. J. Comput. Appl.*, 147, 3, 21, 2016.

36. Agarwal, V. and Kumar, P., UNLization of Punjabi text for natural language processing applications. *Sādhanā*, 43, 6, 87, 2018.

37. Terdalkar, H. and Bhattacharya, A., Framework for question-answering in sanskrit through automated construction of knowledge graphs, in: *Proceedings of the 6th International Sanskrit Computational Linguistics Symposium*, pp. 97–116, 2019.

38. Ravi, S. and Artstein, R., Language portability for dialogue systems: translating a question-answering system from english into Tamil, in: *Proceedings of the 17th Annual Meeting of the Special Interest Group on Discourse and Dialogue*, pp. 111–116, September 2016.

39. Karmegam, N., *Agrisage: An HMM and Ontology based Cross-lingual Question Answering system for the Agricultural Domain*, Doctoral Dissertation, Sri Lanka, 2019.

40. Sankaravelayuthan, R., Anandkumar, M., Dhanalakshmi, V., Mohan Raj, S.N., *A Parser for Question-answer System for Tamil*.

41. Liu, J., Lin, Y., Liu, Z., Sun, M., XQA: A cross-lingual open-domain question answering dataset, in: *Proceedings of the 57th Annual Meeting of the Association for Computational Linguistics*, pp. 2358–2368, July 2019.

42. Thara, S., Sampath, E., Reddy, P., Code mixed question answering challenge using deep learning methods, in: *2020 5th International Conference on Communication and Electronics Systems (ICCES)*, IEEE, pp. 1331–1337, June 2020.

43. Chandu, K., Loginova, E., Gupta, V., Genabith, J.V., Neumann, G., Chinnakotla, M., Nyberg, E., Black, A.W., Code-mixed question answering challenge: Crowd-sourcing data and techniques, in: *Third Workshop on Computational Approaches to Linguistic Code-Switching*, Association for Computational Linguistics (ACL, pp. 29–38, 2019.

44. Selvarasa, A., Thirunavukkarasu, N., Rajendran, N., Yogalingam, C., Ranathunga, S., Dias, G., Short Tamil sentence similarity calculation using knowledge-based and corpus-based similarity measures, in: *2017 Moratuwa Engineering Research Conference (MERCon)*, IEEE, pp. 443–448, May 2017.

45. Rajendran, S., Soman, K.P., Anandkumar, M., Sankaralingam, C., Ontological structure-based retrieval system for Tamil, in: *Applications in Ubiquitous Computing*, pp. 197–223, Springer, Cham, 2020.

46. Ravva, P., Urlana, A., Shrivastava, M., AVADHAN: System for open-domain telugu question answering, in: *Proceedings of the 7th ACM IKDD CoDS and 25th COMAD*, pp. 234–238, 2020.

47. Khanam, M.H. and Subbareddy, S.V., Question answering system with natural language interface to database. *Int. J. Manage. Inf. Technol. Eng.*, 7, 4, 38–48, 2017.

48. Duggenpudi, S.R., Varma, K.S.S., Mamidi, R., Samvaadhana: A telugu dialogue system in hospital domain, in: *Proceedings of the 2nd Workshop on Deep Learning Approaches for Low-Resource NLP (DeepLo 2019)*, pp. 234–242, November 2019.

49. Chandu, K.R., Chinnakotla, M., Black, A.W., Shrivastava, M., Webshodh: A code mixed factoid question answering system for web, in: *International Conference of the Cross-Language Evaluation Forum for European Languages*, Springer, Cham, pp. 104–111, September 2017.

50. Chandu, K., Loginova, E., Gupta, V., Genabith, J.V., Neumann, G., Chinnakotla, M., Nyberg, E., Black, A.W., Code-mixed question answering challenge: Crowd-sourcing data and techniques, in: *Third Workshop on Computational Approaches to Linguistic Code-Switching*, Association for Computational Linguistics (ACL, pp. 29–38, 2019.

51. Danda, P., Jwalapuram, P., Shrivastava, M., End to end dialog system for Telugu, in: *Proceedings of the 14th International Conference on Natural Language Processing (ICON-2017)*, pp. 265–272, December 2017.

52. Singh, J., McCann, B., Keskar, N.S., Xiong, C., Socher, R., Xlda: Cross-lingual data augmentation for natural language inference and question answering, 2019, arXiv preprint arXiv:1905.114.

Part III

SECURITY AND SAFETY ASPECTS WITH DEEP LEARNING

11

Secure Access to Smart Homes Using Biometric Authentication With RFID Reader for IoT Systems

K.S. Niraja* and Sabbineni Srinivasa Rao

Department of Computer Science and Engineering, Koneru Lakshmaiah Education Foundation, Vaddeswaram, Guntur, Andhra Pradesh, India

Abstract

Internet of Things (IoT) had brought us drastic change in every field where especially the drastic change from the invention of radiofrequency identification (RFID) tags, which eliminated line of sight problem. RFID usage has been used not only in smart home but also in many other fields that are smart agriculture, smart health care, etc. With the introduction of IoT device, machine to machine interaction has increased over human to machine. When machine to machine usage had started to develop, we need to protect the data in more secured where authentication is playing a vital role which has been taken more precisely especially with machine-to-machine interaction. RFID tag readers though it eliminates the line of sight, it carries sensitive data as well, so we need to take efficient authentication methods. Artificial intelligence usages have been widely used in every field where we can enhance a framework to efficiently provide more security to smart home applications with different machine learning algorithms to provide more privacy to user data. Hence, we need to prove more secure authentication mechanism for IoT applications. The framework, which we propose, performs better than the already existing approaches with the help of RFID reader along with biometric authentication.

Keywords: Smart health, machine to machine interaction, tag readers, biometric authentication, line of sight problem, framework, privacy

---

*Corresponding author: niraja.ksvce@gmail.com

Rajdeep Chakraborty, Anupam Ghosh, Jyotsna Kumar Mandal and S. Balamurugan (eds.) Convergence of Deep Learning In Cyber-IoT Systems and Security, (233–248) © 2023 Scrivener Publishing LLC

11.1 Introduction

Internet of Things had made everyone's life easy and convenient with more flexibility. IoT had made billion of devices had been connected to Internet where every device has been connected to the World Wide Web easily. The invention of RFID it became more users friendly and eliminated so many problems like line-of-sight problems especially when it comes to business field it eliminated so many problems where the stock updating to maintenance had become very easy. RFID was the technology which was widely used especially when it comes to smart home, smart buildings etc where they track the objects in every field with the help of barcode readers. When it comes to Smart home or smart building RFID reader was used for mostly for authentication purpose. When we consider IoT use case of this smart home there need to have IoT devices with RFID reader along with sensor devices to continuously sense the objects and transmit the data through the server for authentication process. Some of the RFID cases are implemented practically but still they lag in authentication process especially when it comes to smart homes, smart buildings, smart city, smart transportation and smart healthcare systems. RFID tag readers however eliminate the line of sight still they are lacking behind privacy issues as they carry sensitive information such as identification identity information along with location information of user.

The network connected devices are more prone to a variety of attacks as they carry sensitive data especially when the information has been exchanged from tag reader to other parties so more research and study need to be done on this specially to eliminate the privacy issues. IoT-based application mainly have the problem of leakage of data especially with the location-based services which cause for privacy attacks where there is utmost need to protect it. Privacy concerns in RFID authentication is the major contribution of researcher as they have to take care of authentication process still as we have so many existing approach and methods also. When this type problem is solved then there will be more usage of IoT applications improve in real world applications by which our task and applications can be done more easily.

The motivation of our chapter is to discuss about such privacy issues and to propose a framework so that it can have many features like mutual authentication, availability, scalability and forward secrecy. RFID along biometric-based authentication will definitely aim for high level of security. Prototype application platform has been used to implement where python for data science has been used for RFID authentication process. The rest of the book chapter has been divided into the following: section 11.2, Related work; section 11.3,

Framework for smart home use case applications; section 11.4, Control scheme for secure access in smart home case study; section 11.5, Results with proposed and existing framework; section 11.6, conclusion and future work.

11.2   Related Work

In this section, we see the authentication schemes where we study about IoT-based devices using RFID-based authentication mechanism in different integrated applications. Secure localizations for different smart home and smart care application using RFID-based scheme was proposed [1] where they proposed that localization information needed to be more safeguard than the existing as they carry sensitive data. Fusion techniques, along with localization and tracking of objects, which can be used in occupancy has been discussed [2]. Identification of objects along with sensing for distributed approach in obtaining data dynamics is proposed [3]. Access control for efficient energy for smart home and smart buildings along with case study has been proposed [4] along with RFID importance especially in smart cities and its use case study [5] discussed about the theft approaches along with misplaced security issues especially in RFID tags. A similar kind of study has been found in Kuan *et al.* [6], where sensitive information along with leakage information is discussed.

The level of security along with different models in smart home has been proposed [7]. Privacy attacks along with user location information for protecting RFID reader tag data have been discussed in Tuan and Aiello [8]. Integrated applications along with hardware and software in smart cities and smart home applications have been the focus [9]. Authentication mechanisms in IoT use cases have been discussed [10]. RFID and its applications along with its importance have been discussed in Kuzlu *et al.* [11]. Pervasive computing and its applications in IoT where the possibilities of security issues and misusing the tag reader have been discussed [12]. Privacy and security issues, which are mainly essential in safeguarding of IoT devices and its applications, have been discussed in Liang *et al.* [13]. Heterogeneous data and devices along with their standards that have been found along with leakage of sensitive data were discussed [14], they even proposed a framework to protect the system from privacy and security issues [15]. From the review, it is understood in a better way that there is most need for security especially in privacy and end to end communications between different devices, which has to be taken care especially when treating RFID tag readers has been discussed in this chapter.

11.3   Framework for Smart Home Use Case With Biometric

It mainly focuses on different frameworks and scheme where they have to be protected especially when communicating in different smart care IoT applications [16]. The authentication along with system model and many components needed for this model have been described, which include variety set of RFID tag reader, different modem, specifically GSM, variety of servers, microcontroller circuits which have alarms and locks [17].

RFID tag readers are mostly semipassive circuits, the reason why we choose such a circuit is that they have the ability to use the power, which has been generated from different radio waves along with inbuilt battery circuit [18]. The person who carries the RFID tag reader try to enter the zone where nearby camera capture his face and the person information along with capture images are forwarded to a nearby server, which had already been connected with cloud servers when it could able to detect that server checks the images captured to the existing authentication pictures and if there is proper verification done, the door is opened otherwise it raises an alarm and it will not give access to the smart home which identify as intruders or frauds person and which immediately send the notification to the authentication messages to authenticated users or authorized user [19].

The proposed frame work along with its necessary procedure steps are shown in Figure 11.1.

It has been understood that information along with tag reader and human face recognition have been captured by sensor along with camera, which has been compared and has been verified with existing data in the server if the authentication process is successful, door gets opened, if not, an alarm raises along with identifying the authentication process failed and sends an immediate notification to all the authentication users which this dual way authentication the smart home application especially use case if smart home had more secured compared to the existing approaches which we discussed earlier [20].

11.3.1   RFID-Based Authentication and Its Drawbacks

When it comes to RFID-based tag-based scheme and methods we could found so many drawbacks especially when using with specific use cases like smart home and smart health care system which had major effect on such tag-based authentication where there are more possibilities of stolen

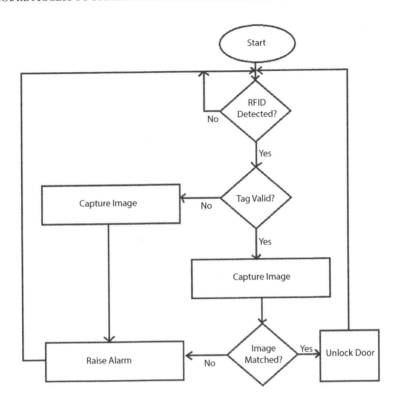

Figure 11.1 Authentication procedure for smart home applications.

tag reader and which can be accessed easily by an unauthorized person treating himself as an authorized person, this is done not only to provide just any security which completely laps since tag readers carry sensitive data along with so many privacy data and issues as well [21]. To overcome such problems in advance we proposed a system to eliminate all the drawbacks with a two-way authentication procedure especially for the use case of smart home where it has shown major improvement compared to all the existing approaches and methods [22].

11.4   Control Scheme for Secure Access (CSFSC)

11.4.1   Problem Definition

RFID tag-based readers may be stolen easily or may be prone to different forgery attacks since it carries location information that can also lead to privacy attacks for authentication since it carries sensitive information [23]. Due to heavy computational issues and complexity, the RFID-based scheme was introduced which may provide harm to tag reader along with their framework and techniques along with existing methods which were not up to the mark that is addressed below.

11.4.2   Biometric-Based RFID Reader Proposed Scheme

Control Scheme for Secure Access (CSFSC) is a method that we propose which provide end-to-end secure communications along with privacy where the tag information will be exchanged between itself. Table 11.1

Table 11.1 Components used in proposed scheme.

Notation described below:
Tag
Reader tag
Server used at backend
Identity which reflects tag
Identity which reflects identity tag with alias reader
Identity with pseudo code reader
Identity which represents server
To Identify random number
To Identify different random number
Key shared between tag reader and server
Emergency tag of server and device
Secret key of device and server
Sequence number tracked
Identification of location information
One way hash function denotation
XOR
Concatenation

below shows how the data have been preserved, which has been built in with components of different methods.

All the components which have been discussed where both the tags were registered from back end server. It was provided with various security keys in advance from the back end server, similarly, back end server is registered with cloud server with all the necessary authentication procedure and facilities where communication between two RFID networks can be done more securely among the servers to carry all the necessary process, which had to be carried among all the communication parties in advance, this is illustrated in Figure 11.2, giving us a brief structure how it carries between the two parties.

CSFSC provides different steps to verify the registration process and to verify it along with different components, like tag reader, server, etc [24]. The server generates sequence number and random number, which has been compared with the pseudo code identity in the form of set of tuples, where it generates pseudo identities. Once whole registration process completes then server sends authorization credentials to the two parties for authentication process if mutual authentication are done, then back server sends required variables like alias key identity, identity for tag reader, and identity for server, which have been bundled along with necessary components or information and will be transferred to receiver.

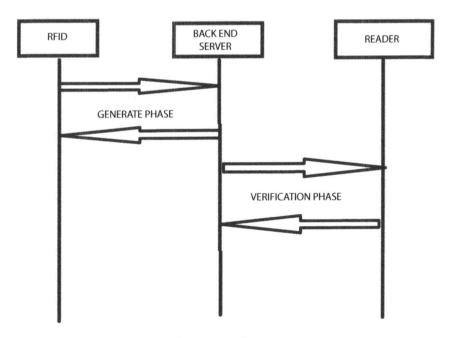

Figure 11.2 Authentication procedure between the communication parties.

11.4.3   Reader-Based Procedures

1. $N_x = K_{ts} \oplus N_t$ (11.1)
2. $AID_T = h \, (ID_{Tj} || K_{ts} || N_t || Tr_{seq})$ (11.2)
   $||$ Operator for concatenation. AID_T is hashing
   function of $ID_{Tj} || K_{ts} || N_t || Tr_{seq}$
3. $EL = LAI_T \oplus h \, (|| K_{ts} || N_t ||)$ (11.3)
   Hashing function to provide secure transmission
4. $V_1 = h \, (AID_T || N_x || K_{ts} || R_i || S_{id} || EL)$ (11.4)
   V_1 hashing function of $AID_T || N_x || K_{ts} || R_i || S_{id} || EL$
   Or
   $pid_j \in PID, \, k_{emj} \in K_{em}$
   $AID_T = pid_j, \, K_{ts} = k_{emj}$

After receiving M_{A1} unknown number, like hash number, it will be generated and computed, and this information is at the backend for secure transmission.

11.4.4   Backend Server-Side Procedures

Generate Nr
Derive $Ny = Krs \oplus Nr$
Ny is Ex OR operation of $Krs \oplus Nr$
Compute $V2$ = hashing $(MA1 || Nr || Krs || LAIr)$
$V2$ Hashing function of $MA1 || Nr || Krs || LAIr$
$AIDT \, Kt, \, Nx, \, Ri, \, Sid$ and checks whether it is equal to $V1$.

It computes after receiving the messages from backend server. The backend server checks and compute with the random number generated information along with hashing function, once verification has been done safely and securely, further process for authentication is done and it is updated with tracking the sequence number [25]. The whole information has been put in a message after receiving it and computed necessary message will be transmitted where the other end the receiving from the server reader computes and verifies with its tag information and then sends it to the server back for authentication process.

11.4.5   Reader Side Final Compute and Check Operations

$$V^* = \text{hash} \, (R || N || K) = V$$ (11.5)

$$V_3^* = \text{is hashing function of } \left(R\|N\|_i\|K\right)_r Tr_{rs}$$

$$N_t = K_{ts} \oplus N_x \, N_r = K_{rs} \oplus N_y \, V_2. \, ? \, V_1. \, ? \, AID_T \text{ and } LAI_t \text{ with } LAI_r$$

$$TR = \text{hashing } (K_{ts}\|ID_{Tj}\|N_t) \oplus Tr_{seqnew}$$

$$V_4 = (Tr\|K_{ts}\|ID_{Tj}\|N_t) \tag{11.6}$$

V_4 is hashing function of $Tr\|K_{ts}\|ID_{Tj}\|N_t$

$$V_3 = \text{h } (Ri\|N_r\|K_{rs})$$

V_3 is hashing function of $Ri\|N_r\|K_{rs}$

$$V^* = \text{hashing } (Tr\|K\|ID\|N) = V \tag{11.7}$$

Compute and update:

$$Tr_{seqnew} = \text{h } (K_{ts}\|ID_{Tj}\|N_t) \oplus Tr$$

Tr_{seqnew} is Ex OR and hashing

$$K_{tsnewf} = \text{hash } (K_{ts}\|ID_{Tj}\| Tr_{seqnew})$$

$$K_{tsnew} = \text{h}(ID_{Tj} \| kem_j) \oplus x, K_{ts} = K_{tsnew}$$

This process provides safe process along with policies for protecting privacy where mutual authentication where information has been provided securely to improve security which provides pseudo code key generation along with forward key secrecy usage for home security in smart applications along with localizations. This approach also helps in preventing the smart home use case by cloning attacks along with denial-of-service attack in normal network as well as distributed denial of service attacks.

11.5   Results Observed Based on Various Features With Proposed and Existing Methods

In this, we have observed the existing methods along with different features or parameters along with our proposed frame work control scheme for secure access model presented in Table 11.2.

As shown in Table 11.2, we made comparison along with performance of different existing models for different attributes and features along with proposed model. Each model has its drawbacks when we try to compare with different parameters especially in providing mutual authentication from reader to end user server along with Table 11.3 where the total time taken to execute among all the communication parties has been indicated.

Total time taken for execution along with existing and proposed model have been compared above where it showed the reflection of each model in terms of milliseconds when it is compared to security features, the proposed method had showed better with 0.94 milliseconds, along with all the existing models. The complexity of the proposed model showed more level of security. The tradeoff value is also given top most priority. The study used for face recognition along with biometric authentication models where we gathered different facial expression and used for experimental studies.

We have collected dataset with different face images and was used for biometric authentication models as shown in Figure 11.3. The tags along with different faces have been saved in the communication party server for verification of these images. From reader side along with backend servers where authentication process checks from all the side and provides an average execution time taken per different sections and its average time. Image matching schemes had been used and compared with different existing model were found more secure, though the execution time is more when compared with different models.

Evaluation of performance with various existing and proposed models was presented in result 1 or Figure 11.4. The time taken for proposed scheme was found very less compared with other model, where it had proven that security is better and had proven that two-way authentication using RFID reader and biometric had been shown more authentication especially in smart home use case system.

Execution time along with average time and its performance are shown in result 2 or Figure 11.5 where existing models showed highest execution time where IMA with proposed scheme performance improvement, though it showed little bit over head. It ensures that secure communications

Table 11.2 RFID-based authentication models.

Methods	Authentication which will be done mutually by all parties	Do the devices provide anonymity	Are the availability of the devices provided	Do the devices provide security	Does the devices provide scalability among themselves	Does the device provide secure localization among themselves
Method 1 using SURF algorithm	Doesn't provide	Doesn't provide	Doesn't provide	Doesn't provide	Doesn't provide	Doesn't provide
Method 2 using SIFT algorithm	Doesn't provide	Doesn't provide	Doesn't provide	Provide	Doesn't provide	Doesn't provide
Method 3 using IMA Algorithm	Provide	Doesn't provide	Doesn't provide	Doesn't provide	Doesn't provide	Doesn't provide
Method 4 using IMA with proposed algorithm	Provide	Provide	Provide	Provide	Provide	Provide

Table 11.3 Total time taken for execution along with existing and proposed model.

Models	Existing and proposed model time taken for execution
Method 1 using SURF Algorithm	0.59
Method 2 using SIFT Algorithm	0.41
Method 3 using IMA Algorithm	0.77
Method 4 using IMA with Proposed Algorithm	0.94

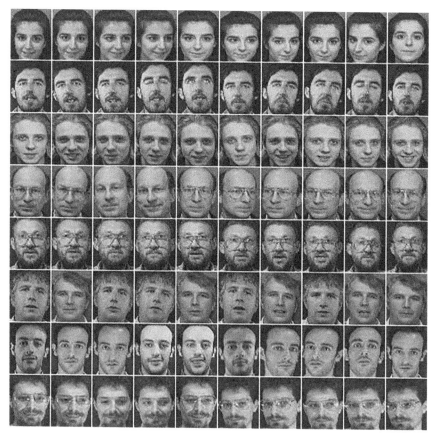

Figure 11.3 Face expression along with various images which was collected from [25].

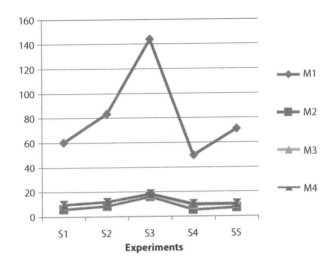

Figure 11.4 Evaluation with various existing and proposed models.

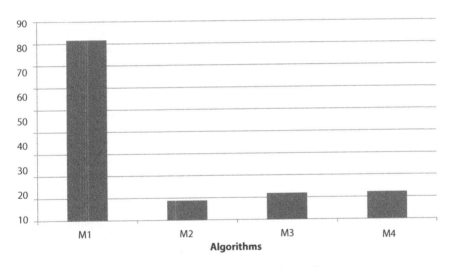

Figure 11.5 Execution time along with average time and its performance.

with different parties along with two-way authentication is proven to be more secured among all the other existing models.

11.6   Conclusions and Future Work

IoT usage has shown a drastic change in many real-world applications where the usage of different IoT devices has increased and has proven that it has been combined along with different entities used in real-world applications. Though some problems, like security among the communication parties along with leakage of privacy, still exist, IoT devices have been widely used in a variety of scenario especially in different use case, like different smart case applications, which have been investigated in this paper. RFID-based biometric authentication approaches have been built, especially in smart home and smart city applications where it ensured security among all of them in communication. Devices which read the data and transmit the data to them along with backend server were made with different random key generators. The proposed model has implemented the best results over the existing models. In the future, more secure methods can be implemented along with AI technology to eliminate leakages policies, especially privacy toward smart applications use cases.

References

1. Gope, P., Amin, R., Hafizul Islam, S.K., Kumar, N., Bhalla, V.K., Lightweight and privacy-preserving RFID authentication scheme for distributed IoT infrastructure with secure localization services for smart city environment. *Future Gener. Comput. Sy.*, 83, 629–637, June 2018.
2. Akkaya, K., Guvenc, I., Aygun, R., Pala, N., Kadri, A., IoT-based occupancy monitoring techniques for energy-efficient smart buildings. *IEEE*, 171, 1943–1952, 2020.
3. Hernández-Ramos, J.L., Victoria Moreno, M., Bernabé, J.B., Carrillo, D.G., Skarmeta, A.F., SAFIR: Secure access framework for IoT-enabled services on smart buildings. *J. Comput. Syst. Sci.*, 81, 8, 1452–1463, December 2015.
4. Ziegeldorf, J.H., Garcia Morchon, O., Wehrle, K., Privacy in internet of things: Threats and challenges. *ACM*, 7, 12, 2728–2742, December 2014.
5. Martínez-Ballesté, A., Pérez-Martínez, P.A., Solanas, A., The pursuit of citizens' privacy: A privacy-aware smart city is possible. *IEEE*, 68, 2, 1–6, 2020.
6. Zhang, K., Ni, J., Yang, K., Liang, X., Ren, J., Shen, X.S., Security and privacy in smart city applications: Challenges and solutions. *IEEE Acess Journal*, 1–8, September 7 2018.
7. Celdrán, A.H., Clemente, F.J.G., Pérez, M.G., Pérez, G.M., SeCoMan: A semantic-aware policy framework for developing privacy-preserving and context-aware smart applications. *IEEE Syst. J.*, 10, 3, 1–14, 2016.
8. Nguyen, T.A. and Aiello, M., Energy intelligent buildings based on user activity: A survey. *Energy Build.*, 56, 244–257, 2013.
9. Arjunan, P., Saha, M., Choi, H., Gulati, M., Singh, A., Singh, P., Srivastava, M.B., *SensorAct: A Decentralized and Scriptable Middleware for Smart Energy Buildings*, IEEE, pp. 1–10, 2015.

10. Mehrotra, S., Kobsa, A., Venkatasubramanian, N., Rajagopalan, S.R., *TIPPERS: A Privacy Cognizant IoT Environment*, IEEE, pp. 1–6, 2016.
11. Kuzlu, M., Pipattanasomporn, M., Rahman, S., *Review of Communication Technologies for Smart Homes/Building Applications*, IEEE, pp. 1–6, 2015.
12. Chen, L., Thombre, S., Järvinen, K., Lohan, E.S., Alén-Savikko, A., Leppäkoski, H., Bhuiyan, M.Z.H., Bu-Pasha, S., Ferrara, G.N., Honkala, S., Lindqvist, J., Robustness, security and privacy in location-based services for future IoT: A Survey. *IEEE*, 5, 1–22, 2017.
13. Liang, K., Liu, J.K., Au, M.H., Lu, R., Privacy-preserving personal data operation on mobile cloud-chances and challenges over advanced persistent threat, future generation computer systems, Elsevier, 79, pp. 337–349, February 2018. https://doi.org/10.1016/j.future.2017.06.021
14. Patra, L. and Rao, U.P., *Internet of Things–Architecture, Applications, Security and other Major Challenges*, IEEE, pp. 1–6, 2016.
15. Cusack, B. and Khaleghparast, R., A privacy gap around the Internet of Things for open source project, IEEE, pp. 1–8, 2015.
16. Das, A.K., Pathak, P.H., Jee, J., Chuah, C.-N., Mohapatra, P., *Non-Intrusive Multi-Modal Estimation of Building Occupancy*, ACM, pp. 1–14, 2017.
17. Ahvar, E., Daneshgar-Moghaddam, N., Ortiz, A.M., Lee, G.M., Crespi, N., On analyzing user location discovery methods in smart homes: A taxonomy and survey. *J. Netw. Comput. Appl.* (Elsevier), 1–34, 2016.
18. Zhao, Z., Kuendig, S., Carrera, J., Carron, B., Braun, T., Rolim, J., Indoor location for smart environments with wireless sensor and actuator networks. *IEEE*, 1–8, 2017.
19. Challa, S., Wazid, M., Das, A.K., Kumar, N., Reddy, A.G., Yoon, E.-J., Yoo, K.-Y., *Secure Signature-Based Authenticated Key Establishment Scheme for Future IoT Applications*, IEEE, pp. 1–16, 2017.
20. Magesh Kumar, K., Vetripriya, M., Brigetta, A., Akila, A., Keerthana, D., Analysis on Internet of Things and its application. *IJSRSET*, 2, 2, 1–8, 2016.
21. Yang, J., Park, J., Lee, H., Ren, K., Kim, K., Mutual authentication protocol for low-cost RFID. *Proceedings of the Workshop on RFID and Lightweight Cryptography*, pp. 17–24, 2005.
22. Tan, C.C., Sheng, B., Li, Q., Secure and server-less RFID authentication and search protocols. *IEEE T. Wirel. Commun.*, 7, 1400–1407, 2008.
23. Cai, S., Li, Y., Li, T., Deng, R., Attacks and improvements to an RFID mutual authentication protocol. *Proceedings of the 2nd ACM Conference on Wireless Network Security*, pp. 51–58, 2009.
24. Cho, J.S., Jeong, Y.S., Park, S., Consideration on the brute-force attack cost and retrieval cost: A hash-based radio-frequency identification (RFID) tag mutual authentication protocol. *Comput. Math. Appl.*, 69, 58–65, 2015.
25. Hopper, Prof A., Cambridge University Computer Laboratory, 2002. https://cam-orl.co.uk/facedatabase.html

12

MQTT-Based Implementation of Home Automation System Prototype With Integrated Cyber-IoT Infrastructure and Deep Learning–Based Security Issues

Arnab Chakraborty

Department of CSE, Netaji Subhash Engineering College, Kolkata, India

Abstract

Smart home automation is an absolute necessity in today's world. The term "smart home automation" refers to a system of interconnected electronic devices that can be operated from a distance and regulate all aspects of a household's activity. Because of technological developments and new innovations in the Internet of Things (IoT), home automation is becoming increasingly popular. Automation of home appliances, such as televisions, refrigerators, and air conditioners, fans, and lights, as well as motor pumps, can be accomplished through the use of local networking or mobile apps. Using artificial intelligence, we can make real-time decisions.

In such situations, denial-of-service attacks, unwanted network access, data leakage, and some other vulnerabilities can all be mitigated by making IoT devices and protocols as safe as possible. The Internet of Things makes use of CAP and MQTT, two protocols for exchanging data over short distances. These protocols are the cause of the DoS attack. DoS attacks can be thwarted by employing the MQTT protocol. A Wi-Fi-based development board, the ESP32 is used in this paper to develop and implement MQTT using sensors and actuators attached to the microcontroller board and a Mosquitto-based MQTT broker to remotely monitor the system and to handle security threats and malicious activity using MQTT protocol, which is based on the protocol.

Keywords: Home automation, MQTT protocol, ESP32, NodeMCU, cyber-IoT system, lightweight protocol, DL-based security issues

Email: arnab125125@gmail.com

Rajdeep Chakraborty, Anupam Ghosh, Jyotsna Kumar Mandal and S. Balamurugan (eds.) Convergence of Deep Learning In Cyber-IoT Systems and Security, (249–268) © 2023 Scrivener Publishing LLC

12.1   Introduction

A smart home system that is monitored and controlled remotely with or without the help of the Internet is not a new concept. By 2020, there are estimated to be 50 billion connected devices [1]. When it comes to home automation, a current example is the use of a web platform to control home appliances through an IoT-cloud-based structure [2]. The HTTP requests are used to control the status of the appliances. The ability to store and analyze data on the status of connected household appliances is a key feature of the IoT-Cloud technique. Smart Home Automated system uses actuators, various sensors, microcontrollers to extend safety, security for the better life of home residents. It can also give the flexibility to handle electronics appliances remotely and also securely with the help of security protocols. A smart home automation system is used to manage and maintain communication between smart devices. Due to the dramatic decline in the price of electronically controlled devices at the end of the twentieth century, microcontrollers have become increasingly important in building a smart home system. We have used remote controls for TVs, lights, fans, and air conditioners in our houses to control them. Using short-range communication channels on mobile devices, such as ZigBee, Bluetooth, as well as GSM modules and wireless LAN networks, users may now operate their home appliances from afar due to the expansion of technical media and networks. Figure 12.1 below represents a model of the smart home automation system.

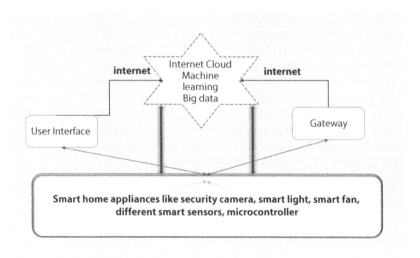

Figure 12.1 IoT cloud-based smart home automation.

An abundance of gadgets may be found in a smart home, all of which communicate with one another and share data over the Internet at random intervals [3, 4]. Protocols, like constrained application protocol (CoAP), XMPP, and MQTT, were created to communicate data between IoT devices and facilitate the transmission of messages in the IoT network. Because of MQTT's lightweight qualities [5] and its ability to work efficiently in low-power, limited memory devices, it is the greatest contender for M2M communication. Specifically, the MQTT protocol is discussed in this work. Data can be exchanged in real-time using MQTT, which has a little impact on the communication network. There are no additional fees associated with using MQTT because it runs through TCP/IP, which is used by all tools and Internet-enabled devices.

Any procedure for publishing and receiving data from the broker is a major factor. A broker is capable of managing a huge number of MQTT clients that can be running at the same time; Home Automation System all depends on how it is implemented. Messages are delivered to clients who have already signed up, after which they are filtered by the broker and organized by topic for each subscriber. Including subscriptions and missed messages, all existing customers' sessions are also saved in the database. Individual clients are also authenticated and authorized by the broker. Because of this, the broker should be simple to keep track of, and capable of coping with setbacks.

Using the MQTT protocol and NodeMCU microcontroller [6, 13] ESP32, this research focuses on the development and implementation of a budget-friendly, secure, and dependable cloud-based home automation system. Secure Socket Layer (SSL) level security is provided via the MQTT protocol, which has built-in security. In order to control household appliances from afar, a user can transmit relevant commands over the Internet via the cloud. Wi-Fi, cloud MQTT, ESP32 [7], relays, and a power supply unit make up this system.

The rest of the document will look like this: In this instance, the home automation system is being used; Section 12.2 explains the basic architecture. Some of the security challenges in home automation and possible solutions using deep learning are discussed in Section 12.3. Section 12.4 explains how the proposed home automation system prototype is implemented. Those results can be seen in section 12.5, and section 12.6 comes to close with a brief exchange of views and a recommendation.

12.2   Architecture of Implemented Home Automation

MQTT [8] is a lightweight connection protocol that follows the publish-subscribe architecture (pub/sub) architecture shown in Figure 12.2. Messages are transferred (or published) from a client-side to a server-side in this system. As a result of this, another client receives the message. Senders must make sure that clients are subscribed to topics they publish in order to ensure that their messages are delivered correctly [9].

It is generally utilized in places where communication channels have limited throughput, such as smart cities, home automation, and monitoring [10]. To the MQTT server, the client posts a message that is relayed to other clients that are subscribed on the same subject as the client. A folder-like structure is used to represent the subject matter, it is also arranged like how files are arranged in folders in a computer's OS. MQTT is a low-overhead messaging protocol that can be used on unstable networks. A single packet's error and flow control are delegated to lower tiers of the network's protocol design because MQTT [8] sits above TCP. MQTT uses a publisher/subscriber-based approach, therefore, information is organized into hierarchical "topic" structures subscribing members will be able to follow lines and nodes. For the sake of message delivery, MQTT likewise provides a QoS (quality of services) level that is adapted to the needs of customers [11]. The secure sockets layer (SSL) and transport layer

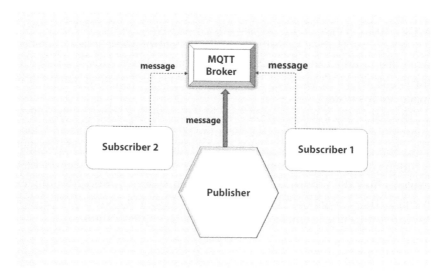

Figure 12.2 MQTT architecture.

security (SSL) control the authenticity of MQTT brokers through the user names and passwords.

A message can be reserved on the MQTT broker for an indefinite amount of time if desired. As soon as a subscriber signs up for a given topic, they get a message with links to the most recent article that contain useful information [12].

If the broker and the clients are still connected or not, and when a single one of them is disconnected, a keep-alive system has been put into operation in MQTT to prevent partial operating status. Transmission times are excessively long or a lack of communication for an extended amount of time triggers this mechanism. The client or broker sends a request status message, which is returned with an appropriate acknowledgment of the request. There is a last will and testament (LWT) [9, 12] notification given to any broker or client who fails to respond within the allotted time period. MQTT does not require a client to be aware of a server's physical identification, in contrast to a traditional client-server architecture. Messages sent over MQTT can be in any format, which is a significant advantage. This implies that the data format must be agreed upon in advance by both the publisher and the subscriber.

12.3   Challenges in Home Automation

The MQTT protocol is not completely safe, and it has various limits and drawbacks that must be considered. The primary drawback of MQTT is that it is heavily dependent on the broker. The whole system's scalability can be affected by the broker. MQTT brokers can support as many networks as they can handle, also it might be a source of failure in an automation system because they are powered by batteries. If the broker experiences a power outage and goes into offline mode, the data sent/received by the devices to it may be affected and may not be able to publish it.

Most IoT devices are points of entry into the home or any corporate network, therefore, the present dangers are associated with information infringement, because private servers hold 80% of the world's data [14]. As long as the attackers have access to such servers, huge damage can occur. In order to protect network security and IT systems from the ever-increasing dangers, a number of aggressive actions can be done. Data integrity, privacy, confidentiality, as well as accessibility of the MQTT messaging protocol should contain IoT security features becoming progressively serious both in terms of averting commercial and personal calamities [15].

12.3.1 Distributed Denial of Service and Attack

DoS attack are those carried out by a single person that prevents users and corporations that are legitimate from obtaining the services and resources they are entitled to. As a result of distributed denial of service (DDoS) attacks, authorized people and organizations are unable to access services. With respect to hardware, m2m, cloud and related devices, and the idea of the Internet of Things (IoT) security including that of embedded devices, is not a new, because the firmware and/or back-end mechanisms of a device are likely to be vulnerable to security threats. DDoS attacks at the application-level, committed by exploited IoT devices are extremely difficult to avoid. A denial-of-service attack on a large scale (DDoS) can be taken care by intercepting the unique subscriber ID and sending it to a "topic" of brokers, or by failing authentication or authorization. It is possible that the server will go down because of this or build a link to the attacker that is completely anonymous. It is important to note that MQTT brokers are the single point mechanism of any IoT architecture, as well as the primary target of DDOS attacks when open-source brokers are used.

12.3.2 Deep Learning–Based Solution Aspects

Devices that are continually linked to the Internet, using sensor data and interacting with external actuators, are referred to as the "Internet of Things" (IoT) [15]. The Internet of Things (also known as IoT) is expected to have 4.5 billion connected devices by 2020 [17, 18]. They have some qualities, as for example, low ability to perform computations and the usage of protocols with a small footprint. While as a result, Internet of Things devices are compact and efficient, it also reduces their ability to protect themselves from hackers. The abnormalities and new vulnerabilities posed by these diversified networked and computerized systems present advanced problems in the field of in cyber security [19, 20]. Assaults like the Mirai botnet, which infected IoT devices and launched distributed denial of service attacks with as many as 400,000 connected devices [21], exploited these weaknesses.

Semisupervised learning and Fuzziness as a basis works about 84% of the time [22], while sequential extreme learning machines can identify network traffic with an accuracy of 95 [23]. Using machine learning to detect network breaches is a smart idea, based on these promising results. New criteria for signature-based IDS can be applied using machine learning approaches to improve the detection method, which provides good results in qualifying frames under assault and also in detecting zero-day attacks [24, 25]. Deep learning [26] concepts are used in the machine learning approaches. Deep learning may be used to find a solution to a variety of oddity-detection issues. Using the DBN (Deep Belief Network) is possible as an extractor of characteristics as an SVM may be used to classify assaults based on the KDD dataset [27].

12.4   Implementation

The MQTT protocol, which is used to communicate amongst IoT devices, is explained in detail. Messages are published under a topic name in this protocol. The message is then delivered to all subscribers under the topic name via a broker.

Our discussion of the project description will take place in this section. A home automation system that is safe, reliable, and easy to customize is the goal of this paper. We use NodeMCU, an open-source IoT device with low costs. Espressif Systems' ESP32 Wi-Fi SoC was used to operate the first software and hardware components. ESP32 32-bit MCU support was introduced later. In terms of development boards for Espressif's Wi-Fi Internet of Things chip, the ESP32, NodeMCU reigns supreme. In order to run user programs on the ESP32 without having to recompile them, it employs the Lua scripting language [12]. An ESP-12E module, a CP2102 chip, and a USB power connector make up the circuit board. The ESP32 feature is described in Table 12.1. Breadboard compatibility is ensured by placing the ESP-12E's pins on a board that is both small and compact. Both the Arduino IDE and the NodeMCU firmware are available to us. Figure 12.3 depicts the ESP32 construction and pin-out diagram.

Figure 12.3 ESP32 NodeMCU.

Table 12.1 ESP32 NodeMCU Feature.

Names of the parts	Specification
ROM flash	4M
Programming language for creating scripts	2 buttons (reset and flash)
Total GPIO pins	17 GPIO
ADC	Ranging from 1 to 10 bits
Operation modes	Sleep mode, Deep sleep modes and Active modes
Operating voltage	Approx. 3.3 V
Internet	IEEE 802.11 b/g/n Wi-Fi
programmer	CP2102 USB-to-UART
Module	ESP-12

12.4.1   Relay

It is a model based on communication between sender and receiver's probabilistic outcomes, supported by few intermediary relay inputs in the relay channel in information theory. Figure 12.4 below shows a replay switch with three inputs and Table 12.2 shows the features of two-input relay circuit individually.

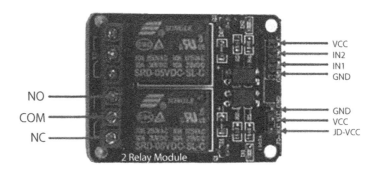

Figure 12.4 2-input relay switch.

Table 12.2 Features of relay.

Name of the components	Specification
Max. flow through a relay contact	AC250V: 10A
Total no of relays	2
Maximum possible current for each relay	20mA
Minimum operating voltage	5v
Contact current capacity of relay	DC30: 10A

12.4.2 DHT11

An inexpensive digital sensor is the DHT11 for measuring temperature and relative humidity. Humidity and temperature readings may be taken instantly using this sensor, which can be used with any microcontroller. It has a sensor where humidity is conductive in nature for the measurement of temperature, as well as a thermistor. The humidity-sensing capacitance uses moisture-holding substrate as a dielectric between both electrodes. The capacitance value varies with variations in relative humidity. Analog resistance levels are measured and processed by the integrated circuit. Figures 12.5 depicts the basic diagram of DHT 11 sensor.

Figure 12.5 DHT 11.

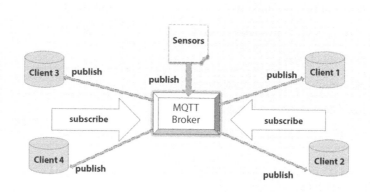

Figure 12.6 Devices connected with MQTT.

The broker service provider determines the quantity of "customers" that can be connected to the broker. In fact, it has the ability to reach a large number of customers who are constantly publishing and subscribing. It is not just that there are a lot of connected devices, but that any one of them can access the data of any other one at any moment. As a result, the potential uses for this readily available data are virtually limitless. It is necessary to enter the server name (io.adafruit.com), port number (1883), username, and unique AIO key in the Arduino IDE, as well as the feed name and the password credential along with the SSID of an Access point for WiFi that has access to the Internet, in order to subscribe or publish to the MQTT server. Compilation and upload of code to the ESP32 have been completed once everything is set up correctly. You will need an MQTT client library in order to use Adafruit IO's MQTT API. It is called MQTT, or message queue telemetry transit, and it is supported by Adafruit. Adafruit's IO may be used with Python, Ruby, and Arduino. How several clients are connected with MQTT is explained in Figure 12.6.

It is possible to use MQTT in libraries. You should look for a MQTT library that supports the MQTT 3.1.1 protocol across multiple operating systems and language.

- Arduino: The Adafruit MQTT
- Python: Adafruit IO Python includes an MQTT Client.

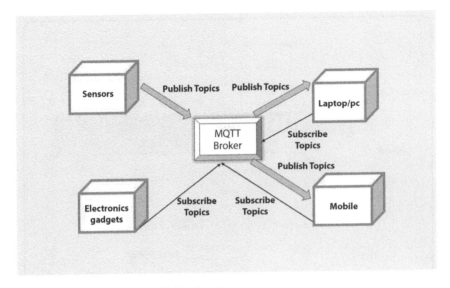

Figure 12.7 MQTT broker publish-subscribe.

- CircuitPython: Adafruit IO CircuitPython includes an MQTT Client class, IO_MQTT.
- MicroPython: MicroPython devices can connect to Adafruit IO using MQTT
- Ruby: Adafruit IO Ruby includes an MQTT client.

"If this, then that" is a programming conditional statement, and that is where the name IFTTT comes from. The company's application, devices information, and services can all be connected to the same software platform. We can use IFTTT with absolutely no change. For the purpose of sending out notifications, we implemented an IFTTT server. Figure 12.7 describes the pub-sub model of MQTT broker and Figure 12.8 is the screenshot of Arduino IDE.

Our project is based on home automation. We tried to control different electronic devices from outside the home even from anywhere in the world using MQTT protocol. We divided our projects into 2 parts:

  i) Controlling Home Devices from Outside
      In this part basically, we tried to control a bulb (electronic device) that is present inside our home from outside. To implement this we used one MQTT server called Adafruit.io. There are many other MQTT servers present, but we chose

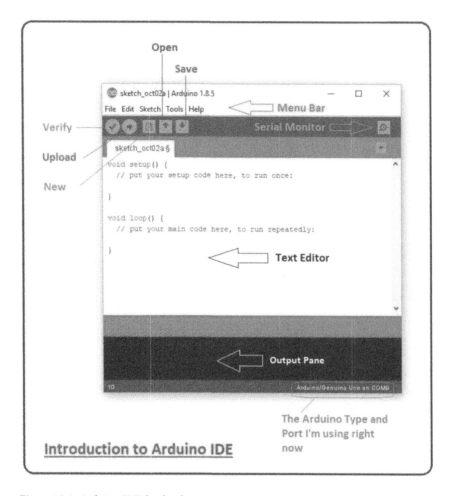

Figure 12.8 Arduino IDE for development.

this because this has a free trial and is easy to implement. Here, as mentioned in Figure 12.9, we connect a Bulb to the NodeMCU Wi-Fi module through a relay circuit. We create a feed (light) in the Adafruit.io dashboard. According to MQTT protocol if we subscribe to that feed, when we publish something then that value will be reflected in the device connected to that feed. It is just like Youtube. In Youtube, if we subscribe to a channel, then when this channel publishes a video that video comes in our Youtube home page.

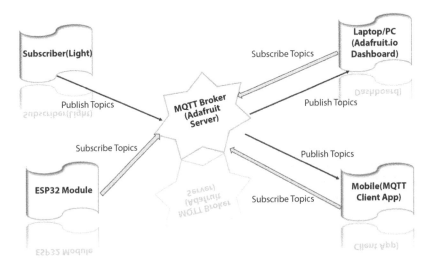

Figure 12.9 Controlling home devices from outside.

Suppose we are outside the home and forgot to switch off our bedroom light. Then we can easily switch off the light from anywhere through the MQTT server. An appropriate commands can be delivered via the Internet's "cloud" from afar, you can operate your household appliances.

ii) Room Temperature and Humidity Measurement

Controlling electronic devices in homes and businesses has never been easier thanks to the Internet of Things (IoT). As a bonus, you can access any sensor's data from anywhere in the world and analyze it in a graphical manner. A simple room temperature monitoring system is implemented in our project. We use the NodeMCU module to read the temperature sensor (DHT11) and upload it to an Adafruit cloud. The DHT11 sensor collects room temperature data, processes it, and transmits it to a NodeMCU Module. The NodeMCU is a Wi-Fi module and one of the most popular platforms for the Internet of Things. It can send data to the IoT cloud (here Adafruit). Additionally, in the Adafruit.io dashboard, add a new feed called "temperature monitor." At this point, the sensor is reading a value every 30 seconds and publishing that value to Adafruit's dashboard, which we can access from any location to see the room temperature logs in real time.

12.5   Results and Discussions

The cloud service eliminates the need for a local gateway, making the proposed system more secure than the current systems. Users and devices benefit from the broker cloud (Adafruit Server) in terms of processing speed. Cryptographic operations between different devices are also reduced by this method. SVC, a machine learning algorithm, learns from users' usage history in order to predict what devices they will need in the future.

To make our home more secure, we also implement a notification system during emergencies. Here we used one SMTP server (IFTTT Maker). The DHT11 sensor continuously reads room temperature from the environment and publishes that value in the Adafruit Dashboard. During that time, we also compare that value falls in between the range we mentioned. If the room temperature is greater than the maximum range or lesser than the minimum range, then it will send a notification mail through IFTTT as an alert, so that we can take precautions. Figure 12.10 below represents detailed results of the MQTT Broker Dashboard.

We created different feeds for controlling our devices and publishing the data.

1. The Light1 is used to control the light connected to NodeMCU ESP32. If we toggle the "Light1" feed to "ON", then the Light will be switch on and if we toggle the "Light1" feed to "OFF", the Light will be switch off. And all the results of this feed are also stored in the Adafruit log in Figure 12.11.

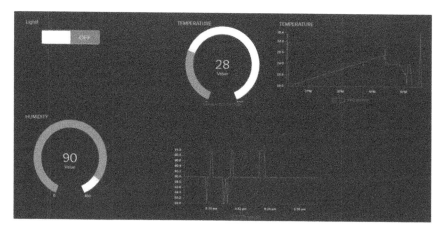

Figure 12.10 Adafruit dashboard.

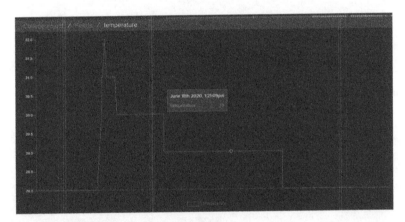

Figure 12.11 Feed log of light 1.

2. We make a feed called "TEMPERATURE" to publish the temperature data in the Adafruit dashboard taken by the DHT11 sensor. The data are represented both in Gauge and in a Linear Graph in Figures 12.12 and 12.13. And all the results of this feed are also stored in the Adafruit log like this:

Figure 12.12 Temperature feed log (graphical).

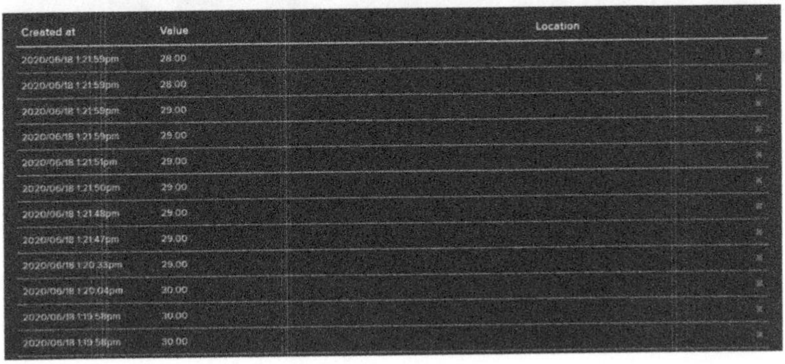

Figure 12.13 Temperature feed log.

3. We make a feed called "HUMIDITY" to publish the Humidity data in the Adafruit dashboard taken by the DHT11 sensor. The data are represented in Figures 12.14 and 12.15 both in Gauge and in a Linear Graph. And all the results of this feed are also stored in the Adafruit log like this

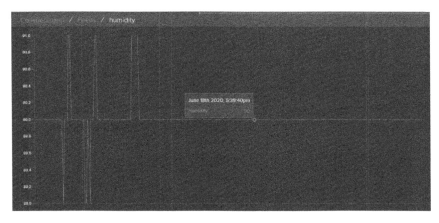

Figure 12.14 Humidity feed log (graphical).

Created at	Value	Location
2020/06/18 5:48:32pm	90.00	
2020/06/18 5:48:27pm	90.00	
2020/06/18 5:48:23pm	90.00	
2020/06/18 5:48:20pm	90.00	
2020/06/18 5:48:09pm	90.00	
2020/06/18 5:48:02pm	90.00	
2020/06/18 5:47:58pm	90.00	
2020/06/18 5:47:50pm	90.00	

Figure 12.15 Humidity feed log.

4. In addition, we introduce a mail notification system shown in Figure 12.16. A temperature reading from the DHT11 sensor is checked to see if it is above or below the threshold value at all times. If the value is higher than the predefined limit, the following message will be sent via IFTTT server.

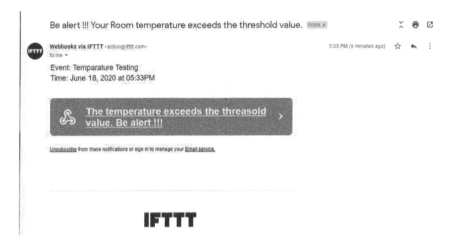

Figure 12.16 Alert mail through IFTTT.

12.6 Conclusion

We have set up a simple implementation of the secure MQTT protocol in a smart home to control a few sensors and lights. Sensors and relay shields can be controlled wirelessly over the Internet using the ESP32 microcontroller. The coverage range of the Wi-Fi router indicates that the Internet of Things (IoT) devices can be utilized properly, and accessed virtually anywhere on our premises. The Adafruit MQTT broker is used to efficiently implement the publish-subscribe model. Each client's connection is encrypted using an SSL port. MQTT's best feature is that when releasing feed data, the option to set a quality of service level (QoS), which is the most important feature. As a result, the proposed system improves automation service and security by verifying whether the data have been made available to the public. It reduces the amount of work required to perform computations. Smart home services and a more secure system are expected to be added in the future. A gateway has been eliminated in favor of using the cloud for intermediate data storage and processing, which has the added benefit of lowering the overall cost of the proposed system.

For our future research, we plan to conduct additional attempts to find out which broker is the most secure that may be applied to establish a connection with IoT gadgets in smart homes' and cities' safety.

References

1. BCC Research, *Sensors: Technologies and global markets*, BCC Research, Wellesley, Massachusetts, United States, 2011.
2. Iqbal, A., Ullah, F., Anwar, H., Kwak, K.S., Imran, M., Jamal, W., A. ur Rahman, G., Noble, B., Sneddon, I.N., Interoperable Internet-of-Things platform for a smart home system using web-of-objects and cloud. *Sustain. Cities Soc.*, 38, 636–646, Apr. 2018.
3. Jabbar, W.A., Alsibai, M.H., Amran, N.S.S., Mahayadin, S.K., Design and implementation of IoT-based automation system for smart home, in: *2018 International Symposium on Networks, Computers, and Communications (ISNCC)*, IEEE, pp. 1–6, 2018.
4. Ning, H., Shi, F., Zhu, T., Li, Q., Chen, L., A novel ontology consistent with acknowledged standards in smart homes. *Comput. Netw.*, 148, 101–107, 2019.
5. Kodali, R.K. and Soratkal, S., *MQTT based Home Automation System Using ESP8266*, Department of Electronics and Communication Engineering, National Institute of Technology, Warangal, India, 2016.
6. Jabbar, W.A., Kian, T.K., Ramli, R.M., Zubir, S.N., Zamrizaman, N.S.M., Balfaqih, M., Shepelev, V., Alharbi, S., Design and fabrication of Smart Home with the Internet of Things enabled automation system, *IEEE Access*, 7, 1–11, https://doi.org/10.1109/ACCESS.2019.2942846"10.1109/ACCESS.2019.2942846.
7. Thirupathi, V. and Sagar, K., Implementation of home automation system using MQTT Protocol and ESP32. *IJEAT*, ISSN: 2249–8958, 8, 2C2, 111–113, December 2018.
8. MQTT.ORG, http://mqtt.org/.
9. MQTT Version 3.1.1. Edited by Andrew Banks and Rahul Gupta. OASIS Standard. Burlington, Massachusetts, United States, 29 October 2014.
10. Perrone, G., Vecchio, M., Pecori, R., Giaffreda, R., *The Day After Mirai: A Survey on MQTT Security Solutions After the Largest Cyber-Attack Carried Out through an Army of IoT Devices*, pp. 246–253, 2017.
11. Soni, D. and Makwana, A., A Survey on MQTT: A protocol of Internet of Things (IoT), Research Gate. Conference: International conference on telecommunication, power analysis and computing techniques (ICTPACT – 2017), 11–16, April 2017.
12. Perry, L., Internet of Things for Architects, Architecting IoT solutions by implementing sensors, communication infrastructure, edge computing, analytics, and security, Packt Publishing. ISBN 1788475747, 1–10, 2018.
13. NodeMCU • GitHub. [Online]. Available: https://github.com/nodemcu [Accessed: 08-Dec-2019].
14. Kotak, J., Shah, A., Shah, A., Rajdev, P., *A Comparative Analysis on Security of MQTT Brokers*, Gujarat Forensic Sciences University, India, 2019.

15. Anthraper, J.J. and Kotak, J., Security, privacy and forensic concern of MQTT Protocol (March 19, 2019), in: *Proceedings of International Conference on Sustainable Computing in Science, Technology and Management (SUSCOM-2019)*, February 26-28, 2019.

16. Locke, D., MQ Telemetry Transport (MQTT) V3.1 Protocol Specification, https://bibbase.org/network/publication/locke-mqtelemetrytransportmq ttv31protocolspecification-2010, MQ Telemetry Transport (MQTT) V3.1 Protocol Specification. Locke, D. Technical Report IBM, August, 2010.

17. Singh, M., Rajan, M.A., Shivraj, V.L., Balamuralidhar, P., Secure MQTT for Internet of Things (IoT). *2015 Fifth International Conference on Communication Systems and Network Technologies*, TCS Innovation Labs, Bangalore, 560066, India, Email:{meena.s1, Rajan.ma, Shivraj.vl, balamurali.p}@tcs.com.

18. Green, J., The Internet of Things Reference Model. *Internet of Things World Forum*, pp. 1–12, 2014.

19. Galán, C.O., Lasheras, F.S., de Cos Juez, F.J., Sánchez, A.B., Missing data imputation of questionnaires by means of genetic algorithms with different fitness functions. *J. Comput. Appl. Math.*, 311, 704–717, 2017.

20. Razzaq, M.A., Gill, S.H., Qureshi, M.A., Ullah, S., Security issues in the Internet of Things (IoT): A comprehensive study. *Int. J. Adv. Comput. Sci. Appl.*, 8, 6, 383, 2017.

21. Kolias, C., Kambourakis, G., Stavrou, A., Voas, J., DDoS in the IoT: Mirai and other Botnets. IEEE *Computer*, Society, 50, 7, 80–84, 2017.

22. Ashfaq, R.A.R., Wang, X.Z., Huang, J.Z., Abbas, H., He, Y.L., Fuzziness based semi-supervised learning approach for an intrusion detection system. *Inf. Sci.*, 378, 484–497, 2017.

23. Singh, R., Kumar, H., Singla, R.K., An intrusion detection system using network traffic profiling and online sequential extreme learning machine. *Expert Syst. Appl.*, 42, 22, 8609–8624, 2015.

24. Alaiz-Moreton, H., Aveleira-Mata, J., Ondicol-Garcia, J., Muñoz-Castañeda, A.L., García, I., Benavides, C., Multiclass classification procedure for detecting attacks on MQTT-IoT Protocol, 2019, Article ID 6516253. Research Institute of Applied Sciences in Cybersecurity (RIASC) MIC, Universidad de León, León, Spain, 1–11, 2019, https://doi.org/10.1155/2019/6516253.

25. Perdisci, R., Ariu, D., Fogla, P., Giacinto, G., Lee, W., McPAD: Multiple classifier systems for accurate payload-based anomaly detection. *Comput. Netw.*, 53, 6, 864–881, 2009.

26. Kwon, D., Kim, H., Kim, J., Suh, S.C., Kim, I., Kim, K.J., A survey of deep learning-based network anomaly detection. *Cluster Comput.* 22, 949–961, Springer, 2017, https://doi.org/10.1007/s10586-017-1117-8.2019

27. Kim, J., Thu, H.L.T., Kim, H., Long short term memory recurrent neural network classifier for intrusion detection, in: *Proceedings of the International Conference on Platform Technology and Service (PlatCon, 2016)*, pp. 1–5, 2016, http://ieeexplore.ieee.org/document/7456805/.

Malware Detection in Deep Learning

Sharmila Gaikwad* and Jignesh Patil

Mct's Rajiv Gandhi Institute of Technology, Mumbai, India

Abstract

Malware is a risk to the privacy of computer users that can cause an economic loss to organizations. Deep learning is subfield of machine learning which concentrate on human brains using artificial intelligence. Nowadays, analyst perform operations and pay their attention on security features. This pandemic situation is changing world working style to different level (work from home). WFM system is increasing production level in huge manner and high growth. There is one serious issue of security third party can make changes in the confidential data. We have learned about different security threats, such as malware, data breach, etc. Intruders and extruders play a role of attacking to make system vulnerable [4]. There are various architectures of malware detection exploring in chapters, such as DSN auto encoder. Attackers play different tactics and methods to reveal confidential data using email attachments and links. In this pandemic situation, huge numbers of data breach conditions were out. India is a country that pays the highest amount for data breach due to lack of security. For this specific condition, a company is in progress of developing their personal VPN for heavy and safe security. Deep learning malware was detected using call sequences, deep neural network using process behavior, efficient dynamic malware analysis using network behavior, convolutional neural network using image processing. Few more concepts are integrated in malware detection using deep learning [2, 3], malware types, impact of malware on system, malware impact in pandemic situation, and case study.

Keywords: Malware, Malware detection, deep learning based malware detection

*Corresponding author: sharmilagaikwad1709@gmail.com

Rajdeep Chakraborty, Anupam Ghosh, Jyotsna Kumar Mandal and S. Balamurugan (eds.) Convergence of Deep Learning In Cyber-IoT Systems and Security, (269–284) © 2023 Scrivener Publishing LLC

13.1 Introduction to Malware

13.1.1 Computer Security

Computer security is the procedure of hiding confidential material from attackers. The attackers can be different categories such as insider and outsider. These types of attackers are badly affecting computers without knowing the owner of the computers or institute. Nowadays, organizations are shifting their aim toward security purpose. Security should be secure, and strong algorithms is applied on the wall of the system. Sometimes, organization innovate their own algorithms to secure database. The key principles of computer security are listed below (Figure 13.1):

- Confidentiality:
  It states that the data which hidden by organization should be read by end user. For example, customer personal details should not share with another third party. Organizations should take care of those things, which will not make serious issues.

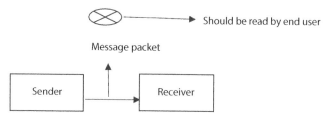

Figure 13.1 Confidential data sending [4].

- Integrity:
  It is the procedure that the packet (internal data) which is sent by an authorize owner should not be change by the third party. Data modification is the threat or malicious act by attacker (Figure 13.2).

Figure 13.2 Integrity [4].

- Availability:
It states that all previous record or data should be available to the owner at any time for strong communication and transaction. If no available information is present, error will occur in the system (Figure 13.3).

Figure 13.3 Data availability [4].

13.1.2   What Is Malware?

We know that information technology has a threat of many things to protect from those company and other institute try to make stronger software platform or software security application. We will study about malware in chapter 1 of the most dangerous during pandemic situation. From 2019 to 2021, n's number of malware cases were found out by google and different institute. "A software application which learns a correct system without knowing a correct system is called as Malware Program."

The aim of malware program is to make harmful program for hacking money stealing and financial crimes. Malware is classified into different categories (Figure 13.4).

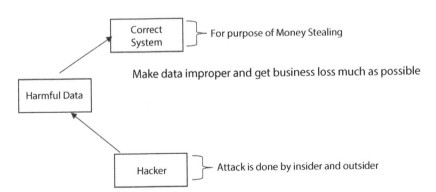

Figure 13.4 General malware idea [5].

Types of Malware

1. Worms: Worms are network viruses that have ability to spread over the network by replicating themselves. Worm attacks: First Love Letter

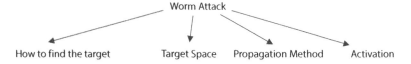

Basic steps for worm attack:
Target is searched by following methods (Selecting Randomly, Sequential Scan, Hit-List Scan, Pregenerated Scan List).
Target space (hosting malware using Internet and email).
Propagation method (exploiting the system very badly).
Activation (spreading the hosted malware)

2. Trojan Horse: It is the most harmful and dangerous, it pretends that it is a useful software but it is one of the most harmful.

Basic Steps for Trojan Horse Attack;
a) Search for victims: random select, check for vulnerable system, input a malicious application
b) Installation: spam link and fake pop-ups which are main source of installing Trojan horse (Figure 13.5)
c) Distribution of malware: After submitting fake pop-ups details, it starts for spreading malware.

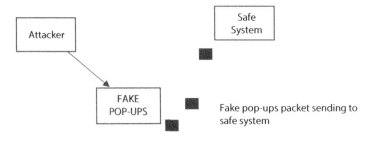

Figure 13.5 Basic diagram of Trojan horse [5].

3. Virus: a code or program is modified and malicious harmful code is attached with it is called as virus. It also gets infected files while transferring and makes security more vulnerable (Figure 13.6).

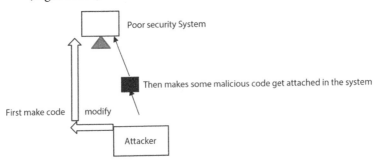

Figure 13.6 Basic diagram of virus [5].

4. Ransomwares: Ransomwares attack are very different attackers, here, the attacker gets the encrypt file modified and does not allow the user to get access information. In current scenario, ransomware is the most attacks done by the attacker (Figure 13.7).

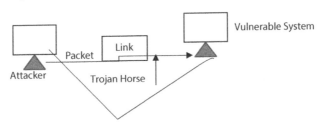

Figure 13.7 Ransomware attack using Trojan horse [6].

Step 1: Here, first, file is encrypted and does not allow the user to access the user details. Step 2: Fake pop-ups invitation are send to the vulnerable system.

5. Data breach: A data breach is security attack which information is retrieved without authorization. There are three basic types of data breach perform.
   1. Research: poor security system are recorded in the list.
   2. Stage Attack: phishing mail
   3. Advantage: if attack is effective on the computer systems or on institute at that time cybercrime operations are performed documents is stolen and money extortion

13.2   Machine Learning and Deep Learning for Malware Detection

13.2.1   Introduction to Machine Learning

Machine learning is the process that make how machine will perform task (give n's number of example to the system will it learn automatically). The basic idea behind is that a machine should work efficiently and smoothly without any human work (Figure 13.8). There are many examples were humans fail at work but ML catches it properly and gives the accurate result.

Some of the common steps designed by the organization while applying the ML project.

1. Define Aim
2. Examination the present system and study for fresh things.
3. Cover all the aspect of the device while designing (security policies, Database and Networking etc).
4. Design the flowchart to work on system.
5. Vision of the system
6. Validate and verify the risks, strategies and establish the cases.
7. Estimate the cost of the system.
8. Implement the system.
9. Modify the system if error is thrown out.
10. Follow back the loop for accurate result.

Architecture of Machine Learning:

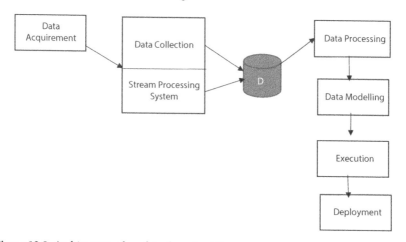

Figure 13.8 Architecture of machine learning [2].

1. Data acquirement: Preparing data and ghettoizing the case scenario based on the tasks and requirement. It is also called as data preprocessing.
2. Data collection: gathering and storing raw material in the form of datasets.
3. Stream processing system: extracting information from database and using it for real-time application.
4. Data warehouse: storing huge amount of the data in the container, this container has n number of data, such as information, images, and videos.
5. Data processing: cleaning, transformation and encoding actions are executed by executor.
6. Data modeling: algorithm and flowchart are executed by the programmer.
7. Execution: testing system, performance of system and decision of system are carried out.
8. Deployment: overall product is thrown out after all possibilities and testing is performed by the teams.

Machine is trained by using three algorithms:

a. Supervised Learning:
   It is used for mathematical model. Supervised learning is ML for acquiring the input relationship information and system based on given set of paired input training samples (Figure 13.9).

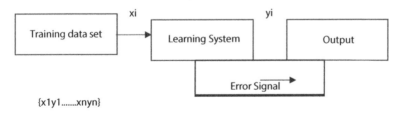

Figure 13.9 Supervised learning [7].

(x1, y1) is a supervised training sample
x represents system inputs y represents system outputs
i indicates index of the training sample xi fed to the learning system
yi generates the output
Error signal is to use for adjusting the signal

b. Unsupervised Learning: Unsupervised learning is a second type more that looks for earlier hidden patterns in a dataset with no pre-existing and with a minimum of human monitoring (Figure 13.10).

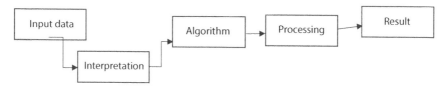

Figure 13.10 Unsupervised learning [7].

Example: Customer Segmentation
i.   Input data: customer segmentation
ii.   Interpretation: analysis of the dataset to track and make strategies for market customer growth.
iii. Algorithm: clustering (finding the similarities between the data item), outlier detection (dataset search for any kind of dissimilarities and anomalies in the data), association rule mining (founds out the most frequently occurring item-sets.
iv.   Processing: execution of algorithm with good accuracy.
v.   Result: displaying output, schedule meeting with heads for verifying and validating end result.

c. Reinforcement Learning:
Reinforcement learning is the area of the ML that deals sequential decision making [11]. It is used for classifying patterns in the data for tasks, such as data compression.

We need ML in following cases:

1. Human expertise is absent.
2. Human are unable to explain their expertise.
3. Solution changes with the time.
4. Problem size is too vast for our limited of reasoning capabilities.

13.2.2   Introduction to Deep Learning

Deep learning is a branch of ML based sets of procedures that crack to system top-level abstraction by using multiple processing. It terms that covers particular approach to building and training neural networks (Figure 13.11).

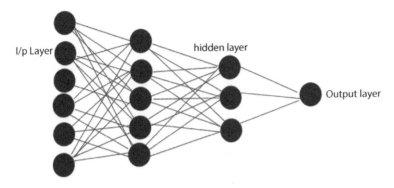

Figure 13.11 Basic layer structure of deep learning [8].

The data are stored in array, which contains of pixel, audio and waveforms. Some operations are performed in execution (Fourier Transform, DIT, FFT). Output predicted by the executor (output is in the form of numbers).

According to the definition, it is considered as the application of multi-layer network with multiple neurons at each layer to perform tasks. System is trained by using three methods in deep learning training dataset, validation dataset, test dataset.

It is also called as shallow network.

1. Input layer: It consists of raw material such as water, milk in tea.
2. Hidden layer: It is the layer between input and output layer called hidden layer
3. Activation function: Activation Function is a transformation
4. Output layer: Actual output is display with accurate input given to system.

We will discuss few types of architecture of deep learning which as follow as:

1. Auto-encoder: Auto-encoder makes target result set and get equal with the input values. The network attempts to restructure its input, which powers the hidden layer to study the finest demonstrations of the input. The hidden layer is used to explain a program, which aids to denote the input. It represents set of data using high dimensional using its subtypes (de-noising auto encoder, Sparse auto encoder, Variation

auto encoder, contractive auto-encoder). It is used in NLP and Complex data representation.

2. Convolutional neural networks (CNN): Basically, CNN first architecture was identifying the features such as edges, after recombination of some features these flow of data is performed (convolutional, pooling and classification). It is used for document analysis and face recognition.

3. Deep stacking networks: DSN is created of mixture of elements which are fragment of the system and architecture. Individual element involves of input zone, hidden zone, and output zone. The information which these system holds a huge number of deep single networks where each network has its specific hidden layers.

4. Long short-term memory: LSTM uses a memory unit called a cell which can stop its value for enough time and its gives it as a task of its feedback. This aids the unit to learn the earlier calculated value. The memory cell created of three ports called gates, which grips stream of data in the cell (first is input port which grips fresh data, second is forgets port handles summarization of the fresh data, and third is output gate which holds the flow of information that is existing in the cell.

5. Recurrent neural network: It takes the earlier memory of input and mock-ups the issues within the seconds. These networks can be changed, modified, and extended with usual backpropagation.

Some advance architecture of deep neural network is nowadays most used:

1. Alex net: The architecture consists of convolutional layers, pooling layers, which are loaded on one another and then tracked by fully interlinked layers on the uppermost.

2. Google net: This architecture single layer handles many types of the feature extractors that benefit the network to perform better.

3. Res net: The residual units are located on single over the other and made positive and whole node to node network.

4. You only look once (YOLO): This architecture resolves image recognition problem, it is used for handling the real time issues.

5. Generative Adversarial Networks: It is a special network architecture which creates fully new and diverse images which are not previously present in the vacant training dataset.

13.2.3 Detection Techniques Using Deep Learning

We have seen architectures of deep learning in Figure 13.11, which show how deep learning is extended his network. Especially new architecture of deep learning is proving stronger and accurate results [8]. In recent years, which method is most use for malware detection using deep learning are listed? (Table 13.1) [1].

Table 13.1 Deep learning methods for malware detection.

Deep learning methods	Description
Deep Neural Network	Accuracy of detection is 95% and false rate is 0.1%.
CNN and LSTM	Used for spatial and temporal signals difficult of malware illustration.
Deep Learning	Mixture of static, dynamic malware analysis is used for recognition.
Deep Belief Network	It represent malware as opcode sequences and then apply DBN
Deep Learning (CNN)	Using image processing for malware detection which convert malware in greyscale binaries and train the CNN.

Methodology for malware detection using CNN [8]:

1. Malware is unpacked
2. Executable file is stripped
3. API calls is extracted
4. Offered an extension by adding another step.
5. Various features are integrated through static analysis (Capturing information from executables without running it) and dynamic analysis (running malware in isolated environment).
6. Most new malware is formed using previous malware changing some things in a code taking these as advantage using image processing techniques will detect malware. Here image processing steps is performed to detect malware.
   i. Converting Malware binary to image
   ii. Apply CNN to Malware image

      iii. Convert CNN into flatten (converting image to column matrix)

      iv. Apply bidirectional long short term memory (BiLSTM) to classify the input.

   7. Machine learning algorithm is less accurate then deep learning [7] because the numbers of layers are more it increase the time of training (Figure 13.12) [10].

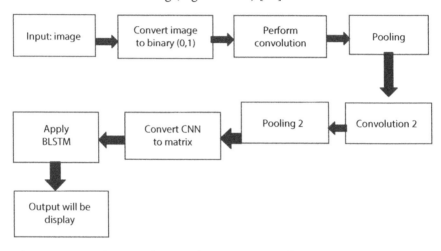

Figure 13.12 Combination of CNN and image processing for malware detection [14].

13.3 Case Study on Malware Detection

13.3.1 Impact of Malware on Systems

Current society relies upon on fundamental infrastructures and offerings enabled the use of modern technologies [6, 16]. The traditional cooperative style of working from an office is also changing. The majority of businesses are embracing Bring Your Own Device (BYOD) and cloud-based applications. On-premise data centers are giving way to cloud-based data centers. The market for cloud offerings issuers reached $186.4 billion in 2018, up 21% year on year [8]. Cloud-based applications allow employees to work from anywhere (home, airport, coffee shop) and have access to the most up-to-date information at any time. This luxury of flexibility comes with new assault floor as well. Many studies have been conducted to understand the threats associated with cloud offerings, such as vulnerability visibility and remediation, data integrity, authentication weaknesses, risk mitigation measurements, activities and incidence management, information privacy and confidentiality in some noticeably virtualized and multitenant environments [9]. Every other topic outside of the scope of this study is cloud security. It is important to note, however, that any cyber-attack structure might have an impact on the organization and financial stability. And, based on recent incidents, it is apparent that data security breaches involving private and sensitive data can have a detrimental impact on the stock market. Agriculture enterprise have adopted modern-day and superior applied sciences, such as far off sensors, gear automation, world positions structures (GPS), place monitoring systems, robotics, computing device learning, part computing, and different conversation community structures to minimize the operations price and to enlarge the productiveness of the farming. Agriculture is now not solely a nonpublic commercial enterprise of a man or woman farmer, it is vitally essential to the nation's usual financial and meals security. The farming community provides food for the entire state as well as financial exports around the world. A cyber-attack on the agriculture sector can have a significant impact on a country's economic structure. SCADA structures are used to modify and display vital infrastructure of a nation, such as electrical energy distribution, gas and oil pipeline transportation, water administration and distribution, site visitors' lights, and other structures in today's civilization. In the RISI database, there are regarded events ranging from a Trojan attack on a Siberian Gas Pipeline explosion in 1982. In 2015, a cyber-attack on a German metal plant occurred. Advanced social engineering was utilized as an attack vector to gain access to the German metal mill community, which resulted in the furnace malfunctioning. Stuxnet is a well-known worm that was discovered in the Iranian nuclear plant at Natanz in 2010 and is regarded as one of the most complex malwares [13, 15].

The Stux net malware was created specifically to exploit Siemens structures and frequency-converter drives used to power centrifuges manufactured by Fararo Paya in Iran and Vacon in Finland. Malware Duqu and Flame are remarkably similar to the Stuxnet malware, which was also developed as a cyber weapon to harm critical infrastructure. Mirai malware [11, 12], a cyberweapon, exploited IoT devices to construct a massive botnet device known as Mirai, which was successful in bringing down OVH cloud carrier corporation by conducting a 1.1 Tbps DDoS assault in 2016. The attack is regarded as one of the most significant DDoS attacks to date.

13.3.2   Effect of Malware in a Pandemic Situation

In these pandemic conditions, almost business and ecommerce sites are attacked with a n number of malware. Big companies with high security also get trapped with the data breach and ransomware attack. In 2021, a huge number of cases of data breach and ransomware are popped out. Malware attacks by means of nonstandard ports additionally fell in 2021 after breaking all records of 2020. These attacks, which intention to make bigger payloads by means of bypassing ordinary firewall technologies, symbolize 14% of all malware tries in the first half of 2021, down from 24% year to date. We will see here some ransomware malware example, which affected those company very badly.

Cybercrime is a rapidly rising, extremely profitable industry. Cybercrime costs would rise 15% every year to US$10.5 trillion by 2025, according to cybersecurity ventures. Ransomware is a kind of financial fraud that turned out to be a full-scale business model for ill-minded people. According to new data, ransomware has overtaken credit card theft as the top form of cybercrime. Almost 1 in 5 incidents in 2019 involved this type of attack, where companies of all sizes found their environments compromised by network encrypting malware and faced a demand from attackers to regain access to the data Ransomware is not the only cyber threat to retail businesses. Quite possibly, the most noticeable gatherings focusing on Internet shopping frameworks is Magecart, utilizing an online Mastercard skimming assault. The gathering has been noticed focusing on everything from online shops to inn booking sites and even US neighborhood taxpayer supported organizations to take client installment data. In large numbers of these cases, the danger entertainers designated the store network and compromised outsider programming from a frameworks integrator (for example, web based business specialist organizations), ordinarily by infusing malevolent contents. The entirety of this exhibits the significance of getting the whole retail biological system from conceivable malevolent assaults. Ransomware administrators may choose to dispatch assaults by means of social designing messages to contaminate an organization's machines with ransomware, or on account of WannaCry, through unpatched frameworks. The Magecart assaults, in which danger entertainers in a roundabout way compromised organizations by focusing on their specialist co-ops, showed that the store network could likewise be an expected objective.

Buffalo public school

In 2020, assaults on the training area rose essentially. That action has not stopped. While numerous schools have been hit by ransomware in 2021, the Buffalo Public School framework in New York serves 34,000 understudies and contains profoundly touchy data that might have been spilled. The ransomware assault on March 12 shut down the whole educational system, dropping both far off and in-person guidance for multi week. Wild ox Schools Superintendent Kriner Cash gave an assertion on March 15 that said the school was "effectively working with network protection specialists, just as nearby, state, and government law authorization to completely explore this online protection assault." The educational system continued procedure on March 22.

Ireland's Health Service Executive (HSE)
On May 14, the public authority association that runs all general wellbeing administrations in Ireland shut down IT frameworks in the wake of a critical ransomware assault, and activities presently cannot seem to get back to business as usual. While HSE frameworks were constrained disconnected as a prudent step in particular, and the National Ambulance Services were working as would be expected, admittance to numerous wellbeing administrations was disturbed. Since frameworks were not working obviously, patients experienced postponements and, sometimes, cancellations. It was not until June 30 that online enrollment for clinical cards was re-established. Moreover, medical services places requested that patients get paper archives since PC records were unavailable. In spite of the disturbances, Ireland's general wellbeing network said it would not pay the payment and neither would the government. However, there was proof that patient and staff data was gotten to in the digital assault and that a portion of the information was spilled. The association contains more than 100,000 workers, notwithstanding all patients it serves. Released individual information could incorporate names, addresses, contact telephone numbers, and email addresses. Clinical data could incorporate clinical records, notes, and treatment narratives.

13.4   Conclusion

Thus, we implemented successfully a malware detection model. We discuss the importance of the malware detection system in world perspective.

References

1. Cakir, B. and Dogdu, E., Malware classification using deep learning methods. *ACMSE*, Richmond, KY, US, 1–6, 2018.
2. Rathore, H., Agarwal, S., Sahay, S.K., Sewak, M., *Malware Detection Using Machine Learning and Deep Learning*, 2014.
3. Kumar, G.S. and Bagane, P., Detection of malware using deep learning techniques. *Int. J. Sci. Technol. Res.*, 9, 01, 1688 and 1691, January 2020.

4. Ganapathi, P. and Midhunchakkaravarthy, D., A survey on various security threats and classification of malware attacks, Vulnerabilities and Detection Techniques. *TIJCSA*, 2013.

5. Anusmita Ray Dr. Asoke Nath. Introduction to malware and malware analysis: A brief overview, *International Journal of Advance Research in Computer Science and Management Studies (IJARCSMS)*, 24–30 October 2016.

6. Saeed, M.A.H., Malware in computer systems: Problems and solutions. *IJID, International Journal of Advanced Computer Science and Applications (IJACSA)*, 11, 2, 2020.

7. Rathod, N. and Wankhade, S., An enhanced extreme learning machine model for improving accuracy, in: *Proceedings of Integrated Intelligence Enable Network and Computing*, Springer, pp. 613– 621.

8. Pream Sudha, R. Kowsalya, A survey on deep learning techniques, applications and challenges, *International Journal of Advance Research In Science And Engineering (IJARSE)* http://www.ijarse.com, 4, 3, 315 and 317, 2015.

9. Vijayanand, C.D. and Arunlal, K.S., Detection of malware using deep learning techniques, Garminla Sampath Kumar, Pooja Bagane (eds.) International Journal of Scientific & Technology Research, 9, 01, 1-5, 2020. ISSN 2277-8616.

10. Hama Saeed, M. A. Malware in computer systems: Problems and solutions. *International Journal on Informatics for Development (IJID)*, 9, 1, 1–8, 2020.

11. Mariga, G. and Kamiri, J.Research methods in machine learning: A content analysis, *International Journal of Computer and Information Technology*, (ISSN: 2279–0764), 10, 2, 78–91, March 2021.

12. Pandey, A.K., Khan, M.W., Tripathi, A.K., Agrawal, A., Kapli, G., Kumar, R., Singh, V., Khan, R.A., Trends in malware attacks: Identification and mitigation strategies, Research Gate, 2020.

13. Datta, A., Kumar, K.A., Aju, D. An emerging malware analysis techniques and tools: A comparative analysis, *International Journal of Engineering Research & Technology (IJERT)*, 10, 04, 111–117, April 2021.

14. Awan, M. J., Masood, O. A., Mohammed, M. A.,Yasin, A., Zain, A. M., Damaševicius, R. and Abdulkareem, K. H. Image-based malware classification using VGG19 network and spatial convolutional attention, 1-9, 8 October 2021. https://doi.org/10.3390/electronics10192444

15. Pratama, A. and Rafrastara, F.A., Computer worm classification. *IJCSIS*, 2020.

16. Nitish, A. and Hanumanthappa, J., Deep learning for malware analysis. *IJRECE*, 7, 2, 1197–1199, April-June 2019.

14

Patron for Women: An Application for Womens Safety

Riya Sil*, Snatam Kamila, Ayan Mondal, Sufal Paul, Santanu Sinha and Bishes Saha

Adamas University, Kolkata, India

Abstract

India—"The land of culture and diversity" is a name given to a nation that is home to several communities with distinct cultures and traditions. Despite of such rich background, the amount of violence against women has increased by many folds in the past few decades. Women's safety has become one of the major concerns in Indian society. Some of the foremost reasons for these crimes include societal pressure and shame that does not let women report to police, slow pace of operations in courts, police unable to locate the crime location on time, and many more. In this modern era, where the whole world is dependent on technology, an advanced system is required at the earliest as the cases involving women safety are increasing drastically. In recent years, the use of smartphones has increased rapidly, making it an imperative part of our daily life. In this paper, authors have proposed an application named "Patron for Women" to reduce the crime rate against women. The application stores the emergency contact details of the user while signing up. This information is used later on in emergency situation with a pre-loaded message. Another feature includes minimum number of clicks while sending GPS location to the contacts. The unique feature of this application is "gesture control" that reduces the consumption time in operating the application.

Keywords: Women safety, android application, GPS location, gesture control, privacy, location tracking, offline

**Corresponding author*: riyasil1802@gmail.com

Rajdeep Chakraborty, Anupam Ghosh, Jyotsna Kumar Mandal and S. Balamurugan (eds.) Convergence of Deep Learning In Cyber-IoT Systems and Security, (285–302) © 2023 Scrivener Publishing LLC

14.1   Introduction

The 21st century has seen a lot of change in the society that includes women being engaged in various activities alongside men where women have been equally contributing to the wellbeing of the society [1]. Even after such great contribution to the society, women are not being able to move freely due to harassment and sexual abuse [2] which is one of the major incidents of women empowerment. According to the National Crime Records Bureau (NCRB) report, in the year 2019, there has been an average of 87 rape cases per day and around 400,000 cases of crime against women during the year. Apart from this Delhi reported the highest number of harassment cases against women, i.e., over 430 cases [3]. This type of incident reported increased 7% from 2018 [4]. In this paper, authors have developed women's safety application named "Patron for Women" that ensures women's safety from danger and accordingly identifies the location of the person at the time of critical situation. The main purpose of this application is to provide safety to women during their critical safety situations. The application is operated in the following process. The user should keep the application turned on. The first page shows two options—sign-up and sign-in button. If the user is new to this app, she must register with her name, email id, and password. And if she is an existing user, then she might continue with her existing email-id and password for logging in. After sign up or log in there is three option which includes—Guardians' Details, Check Location and Emergency button. Whenever the user faces any unavoidable situation, she can press the emergency button and send the emergency message along with the current location to the registered contact person. And all this works both offline and online. The objective of this system is to develop a cost-effective GPS based women tracking system.

Section 14.2 states the background of the work. Section 14.3 focuses on the literature survey related to women safety application. Section 14.4 thoroughly explains our proposed methodology and its performance analysis. Section 14.5 discusses about the results and analysis. Section 14.6 concludes our paper with a direction to future scope of this research work.

14.2   Background Study

In the past few years, numerous researches have been performed for the prevention of crime against women using various technologies. Many researchers have created innovative applications to reduce this problem. One such innovation has been done by Narang *et al.* [5], who developed an application that includes sending updated location link message to the emergency contact person when the application is opened. GPS technology is used to track the location of the user, and a link is sent to emergency contacts. It provides continuous location tracing after every 30 seconds and shows the information of nearby police stations in case of greater danger if police protection is required. When the panic button is pressed, the camera will automatically switch-on and a snapshot is captured, which may be useful for further investigation. This app will need continuous access to the Internet for tracking location. Similarly, few other applications have been built for the safety of women, such as the VithU application [6], Street Safe application [7], Safetipin application [8], and many more. AESHS (Advanced Electronics System for Human Safety) [9] is a similar type of device that helps in victim's location tracking using GPS through application. Guardly [10] is application, developed with the intention of women safety. Few features include instant location and emergency hit providing victim's location to the selected contacts. For registration, one has to give details in profile sheet. These are few of the examples related to women safety applications developed to reduce the crime rate and protect women in the best way possible.

In this paper, the authors have designed an application and have tried to enhance by adding new features and remove the existing problems. The main objective of this application is to provide the user with an improved safety environment through smartphones/smart devices.

14.3   Related Research

In the related research section, authors have investigated on some of the existing applications that provide similar service to the society.

14.3.1   A Mobile-Based Women Safety Application (I safe App)

Mandapati *et al.* [11] have designed an application named "I safe App" that takes the name and contact number of the person as input with whom she wants to connect at the time of her emergency. Users are able to add multiple contacts in the emergency contact list. In case of any emergency, notification will be sent to the said contact list. As soon as the user press the provided SOS button, an emergency message will be sent to the respective contact person followed by the GPS location of the victim's mobile device.

The user will be able to make audio or video calls through this application. It also provides few necessary first aid precautions that needs to be taken during unavoidable situations. Continuous supply of Internet connection is required for the application to run smoothly.

14.3.2   Lifecraft: An Android-Based Application System for Women Safety

Khandekar *et al.* [12] have designed a system named "Lifecraft" where user login with their respective registered email id and password. User can provide up to three contact details of their choice manually. Each time the user starts the application by turning on the on/off button. The application starts by pressing SOS key or voice command and accordingly alert message is sent to the registered contacts that contains the user's name with their location. The location details of the victim is dynamic and, therefore, will be sent in every 5 minutes to their respective contacts so that the updated location of the victim can be tracked. Live streaming is done that provides the current position of the person to the registered contacts and also audio recording facility is there. For the first 5 minutes surrounding of the victim is captured for future use after receiving the SOS command. User can avail safe zone option where user can find nearby police stations through map. Also, the user can use offline mode feature to send alert messages. In this application if the users get any trouble in the network, then it will lead to a big problem since the message along with the location can only be sent through Internet connection, and if at all the Internet accessibility is not possible, then it will not provide the location.

14.3.3   Abhaya: An Android App for the Safety of Women

Yarrabothu *et al.* [10] developed another similar android application named "Abhaya" where the application will start working with a single click. Using GPS location can be identified and accordingly send location URL to registered contacts list and call the first registered contact for help in emergency situation. One of the significant features of this application is to send alert messages to the registered contact person continuously on every 5 minutes interval until the SOS button in the application is pressed. It provides with dynamic location service of the user for which stable Internet connection is required. Any trouble in the network will lead to discontinuation of location service since the only way to give the information to the registered number is through the Internet.

Table 14.1 Comparison table on the basis of certain parameters.

Apps name	Requires internet	Alert	Send SMS	Without internet
Lifecraft app	Yes	Yes	Yes	Yes but no map
ISafe app	Yes	Yes	Yes	No
Abhaya app	Yes	No	Yes	No
Sakhi—The Saviour app	Yes	Yes	Yes	No

14.3.4 Sakhi—The Saviour: An Android Application to Help Women in Times of Social Insecurity

Through this application, the location of the user should also be precisely known to the person to whom the message is sent [13]. This application includes sending updated location link messages to the emergency contact when the application is opened. GPS technology is used to track the location of the user, and a link is sent to emergency contacts [14]. It provides continuous location tracking for every 30 seconds. It shows the information of nearby police stations in case of greater danger and when the user needs police protection. When the panic button is pressed, the camera will turn on and a snapshot is captured which may be useful for further investigation. This app will need continuous access to the Internet for tracking location [15]. If the victim is in danger, it is not possible to touch the panic button to give alert. The problem can be reduced by providing SMS feature without the Internet and making app more comfortable to use.

As a part of literature review [16–19], we have investigated some applications of safety that already exist in the market. The main motive is to observe how these applications work and to see how they are different and how they can be improved [20].

Table 14.1 shows a basic comparison of various applications based on certain parameters that includes requirement of Internet, alert message, and others.

14.4 Proposed Methodology

In this section, authors have discussed about the proposed Android-based women safety application and provided a clear view of the design for the safety purpose of women.

Subsection 14.4.1 discusses about the motivation and objective of the proposed system. Subsection 14.4.2 provides a detailed view of the proposed system. Subsection 14.4.3 focuses on the System flowchart. Subsection 14.4.4 thoroughly explains the use-case models. Subsection 14.4.5 discusses about the novelty of the work. Subsection 14.4.6 compares the proposed system with the existing systems.

14.4.1 Motivation and Objective

Women safety has become a huge concern in today's society. 10% of all the crimes in India are those of women abuse. According to a report, in every 20 minutes, a woman is raped in India [21]. In this era of technology, almost every person has at least one smartphone.

Most of the women these days carry their Smartphones with them, so it is important to have one safety application installed in their Smartphones [22–24]. Our team members are going to develop one mobile application. Our main intention is to provide safety in the simplest way possible. Our motivation is to contribute something good for women. There will be some features in our application, like offline mode, gesture control, location tracking, messaging, etc., which is useful for women safety [25–28].

14.4.2 Proposed System

In this paper, authors have designed a system different from the existing applications that have been designed till date. The following steps are performed for using the proposed system: (i) The application named 'Patron for women' is downloaded in Android phone. (ii) In the welcome screen, user's email id needs to be confirmed after which the registration screen opens. (iii) The registration screen gives birth to two conditions, i.e., whether the user is already registered or not. If registered, further process will be held and if not, then the application exits and revisits the welcome screen. (iv) A warning/attention command appears for the permission to access Internet connection and current location of the device. (iv) A dashboard will open where operator's current location, add emergency contact number and emergency button will be displayed on the application screen. In case of any emergency situation, the user can activate the system by touching the emergency button or by operating the gesture control according to the operator's requirement. The application sends notification to all the emergency contact list via SMS or E-mail. The distance between both the operator and guardian are displayed on the guardian's side of the map in Km/m and operator will be helped as early as possible. Our application will also work in offline mode. Suppose due to some reasons if there is any network glitch then also the notification will be sent to the caregivers with the map link. But as the Internet is not working at that moment, it will send the emergency contact person the previous location whenever the Internet was working previously.

14.4.3   System Flowchart

The application can be activated in two ways: (i) Through the emergency button or SOS button in app. (ii) Through gesture on the screen of smartphone. When the emergency button or SOS button is pressed, the system checks whether the GPS is on or not accordingly the app will switch on the GPS location service if it is off. After the activation of the emergency button or SOS button, the app will send an alert message along with the location details of the victim to all the registered contacts. As a result, the victim will get help from the volunteers. The system flowchart of the model has been shown in Figure 14.1.

14.4.4   Use-Case Model

Figure 14.2 shows outline of the System Models. It is known as context diagrams, are the most basic data flow diagrams. It provides a broad view of the system with little details. Here it shows how any user authenticate themselves and send the emergency alert to her close one.

Figure 14.3 shows the separation of all external modules, relationship between those modules and the application. In level 1 data flow diagram, the single process node broken down into several subprocesses. The above figure shows the separation of all external modules, relationship between those modules and the application where it shows how all the details like registration, login, contact details, message details, location details go and store into the database which can help police to find the victim very easily.

Figure 14.4 shows differentiates the modules frontend and backend. simply break processes down into more detailed subprocesses. It is also an illustration of our application where it shows the main feature of our app that is the offline mode, which can help to send the alert message without Internet if she faces any network issues during her emergency time.

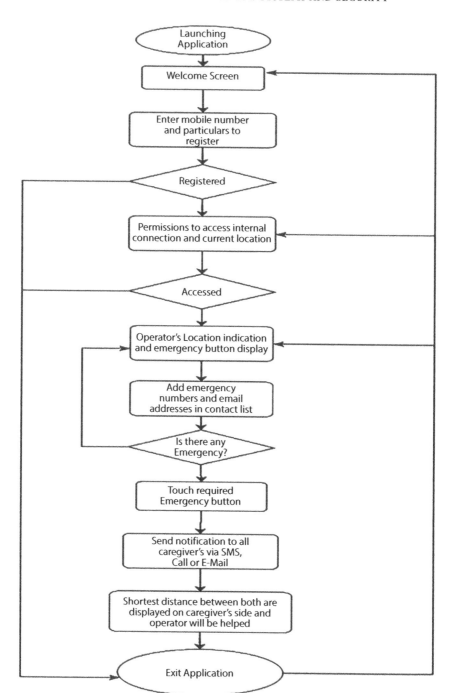

Figure 14.1 System flowchart of the model.

Figure 14.2 Outline of the system models.

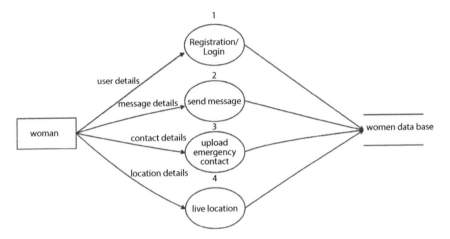

Figure 14.3 Separation of all external modules, relationship between those modules and the application.

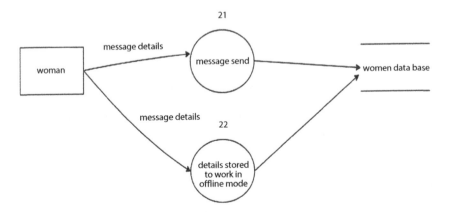

Figure 14.4 Differentiates the modules frontend and backend.

Table 14.2 Comparison table between various applications

Sl no.	Name	Advantages	Limitations
1	Safety Pin	Live GPS tracking, alert message with location URL	No offline mode, no gesture control system
2	Abhaya	Live GPS tracking	No offline mode, no gesture control system
3	I Go Safety	Works offline	No offline mode, no live GPS tracking, no gesture control system
4	Proposed System (PATRON FOR WOMEN)	Works offline, has gesture control feature, send alert message with location URL, live GPS tracking	-

14.4.5 Novelty of the Work

The main concern of this research is women's safety. One of the primary features of this application is that it can work both in online and offline mode. Using the location of the victim, assistance can be provided to them by volunteers and caregiver. Another highlighted and unique feature of this application includes alert message by the user through gestures when in unexpected trouble. Faster help is provided to the user as optimization of the application has been done, such that it can utilize all system resources efficiently and thus provide an expected, speedy outcome.

14.4.6 Comparison with Existing System

Below, in Table 14.2 authors have discussed about the advantages and limitations of various applications.

14.5 Results and Analysis

In this section, authors have provided few of the screenshots of the UI interfaces of the women safety application named "Patron for women." These figures will provide a clear view of the proposed system.

Figure 14.5 shows the signup form of the application. Here user has to provide e-mail, name and password. After filling the form, the details of the user will be saved into the database, which will later be used.

Figure 14.6 represents the screenshot of Login page in which the registered user can login and continue with the process.

Figure 14.7 depicts the User interface of our application. Here are "guardian details" where user can register the details of emergency contacts, in the field of "check location" user can check the location where is she right now, in the "emergency" section, if user faces any dangerous situation, she has to press the "emergency" button and alert message along with location of the user will be sent to the registered contacts.

Figure 14.8 represents the emergency contact details of the application. In the "add guardian" section, user has to provide the details of the Emergency contact. In the field of "guardian information" user can see and edit the details of the emergency contacts.

Figure 14.9 represents the current location of the user. By clicking on "check location" user can see her current location.

Figure 14.10 shows alert message with location URL.

Figure 14.5 Sign up form.

Figure 14.6 Login page.

Figure 14.7 UI interface.

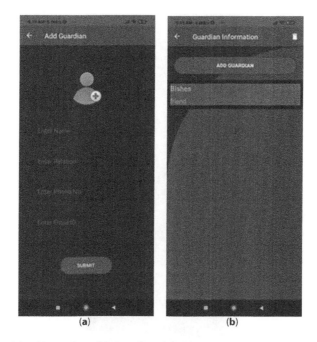

Figure 14.8 (a) Add guardian. (b) Guardian details.

Figure 14.9 Screenshot of current location.

Figure 14.10 Screenshot of alert message.

14.6   Conclusion and Future Work

In this section, authors have provided few of the screenshots of the UI interfaces of the proposed application named "Patron for Women" can reduce risk of women safety. Using a safety system, women can get quick support through safety application anytime whenever they are in danger. In this paper, authors have focused on providing security to its users by providing services based on location, SMS services and GPS service. This application can be the easier and faster way to provides the necessary safety and security to any individual in just few clicks who might face social threats and can prove to be a useful tool for women safety and Empowerment.

In future, the authors will launch a new role, i.e., caregiver role in the portal which will be a voluntary service. These caregivers can be the front liners beside the police. Once the user enables the SOS button, the emergency message is sent to the nearby police stations and the caregivers located in same area so that the victims can be located and helped on right time. Authors will also add a toll-free no for users in future without a smart phone so that they can register themselves in our portal with their contact no, name, emergency contacts. After registering, in case of any emergency situation dialing or messaging the toll-free number will lead to the tracking of every incident. Our team along with caregivers will collect the case report from the police and submit a final report of the case with declaration from victim and the guardian. To provide better security and convenience to the people, voice control and other accessibility features will be added in our application.

References

1. Rakesh, P.S., Women safety application using machine learning. *Int. J. Res. Appl. Sci. Eng. Technol.*, 9, 5, 1295–1303, 2021. https://doi.org/10.22214/ijraset.2021.34542.
2. Sil, R., Labib Chy, S.S., Bose, S., Kabir Mollick, H., A Study on interactive automated agent based response system over legal domain. *SSRN Electronic J.*, 50–57, 2021. https://doi.org/10.2139/ssrn.3768280.
3. ncrb.gov.in
4. The Wire, Average 87 rape cases daily, over 7% rise in crimes against women in 2019: NCRB Data, September 30 2020, https://thewire.in/women/average-87-rape-cases-daily-over-7-rise-in-crimes-against-women-in, 2019-ncrb-data, accessed on 10/06/2021
5. Narang, A., 'Help anytime anywhere': An android application providing help and safety. *Int. J. Psychosoc. Rehabil.*, 24, 4, 6532–6539, 2020. https://doi.org/10.37200/ijpr/v24i4/pr2020463.
6. Save, S., Gala, M., Patil, S., Kalbande, D.R., Applying human computer interaction to individual security using mobile application. *2015 International Conference on Communication, Information & Computing Technology (ICCICT)*, 2015, https://doi.org/10.1109/iccict.2015.7045691.
7. Chaudhari, P., Kamte, R., Kunder, K., Jose, A., Machado, S., 'Street smart': Safe Street app for women using augmented reality. *2018 Fourth International Conference on Computing Communication Control and Automation (ICCUBEA)*, 2018, https://doi.org/10.1109/iccubea.2018.8697863.
8. Viswanath, K. and Basu, A., SafetiPin: An innovative mobile app to collect data on women's safety in Indian cities. *Gend. Dev.*, 23, 1, 45–60, 2015. https://doi.org/10.1080/13552074.2015.1013669.
9. Harikiran, G.C., Menasinkai, K., Shirol, S., Smart security solution for women based on Internet of Things (IoT). *2016 International Conference on Electrical, Electronics, and Optimization Techniques (ICEEOT)*, 2016, https://doi.org/10.1109/iceeot.2016.7755365.
10. Yarrabothu, R.S. and Thota, B., Abhaya: An android app for the safety of women. *2015 Annual IEEE India Conference (INDICON)*, 2015, https://doi.org/10.1109/indicon.2015.7443652.

11. Mandapati, S., Pamidi, S., Ambati, S., A mobile based women safety application (I safe apps). *IOSR J. Comput. Eng. (IOSR-JCE)*, 17, 1, 29–34, 2015. https://doi.org/10.9790/0661-17112934.

12. Khandoker, R.R., Khondaker, S., Fatiha-Tus-Sazia, Nur, F.N., Sultana, S., Lifecraft: An android based application system for women safety. *2019 International Conference on Sustainable Technologies for Industry 4.0 (STI)*, 2019, https://doi.org/10.1109/sti47673.2019.9068024.

13. More, M.A., Gawade, M.K., Guled, M.P., Chippa, M.S., Galgurgi, M.V., Chinchawade, A., Sakhi-the saviour: An android application to help women in times of social insecurity. *Int. Res. J. Eng. Technol.*, 8, 564–568, 2021.

14. Hussain, S.M., Nizamuddin, S.A., Asuncion, R., Ramaiah, C., Singh, A.V., Prototype of an intelligent system based on RFID and GPS technologies for WOMEN safety. *2016 5th International Conference on Reliability, Infocom Technologies and Optimization (Trends and Future Directions) (ICRITO)*, 2016, https://doi.org/10.1109/icrito.2016.7784986.

15. Karakus, S. and Kucukkomurler, S., The application of women towards food safety. *TAF Prev. Med. Bull.*, 11, 6, 651, 2012. https://doi.org/10.5455/pmb.1-1324455613.

16. Prakash, N., Udayakumar, E., Kumareshan, N., Gowrishankar, R., GSM-Based design and implementation of women safety device using Internet of things, in: *Intelligence in Big Data Technologies—Beyond the Hype*, pp. 169–176, 2020, https://doi.org/10.1007/978-981-15-5285-4_16.

17. Chitkara, D., Sachdeva, N., Dev Vashisht, Y., Design of a women safety device. *2016 IEEE Region 10 Humanitarian Technology Conference (R10-HTC)*, 2016, https://doi.org/10.1109/r10-htc.2016.7906858.

18. Hebbar, R., Anisha, A., Hashiya, B., Chaithra, L., Kauser, F., Suraksha women safety device and application. *Int. J. Innov. Res. Electr. Electron. Instrum. Control Eng.*, 5, 5, 252–255, 2017. https://doi.org/10.17148/ijireeice.2017.5538.

19. Design and implementation of children safety system using IoT. *Int. J. Eng. Adv. Technol.*, 9, 4, 1422–1425, 2020. https://doi.org/10.35940/ijeat.d7345.049420.

20. Umamaheswari, K.M., A smart approach to provide the women safety by using smart security devices. *Int. J. Psychosoc. Rehabil.*, 24, 4, 4039–4045, 2020. https://doi.org/10.37200/ijpr/v24i4/pr201516.

21. Eeshwaroju, S., Ganesan, S., Praveena, J., Rakshak – An IoT based wearable device for women safety. *Int. J. Eng. Adv. Technol.*, 9, 4, 2068–2077, 2020. https://doi.org/10.35940/ijeat.d8758.049420.

22. Sarosh, M.Y., Yousaf, M.A., Javed, M.M., Shahid, S., MehfoozAurat. *Proceedings of the Eighth International Conference on Information and Communication Technologies and Development*, 2016. https://doi.org/10.1145/2909609.2909645.

23. Sarosh, M.Y., Yousaf, M.A., Javed, M.M., Shahid, S., MehfoozAurat. *Proceedings of the Eighth International Conference on Information and Communication Technologies and Development*, 2016. https://doi.org/10.1145/2909609.2909645.

24. Ceccato, V. and Loukaitou-Sideris, A., Fear of sexual harassment and its impact on safety perceptions in transit environments: A global perspective. *Violence Against Women*, 28, 2021. https://doi.org/10.1177/1077801221992874

25. Chand, D., Nayak, S., Bhat, K.S., Parikh, S., Singh, Y., Kamath, A.A., A mobile application for women's safety: Wosapp. *TENCON 2015 - 2015 IEEE Region 10 Conference*, 2015, https://doi.org/10.1109/tencon.2015.7373171.

26. Ogata, M., Guttman, B. and Hastings, N., Public safety mobile application security requirements workshop summary, NIST Interagency/Internal Report (NISTIR), National Institute of Standards and Technology, Gaithersburg, MD, 2015 [online], https://doi.org/10.6028/NIST.IR.8018

27. Prashanth, D.S., Patel, G., Bharathi, B., Research and development of a mobile based women safety application with real-time database and data-stream network. *2017 International Conference on Circuit, Power and Computing Technologies (ICCPCT)*, 2017, https://doi.org/10.1109/iccpct.2017.8074261.

28. Fernando, M.C., Streetwatch: A mobile application for street crime incident avoidance and safety solution. *TENCON 2015 - 2015 IEEE Region 10 Conference*, 2015, https://doi.org/10.1109/tencon.2015.7372756.

15

Concepts and Techniques in Deep Learning Applications in the Field of IoT Systems and Security

Santanu Koley* and Pinaki Pratim Acharjya

Department of Computer Science and Engineering, Haldia Institute of Technology, Haldia, India

Abstract

Deep learning (DL), a subdivision of machine learning (ML), i.e., an integral part of artificial intelligence used in various applications in today's life. At present, machine learning approach is almost completely dependent on DL techniques, which produce accurate results with the help of human centric nature of learning. It has gone off in the community awareness, mostly as extrapolative and analytical products that saturate our planet in most useful, organized, and time- and cost-competent method of ML approach. There are some algorithms, like generative adversarial networks, multilayer perceptions, convolution neural networks, or self-organizing maps, that have entirely changed the thinking toward information processing means. Currently, DL is using in numerous domains like knowledge, commerce, science, administration sectors; it can be employed on novel corona virus prediction, detection, and analysis of clinical and method logical characteristics too is also a matter of discussion here. Our work is absolutely displays on the notion of crucial sophisticated design, method, inspirational characteristics and constraint of DL. This writing section describes a detailed analysis of chronological and modern trailblazing approaches to the distribution of conjecture, myth, and text; social network analysis; and innovative advances in natural language processing, extensive research around spin, and in-depth learning activities. The main target of this work is to describe the newly developed DL techniques for Internet of Things (IoT) architecture and its security. IoT security threats associated with the underlying or newly introduced threat are talked about and diverse possible IoT system attacks and probable threats connected to all facets are thrashed out.

---

*Corresponding author: santanukoley@yahoo.com

Rajdeep Chakraborty, Anupam Ghosh, Jyotsna Kumar Mandal and S. Balamurugan (eds.) Convergence of Deep Learning In Cyber-IoT Systems and Security, (303–348) © 2023 Scrivener Publishing LLC

The possibilities, advantages, and limitations of both systems are illustrated systematically by analyzing the DL strategy aimed at IoT security. We provide perspectives and related issues regarding IoT security from ML/DL. Discussed approaches and problems of potential expectations can serve as research guidelines for the future endeavor.

Keywords: Deep learning (DL), Internet of Things (IoT), machine learning (ML)

15.1 Introduction

Current developments in communication technology, e.g., the IoT has strangely surpassed the conventional theoretical concept of the neighboring atmosphere. Rapid growth of several technical features of wireless sensor networks (WSN), Mobile Communications, Radio-Frequency Identification (RFID), and numerous lightweight protocols recommend the idea of the IoT. The basic principle of IoT self-transmitted interconnections of billions of varied elements or objects revolve everywhere. The ecosystem transmits wired or wireless through intelligent support Sensors, actuators and additional components. These elements intertwine to create the state of things and, therefore, give people around the world a huge amount of money back and easy. IoT technology can enable modernization that improves quality of life [1] and the ability to integrate, calculate and recognize neighboring atmospheres. This situation facilitates innovative communication between things and individuals and therefore strengthens the consciousness of smart cities [2]. The numbers indicate that the IoT market (as a combination of SaaS, Connectivity, Devices, etc.) gained about $222 billion in 2021, opened with just $2 billion in 2006 then is projected towards $318 billion in 2023 [3]. The results of this computerization have established the existence of clever and intellectual subjects, as a result of which a strategy has been identified in all domains: smart city, healthcare, finance, manufacturing, academia, etc. The application of IoT with the implementation of ratios on various grounds is presented in Figure 15.1 [3].

IoT is, as a result, the integration of diverse technologies at multiple levels, consisting of a wide range of frequent and continuous computing optimizations across different sub-regions. The cross-cutting and large-sized nature of the IoT system has announced new security challenges in the complex components of various systems. IoT systems understand versatility and integration systems. As a result, maintaining security obligations in the event of an external outbreak of the IoT system is a matter of

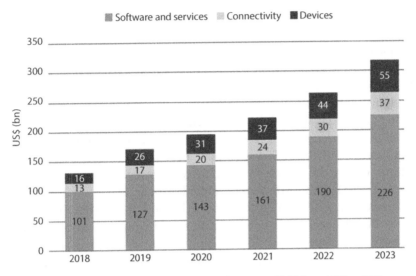

Figure 15.1 Previous and predictive data about the usage of IoT from 2018 to 2023.

concern. Resolution requirements include full discussion to satisfy security preconditions. Nevertheless, IoT devices usually endeavor in an unnecessary environment. Thus, an interlocutor can significantly recognize such mechanisms. IoT systems are traditionally coupled to a wireless network wherever a trespasser can hear additional information against a communiqué channel. IoT equipment cannot specify their partial calculations and power resources for multitasking assemblies [4].

IoT's complex security framework includes not just restricted computing, correspondence then power resources then again reliable collaboration through a physical area, especially the behavior of a physical setting in indefinite and volatile means, Since the IoT scheme is similarly a piece of an Internet-based physical structure; Initially, IoT schemes necessarily continue then survive as a priority through security in a special and possible way, especially in the vicinity where health-threatening situations may arise [5]. In addition, the new facial attack surface is presented through IoT atmosphere. This type of attack is triggered with code-dependent as well as compatible environment of external IoT. Therefore, security risks are higher in IoT arrangements in comparison to additional structure of computing. Conventional resolutions might remain useless for this type of structure [6].

ML as well as DL may be common approaches to investigate the data to study around 'usual' as well as 'unusual' compression, referring towards what manner IoT mechanisms then gadgets relate to each other in the IoT atmosphere. The data to be taken as input for the individual parts of the IoT structure perhaps designed as well, also searched for standard design control of communication, thus recognizing poor performance in the early stages. In addition, ML/DL approaches can be significant in anticipation of new outbreaks, which often translate to earlier intrusion, since they can anticipate the coming unknown event through knowledge after the conventional parable. Accordingly, the requirements of the IoT system have evolved to enable secure declarations within the device from security-oriented intellect empowered through the DL and ML method aimed at operative besides protected schemes only. Although basically a section of DL ML, this paper delivers to the reader in their two separate parts through in-depth analysis, inclusive assessment and possible application of mutually traditional theoretical ML as well as DL approaches meant for IoT protection [7, 8]. Figure 15.2 demonstrations a confined classification [9] of ML and DL designed for IoT safekeeping and Figure 15.3 demonstrates basic deep learning concepts.

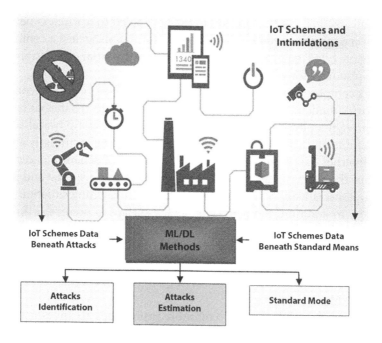

Figure 15.2 Probable appearance of ML/DL approaches in IoT safekeepings.

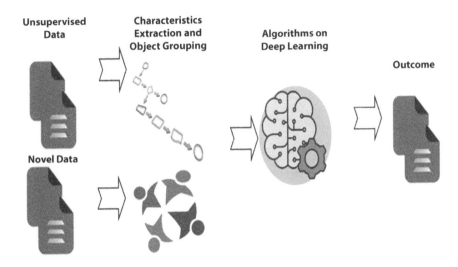

Figure 15.3 Basic deep learning concepts.

15.2   Concepts of Deep Learning

DL is a subcategory of Artificial Intelligence (AI) which is a ML procedure which educates the logical operation of computers and devices. DL derives from the name that it penetrates deeply into numerous layers of the network, including a secret layer. The much deeper one can dive; Added compound information can be extracted. DL strategies rely on a variety of composite programs to replicate the intelligence just like human beings. These distinct processes teach computers to design consequential designs and are thus categorized into different types. Pattern recognition is an important component of DL, besides credit to ML; Computers do not require any widespread programming. During DL, the machines may engage in image, text or audio files to perform then act upon a few tasks in a human-like manner.

Some of the industrial applications of DL may include virtual assistants, chatbots, healthcare, entertainment, news aggregation, composing music, image coloring, robotic, image captioning, advertising, etc. If properly organized computers can efficiently replicate human performance within a given period of time, produce special results. DL emphasizes repetitive learning approaches that uncover machines to massive sets of data. As such, it assists computers recognize qualities and adapt to change. Supports recurring identification changes of data sets, understands the causes and spreads a reliable data conclusion. DL is currently advancing for more

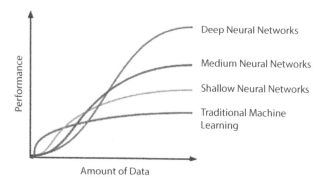

Figure 15.4 Basic deep learning concepts.

reliable development with compound functions. It is not surprising that this particular region is collecting a lot of significant, thus gaining a lot of attraction by emerging experts.

DL is an important aspect of human life today as it is gaining increasing acceptance around the world. It makes daily life more convenient than before, furthermore; it will increase in the future, whether it's a self-driving car or DL aspect of language recognition is driving numerous computerizations in the present era. Nevertheless, the significance of DL can be maximized with the statistics that the world today is producing an indicative amount of data, which requires a large-scale structure. DL uses increasing volume and accessibility of information is most appropriately used. All data formed from this data are accustomed to achieve 100% accurate results completed by repetitive learning prototypes.

Frequent analysis of large datasets eliminates errors and inconsistencies in judgments that ultimately lead to a consistent estimate. DL will endure to make an impression both commercially and individually and create lots of job opportunities in the future. Figure 15.4 shows basic deep learning concepts.

15.3   Techniques of Deep Learning

There are some complex problems that are very difficult for the human brains. Various aspects of the DL method remain equally accurate and operative in dealing with such complications. Here's how diverse kinds DL Methods cast-off:

15.3.1   Classic Neural Networks

Classic neural network (CNN) is also recognized as fully connected neural networks (FCNN) that frequently acknowledged through the issue of multilayer perceptions, wherever neurons remain associated at uninterrupted levels. It was designed in 1958 by the American psychologist Fran Rosenblatt [9]. Besides input and output layers, there are hidden layers exists. Figure 15.5 below describes the story.

This includes the transformation of the model to the required binary data contribution. This model involves three functions [10], namely:

15.3.1.1   *Linear Function*

To be correct, it identifies a solitary row that multiplies the input by an unchangeable factor.

15.3.1.2   *Nonlinear Function*

Any conclusion in use is necessarily non-linear in nature. Contrasting a decision means diversity, as well as following one of them. Additional options in the decision position are unexpectedly closed. Thus, it is not

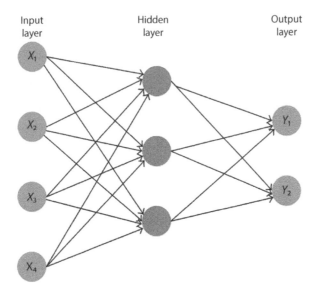

Figure 15.5 Basic architecture of classic three-layer neural network.

surprising that neural networks are essential for non-linearity, as they have to make decisions to control the flow of calculations.

15.3.1.3   Sigmoid Curve

This is a capacity that makes an interpretation from 0 to 1 as a S-molded bend between its sections. The exaggerated digression (tanh) notices to the S-molded bend which differs from −1 toward 1 [11].

15.3.1.4   Rectified Linear Unit

Rectified linear unit (ReLU) is a solitary point work that profits 0 if the information cost is not exactly the predefined esteem along these lines making a straight numerous if the info esteem is more prominent than the predetermined worth. The best way to deal with some table datasets is to design lines and segments in CSV arrangement and issue relapse by genuine expense input [12]. Any model is best with maximum flexibility, just like Artificial Neural Networks (ANNs).

15.3.2   Convolution Neural Networks

Convolution Neural Network (CNN) is a modern then immense conceivable sort of normal ANN model. Subsequently, intended to address more noteworthy complexity, preprocessing and information total. It holds references after the succession of neurons exist in the visual cortex of a creature's cerebrum.

It [13] perhaps measured as the highly effective adaptable model for concentrating in image along with non-pictorial information. There are following associations (as shown in Figure 15.6 also):

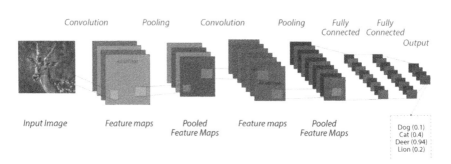

Figure 15.6 Convolution neural networks (CNN) working procedure.

i. It consists of a solitary input layer, usually a 2D collection of neurons meant for data analysis of the main image, which is related to the pixels of the image.

ii. Some CNNs have a 1D surface (layer) of the final product neuron that processes digital photos at inputs via an extended linked dividing surface area.

iii. CNNs additionally have a third layer, perceived as an example layer, to tie the quantity of neurons in the equivalent network layers.

iv. For the most part, CNNs have single or different associated layers that convey the example to the final yield layer.

This network model can assist and extract suitable data about image in a method of fewer components or parts. As soon as the data to be taken as input is introduced into the convolutional model, there are four phases associated with the formation of CNN:

15.3.2.1   Convolution

The technique produces include maps from input information, followed by a capacity that chips away at this guide.

15.3.2.2   Max-Pooling

This assists CNN understand an image built on specific variations.

15.3.2.3   Flattening

Therefore, the data engendered is then compressed for a CNN to examine. Therefore, the data generated for a CNN test are compressed.

15.3.2.4   Full Connection

This is over and again assigned as a secret layer that joins the misfortune work for a model.

CNNs with picture identification, picture investigation, picture division, video examination, and normal language handling are adequate for obligation. On the other hand, where the CNN network can be a valuable estimate, there may be additional settings:

Photo datasets revolve around OCR document analysis at this moment. One-dimensional can be added by changing any two-dimensional input data for quick analysis. The model wants to be concerned with its structural design in order to produce the output.

15.3.3   Recurrent Neural Networks

Recurrent neural networks (RNNs) are primarily conceived to aid the prediction sequence. This type of networks relies completely on arrangements of data of variable input spans as shown in Figure 15.7.

RNN determines [14] the acquired information as an input value for existing estimates as opposed to its previous class. Therefore, it very well may be gainful to acquire momentary memory in an organization, impact the employable authority of stock value deviations, or extra time-arranged information plans.

There are two common types of RNN techniques work extensively to assess a problem. Such type of systems namely:

15.3.3.1   LSTMs

They are convenient to predict data in time progressions through memory. The input, output and forget are three different gates.

15.3.3.2   Gated RNNs

They are similarly valuable in anticipating information of time arrangements through memory. The first is an update and the second is a reset within the dual gates.

RNNs work finest within:

i.   One to one: A sole input associated with only output, such as an image organization.

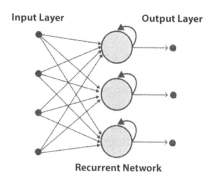

Figure 15.7 Recurrent neural network (RNN) structure.

    ii.   One to many: The solitary input is associated with the output frameworks, identified with picture inscribing that contains various contentions from a sole picture.

   iii.   Many to one: A grouping of data sources that produce a solitary output, for instance: word feeling order.

   iv.   Many to many: Succession of data sources creating legacy of outputs like video recording. It rehearses language interpretation, discussion displaying just as more widely.

15.3.4   Generative Adversarial Networks

Generative Adversarial Network is an intersection of two DL techniques for neural organizations, to be specific: a generator and a discriminator. Albeit the generator network gathers counterfeit data, the discriminator administrations segregate among real and wrong information.

Commonly networks are feasible [15], in light of the fact that the generator creates fake information separate from the genuine information - other than the discriminator sees interminably genuine just as incredible information without segregation (Figure 15.8). There are circumstances where the need to make a library of images is vital, the generator organization will make recreated information in solid pictures. A short time later, a de-convolution neural organization is made.

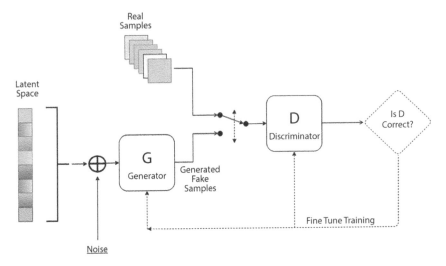

Figure 15.8 Recurrent Neural Network (RNN) structure.

Here, an image detector network is introduced to distinguish among original then bogus images. Initially through an attempt of 50% exactness, the detector wants to establish the value of its cataloging because the generator will make its artificial image improved within generations. Such competition will complete the subsidy on the efficiency and speed of the network.

These drives are finest in image and text formation, improvement of images, innovative drug detection methods.

15.3.5   Self-Organizing Maps

Self-organized maps (SOMs) as shown in Figure 15.9 are unproven data support efforts that reduce the quantity of arbitrary variables within a prototypical. The output quantity is mobile as a two-dimensional model, since the individual synapses are connected to its i/o nodes.

Since the individual data points participate in the model illustration, SOM [16] keeps track of the weight of the adjacent nodes or the Best Matching Units (BMUs). Built near the BMU, the value for the weight deviates. Since weights are recognized like a property of a node, the cost indicates the place where the node is placed within network.

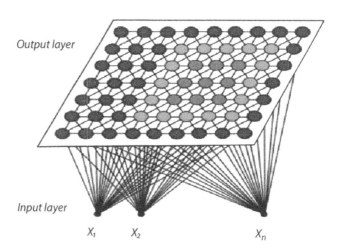

Figure 15.9 Basic model of self-organizing map neural network.

15.3.6   Boltzmann Machines

Aforementioned network model does not appear in either determined order then as a result the nodes are linked in a rounded pattern [17] as shown in the figure. From such uniqueness, these DL methods are produced model limitations. Unlike its predecessors in the fully determinant network model, the Boltzmann machine model is (shown in Figure 15.10) characterized as stochastic.

It makes relentless efforts in monitoring the system, introducing binary endorsement platforms, detailed dataset analysis, step-by-step approach to AI structure formation.

15.3.7   Deep Reinforcement Learning

Such learning denotes the method where an agent reaches out with the environment for considering the state of deep reinforcement learning to adjust its state. Agents can be witnesses and fair measures, as a result, help agents give a network its purpose through state cooperation [18] as shown in Figure 15.11.

This network model contains an input layer, an output layer, then various secret layers, while the condition of the actual surrounding is the input layer. Such model endeavor in a consistent work to expect the approaching compensation of individual accomplishment held in the circumstance accepted. It attempts its best in board games namely chess, poker, self-drive vehicles, mechanical technology, stock administration, resource evaluating and so forth.

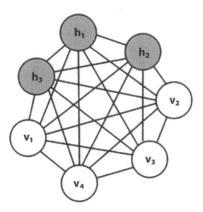

Figure 15.10 Boltzmann machine.

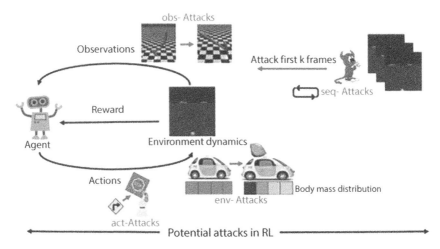

Figure 15.11 Deep reinforcement learning.

15.3.8 Auto Encoders

Among the highest level of regular routine areas for the DL practice, this model works mechanically remain on its bits of feedbacks, already satisfying an enactment capacity and completing yield deciphering [19]. Along these lines, building up a boundary peril creates less sorts of information and augments the increase of the inward information structure shown in Figure 15.12.

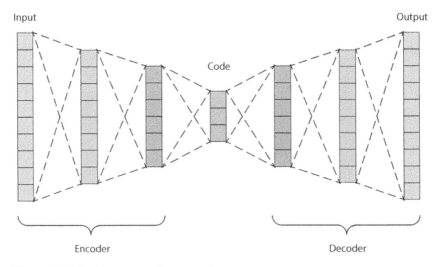

Figure 15.12 Basic structure of auto encoder.

There are different kinds of auto-encoders as shown in Figure 15.13:

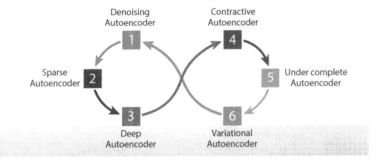

Figure 15.13 Different types of autoencoder.

15.3.8.1 Sparse

Where secret layers surpass the input level produces space to diminish over fitting with the objective of speculation. This confines the expense work, accordingly totally keeps away from the auto encoder in the wake of exaggerating its hubs.

15.3.8.2 Denoising

Now, an advanced type of input is randomly converted to 0.

15.3.8.3 Contractive

It is adding a penalty factor to the damage function for over fitting the hidden layer and copying the data to hide the input layer.

15.3.8.4 Stacked

In an autoencoder, when additional hidden layers are added, it takes two stages of encoding at one stage of decoding.

It makes the best effort in character identification, establishes a mandatory recommendation model, and improves the structure of huge datasets.

15.3.9 Back Propagation

In DL, the back-prop method is mentioned by way of a necessary tool for neural networks to find little mistakes in data estimates. Propagation, alternatively, refers to the communication of data in a certain way through a devoted network. The whole structure can strive to deliver signals in the

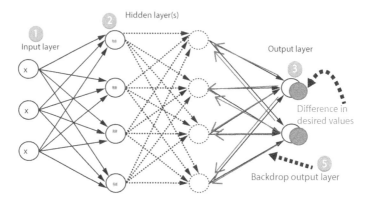

Figure 15.14 Back-prop procedure.

way of instantaneous progress of the conclusion and in contrast leads behind any data related to the limitations of the network (Figure 15.14).

Initially, the network evaluates the constraints and resolves the data, next, it is weighed by a loss function, thirdly, the recognized error is propagated backwards to self-adjust any inappropriate constraints. It tries its finest in data debugging.

15.3.10   Gradient Descent

A gradient mention to an opal that has quantifiable perceptions then might point to an association between variables in a mathematical context. In this method of DL, the connection between the errors that occurred with the data parameter in the neural network perhaps identified as "x" then "y." Variables are already changing frequently in a neural network, so the error may be magnified otherwise reduced by small size deviations (Figure 15.15).

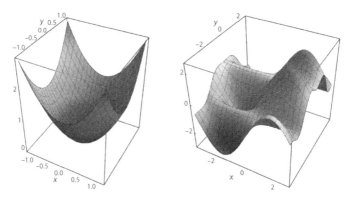

Figure 15.15 Gradient descent with dimensions.

Numerous experts have envisioned the method as a stream route coming down the approach gradient. A similar strategy is to get the neutral best resolution. Subsequently some local minimum resolutions exist in a neural network, where data can be stuck then slowly, leading to inappropriate storage. There is a practice of refraining from such measures.

15.4   Deep Learning Applications

This segment defines the basis of this discussion on a number of grounds that are realistic with the DL algorithm.

15.4.1   Automatic Speech Recognition (ASR)

Google has publicized that Google Voice Search has improved its services, using Deep Neural Networks (DNN) in 2012 as a necessary technology to model words in a language. DNN has exchanged Gaussian blending models that have been in the industry for 30 years. Similarly, DNN has shown that it is more intelligent to measure what words a user is generating at each prompt in a timely manner, and by doing so, they clearly bring enhanced speech recognition accuracy as shown in Figure 15.16.

In 2013, DL ASR and ML together increased the total pair. DL is primarily related to the practice of different levels of non-linear revolution for the production of speech structures, although there are examples-based figure exercises for speech structures through thin layer learning that have high levels but are characteristically empty.

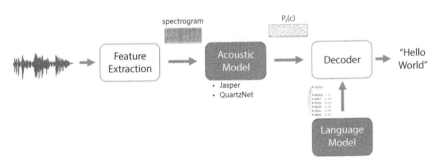

Figure 15.16 An automatic speech recognition (ASR) technique.

15.4.2   Image Recognition

Deep max-pooling involuntary neural networks are practiced to understand mitosis in breast histology images as shown in Figure 15.17. Mitosis is really hard to recognize. Indeed, mitosis is a compound process in which the nucleus of a cell undergoes numerous changes. In this style, DNN is used as a conventional pixel classifier that enables raw pixel values and does not require any human input. Subsequently, DNN inevitably acquires a set of graphic structures from the training data. DNN knowingly overcomes a completely challenging system through a well-established and controlled computational effort on a widely accessible dataset: a typical laptop has insufficient minutes to process a 4MPixel image.

The ImageNet LSVRC-2010 Encounter completes a large and deep CNN to categorize 1.2 million high-resolution images into 1000 diverse categories. According to the assessment data, they have accomplished top 1 and top 5 error rates of 37.5% and 17.0%, which have improved significantly in earlier practices. From all tests, introduction of faster GPUs as well as use of larger datasets can enhance the results.

15.4.3   Natural Language Processing

Nowadays, an assortment of language and information retrieval applications uses DL methods in a large scale as shown in Figure 15.18.

Utilizing deep architecture, DL techniques hide structures from training information and features are suitable for any work of different levels of abstraction. A succession of deep structured semantic models (DSSM)

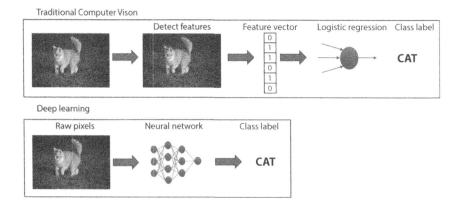

Figure 15.17 Traditional vs. DL image recognition technique.

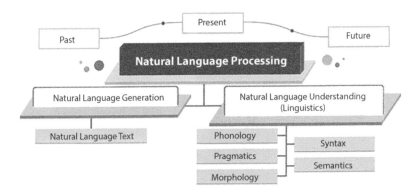

Figure 15.18 Basic structure of natural language processing.

was planned for Web search was introduced in 2013. Precisely, the use of DNN to rank several credentials (documents) for a specific query described here:

Initially, a nonlinear scheme is achieved so that the query can be mapped to a shared semantic space alongside the document. Previously, specified the importance of specific documents, the query was designed as cosine parallels among their vectors in that semantic space.

Neural network presentation is individually very efficient. They use click-through data as a temporary possibility of the document being clicked. Here it is given that the question is capitalized as required. New models in a web document position job are evaluated through an attested and actual data set.

15.4.4   Drug Discovery and Toxicology

Quantitative structure analysis/predictive analysis (QSAR/QSPR) are an attempt to formulate mathematical models related to the physical and chemical properties of composites in their chemical composition (Figure 15.19). Multi-task learning is effective for QSAR using several neural network presentations. They utilized a counterfeit neural organization to con- centrate on a capacity that anticipated the activity of a composite for a long time simultaneously. The plan has been joined through elective procedures and has recently been depicted to represent those neural organizations, including performing various tasks, which can convey provocative great outcomes in the pattern of shapes through irregular forest.

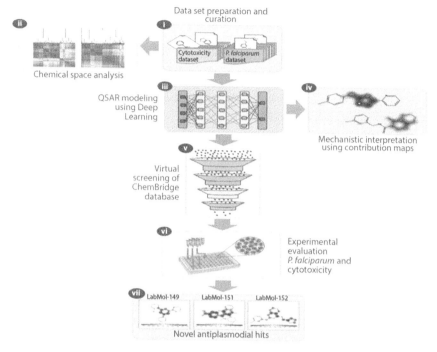

Figure 15.19 Steps of drug discovery using DL.

In 2015, AtomNet has been presented as unique construction-based, profound CNN which intended to anticipate the bioactivity of little particles for drug disclosure submissions. This paper additionally shows how to apply the convolutional ideas of component area and various leveled structure to the demonstrating of bioactivity and compound communications. AtomNet outflanks past docking approaches on an assorted arrangement of benchmarks by a huge degree, accomplishing an AUC more noteworthy than 0.9 on 57.8% of the objectives in the DUDE standard.

15.4.5   Customer Relationship Management

A structure for independent control of a client relationship, the board framework been outlined. Initially, an altered adaptation of the broadly acknowledged Recency-Frequency-Monetary Value arrangement of measurements can be utilized to characterize the state space of customers or givers are investigated. Second, a strategy to decide the ideal direct promoting activity in discrete and nonstop activity space for the given individual, in view of his situation in the state space is portrayed.

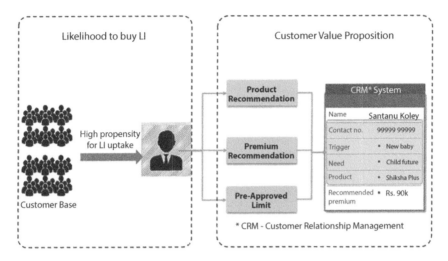

Figure 15.20 Customer relationship management in DL.

The system includes the utilization of sans model Q-figuring out how to prepare a profound neural organization that joins a customer's situation in the state space to accolades related with conceivable advertising exercises. The assessed esteem work over the customer state space can be deciphered as client lifetime esteem (CLV), and subsequently considers a fast module assessment of CLV for a given customer. Test results are introduced, in light of knowledge discovery and data mining tools competition, mailing dataset of gift requesting as shown in Figure 15.20.

15.4.6   Recommendation Systems

Programmed music suggestion has turned into an undeniably important issue as of late, since a ton of music is presently sold and devoured carefully. Most recommender frameworks depend on collective sifting. In 2013, proposed to utilize an idle factor model for suggestion, and anticipate the inert variables from music sound when they can't be gotten from utilization information. Conventional methodology is looked at utilizing sack of-words portrayal of the sound signs with profound convolutional neural organizations, and the expectations is assessed by quantitatively and subjectively on the Million Song Dataset. The outcome shows that the new advances in DL make an interpretation of to the music proposal setting, with profound convolutional neural organizations essentially outflanking the conventional methodology as shown in Figure 15.21.

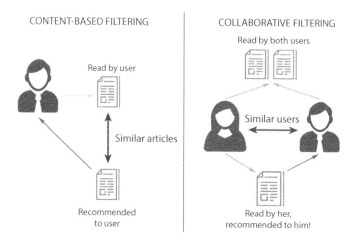

CONTENT-BASED FILTERING

Read by user

Similar articles

Recommended
to user

COLLABORATIVE FILTERING

Read by both users

Similar users

Read by her,
recommended to him!

Figure 15.21 Recommendation system structure in DL.

Ongoing Internet-based administrations depend vigorously on programmed personalization to prescribe significant substance to an enormous number of clients. This expects frameworks to scale quickly to oblige the flood of new clients visiting the web-based administrations interestingly. In 2015 proposed a substance-based suggestion framework to address both the proposal quality and the framework adaptability. They additionally proposed to utilize a rich list of capabilities to address clients, as indicated by their web perusing history and search inquiries. They utilize a DL way to deal with map clients and things to a dormant space where the similitude among clients and their favored things is expanded. Versatility investigation show that the multi-view DNN model can without much of a stretch scale to incorporate large number of clients and billions of thing passages.

15.4.7   Bioinformatics

The explanation of genomic data is a significant test in science and bioinformatics. Existing information bases of realized quality capacities are deficient and inclined to mistakes, and the bimolecular analyses expected to further develop these data sets are slow and expensive. While computational strategies are not a substitute for trial confirmation, they can help in two ways: calculations can support the duration of quality explanations via naturally proposing errors, and they can anticipate beforehand unidentified quality capacities, speeding up the pace of quality capacity disclosure as shown in Figure 15.22.

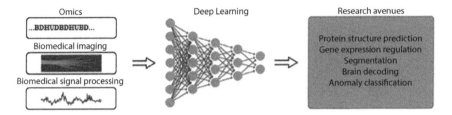

Figure 15.22 Bioinformatics in DL.

The objective utilizing profound auto encoder neural organizations is created. With probes quality explanation information from the Gene Ontology project, it shows that profound auto encoder networks accomplish preferred execution over other standard AI techniques, including the famous shortened particular worth deterioration.

15.5   Concepts of IoT Systems

Basically, the Internet of Things is the idea of associating any gadget (insofar as it has an on/off change) to the Internet and to other associated gadgets. The IoT is a goliath organization of associated things and individuals—all of which gather and offer information about the manner in which they are utilized and about the climate around them.

That incorporates an unprecedented number of objects, everything being equal, and sizes – from brilliant microwaves, which consequently cook your nourishment for the right timeframe, to self-driving vehicles, whose complicated sensors recognize objects in their way, to wearable wellness gadgets that action your pulse and the quantity of steps you've required that day, then, at that point, utilize that data to propose practice plans customized to you. There are even associated footballs that can follow how far and quick they are tossed and record those measurements by means of an application for future preparing purposes.

Gadgets and items (Figure 15.23) with worked in sensors are associated with an Internet of Things stage, which incorporates information from the various gadgets and applies investigation to impart the most important data to applications worked to address explicit requirements.

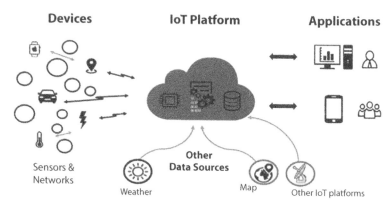

Figure 15.23 IoT platform with devices and applications.

These incredible IoT stages can pinpoint precisely what data is valuable and what can securely be overlooked. This data can be utilized to recognize designs, make proposals, and identify potential issues before they happen. For instance, on the off chance that I own a vehicle fabricating business, I should know which discretionary parts (calfskin seats or combination wheels, for instance) are the most famous. Utilizing Internet of Things innovation, I can: use sensors to distinguish which regions in a display area are the most famous, and where clients wait longest; drill down into the accessible deals information to recognize what parts are selling quickest; automatically adjust deals information to supply, so well-known things do not leave stock. The data by associated gadgets empower me to settle on shrewd choices concerning what parts to load up on, in light of continuous data, which assists me with setting aside time and cash.

With the insight provided by advanced analytics comes the power to make processes more efficient. Smart objects and systems mean you can automate certain tasks, particularly when these are repetitive, mundane, time-consuming or even dangerous. Let us look at some examples to see what this looks like in real life.

15.6 Techniques of IoT Systems

15.6.1 Architecture

The essential part of an operating system is the kernel. The organization of the kernel consists of the OS structure that impacts both the size of the application programs and the manner in which it provides services. Some familiar operating system architectures are monolithic, modular, micro-kernel and layered. Monolithic has a single huge process. It runs solely in a single address space of memory, and it does not have any specific structure. In this type of architecture, the services are applied separately, and each service presents an interface for others. The cost of monolithic OS module is low, therefore, the system is difficult to understand and maintain. Another problem of monolithic kernel is that the code is too long and complex, therefore, it is difficult to configure and understand. Because this type OS architecture is unreliable, it is not a good choice for IOT devices.

The architecture of microkernel has a simple structure. Microkernel architecture has separate process which is known as server. Some servers operate in user-space while others operate in kernel space. A microkernel is the best choice for many embedded operating systems. It is due to the tiny size of kernel and small number of context switches. Due to minimum functionalities the kernel size is reduced significantly. Moreover, this type of architecture offers higher reliability, customization and ease of expansion since most of the OS features, such as time and memory server, are delivered via user-level servers.

The modular architecture is, however, much better than monolithic, because a single module failure does not result in a complete system crash. The layered architecture method is less modular than the microkernel method. It is more stable and less complex than the monolithic kernel.

15.6.2   Programming Model

The programming model decides how the program can be modeled by an application developer. Typical programming models can be split into event-driven and multithreaded schemes for IoT operating systems. An external event like an interrupt must trigger each job in an event-driven scheme as shown in Figure 15.24.

A multi-threaded programming system offers the chance to interact between the functions using an interprocess communication (IPC) and to perform each job in its own thread context. The programming language should be developed in such a way that programmers can use the system efficiently. The selection of programming model is influenced by many variables as shown in Figure 15.25.

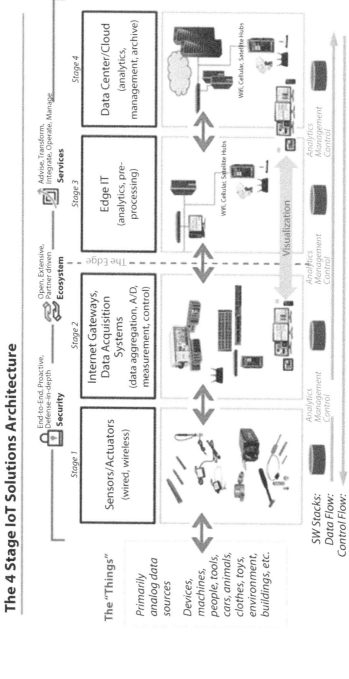

Figure 15.24 Different stages of IoT Architecture.

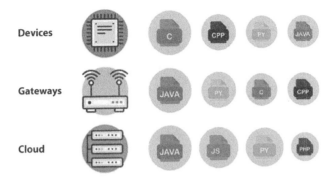

Figure 15.25 IoT programming model.

Particularly parallelism, hierarchy of memory and competition decide which model to use. The model of programming in turn impacts the efficiency and productivity of the scheme. Assembly language is the finest hardware interface option, but high-level language support is required to render it easy to create. However, it is difficult to provide high-level languages on restricted platforms.

15.6.3   Scheduling Policy

Scheduling strategy is the main factor that determines system performance. The scheduling algorithm depends on the latency (response time, turnaround time), performance, energy efficiency, real-time capacities, fairness and waiting time. Two kinds of schedulers are available, i.e., preemptive and cooperative. Preemptive scheduler is the one that allocates CPU time to each task while in cooperative model different jobs take different CPU time (as shown in Figure 15.26).

Several applications exist with strict time limits due to the variety of IoT tasks. The scheduler should handle real-time tasks in order to fulfill the deadlines and to complete the activities within certain time limits. In addition, the schedulers in IoT systems should be multitasking and energy efficient.

15.6.4   Memory Footprint

Memory management offers an idea of managing memory allocation, deallocation, caching, logical and physical address mapping, memory security, and virtual memory. As devices are limited in number so an OS must have low memory and processing requirements.

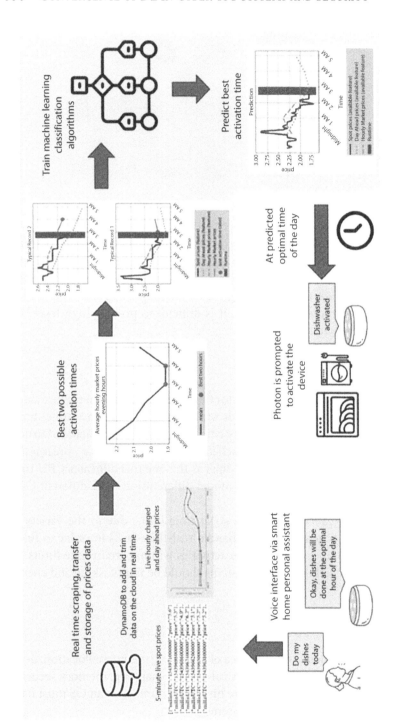

Figure 15.26 IoT scheduling.

IoT devices typically provide a few kilobytes of memory, millions of times less than connected machines (smartphones, laptops, tablets, etc.). The amount of memory management requirement relies on the type of application and the underlying platform support. The distribution of memory may be static or dynamic. Memory distribution is easier through static method, but dynamic strategy can provide flexibility in runtime memory acquisition as shown in Figures 15.27 and 15.28.

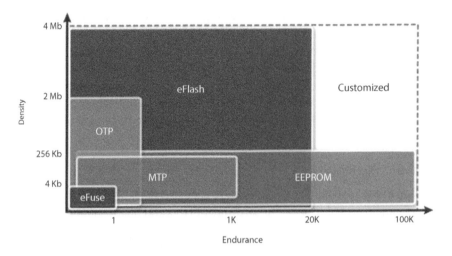

Figure 15.27 IoT memory footprints.

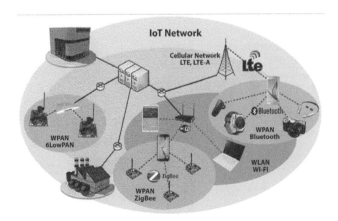

Figure 15.28 Networking in IoT.

15.6.5 Networking

Connectivity of Internet is a basic condition for IoT devices. It should be possible for the IoT organizations to communicate with low power consumption. OS supports various protocols of connectivity, such as Wi-Fi, Ethernet, BLE, IEEE 802.15.4, etc. IoT is not appropriate for traditional TCP/IP stacks or WSN networking technologies. While the previous expert's fails to attain the objectives of less memory, less complexity, and low power, the latter requires intermediate proxies to allow various communication platforms to talk to end to end users.

In addition, WSN protocols, such as ZigBee, Bluetooth, Wavenis, Z-Wave, etc., comply with the specific demands of smart systems, but do not meet IoT's broad-based communication criteria [9]. To allow effective seamless Internet communication, we need an open standard. The IoT stack must be flexible in order to be configured to satisfy the requirements of a broad spectrum of IoT apps with minimal modifications. In IoT schemes, support for Ipv6 is compulsory to have distinctive identities in huge networks.

15.6.6 Portability

OS separates applications from software specifics as shown in Figure 15.29. OS is usually ported to separate hardware devices and board support package (BSP) interfaces in a conventional manner. The operating system should be easily connected to different hardware systems. The big range of hardware architectures should be supported. The IoT microcontrollers used variety between 8-bit and 32-bit.

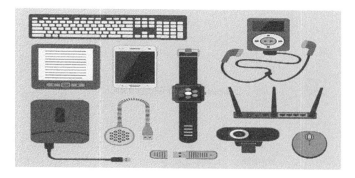

Figure 15.29 Some portable devices used in IoT.

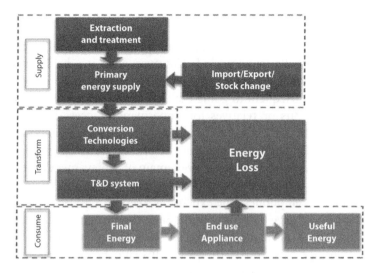

Figure 15.30 Energy efficiency in IoT.

The OS should be prepared to exploit the design that underlies it. In addition, IoT is a future with a broad spectrum of apps in various fields. The OS should be adaptable to the application's specific requirements and provide sensible abstraction to the background information. In addition, IoT is a future with a broad spectrum of apps in various fields. The OS should be adaptable to the application's specific requirements and provide sensible abstraction to the background information.

15.6.7   Energy Efficiency

Energy efficiency becomes crucial for battery-powered IoT systems and should be considered when developing an IoT OS. Most IoT systems are resource-bound in nature. Therefore, battery or other constrained energy sources are used to operate it (Figure 15.30).

Scenarios for IoT implementation are varied, difficult, and sometimes very distant. Humongous IoT network size requires IoT OS to operate the IoT equipment for many years to be power efficient.

15.7   IoT Systems Applications

There are numerous applications for IoT systems in daily life to life support systems, even agriculture and poultry farming get benefited from it. Some of them are discussed herein:

15.7.1   Smart Home

Reports are flowing through IoT that the "brilliant home" is an element of Google's eventually explored IoT. However, what is a brilliant home? Everybody can switch on the cooling prior to arriving at home or mood killer the lights subsequent to going out. Or, on the other hand, make the way for companions or relatives for impermanent access in any event, when nobody is home. Try not to be amazed if IoT organizations are making items to make life simpler and more helpful as shown in Figure 15.31.

Keen homes have made an inventive remain of achievement in the lodging space and it is being theorized that brilliant homes will be just about as reasonable as cell phones. The expense of keeping a house is the significant cost of a mortgage holder's lifetime. Savvy home items guarantee time, energy and cash investment funds. To give some examples, with savvy home organizations like Nest, Smart Things, Philips Hue, Ecobee, Belkin Wemo, Sonos, Lutron family brands will create and plan to never figure it out.

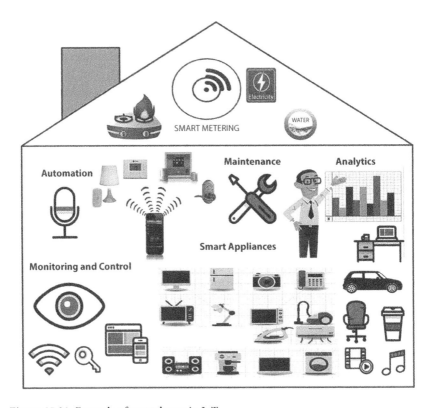

Figure 15.31 Example of smart home in IoT.

15.7.2   Wearables

There is a huge demand for wearable materials in the worldwide market. Companies like Google and Samsung have heavily funded the construction of such devices. Wearable devices are connected to sensors and software that collects data and information around users. These data are then preprocessed to extract important concepts around the handler.

These devices basically cover fitness, health and recreation requirements (as shown in Figure 15.32). The essential for IoT innovation for wearable applications should be profoundly control effective or super low force and irrelevant size.

15.7.3   Connected Cars

Automotive digital technology is focused on enhancing the core functionality of the vehicle. But then again today, the interesting aspects involved in this consideration car are growing. An attached car is a vehicle that is capable of improving its special processes, maintenance, as well as the luxury of travelers through onboard sensors and Internet connection (as shown in Figure 15.33).

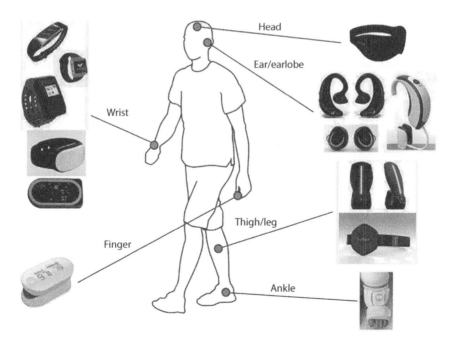

Figure 15.32 Smart wearables in IoT.

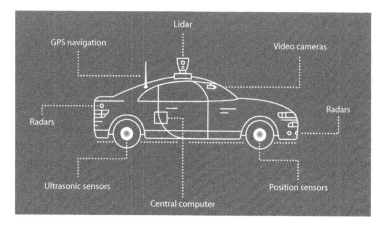

Figure 15.33 IoT applications in a modern car.

Most of the big auto manufacturers are employed in the respective vehicle resolutions as some big bold startups.

15.7.4   Industrial Internet

The industrial Internet is an extravagant buzz in the modern portion, otherwise called the Industrial Internet of Things (IIoT) (shown in Figure 15.34). It is permitting modern designing to make astounding innovation with sensors, programming and huge information investigation. IoT is a "delightful, alluring and investable power," said Jeff Immelt, CEO of GE Electric. The way of thinking behind IIoT is that shrewd machines are more precise and solid than people in conveying through information. Also, these information organizations can focus on inadequacy and intricacy.

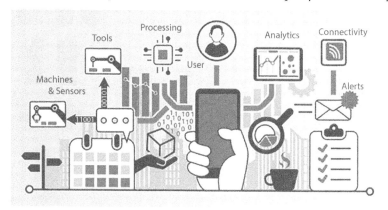

Figure 15.34 Industrial Internet of Things (IIoT).

IIoT holds extraordinary potential for quality control and toughness. Accommodation for impending items, continuous data trade around stock among providers and retailers, and computerized conveyance will expand the adequacy of the store network. The usefulness of the advancement business to GE will produce $10 trillion to $15 trillion in widespread GDP in 15 years.

15.7.5   Smart Cities

Smart city is the additional commanding deposit of IoT that creates questioning among the people of the world as shown in Figure 15.35. Examples of IoT applications for smart surveillance, automated transportation, smart energy administration systems, water distribution, urban security, and environmental intensive care smart cities. IoT pollution, traffic jams and lack of power supply will explain the biggest difficulties faced by people living in the city. The comparative cellular communication-enabled smart belly trash will alert the municipal facilities before emptying a garbage container requirement.

By introducing sensors and afterward utilizing the web application, occupants can look for nothing available spots across the city. Likewise, sensors can identify meter altering issues, generally speaking blunders and any issues with establishment in the electrical framework.

15.7.6   IoT in Agriculture

With the continuous rise of the world's inhabitants, the order of food sources has greatly expanded. The government is serving farmers to

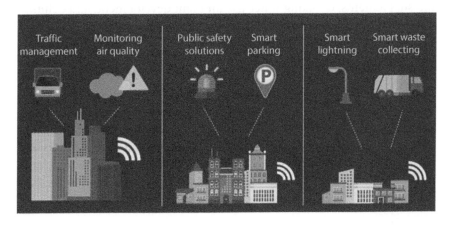

Figure 15.35 Smart city applications of IoT.

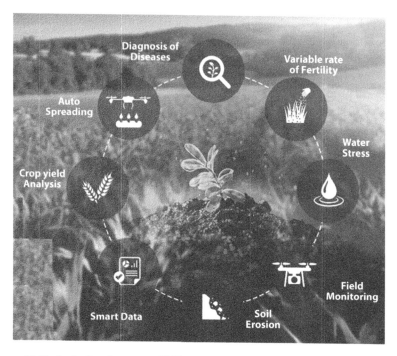

Figure 15.36 Agricultural aspects of IoT.

practice progressive methods and is investigating to intensify food production. Smart agriculture is one of the legitimate mounting arenas of IoT as shown in Figure 15.36.

Ranchers are utilizing informative ideas from information to gather further developed profits from speculation. Distinguishing soil dampness and supplements, checking water use for plant development, and defining regular supplements are a portion of the normal acts of IoT.

15.7.7 Smart Retail

The potential for IoT in the retail area is gigantic as shown in Figure 15.37. IoT gives likelihood to sellers to expand store commitment with clients. Cell phones will be a way for retailers to keep connecting through their customers and surprisingly outside the store. Utilizing interrelationships and signal innovation on cell phones can assist retailers with bettering serve their clients. They can follow clients on a store and mastermind in-store stores and spot the best items in superior execution regions.

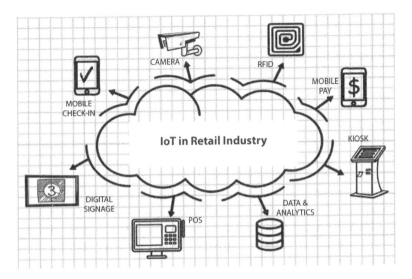

Figure 15.37 IoT in smart retail industry.

15.7.8 Energy Engagement

Future force matrices will not just be astutely enough, they will likewise be exceptionally viable as shown in Figure 15.38. The idea of shrewd network is very boundless everywhere. The essential information behind shrewd networks is to gather data in a robotized way just as to test the conduct or power shoppers and providers for effectiveness just as the economy of force utilization.

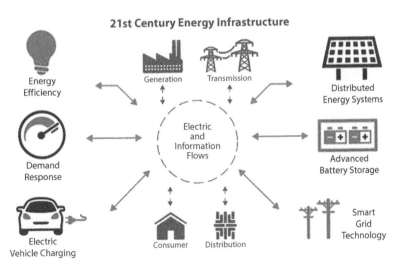

Figure 15.38 IoT in energy engagement.

The smart grid will similarly be able to realize the basis of power outages more quickly and similar solar panels on individual domestic planes, creating imaginable distributed power systems.

15.7.9   IoT in Healthcare

Combined healthcare has so far endured the snoozing of IoT requests enormously. Impressions of related healthcare structures and smart medical devices are possible not only for business, but also for the well-being of the common man as shown in Figure 15.39.

The research will show IoT in healthcare at the turn of the decade. The purpose of healthcare systems in IoT is to allow individuals to lead better lives so that the associated strategies are exhausted. The data will help in analyzing a person's health and provide a comprehensive plan for the fight against the disease.

15.7.10   IoT in Poultry and Farming

The expert care of cattle is animal farming and affordable. The exploitation of IoT deposits to collect information on animal health and well-being, supplementing, and assisting early-recognized farmers in the vicinity of sick animals

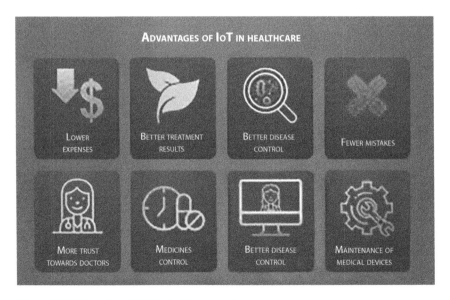

Figure 15.39 Benefits of IoT in healthcare systems.

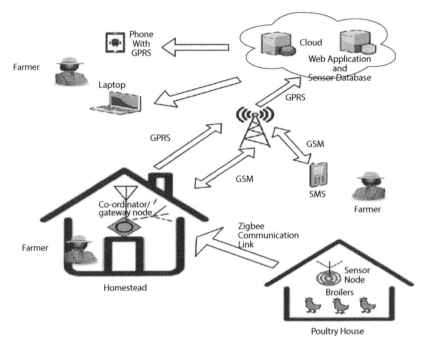

Figure 15.40 IoT in poultry and farming.

to avoid large amounts of sick cattle. Thus, animal husbandry can be profitable and smartly managed with the help of IoT as shown in Figure 15.40.

15.8   Deep Learning Applications in the Field of IoT Systems

DL deposits on IoT devices have repeatedly challenging real-time requirements. For example, security camera-based object-recognition work typically requires a detection potential of less than 500 ms (milliseconds) to respond to arrests and targeted activities. However, approving DL on the side of the device is problematic. Of course, the key aspect of portable IoT devices is low power consumption, which usually balances limited computing power and insignificant memory sizes, and conversely, DL requires high-performance computing and high-power consumption. Therefore, conventional DL libraries have nothing to do with IoT devices. The successful system is a unique architecture of the Convolution Neural Network (CNN):

i.   It creates a feature vector by examining a convolution layer input image.

ii.   An activation level controls which feature of the vector should start for the image below.

iii.   A pooling layer property reduces the vector size.

iv.   The fully attached layer links individual potential labels to all outputs of the pooling layer.

An operative method of reducing power feeding is offloading to the cloud. However, offloading also leads to a delay of at least 2 seconds and dormancy can be as high as 5 seconds which does not face a real-time constraint of 500 ms. Therefore, with the current Internet speed, offloading to the cloud is not yet a possible explanation for real-time DL responsibilities.

By invalid offloading, one choice is to navigate existing DL platforms to IoT devices. Nonetheless, it is actually a daunting task and raises the question of whether it is more valuable to pull a platform out of scratch than to make it an existing port. Deprived of the basic structure, such as the convolution operator, it is extremely problematic. In addition, an extrapolation engine built after scratch cannot go beyond a well-tested DL framework.

15.8.1   Organization of DL Applications for IoT in Healthcare

This piece provides an evaluation of specific DL requests for IoT in the field of healthcare for the inspections obtained in the systematic literature review. Figure 15.41 prescribes a complete system of DL submission for IoT in healthcare domains, which includes medical diagnosis and individual requests, home-based and individual healthcare requests, disease prediction tenders, and human behavior recognition requests.

Analysis of other research papers describes the complexity of the challenges associated with DL requests in healthcare. For example, individual healthcare and home-based submissions based on smart phone sensor data, chronic patients with multiple diseases, learning the patient's physiological signals, smart dental health-IoT systems, fall detection models, sports injury, and nutrition monitoring systems.

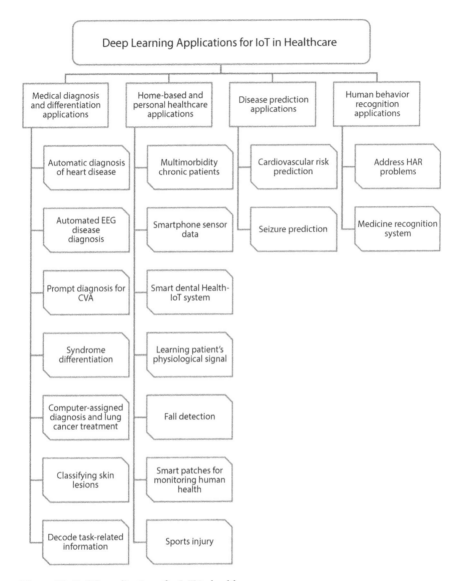

Figure 15.41 DL applications for IoT in healthcare.

15.8.2   DeepSense as a Solution for Diverse IoT Applications

An overall DL context for inputting data from various IoT submissions, called DeepSense. The outline covers all the important basics then can be modified for the learning needs of numerous IoT applications as shown in Figure 15.42.

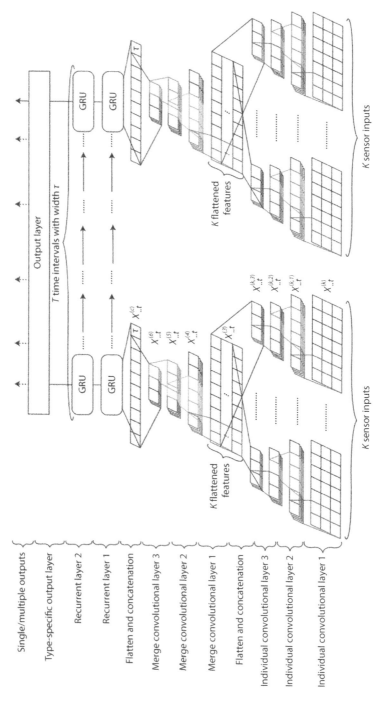

Figure 15.42 Key architecture of the DeepSense framework.

DeepSense built algorithms (including DeepSense and its three options) surpass additional baseline algorithms by a huge margin, which can be realized in the following two evaluation charts Figure 15.43 and Figure 15.44.

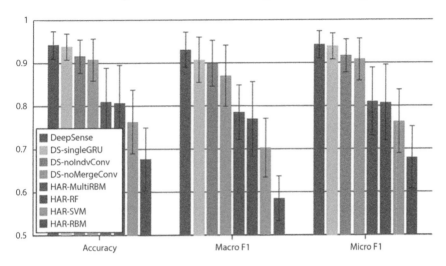

Figure 15.43 Performance metrics of heterogeneous human activity recognition (HHAR) task with the DeepSense framework.

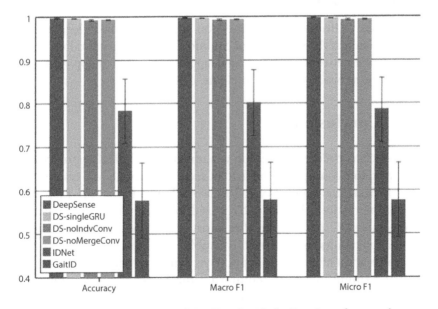

Figure 15.44 Performance metrics of UserID task with the DeepSense framework.

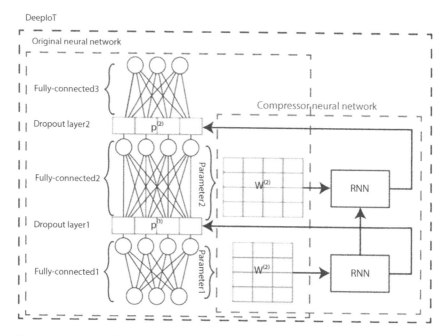

Figure 15.45 Embedded deep learning.

15.8.3 Deep IoT as a Solution for Energy Efficiency

A particularly effective DL compression algorithm, called DeepIoT, can directly compress the structures of commonly used deep neural networks. It "thins" the network structure by dropping hidden elements and compressing the network as shown in Figure 15.45.

15.9 Conclusion

This work has been explained on a number of technical approaches to improving IoT concepts in the field of security through IoT systems and in-depth learning applications. This work hopes to explore many features of the platform based on DL-based IoT technology and structure, architecture, DL. In addition, the effort is complete on how to tackle smart applications in domestic, wearable, car, city, retail, energy bustle, health and environment supportive living systems, agriculture and poultry farming, machine monitoring methods in various industries through in-depth learning. For many more philosophical observations, inspections streamline DL deposits for IoT. So that DL requests can be healthily appreciated, this learning reflects irregular testing and improves them on a variety of features such as characteristic extraction, recognition, cost, delay, calculation load, and so on. Nevertheless, QoS still has almost the potential to increase limitations, privacy and distribution, which can be talked about in future works. Overall, the results of this writing are expected to be realistic for scholars, engineers, healthcare professionals and policy makers who want to make some effort in the field of IoT.

References

1. Belli, L., Cilfone, A., Davoli, L., Ferrari, G., Adorni, P., Di Nocera, F., Dall'Olio, A., Pellegrini, C., Mordacci, M., Bertolotti, E., IoT-enabled smart sustainable cities: Challenges and approaches. *Smart Cities*, 3, 1039–1071, 2020.
2. Syed, A.S., Sierra-Sosa, D., Kumar, ., Elmaghraby, A., IoT in smart cities: A survey of technologies, practices and challenges. *Smart Cities*, 4, 429–475, 2021. https://doi.org/10.3390/smartcities4020024.
3. https://www.windpowerengineering.com/global-iot-market-to-reach-318-billion-by-2023-says-globaldata/, Last Accessed August, 2021.
4. Hameed, S., Khan, F., II, Hameed, B., Understanding security requirements and challenges in Internet of Things (IoT): A review. *J. Comput. Netw. Commun.* Hindawi, 2019, 2090–7141, 2019. https://doi.org/10.1155/2019/9629381.
5. Serpanos, D., The cyber-physical systems revolution. *Computer*, 51, 3, 70–73, 2018.
6. Bertino, E. and Islam, N., Botnets and Internet of Things security. *Computer*, 50, 2, 76–79, 2017.
7. Xin, Y., *et al.*, Machine learning and deep learning methods for cybersecurity. *IEEE Access*, 6, 35365–35381, 2018.
8. Chen, X.-W. and Lin, X., Big data deep learning: Challenges and perspectives. *IEEE Access*, 2, 514–525, 2014.
9. Wang, H. and Raj, B., On the origin of deep learning, arXiv, Vol. abs/1702.07800, pp. 1-81, 2017.
10. Albawi, S., Mohammed, T.A., Al-Zawi, S., Understanding of a convolutional neural network. *2017 International Conference on Engineering and Technology (ICET)*, pp. 1–6, 2017.
11. Han, Z., Francesca, C., Nikolic, K., Mirza, K., Toumazou, C., Signal identification of DNA amplification curves in custom-PCR platforms. *2021 IEEE International Symposium on Circuits and Systems (ISCAS)*, pp. 1–5, 2021.

12. Ying, Y., Su, J., Shan, P., Miao, L., Wang, X., Peng, S., Rectified exponential units for convolutional neural networks. *IEEE Access*, 7, 101633–101640, 2019.

13. Isono, T., *et al.*, A 12.1 TOPS/W mixed-precision quantized deep convolutional neural network accelerator for low power on edge/endpoint device. *2020 IEEE Asian Solid-State Circuits Conference (A-SSCC)*, pp. 1–4, 2020.

14. Heck, J.C. and Salem, F.M., Simplified minimal gated unit variations for recurrent neural networks. *2017 IEEE 60th International Midwest Symposium on Circuits and Systems (MWSCAS)*, pp. 1593–1596, 2017.

15. Bin, K., Luo, S., Zhang, X., Lin, J., Tong, X., Compressive data gathering with generative adversarial networks for wireless geophone networks. *IEEE Geosci. Remote Sens. Lett.*, 18, 3, 558–562, 2021. doi: 10.1109/LGRS.2020.2978520.

16. Yin, H., The Self-organizing maps: Background, theories, extensions and applications, in: *Computational Intelligence: A Compendium. Studies in Computational Intelligence*, vol. 115, J. Fulcher, and L.C. Jain, (Eds.), Springer, Berlin, Heidelberg, 2008, https://doi.org/10.1007/978-3-540-78293-3_17.

17. Hinton, G., Boltzmann Machines, in: *Encyclopedia of Machine Learning*, C. Sammut, and G.I. Webb, (Eds.), Springer, Boston, MA, 2011, https://doi.org/10.1007/978-0-387-30164-8_83.

18. Mousavi, S.S., Schukat, M., Howley, E., Deep reinforcement learning: An overview, in: *IntelliSys 2016: Proceedings of SAI Intelligent Systems Conference (IntelliSys) 2016, Lecture Notes in Networks and Systems*, vol. 16, Cham, Springer, 2018, https://doi.org/10.1007/978-3-319-56991-8_32.

19. Yusiong, J.P.T. and Naval, P.C., Multi-scale autoencoders in autoencoder for semantic image segmentation, in: *ACIIDS 2019: Intelligent Information and Database Systems, Lecture Notes in Computer Science*, vol. 11431, Springer, Cham, 2019, https://doi.org/10.1007/978-3-030-14799-0_51.

Efficient Detection of Bioweapons for Agricultural Sector Using Narrowband Transmitter and Composite Sensing Architecture

Arghyadeep Nag[1], Labani Roy[1], Shruti[2], Soumen Santra[2]* and Arpan Deyasi[3]

[1]*Department of Physics, A.P.C. College, West Bengal, India*
[2]*Department of Computer Application, Techno International New Town,*
West Bengal, India
[3]*Department of Electronics and Communication Engineering, RCC Institute of*
Information Technology, West Bengal, India

Abstract

Bioweapons, nowadays, become a potential method to destroy the food production of any agricultural field at a large scale, which can bring economic calamity to a country. These are precisely the locusts, which can cause severe damage on vast quantity of crops when made attacks, and therefore, prevention at the highest level is required to protect agricultural yields from them. Extensive research showcased that each and every insect have their distinct properties to make them different from others based on some parameters, such as releasing substances (chemical compounds), humming noise (intensity, pitch, frequency), absorbing ability (range of different wavelength), average number of insects in a group, velocity range, maximum/average distance covered, etc. Based on the properties, the present work proposes one novel transmitter associated with a few sensors, which is able to detect the insects based on specific characterization of a particular species. Based on the noise properties, it is possible to detect their expected arrival time along with statistical number of elements (insects) much earlier so that early precaution can be easily carried out. The proposed transmitter will emit specific narrowband wavelength range, which is close to absorbing range of locusts. Based on the absorbing spectrum, we can compute the velocity of gang as well as number

**Corresponding author:* soumen70@gmail.com

Rajdeep Chakraborty, Anupam Ghosh, Jyotsna Kumar Mandal and S. Balamurugan (eds.) Convergence of Deep Learning In Cyber-IoT Systems and Security, (349–366) © 2023 Scrivener Publishing LLC

of species present in that group using deep learning. This detection becomes critically important for the agricultural-based countries. Different spectrum will be produced based on the possible locust attacks, and therefore, a single architecture can be used for multiple attacks.

Keywords: Bioweapon, narrowband spectrum, composite sensing architecture, absorbing wavelength, agricultural sector

16.1 Introduction

Bioweapons are artificial man-made organic weapon acts as a silent killer or acts as the manufacturer wants. Since we are talking about the agricultural sector, we bounded those bioweapons that are involved in this sector [1]. It has been observed that locusts have been used the most as bioweapon. Also, other insects have been used as a bioweapon. Like many other countries, India is also based on agriculture. Adequate agricultural production is needed to provide plenty of food to every category of people of our society in this huge population, that is to say, adequate supply of essential elements for human life and its distribution at low cost is desirable to every human being. But if an enemy country disrupts the agricultural production of countries like India by using their bioweapons, then there will be food crisis, and all food-related systems will collapse, food prices will increase, people in poor countries, like India, will not eat, at last, the economic structure of the country will collapse.

Agriculture is the most common occupation on the planet. This field affects the lives of many people. However, as a result of the state of nature and changes in the environment, more issues occur, posing a threat to farmers. Smart agriculture was implemented to handle these difficulties in an effective and intelligent manner [2]. Every day, a new technology is implemented to overcome agricultural challenges that can be overcome utilizing technology. Smart agriculture assists framers with information accuracy, as well as being dependable and adaptable to changes [3].

Each and every insect has their distinct properties to make them different from others based on some parameters, such as releasing substances (mostly chemical but may be other), humming noise (intensity, pitch, frequency), absorbing ability (range of different wavelength) [4], lifespan (duration, different phases of life cycle) size, shape, average number of insects in a gang, velocity range, maximum/average distance covered, fearing elements/destroying elements involved. Destruction of small elements can be well compared with the identification and detection of small elementary cells inside the body, which are potentially hazardous

[5–7]. Based on different properties (as describe above) of the insects we can sense out them by using appropriate sensors. Each and every insect releases some chemical substances (has definite composition), mainly to maintain their long-range travelling path when they are travelling in a gang [8]. So, we can use an appropriate sensing kit, which can sense out the chemical and detect the insects based on specific characterization of a particular species. If we catch the noise intensity, pitch or frequency, which have produced by the gang of insects, then we can calculate the velocity of the movement of that gang [9]. It can easily help to find that how much time has in our hand to prevent them. So that we can get enough time to take necessary actions. From here, also, we can calculate the number of species present in that gang by using statistical average calculation. Using the properties of absorbing ability of some species means they can absorb different kind of wavelengths range [10]. It is a narrow-thought process because, initially, we guess that the attacked consists of a particular type of insect, i.e., LOCUSTS; so, we know that the absorbing range of wavelength for locusts. Now if we use a transmitter, which can produce and emit particular wavelength signal and we can tuned it and fixed at a certain range. Now, when the gang of locusts passing through the region they must absorb that signal wavelength [11]. Thus, there will be energy loss due to frequency absorbing. From this energy loss and rate of energy loss, we can measure the velocity of gang, number of species present in that gang, etc. But, it has some difficulties as the transmitter created a fixed wavelength signal thus it can trace particular those species, which have absorb this signal. So, working region is fixed and definite.

The main objective of this project is to save the country from the bio-weapons of foreign enemies in the future and to make the agricultural sector of the country more secure. Corresponding flow diagram of the proposed work is described in Figure 16.1. Here, we are sensing the gang of locusts and taking some necessary actions to prevent them [12]. If the transmitter has a wide range of emitted signal, it means it can produce various wavelengths consecutively and also measure the energy loss consecutively. Now, suppose energy loss occur, then find the particular wavelength for which the energy loss produces, then the emitter/transmitter fixed at that wavelength and emit that particular wavelength only. Then, by absorption of the signal, energy loss occur, and calculating this, we can find out velocity, number of species present in that gang, etc.

Basic objective of this project are in two steps.

    i. Sensing the gang of locusts.
    ii. Taking some necessary actions to prevent them.

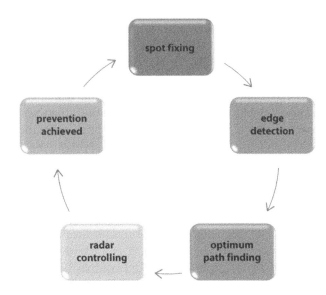

Figure 16.1 Flow diagram for proposed work.

Like many other countries, India is also based on agriculture. Adequate agricultural production is needed to provide plenty of food to every category of people of our society in this huge population, that is to say, adequate supply of essential elements for human life and its distribution at low cost is desirable to every human being. But if an enemy country disrupts the agricultural production of countries, like India, by using their bioweapons, then there will be a food crisis, and all food-related systems will collapse, food prices will increase, people in poor countries, like India, will not eat, at last, the economic structure of the country will collapse.

Farmers are entered into this apps interface by putting their proper details of their lands. Based on the government records and their given credentials find the land details, in this way fixed the spot. Detect the boundary region of the field of the farmer by edge detection method. Also, it can be done by processing of the satellite images. Calculate and find the optimum travelling path for the locust's gangs. Install the radar at that particular path (the information of the installation spot is provided through the apps by government organization by providing longitude & latitude data). Once radar is installed at the perfect position, then it starts its activity by continuous sending images. By analyzing the images, government organization can take preventive actions as well as alert the user. It can produced a humming noise (.....dB) so that locusts gangs are deviated from their original path. As well as it can continuously send the images so that government organization can trace the type of locust, and from there, they can control the frequency/amplitude of the radar. To make it more versatile the controlling option may have into the government organization hand because all the farmers are not trained to control the frequency of the radar's noise, and it cannot be fixed, it can depend on the different type of locusts. So by tracing that, government organization can control this. The main objective of this project is to save the country from the bioweapons of foreign enemies in the future and to make the agricultural sector of the country more secure.

16.2   Literature Review

Neenu *et al.* [13] and Huang [14] described the locust behavior and their monitoring system, which is implemented by IoT sensor simulation technique. Here the methodology identified a locust or fungus and, after recognition of proper object, sent signal to the farmer for alert purpose by an alarm system. In this paper, they used a spraying technique to demolish the object but this kind of chemical not good for corps and human health. Waldner *et al.* [15] introduced a new feature of technology which monitoring the behavior of the locust. They described the colorimetric map of paddy field and explained how desert locust identifies the target corps through their habits, which comes by nature. All kinds of insects like locust, bee, flies, butterfly, grasshopper, ant, etc. uses their various kinds of behavior for the survival of life in earth. Their activities possess as their optimization technique by which they find out their way of life for different purposes, such as finding food, searching for nest, looking for hive, etc. Here, they described all kinds of assessment parameters for the accuracy checking of the system. Yao *et al.* [16] introduced a web based combination of decision based system and geographic information system which tracks the locust network rapidly and accurately. Klein *et al.* [17] predicts the locust outbreak and habitats. In this paper, they described the migration strategy of locust and destructive species.

Utkarsha *et al.* [18] describes the challenges of IoT to introduce the biological warfare entities and fast recognition through object detection and elimination from nature. Miroslav *et al.* [19] explains the working mechanism of biosensors over biological microorganisms, such as different types of bacteria. They calculated various important assessment parameters, i.e., sensitivity, accuracy, specificity etc to show the efficient performance of biosensors over biological warfare entities. Marion *et al.* [20] propagate the knowledge of linkages between locust and human. It compares around 19 species of grasshoppers and their activities over grazing. It also has introduced a tele-coupling process, which related with ecology environment. Chudzik *et al.* [21] developed a deployment framework, which implemented based on deep learning algorithms. Here, it detected the image of grasshopper using deep learning methodology and destroyed them before their movement and break their life cycles. For the identification of various types of images of various species of grasshoppers we require deep learning approaches and predict their flying stages or status and then apply methodology for their destroy.

Connor *et al.* [22] identified the presence of electrochemical agent or substances present in entity, which is considered as biowarfare agent. This electrochemical substance is such a hybrid mutant composition which is not possible to control by human being. If this kind of substance is present in the gang of locust, then it is very much difficult to control or monitor their movement and habitat as well as their stimulus is not only poisonous for corps whether it also affects health of human being. So it creates a threat for the health and economic environment of a country. Longlong *et al.* [23] described the migratory strategies of locust over the agricultural field and analyzed their destructive activities on the paddy field. It also focused on locust distribution strategy with their habitat factors. It introduces a patch-based analytic hierarchy process (Pb-AHP) which introduces a concept of deep learning methodology later. Krishna *et al.* [24] designed a mobile based robotic smart agriculture system which monitored the paddy field and measured different external environmental parameters and based on these measurements analysis and performed several activities which are related with paddy field. A few common examples are sensing of moisture, scaring animals and birds, spraying chemicals (pesticides), circular or translational motion (forward/backward) and switching ON/OFF of the electric motor. Cogato *et al.* [25] describes how the extreme weather event connects with 19 types of corps species. It was a review work, which focused upon the different categories of corps species and explained how they attracted the entities. Graham *et al.* [26] worked upon remote unpopulated or unmanned area where average rainfall is higher rather than others. It measured the locust concentration and applied recent trends to destroy or control them to outbreak the locust movement. Ankita *et al.* [27] introduced a new methodology based on Particle Swarm Optimization (PSO) to detect the locust gang in the paddy field based on image processing technique. Diego *et al.* [28] applied machine learning methodologies to identify the desert locust and measure the parameters to destroy them.

16.3   Properties of Insects

Each bug has its own set of characteristics that distinguishes it from the others. Locusts are a type of short-horned grasshopper that has a swarming colony phase [29]. These insects are mainly migratory-based species that can fly in a disciplined manner when they develop. However, under some circumstances, they become more arbitrary and change their behavior, habitats, and activities in a mutant manner, which is damaging [30]. The basis for the recognition of locust and other grasshopper species creates swarms under intermittently favorable conditions [31], but no taxonomic differentiation is recognized between them [32]. However, when drought is combined with rapid vegetation growth, serotonin in their brains initiates a dramatic sequence of changes: they begin to breed in large numbers, eventually becoming destructive and migratory once their populations grow large enough [33]. They create swarms of winged adults after forming high-bands of wingless nymphs. Both the bands and the swarms move around, destroying fields and causing crop loss. The adults are large nymphs in flight mode, able to travel long distances and consume the majority of the green plants wherever the swarm settles [34]. We will go over the algorithm for distracting locusts from an agriculture area in this article. Figure 16.2 describes the life-cycle of the locust.

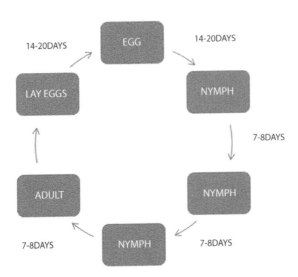

Figure 16.2 Life cycle of locust.

Some properties/parameter:

→ Releasing substances (mostly chemical but may be other)
→ Humming noise (intensity, pitch, frequency)
→ Absorbing ability (range of different wavelength)
→ Lifespan (duration, different phases of life cycle)
→ Size, shape, average number of insects in a gang
→ Velocity range, maximum/average distance covered
→ Fearing elements/destroying elements involvement

Basically, in this chapter, we are trying to implement the detection of bioweapons using narrowband transmitter and take necessary action to prevent the damage. The steps involves are shown in Figure 16.3 schematic diagram in an overview.

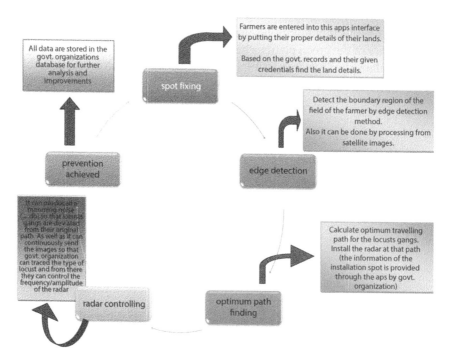

Figure 16.3 Schematic steps for locust prevention and destruction.

16.4 Working Methodology

16.4.1 Sensing

Based on different properties (as describe above) of the insects we can sense out them by using appropriate sensors.

Each & every insects release some chemical substances (has definite composition) mainly to maintain their long-range travelling path when they are travelling in a gang.

So, we can use an appropriate sensing kit, which can sense out the chemical and detect the insects.

16.4.1.1 Specific Characterization of a Particular Species

[i] If we catch the noise intensity, pitch or frequency, which have produced by the gang of insects, then we can calculate the velocity of the movement of those gangs.

[ii] It can easily help to find that how much time has in our hand to prevent them. So that we can get enough time to take necessary actions.

[iii] From here, we can also calculate the number of species present in that gang by using statistical average calculation.

16.4.2 Alternative Way to Find Those Previously Sensing Parameters

Using the properties of absorbing ability of some species means they can absorbs different kind of wavelengths range. It is a narrow thought process because, initially, we guess that the attacked consists by a particular type of insect. Say, LOCUSTS; so we know that the absorbing range of wavelength for locusts. Now if we use a transmitter that can produce and emit particular wavelength signal, we can tune it and fix it at a certain range. Now, when the gang of locusts passing through the region, they must absorb that signal wavelength. Thus, there will be energy loss due to frequency absorbing.

From this energy loss and rate of energy loss, we can measure the velocity of gang, number of species present in that gang, etc. But it has some difficulties as the transmitter created a fixed wavelength signal, thus it can trace particularly those species that have absorbed this signal. So, working region is fixed and definite.

16.4.3   Remedy to Overcome These Difficulties

If the transmitter has wide range of emitted signal means it can produce various wavelengths consecutively and also measure the energy loss consecutively. Now, suppose energy loss occur, then find the particular wavelength for which the energy loss produce, then the emitter/transmitter fixed at that wavelength and emit that particular wavelength only. Then, by absorption of the signal energy loss occur & calculate this we can find out velocity, number of species present in that gang etc. Geographical territory of the locust movement is described in Figure 16.4.

16.4.4   Take Necessary Preventive Actions

There are two different way to prevent the attack of insects:

[i] Active Preventive Mode/Method or Direct Preventive Mode/ Method

[ii] Passive Preventive Mode/Method or Indirect Preventive Mode/ Method

[i] Active or Direct Preventive Mode/Method: In this method, the action should be taken on that particular area or zone, which is the target area of insects. That means, though the insects reach at their target

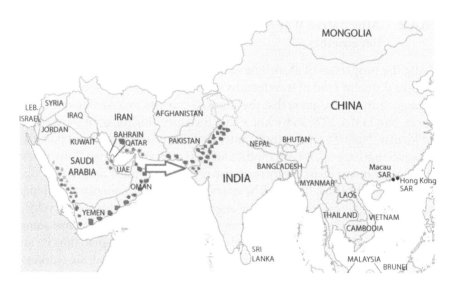

Figure 16.4 Geographical territory for locust movement.

region but we protect that field from insects, so that they cannot do any damage to the crop. Based on this phenomenon we can make the preventive apparatus.

[ii] Passive or Indirect Preventive Mode/Method: In this method, the action will have taken at a certain distance from the target area, such that the gang of insects cannot move forward.

Some possible situation can be created when they can't move forward:

[i]   May their trajectory be changed
[ii] May they can be reflected back from that particular distances
[iii] May they can be destroyed by something
[iv] May they can be trapped

Basic differences is, in active method, we can allow the gang of insects to reach the target zone only focus that how to protect that zone. On the other hand, in passive method, we cannot allow the gang of insects to reach the target zone and focus that how to restrict their movement or path.

16.5   Proposed Algorithm

Based on our proposal, we have devised the following algorithm in accordance to the diagram represented in Figure 16.3:

Step 1: Read the image.
Step 2: Convert the RGB image to Gray Scale image.
Step 3: Resize the image for normalize the array size.
Step 4: Find out Edge using Sobel Edge Detection Filter.
Step 5: Find out Edge using Canny Edge Detection Filter.
Step 6: Convert the image into double precision.
Step 7: Find the size of the image
Step 8: Find total number of rows and total number of columns
Step 9: Create array of all zeroes with corresponding size with proper rows and columns.
Step 10: Apply Mask detection using Edge detection filter based on Ant-Colony Optimization Technique.

Step 11: Procedure Ant Colony Optimization based on eight neighbor components:
Initialize require parameters and pheromone trials;
    while not exit do:
        Generate population of Ants;
        Calculate fitness values for each ant;
        Find Optimum solution through selection methods;
        Update for each iteration pheromone trial;
    end while
    end procedure
Step 12: Segment the edge from background based on threshold value (such as 0.1)
Step 13: Find number of zero elements Detect total end points.
Step 14: Initialize the position of Ants.
Step 15: Find out the intensity of difference between matrixes without Normalization
Step 16: Based on Ant movements find out probabilistic distribution.
Step 17: Find out the touching track through this Probabilistic Distribution
Step 18: Find out Adaptive Tubulise to store each vector value.
Step 19: Show the Image with edge based on this vector value
Step 20: Exit

16.6   Block Diagram and Used Sensors

In the first block diagram, we have briefly outlined how the relay and sensor modules are associated with the system. From the diagram, it is seen that simulation data after initial processing is sent to the microcontroller, which is transferred simultaneously to both the display system and main IoT module. The processed signal is therefore sent to the camera (for visual imaging), motion sensor (for trajectory detection), and relay module (for operation and control). Based on the active state of relay, the warning sound system will work. Accuracy of the total system will depend on initial capturing of data, and therefore simulation based on our proposed algorithm is extremely critical. Figure 16.5 describes the working procedure of the system with various sensors and relay.

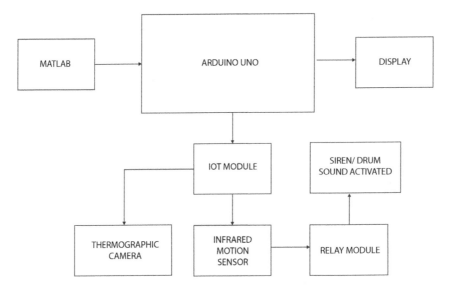

Figure 16.5 Sensor and relay working procedure with the system.

The major associated components for the system are the microcontroller and infrared sensor. Also, thermographic camera and relay module are essential for data processing and output information. In this following section, we briefly describe each of the major components utilized in this system:

16.6.1   Arduino Uno

The Arduino Uno is a commercially free microcontroller board architectured by Arduino.cc and based on the Microchip ATmega328P microprocessor. The board is well equipped and constructed with digital portable and analogue input/output (I/O) pins that may be connected to a variety of extended boards (shields) and other circuits. The board features 14 digital I/O pins (six of which are capable of PWM output), 6 analog I/O pins, and is programmable through a type B USB cable using the Arduino IDE (Integrated Development Environment). It can be powered by a USB cable or an external 9-volt battery, with voltages ranging from 7 to 20 volts. It is similar to the Arduino Nano and Leonardo microcontrollers. The hardware reference design is available on the Arduino website under a Creative Commons Attribution Share-Alike 2.5 licence. Some versions of the hardware have layout and manufacturing files available as well.

16.6.2   Infrared Motion Sensor

PIR sensor, commercially known as passive infrared sensor (PIR sensor) is a type of electronic sensor that detects infrared (IR) light emitted by objects in its field of vision. They are most commonly found in motion detectors with a PIR sensor. PIR sensors are widely utilized in security alarm systems and automatic lighting systems. PIR sensors detect movement in general but do not reveal who or what moved. An imaging infrared sensor is required for this. PIR sensors are usually referred to as "PIR" or "PID," which stands for "passive infrared detector." The name "passive" refers to the fact that PIR devices do not emit energy for the purpose of detection. They only detect infrared radiation (radiant heat) released by objects. The whole work is entirely dependent on detection of infrared radiation or light reflected from objects.

16.6.3   Thermographic Camera

A thermographic camera (also known as an infrared camera, thermal imaging camera, or thermal imager) is a device that uses infrared (IR) radiation to create an image, similar to how a regular camera uses visible light to make an image. Infrared cameras are sensitive to wavelengths ranging from about 1,000 nm (1 micrometre or m) to about 14,000 nm (14 m) instead of the visible light camera's 400–700 nm range. Thermography is the process of acquiring and evaluating the data they offer.

16.6.4   Relay Module

Relay module is used here to control the siren volume and when the siren will be activated. It works as alarming purpose for the farmers. Here, below, we have shown few more sensors that are working upon locust gang and electrochemical substance present in it.

16.7   Result Analysis

Here, we have shown the measurement analysis of mobility power of locust gang on the basis of changes of temperature and humidity of paddy field. As we know, temperature and humidity of paddy field of tropical countries attracted the locust gang. But here, our simulation decreases the mobility power or migratory approach of locust gang gradually which helps to divert their way from the paddy field. Simulated variations are given in Figure 16.6.

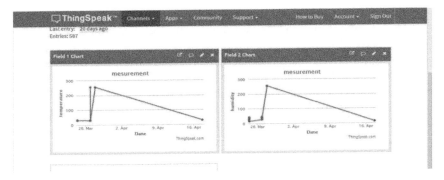

Figure 16.6 Measurement tracking in different time for a consecutive period.

16.8 Conclusion

Here, we introduced a new technology that reduces the possibility of attack of locust gang to paddy field. Here our methodology track the path of locust gang through sensing the intensity stimulus of locusts' gang and compare the total edge of paddy field of agriculture region. There is a map of all mixed connected paddy field, which is compare with the previous traversed field of locust gang and predict the new upcoming tracking path of the new coming locust gang. Based on these predicting path our system create a fencing zone or boundaries and recognize the branching point or junction where we install the sensing radar technology to divert the locust. At junction point, the radar propagates the signal by sensing the high intensity of stimulus of locust and that signal disturbs the locust and force to divert their way and break the gang. This kind of device is very significant for the country, which fully depends on agriculture and cultivation like India. Here the tracking path of locust gang evaluate by combination of ant colony optimization, grasshopper optimization. Determination of area of mixed connected paddy field done by combination of Sobel and Canny edge detection techniques, sensing of intensity of stimulus of locust gang predicting the new path of them done by Bee-colony Optimization and radar technology done by Internet of Things (IoT) techniques. With a great ease of this technology, we can get high impact of societal affect in farmers' life.

References

1. Wheelis, M., Casagrande, R., Madden, L.V., Biological attack on agriculture: Low-tech, high-impact bioterrorism: Because bioterrorist attack requires

relatively little specialized expertise and technology, it is a serious threat to US agriculture and can have very large economic repercussions. *BioScience*, 52, 7, 569–576, 2002.

2. Srivastava, R., Sharma, V., Jaiswal, V., Raj, S., A research paper on smart agriculture using IoT. *Int. Res. J. Eng. Technol.*, 7, 7, 2708–2710, 2020.

3. Friha, O., Ferrag, M.A., Shu, L., Maglaras, L., Wang, X., Internet of Things for the future of smart agriculture: A comprehensive survey of emerging technologies. *IEEE/CAA J. Autom. Sin.*, 8, 4, 718–752, 2021.

4. Adhikary, P., Halder, A., Gupta, N., Deyasi, A., Design of smart system for detecting proximity of obstacles at acute and obtuse angles. *IEEE 3rd International Conference on Electronics, Materials Engineering & Nano-Technology*, Kolkata, India, Aug 29–31 2019.

5. Bhattacharjee, J., Santra, S., Deyasi, A., Novel detection of cancerous cells through an image segmentation approach using principal component analysis, in: *Recent Trends in Computational Intelligence Enabled Research: Theoretical Foundations and Applications*, pp. 171–195, 2021.

6. Bhattacharjee, J., Santra, S., Deyasi, A., Chapter 13 A metaheuristic approach for image segmentation using genetic algorithm, in: *Lecture Notes in Networks and Systems, 6th International Conference on Opto-Electronics and Applied Optics*, vol. 165, pp. 125–134, 2021.

7. Santra, S., Bhattacherjee, J., Deyasi, A., Chapter 2 Cancerous cell detection using affine transformation with higher accuracy and sensitivity, in: *Book Series: Advances in Intelligent Systems and Computing: Intelligent Computing: Image Processing based Applications*, vol. 1157, pp. 17–34, 2020.

8. Madau, F.A., Arru, B., Furesi, R., Pulina, P., Insect farming for feed and food production from a circular business model perspective. *Sustainability*, 12, 5418, 2020.

9. Gorbonos, D., Ianconescu, R., Puckett, J.G., Ni, R., Ouellette, N.T., Gov, N.S., Long-range acoustic interactions in insect swarms: An adaptive gravity model. *New J. Phys.*, 18, 073042, 2016.

10. Hori, M., Shibuya, K., Sato, M., Saito, Y., Lethal effects of short-wavelength visible light on insects. *Sci. Rep.*, 4, 7383, 2014.

11. Santra, S., Mukherjee, P., Halder, P., Mandal, S., Deyasi, A., Chapter 7 Object detection in clustered scene using point feature matching for non-repeating texture pattern, in: *Lecture Notes in Electrical Engineering: Conference on Control, Signal Processing And Energy System*, pp. 79–96, 2020.

12. Saha, A., Ghosh, S., Bhattacharyya, S., Deyasi, A., Environmental condition based auto-adjusted robot design for agricultural purpose. *IEEE 3rd International Conference on Electronics, Materials Engineering & Nano-Technology*, Kolkata, India, Aug 29-31 2019.

13. Neenu, P.A., Ashvitha, Aparajitha, C., Karpagam, S., Locust monitoring system based on using IoT. *Int. J. Innov. Sci. Res. Technol.*, 6, 2, 839–841, 2021.

14. Huang, K., Shu, L., Li, K., Yang, F., Han, G., Wang, X., Pearson, S., Photovoltaic agricultural Internet of Things towards realizing the next generation of smart farming. *IEEE Access*, 8, 76300–76312, 2020.

15. Waldner, F., Ebbe, M.A.B., Cressman, K., Defourny, P., Operational monitoring of the desert locust habitat with earth observation: An assessment. *ISPRS Int. J. Geo-Inf.*, 4, 2379–2400, 2015.

16. Yao, X., Zhu, D., Yun, W., Peng, F., Li, L., A WebGIS-based decision support system for locust prevention and control in China. *Comput. Electron. Agr.*, 140, 148–158, 2017.

17. Klein, I., Oppelt, N., Kuenzer, C., Application of remote sensing data for locust research and management—A review. *Insects*, 12, 233, 2021.

18. Mahajan, U., Role of Internet of Things in biological warfare. *CBW Mag.*, 14, 2, 29–34, January-June 2021.

19. Pohanka, M., Current trends in the biosensors for biological warfare agents assay. *Materials (Basel)*, 12, 14, 2303, 2019.

20. Le Gall, M., Overson, R., Cease, A., A global review on locusts (Orthoptera: Acrididae) and their interactions with livestock grazing practices. *Front. Ecol. Evol.*, vol. 7, article 263, July 23 2019.

21. Chudzik, P., Mitchell, A., Alkaseem, M., Wu, Y., Fang, S., Hudaib, T., Pearson, S., Al-Diri, B., Mobile real-time grasshopper detection and data aggregation framework. *Sci. Rep.*, 10, 1150, 2020.

22. O'Brien, C., Varty, K., Ignaszak, A., The electrochemical detection of bioterrorism agents: A review of the detection, diagnostics, and implementation of sensors in biosafety programs for class a bio-weapons. *Microsyst. Nanoeng.*, 7, 16, 2021.

23. Geng, Y., Zhao, L., Dong, Y., Huang, W., Shi, Y., Ren, Y., Ren, B., Migratory locust habitat analysis with Pb-Ahp model using time-series by satellite images. *IEEE Access*, 8, 166813–166823, 2020.

24. Krishna, K.L., Silver, O., Malende, W.F., Anuradha, K., Internet of Things application for implementation of smart agriculture system. *IEEE International Conference on I-SMAC*, Palladam, India, Feb 10-11 2017.

25. Cogato, A., Meggio, F., Migliorati, M.D.A., Marinello, F., Extreme weather events in agriculture: A systematic review. *Sustainability*, 11, 9, 2547, 2019.

26. Matthews, G.A., New technology for desert locust control. *Agronomy*, 11, 6, 1052, 2021.

27. Harkare, A.H. and Neole, B.A., A system for detection of locusts swarms in farms using IoT. *Proceedings of the International Conference on Smart Data Intelligence*, 2021.

28. Gomez, D., Salvador, P., Sanz-Justo, J., Casanova, C., Machine learning approach to locate desert locust breeding areas based on ESA CCI soil moisture. *J. Appl. Remote Sens.*, 12, 03, 36011, 2018.

29. Pramod, A., Deeksha., R., Neha, H.C., Munavall, J.R., Automated real-time locust management using artificial intelligence. *IJEAST*, 5, 4, 133–138, 2020.

30. Sharma, A., Locust control management: Moving from traditional to new technologies–An empirical analysis. *Entomol. Ornithol. Herpetol.*, 4, 1, 1000141, 2014.

31. Vineela, T., Harini, J.N., Kiranmai, C., Harshitha, G., AdiLakshmi, B., IoT based agriculture monitoring and smart irrigation system using RaspberryPi. *Int. Res. J. Eng. Technol.*, 5, 1, 1417–1420, 2018.

32. Maiya, S.R. and Aishwarya, P., Smart agriculture using IoT. *Int. Res. J. Eng. Technol.*, 7, 4, 3215–3217, 2020.

33. Sandeep, M., Nandini, C., Bindu, L., Champa, P., Deepika, K.H., Anushree, N.S., IoT based smart farming system. *Int. Res. J. Eng. Technol.*, 5, 9, 1033–1036, 2018.

34. Pendyala, H., Rodda, G.K., Mamidi, A., Vangala, M., Bonala, S., Korlapati, K.K., IoT based smart agriculture monitoring system. *Int. J. Sci. Eng. Res.*, 9, 7, 31–34, 2021.

17

A Deep Learning–Based Malware and Intrusion Detection Framework

Pavitra Kadiyala and Kakelli Anil Kumar*

SCOPE, Vellore Institute of Technology, Vellore, India

Abstract

Cyberattacks have increased a lot in the past few years. There are numerous cyber-attacks, such as ransomware, DOS, DDoS, Phishing, BOTS, etc. These attacks have serious consequences, steal and damage confidential data. The usage of web applications has expanded and resulted in more malware attacks. Subsequently, it is essential to prevent emerging malware and attacks. An Intrusion Detection System (IDS) is a highly crucial part of network security IDS monitors the network and data traffic. Attacks are taken place on the IDS. A few examinations have been done in this field, yet profound and comprehensive work is still ongoing. Machine learning and deep learning models are helpful in the cyber security domain. This paper introduces a web application for IDS and malware attack detection using machine learning (logistic regression and random forest classifier) and deep learning (artificial neural network) models. To examine the blends of the vast majority of components that help detect the attacks, we trained our proposed model using existing datasets to predict the security attack.

Keywords: Intrusion detection, malware detection, cyber security, machine learning, deep learning, logistic regression, neural networks, flask

17.1 Introduction

In the past couple of years, the utilization of the internet has expanded a lot. Due to the global pandemic, everything has become online, and so has the usage of the Internet and web services. There is a massive increase in

---

*Corresponding author: anilsekumar@gmail.com

Rajdeep Chakraborty, Anupam Ghosh, Jyotsna Kumar Mandal and S. Balamurugan (eds.) Convergence of Deep Learning In Cyber-IoT Systems and Security, (367–380) © 2023 Scrivener Publishing LLC

the use of the Internet and multiple software and applications. The storing of all the data has become online more than manual for ease of data transfer. But the increase in usage has led to a rise in security threats as well. An intrusion detection system keeps our network secure as it tells us about any suspicious activity. It is essential to build a network intrusion detector that tells us about the good and malicious traffic on the web.

Similarly, the amount of malware attacks has increased. There are multiple types of malware, such as viruses, ransomware, Trojans, etc. This is a very common attack and can steal a lot of sensitive data. This would result in a lot of damage to confidential data. Many methods have been proposed for detection and securing the devices and network traffic.

In this paper, we focus on proposing a web framework for intrusion detection, i.e., detecting if the network is safe or unsafe and malware detection using machine learning and artificial intelligence. Machine and deep learning can play a significant role in helping detect cyberattacks. We use ML and DL models to predict and integrate the same with a website to make it easier to use for users.

Organization of the Paper

1. Abstract
2. Introduction
3. Literature Survey
4. Overview of Proposed Work
5. Implementation
6. Result
7. Conclusion and Future Work
8. References

17.2 Literature Survey

This work [1] gives us the importance of an intrusion detection system. It tells us that an intrusion location framework is a piece of the protective activities that supplements the protections like firewalls, UTM and helps detect any anomaly or unknown source. It states that the intrusion identification frameworks are regularly arranged as attack identification and peculiarity recognition frameworks.

The paper [2] has proposed a fundamental framework containing frequency runs, association, and classification rules, that uses data mining methods for intrusion detection. This framework can be helpful to build models. They experimented on Sendmail. These assessments on Sendmail structure call data and network TCP dump data showed the practicality of classification models in distinguishing anomalies. The precision of these models depended upon good planning data and good features. They proposed that the association runs and frequency run estimations can be utilized to read the consistent details from survey data. These regular models structure a blueprint of a review trail and thus can be used to direct the survey data gathering measure, offer help to incorporate assurance, and discover instances of interference. Starter tests of using these estimations on the TCP dump data showed them promising results.

The work [3] analyzed the contrasts between the organization intrusion identification issue and different zones where AI routinely discovers more achievement. Their primary case is that the errand of discovering attacks is, on an elementary level, unique in relation to these different applications, which makes it altogether harder for the intrusion identification local area to utilize AI viably. They support this case by recognizing moves specific to organize intrusion identification and provide many rules intended to fortify future examination on abnormality location.

In this paper [4], they have done a point-by-point examination and investigation of different AI strategies to discover the reason for issues related to other AI methods in intrusion detection. Attacks order and planning of the attack highlights are given relating to each attack. They examine challenges identified with recognizing low-recurrence attacks utilizing network attack datasets and propose suitable strategies for development. AI methods have been broken down and analyzed as far as their location ability for identifying the different classifications of attacks. They also discuss limits related to each of them. Other data mining tools, such as Scikit-learn, KMINE for AI, have also been discussed. This paper suggests that clustering helps detection accuracy and that the same approach may not work for all types of attacks. It also indicates that multiple classifiers with needed features work better than other classifiers.

In this paper [5], the authors have researched showing an ID framework on the principle of profound learning. They propose a deep learning approach, using Recurrent Neural Networks, for an intrusion recognition system. In addition, they studied the model's performance in similar gathering and multi-class course of action, and the quantity of neurons and specific learning rate impact the introduction of the proposed model. They contrast it with J48, support vector machine, and other AI strategies presented by past researchers. Their research outcome shows that RNN-IDS is sensible for exhibiting a high-precision portrayal model. Its show is superior to that of ordinary AI gathering systems in both matched and multiclass plans. RNN-IDS model improves the precision of the intrusion location and gives another exploration strategy to intrusion recognition.

The work [6] presented a structure for equipment that helped malware discovery dependent on checking and ordering memory access designs using AI. This research includes expanded mechanization and inclusion through lessening client contribution on explicit malware marks. The critical understanding of their work depends on malware changing control streams or possibly data structures, leaving traces on program memory. Developing this, they propose an online construction for distinguishing malware that usages AI to bunch malware on virtual memory access plans. Novel parts of the structure incorporate strategies for gathering and summing up per-work memory access designs and a two-level grouping engineering. Their test assessment centers around two significant classes of malware, namely part rootkits and memory defilement attacks on client programs. The system has a discovery pace of 99.0% with under 5% false positives and beats past recommendations for equipment helped malware recognition.

The work has proposed to analyze the malware reports [7]. They preprocessed this data into vector models for additional AI (order). The classifiers they utilized are k Nearest Neighbors (KNN), Naive Bayes, J48 Decision Tree, Support Vector Machine, and Neural Networks. J48 had the best result with an accuracy of 97.3%. It had a recall and precision of 95.9% and 96.8%, respectively, and a false positive of 2.4%.

The authors [8] have utilized opcode recurrence as a component vector and applied unaided learning notwithstanding administered learning for malware recognition. Their main point of this was to introduce their work on identifying malware with various machine learning calculations and profound learning models. Their outcomes show that the Arbitrary Backwoods beats Profound Neural Organization with opcode recurrence as an element. Likewise, in include decrease, Profound Auto-Encoders are over the top excess for the dataset, and rudimentary capacity like Difference Edge perform better compared to other people. Notwithstanding the proposed procedures, they likewise examine the different issues and the novel difficulties, open exploration issues, limits, and future bearings.

The proposed [9] machine learning-based malware examination framework comprises of information handling, dynamic, and new malware identification modules. The first part manages dark scale pictures, Opcode n-gram, and import capacities which they use to extricate the highlights of the malware, whereas their second part uses the highlights to order the malware and to distinguish dubious malware. At last, they use SSN clustering calculation to find new malware types. They assess their method on more than twenty thousand malware examples gathered by Kingsoft, ESET NOD32, and Anubis. The outcomes show that their framework could adequately arrange the unknown malware with the accuracy of 98.9% and effectively distinguishes 86.7% of the new/unknown malware.

The research [10] can utilize distinctive AI calculations to effectively recognize malware records and clean documents while keeping the false outcomes as low as possible. This paper presents their structure by handling coarse, uneven perceptrons and, with course, kernelized uneven perceptrons. This work has been effectively tried on medium-size datasets of malware and clean documents, which empowered them to work with vast malware datasets.

Due to the increase in attacks, many serious consequences can occur, such as confidential data leakage and damage. Hence an efficient system is needed for prevention and detecting such attacks.

17.3   Overview of the Proposed Work

17.3.1   Problem Description

Due to emerging security attacks, it is highly essential to introduce an emerging and highly accurate detection model. Hence, we have modeled our proposed model with three emerging algorithms with two datasets and also integrated our model with a web application for ease of use. This framework would detect malware attacks effectively.

17.3.2   The Working Models

1. Logistic Regression
2. Random Forest Classifier
3. Neural Network

17.3.3   About the Dataset

The primary dataset is malware detection dataset. A few of the parameters of this dataset are hash, millisecond, classification, state, usage counter, prio, static, normal, policy, the total number of pages, shared and executable pages, address space, size, system time.

The secondary dataset is intrusion detection dataset. A few parameters of this dataset are bytes, the type of protocol, buffer, duration(of connection), if it is a host or guest login, error rate, It also has features, such as number of wrong fragments or urgent packets, status of the connection, number of access by root and number of operations taken place and the SYN and REJ errors.

Figure 17.1 gives a glance at the malware dataset and Figure 17.2 provides a glance at the intrusion dataset. Similarly, Figures 17.3, 17.4, and 17.5 provide more visualization information of these datasets.

hash	millisecond	classification	state	usage_counter	prio	static_prio	normal_prio	policy	vm_pgoff	...	nivcsw	min_flt	maj_flt	fs_excl_co
0b9c914...	0	malware	0	0	3069378560	14274	0	0	0	...	0	0	120	
0b9c914...	1	malware	0	0	3069378560	14274	0	0	0	...	0	0	120	
0b9c914...	2	malware	0	0	3069378560	14274	0	0	0	...	0	0	120	
0b9c914...	3	malware	0	0	3069378560	14274	0	0	0	...	0	0	120	
0b9c914...	4	malware	0	0	3069378560	14274	0	0	0	...	0	0	120	

Figure 17.1 Snippet of malware dataset.

	duration	protocol_type	service	flag	src_bytes	dst_bytes	land	wrong_fragment	urgent	hot	...	dst_host_same_srv_rate	dst_host_diff_srv_rate	ds
0	0	tcp	http	SF	181	5450	0	0	0	0	...	1.0	0.0	
1	0	tcp	http	SF	239	486	0	0	0	0	...	1.0	0.0	
2	0	tcp	http	SF	235	1337	0	0	0	0	...	1.0	0.0	
3	0	tcp	http	SF	219	1337	0	0	0	0	...	1.0	0.0	
4	0	tcp	http	SF	217	2032	0	0	0	0	...	1.0	0.0	

5 rows × 43 columns

Figure 17.2 Snippet of intrusion dataset.

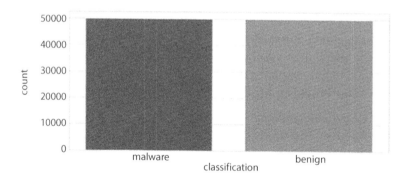

Figure 17.3 Malware dataset visualization.

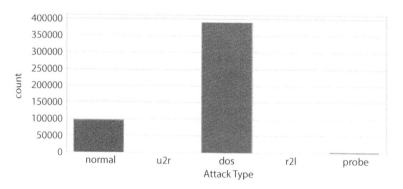

Figure 17.4 Intrusion dataset visualization.

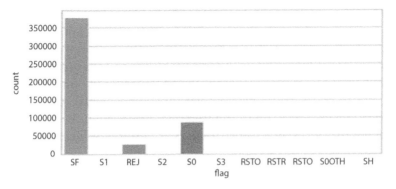

Figure 17.5 Intrusion dataset visualization.

17.3.4   About the Algorithms

Logistic Regression: It tells the relation between the independent variables(input) and the dependent(output). It is a game plan issue where your target part is outright. Unlike Linear Regression, in Logistic Regression, the yield required is tended to in discrete characteristics like binary 0 and 1. It checks the association between a dependent variable (target) and one free factor (pointers) where the subordinate variable is categorical. One can import it from sklearn.linear-model import LogisticRegression.

    Random Forest Classifier: The gathering of decision trees is a random forest. It is an ensemble algorithm and can be used for classifiers and regressors. Like other AI methodologies, random forests use getting ready data to sort out some way to make assumptions. Capacities are honorably out of the holder without tuning any limits. Various models may have settings that require enormous experimentation to find the most desirable characteristics. Tend not to overfit. The patterns of randomizing the data and elements across various trees infer that no single tree sees all the data. This helps with focusing on the general models inside the readiness data and diminishes the affectability to clatter. It can manage non-direct numeric and hard and fast markers and results. Various models may require numeric wellsprings of information or anticipate linearity. Accuracy decided from out-of-pack tests is a middle person for using an alternate test instructive assortment. The out-of-sack tests are those not used for setting up a specific tree and, as such, can be used as a reasonable extent of execution. One can import this library from sklearn.ensemble import RandomForestClassifier.

    Neural Network: It is a series of calculations that attempts to find fundamental connections in the given arrangement of information through a cycle that emulates how a human brain works. Presently assuming we examine Human Brain similarity, this alludes to neurons. These assist us with grouping and arrange the given information. There are numerous sorts of neural networks accessible or that may be in the improvement stage. We can characterize them relying upon their: Structure, Datastream, Neurons utilized and their thickness, Layers and their profundity initiation channels, and so on. A neural network has three fundamental parts: forward propagation, loss calculation, and backward propagation. We can use different libraries for Neural Networks such as TensorFlow, Keras, PyTorch.

Organization of this section

1. Problem Description
2. Working Model Overview
3. About the dataset
4. About the Algorithms

17.4   Implementation

17.4.1   Libraries

Seaborn: Seaborn is a data portrayal library for quantifiable plans plotting in Python. It gives magnificent default styles and concealing reaches to make verifiable plots engaging. It depends on the most important place of the matplotlib library. We can use it closely by matplotlib to make our plots seriously engaging. Scarcely any features consolidate Histogram, Plots (Bar, Count, Point, Violin, Joint, Reg, Box), Heatmap, etc. We can install using the command pip install seaborn, and we can import it by import seaborn as sns.

SciKit Learn: Scikit-learn is a Python module joining many top-tier AI computations for medium-scale directed and independent issues. This group revolves around carrying AI to non-specialists using a generally valuable irrefutable level language. The highlight is put on ease of use, execution, documentation, and API consistency. It has unimportant conditions and is spread under the enhanced BSD license, enabling its use in academic and business settings. It has multiple inbuilt features. It has many inbuilt algorithms, which can be imported directly using SciKit Learn.

Tensorflow: TensorFlow is a beginning-to-end open source stage for AI. TensorFlow is a framework for dealing with all bits of an AI structure; notwithstanding, this class spins around utilizing a specific TensorFlow API to make and arrange AI models. Its APIs are arranged logically, with the certain level APIs dependent on low-level APIs. Simulated intelligence researchers use low-level APIs to make and explore new AI estimations. One will use an

API named tf.keras to describe and plan AI models and make assumptions. tf. keras is the TensorFlow variety of the open-source Keras API. TensorFlow is the subsequent AI system that Google made and used to configure, fabricate, and train profound learning models. One can utilize the TensorFlow library to do mathematical calculations. These calculations are finished with information stream charts. Here, centers address mathematical errands, while the edges address the data, which by and large are multidimensional data groups or tensors that are granted between the edges. We import the TensorFlow library as tf. We can choose the version we want while downloading.

Numpy: NumPy addresses Numerical Python. It is a pack for data examination and sensible enrolling with Python. NumPy utilizes a multidimensional show object and has cutoff points and instruments for working with these gatherings. The n-dimensional presentation in NumPy speeds up information status. NumPy can feasibly be interfaced with other Python bundles and provides mechanical gatherings for melding other programming vernaculars like C and C++. NumPy displays are taken care of at one relentless spot in memory, unlike records, so cycles can gain to and power them gainfully. This lead is known as the area of reference in programming. Moreover, it is smoothed out to work with the latest CPU structures.

Padas: The library is consolidated for performing essential data controls and assessments on such instructive records. It means to be the focal layer for the destiny of verifiable figuring in Python. It fills in as a solid enhancement to the current intelligent Python stack while executing and upgrading such data control contraptions found in other actual programming vernaculars like R. We can install this using the command pip install pandas and import using import pandas as pd.

Flask: Flask is a miniature web system that is written in Python. It is named a micro framework on the grounds that it does not need specific devices or libraries. It has no data set reflection layer, structure approval, or other segments where previous outsider libraries give standard capacities.

HTML (Hypertext markup language) and CSS (cascading style sheets): We used HTML and CSS for the front-end development of the web application. They are integrated with a flask to predict the output from the given input details through forms on the HTML page. We used CSS to add color and features to the HTML Page.

Python: Python is a very popular programming language. Python can be utilized on a framework software to code web applications, close by programming to make few functions and processes, can work along with data set frameworks. It can, likewise, peruse and change documents. It can be used to deal with massive information, perform complex arithmetic, quick prototyping, or create programming improvement.

Framework: We have used VS CODE and Jupyter Notebook for implementing the proposed framework.

17.4.2 Algorithm

1. Import the necessary libraries
2. import the dataset
3. Data Visualization of the data
4. EDA (Exploratory Data Analysis): Encoding the data, Looking out for missing values, Normalization and Standardization of the data, Feature Scaling
5. Choosing the necessary parameters needed for the data modeling
6. Splitting the dataset
7. Defining the Logistic Regression Model and training the data on train dataset and testing on the test dataset.
8. Similarly, operations with Random Forest Classifier
9. Then initialize Neural Network Model, Add the input, and first and second hidden layer, and finally output layer (dense layers)
10. Compile the Neural network and train on the training dataset.
11. Find the accuracy for these models. Plot the accuracy graph.
12. Save the model with the highest accuracy.
13. Integrate this model with a web application using HTML, Cs, flask.
14. Run the app on the localhost and give input to get the output if safe or unsafe.
15. Deploy for large scale (Optional)

Organization of this section

1. Libraries used
   (Seabron, Scikit Learn, Tensorflow, Numpy, Pandas, Flask, HTML CSS, Python, Framework)
2. Algorithm

17.5 Results

We tried various algorithms and deployed the model on a flask framework. We used python programming language for the same.

```
Epoch 42/50
2500/2500 [==============================] - 2s 889us/step - loss: 1.6663e-06 - accuracy: 1.0000
Epoch 43/50
2500/2500 [==============================] - 2s 865us/step - loss: 1.2503e-06 - accuracy: 1.0000
Epoch 44/50
2500/2500 [==============================] - 2s 860us/step - loss: 3.7402e-04 - accuracy: 0.99990s - loss: 1.1140e
Epoch 45/50
2500/2500 [==============================] - 2s 850us/step - loss: 2.8739e-06 - accuracy: 1.0000
Epoch 46/50
2500/2500 [==============================] - 2s 934us/step - loss: 1.0572e-06 - accuracy: 1.0000
Epoch 47/50
2500/2500 [==============================] - 2s 847us/step - loss: 6.3647e-07 - accuracy: 1.0000ls - loss: 7.273 - ETA:
0s - 1
Epoch 48/50
2500/2500 [==============================] - 2s 862us/step - loss: 3.8989e-04 - accuracy: 0.9999
Epoch 49/50
2500/2500 [==============================] - 2s 845us/step - loss: 3.1722e-04 - accuracy: 1.0000
Epoch 50/50
2500/2500 [==============================] - 2s 912us/step - loss: 1.0494e-04 - accuracy: 0.9999
```

Figure 17.6 Malware detection.

```
12351/12351 [------------------------------] - 13s 1ms/step - loss: 0.0010 - accuracy: 0.9995
Epoch 42/50
12351/12351 [==============================] - 13s 1ms/step - loss: 0.0017 - accuracy: 0.9995
Epoch 43/50
12351/12351 [==============================] - 13s 1ms/step - loss: 0.0017 - accuracy: 0.9995
Epoch 44/50
12351/12351 [==============================] - 13s 1ms/step - loss: 0.0017 - accuracy: 0.9995
Epoch 45/50
12351/12351 [==============================] - 13s 1ms/step - loss: 0.0016 - accuracy: 0.9995
Epoch 46/50
12351/12351 [==============================] - 13s 1ms/step - loss: 0.0016 - accuracy: 0.9996
Epoch 47/50
12351/12351 [==============================] - 13s 1ms/step - loss: 0.0016 - accuracy: 0.9996
Epoch 48/50
12351/12351 [==============================] - 13s 1ms/step - loss: 0.0016 - accuracy: 0.9995 0s - loss:
Epoch 49/50
12351/12351 [==============================] - 13s 1ms/step - loss: 0.0016 - accuracy: 0.9995
Epoch 50/50
12351/12351 [==============================] - 13s 1ms/step - loss: 0.0016 - accuracy: 0.9996
```

Figure 17.7 Intrusion detection.

17.5.1   Neural Network Models

Below is the neural network model for both datasets. Figure 17.6 depicts the Malware Detection neural network model, and Figure 17.7 depicts the intrusion detection neural network model.

17.5.2   Accuracy

Below is the accuracy of the machine learning and the accuracy graph for the deep learning model. Figures 17.8 to 17.10 show the accuracies of the model for malware, whereas Figures 17.11 to 17.12 show the accuracies for the intrusion detection model.

17.5.3   Web Frameworks

Below are the web page snippets. We give the input in Figure 17.13, and we get the output in Figure 17.14 for malware detection. Similarly, Figure 17.15 depicts the intrusion detection framework.

```
accuracy_score(logreg_predict,y_test)
0.94035
```

Figure 17.8 Malware detection: logistic reg.

```
accuracy_score(rfc_predict,y_test)
1.0
```

Figure 17.9 Malware detection: random forest.

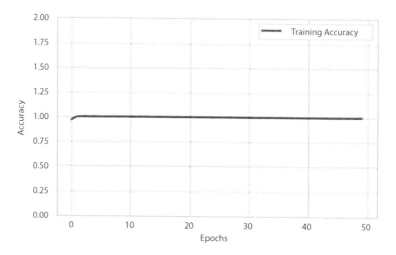

Figure 17.10 Malware detection: neural network.

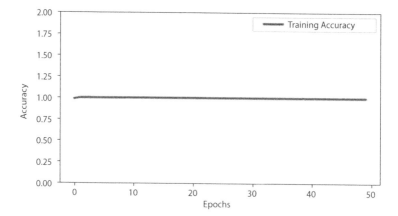

Figure 17.11 Intrusion detection: neural network.

```
from sklearn.metrics import confusion_matrix, accuracy_score
accuracy_score(logreg_predict,y_test)

0.9957087191943728
```

Figure 17.12 Intrusion detection: logistic regression.

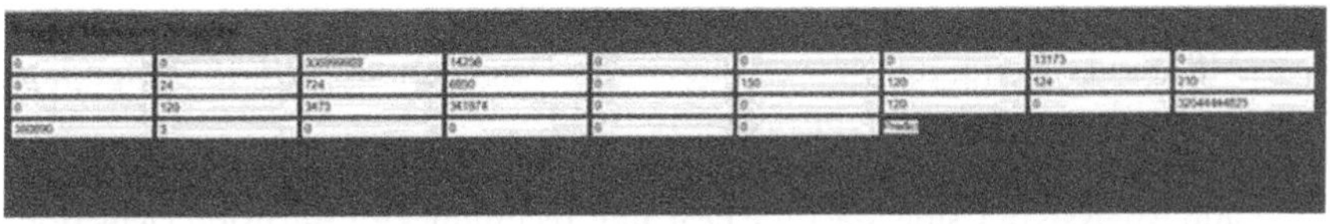

Figure 17.13 Malware detection.

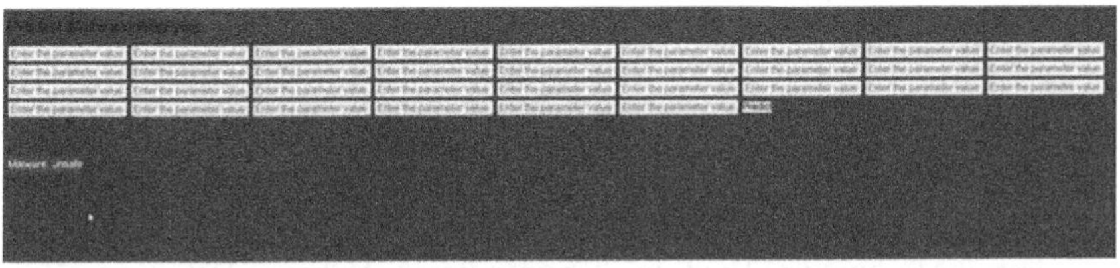

Figure 17.14 Malware predicted.

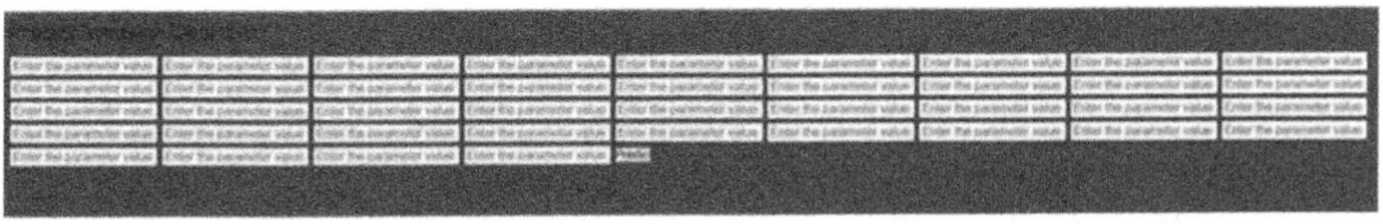

Figure 17.15 Intrusion detection snippet.

17.6   Conclusion and Future Work

Our proposed model helps detect various types of attacks and classify suspicious activities that may be safe or unsafe. Our model has also achieved better accuracy for larger-scale data sets and could be easily integrated into web-based systems for efficient monitoring and decision making to reduce human effort and errors in decision-making systems. The proposed model has achieved high accuracy for detecting and categorizing malware attacks, which can be helpful for the prevention of malware attacks and network intrusions.

References

1. Ashoor, A.S. and Gore, S., Importance of Intrusion Detection System (IDS). *Int. J. Sci. Eng. Res.*, 2, 1–4, January 2011.
2. Lee, W. and Stolfo, S.J., Data Mining Approaches for Intrusion Detection. *Proceedings of the 7th USENIX Security Symposium.*
3. Sommer, R. and Paxson, V., Outside the Closed World: On Using MachineLearning for Network Intrusion Detection. *2010 IEEE Symposium on Security and Privacy*, pp. 305–316, 2010.
4. Mishra, P., Varadharajan, V., Tupakula, U., Pilli, E.S., A Detailed Investigation and Analysis of Using Machine Learning Techniques for Intrusion Detection. *IEEE Commun. Surv. Tut.*, 21, 1, 686–728, Firstquarter 2019.
5. Yin, C., Zhu, Y., Fei, J., He, X., A Deep Learning Approach for IntrusionDetection Using Recurrent Neural Networks. *IEEE Access*, 5, 21954–21961, 2017.
6. Xu, Z., Ray, S., Subramanyan, P., Malik, S., Malware detection using machine learning based analysis of virtual memory access patterns. *Design, Automation Test in Europe Conference Exhibition (DATE), 2017*, pp. 169–174, 2017.
7. Firdausi, I., Lim, C., Erwin, A., Nugroho, A.S., Analysis of Machine learningTechniques Used in Behavior-Based Malware Detection. *2010 Second International Conference on Advances in Computing, Control, and Telecommunication Technologies*, pp. 201–203, 2010.
8. Rathore, H., Agarwal, S., Sahay, S.K., Sewak, M., Malware detection using machine learning and deep learning. *Lect. Notes Comput. Sci.*, 11927, 402–411, 2018.
9. Liu, L., Wang, B.S., Yu, B. *et al.*, Automatic malware classification and new-malware detection using machine learning. *Front. Inf. Technol. Electron. Eng.*, 18, 1336–1347, 2017.
10. Gavrilut, D., Cimpoesu, M., Anton, D., Ciortuz, L., Malware detection using machine learning. *2009 International Multiconference on Computer Science and Information Technology*, pp. 735–741, 2009.

18

Phishing URL Detection Based on Deep Learning Techniques

S. Carolin Jeeva[1]* and W. Regis Anne[2]

[1]Karunya Institute of Technology and Sciences, Coimbatore, India
[2]PSG College of Technology, Coimbatore, India

Abstract

In the digital era, online communication has seen tremendous growth worldwide for the past decade. Over the last years, the web has seen a massive growth, and due to pandemic, the usage has increased a lot. In today's scenario, all types of transactions are done through the web, which was previously thought to be impossible. This has led the Internet users becoming targets of cyber threats. Among all the cyber-attack available, phishing is the most common technique to capture sensitive information like user name and password in websites without the knowledge of the end user. Report by antiphishing working states that the phishing attacks have doubled over the course of the year 2020. Due to the pandemic, the online usage has seen a tremendous growth ever before. Internet has become the mode of phishing is a form of cyber-attack that has laid the path for hackers to obtain the sensitive information from the user by impersonate as legitimate website. However, identifying phishing URL is a challenging task. This chapter focuses on detecting phishing URL using convolutional neural network. The phishtank dataset is considered, and the features of the URL are extracted. Finally, the deep learning classifier is used to detect if the URL is phishing or legitimate URL. The performance of the classifier is evaluated based on the accuracy, precision, recall, and F1 score.

Keywords: Phishing, social engineering, cyber security, deep learning, cybercrime, cyber-attack, accuracy

Corresponding author: caroljeeva@gmail.com

Rajdeep Chakraborty, Anupam Ghosh, Jyotsna Kumar Mandal and S. Balamurugan (eds.) Convergence of Deep Learning In Cyber-IoT Systems and Security, (381–396) © 2023 Scrivener Publishing LLC

18.1   Introduction

Information communication technology (ICT) has reformed various aspects of human life and thereby made life simpler. Nowadays, computers and Internet-equipped devices have turn out to be an essential part of human life. The World Wide Web technologies enable users around the globe to get involved in viable activities throughout the day and the place they reside. Today, the Internet has become the utmost necessity in everyone's life. As a result, the cyber-crimes have increased a lot and thereby many security companies have used new technology to protect their asserts from the hackers. Internet services are used to communicate and to perform mission critical system for various businesses. The web has made communication easier and quicker and thereby enlarges its usage boundaries. The resources hosted in the web are interconnected through hypertext and are accessed through the web browser. These webpages are navigated through the hyperlinks available in the webpage. A set of related webpages are known as website and are from the single web domain. These days, all the work is done through websites. E-commercial websites, such as amazon, and online auction websites, such as eBay, provide an online platform where millions of products are exchanged per day.

Phishing is a cybercriminal attack that captures the personal information from the user by sending an e-mail that has a link to gather sensitive details from the online users for further transaction. A phisher creates a fake webpage that resembles the legitimate webpage and thereby probe the user to enter the sensitive details like user name and password, and it is transferred to the hacker's server. As most of the user prefer online transaction than off line transaction the cyber-crime threats have increased a lot. According to the report by Proofpoint's 75% of the organizations experienced phishing attack during the year 2020.

18.1.1   Phishing Life Cycle

According to the antiphishing working group, the use of "ph" in the terminology is related to the replacement of the character 'f' in the word "fishing," where the early hacker used the term "phone phreaking," a technique used to gather sensitive details by making long-distance phone calls. The term "phreaks" was coined in the year 1996 where the hackers were stealing America Online accounts (AOL) by capturing passwords by hacking the telephonic conversation from unsuspecting AOL users. The APWG states that "phishing" originally comes from the analogy that initial

Internet convicts used email that traps to "fish" toward password gathering, financial data from the oceanic of Internet users.

The Phishing attacker's trick users with different tactics such as threatening to suspend user account. An attacker presents as a modest and liable individual with social ethics. The phisher uses social engineering techniques, indulge the user to produce their user's name and password within a particular period of time. The forged webpage typically comprises of a login editable screen, and when an online user unlocks the counterfeit webpage and inputs nonpublic facts, these details are accessed by the attacker. To warfare phishing, the various steps involved in phishing attack must be investigated. The following are the activities involved in phishing attack.

18.1.1.1   Planning

Usually, phishers initiate an attack by developing a forged copy of the legitimate internet site by identifying their victims, the details to be extracted and the technique to follow to obtain the same. The intension of the phisher is to identify the users targets and steps to achieve maximum profit with minimum risk. The criminal gathers the employee database from the organization and from social networking sites. The most commonly used way to make interact between the attacker and the victims is through the social networking sites including electronic mail and instant messaging.

A traditional phishing attack involves two components; they are reliable-looking email and illegitimate web page. The contents of the phishing email are portrayed to confuse the recipient. The illegitimate webpage normally has the appearance of a genuine webpage that is created by having alike logo of the legitimate company and its page layout. The term phishing was coined in 1995, where the scammers sent mail of hard-crafted, incorrect messages and dupe the users to connect to the link or opening a malevolent add-on provided in the email. The malicious email pays a way for gaining a base to initiate an attack. A report by Tom *et al.* (2007) indicated that online users are 4.5 times expected to be victims of the phisher. This is the reason why the phishers are targeting social networking websites. The main comparison between spam emails and phishing emails are the spam emails are exasperating emails forwarded to publicize products. Alternatively, phishing emails are dispatched to the sufferers to obtain sensitive data. Normally, the attacker adapts tactics to capture confidential details from the web user.

18.1.1.2   Collection

As soon as the victims are convinced to make an action to an information theft, he is insisted to produce the data through a mimicking site. Usually, the counterfeit website is hosted on a compromised server and thereby gain information from the victims. Occasionally, the phisher uses free cloud application, namely Google spreadsheets with the intention of hosting fake websites. The report by APWG (2003) in order to diminish the possibility of the phisher being caught the phishers will abuse web servers that lack in security and the countries those have inadequate law execution resources.

18.1.1.3   Fraud

Lastly, when the hacker has attained the task by obtaining the credentials and involves them by impersonating the victims. The fraud can be done by the phisher or he can sell the credential to the buyer and he uses mules to transfer money. The common phases involved in phishing attack are shown in Figure 18.1.

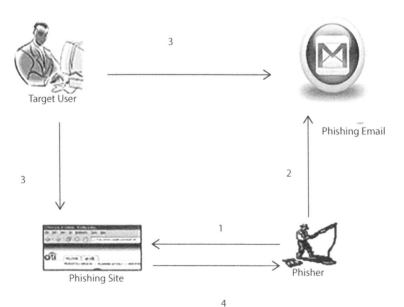

Figure 18.1 Common phases involved in phishing attack.

Step 1: The attacker makes duplicate copy of the well-known legitimate internet site and creates the phishing website by editing the valid internet site.

Step 2: The phisher creates an electronic mail and incorporate the hyperlink of the fake websites, thereby prompting the user to click the hyperlink provided in the email.

Step 3: Unknowingly, the user enters the phishing URL and provides the login details assuming that the website is legitimate.

Step 4: The hacker obtains the confidential details from the user through the illegitimate website and makes use of this details to carry out further process.

Phishing offends internet users, brands and organizations in numerous aspects. The subsequence of this phishing attack leads the user in many ways RSA (2013).

a. The phishing result reveals online users' personal information like (username, password, or the sensitive details of the users' credit cards) and thereby causes economic losses.

b. Destroy users believe in online interactions and create a negative image in the minds of the consumer.

c. Phishing causes a continuing avoidance of internet purchase and banking and thus hampers the growth of e-commerce.

d. Phishing has a damaging effect on stakeholders, which results in failure to preserve the brands and, subsequently, results in bankruptcy.

Phishers can offend the trust in Internet business by stealing sensitive information from the users. Online frauds have made the people slowly lose their trust and confidence toward Internet interactions. People believe that the usage of e-banking increases the likelihood of phishing attack that results in financial losses. Overall, phishing is a type of fraud that is considered to be the most hazardous threat around the world.

18.2 Literature Survey

Phishing has become a foremost hazard to online users. The speedy boom and increase of phishing approaches generate a huge risk to online transactions and thereby needs production to the end users. Routhu Srinivasa Rao and Alwyn Roshan Pais [1] proposed machine learning model in detecting phishing URL. The detection of the URL is carried out based on the heuristic features from the URL, third party service, and source code. Carolin Jeeva and Elijah Blessing Rajasingh [2] proposed heuristic features and based on the relationship of phishing URLs and rules are generated. Neda *et al.* [3] proposed rule-based classification and features are generated based on human experience instead of using data mining techniques. The proposed technique by Jain A.K and Gupta [4] uses automatic update of legitimate websites and warns the online user of sensitive keywords.

The legitimacy of the webpage is accessed based on 1) IP address and domain matching module, 2) Hyperlinks features from source code. Few antiphishing technologies rely on the combination of blacklist and whitelist-based approaches. These approaches are deployed as toolbars or browser extensions. The whitelist using aural and visual similarity of web pages is proposed by Sonowal *et al.* [5]. The drawbacks in visual similarity-based approach arise due to the dependency on source code and can be rectified by analyzing the features in captured images of legitimate and suspicious websites.

A predictive black list-based approach is proposed to identify phishing websites [6]. The blacklist-based approach is effective, and it depends on the excellence of the list maintained. The advantage of using Black list-based approach is that it can be implemented easily. The downside of using a blacklist-based approach is that it cannot identify the sites not listed, which yields a low positive rate. After the phishing website is launched, the particular URL is updated in the blacklist, which is a major disadvantage. Frequent updates are done but still new phishing sites are not done timely. The shortcoming of the traditional black list method cannot recognize the non-blacklisted sites and thereby does not deal with the new phishing sites. Like black list, white list–based approach also needs to update its information on a large scale. Unfortunately, the white list could not contain all the legitimate sites. Although the approach of using black list and white list is efficient, checking in black list alone is not an efficient method because the recent phishing URLs are not maintained in the black list. If the system is having any technical issues in connecting with the black list database, then the system cannot respond and this leads to incorrect results.

An approach that uses search engine was proposed by Huh *et al.* [7] for phishing detection but in a lighter way. The full URL string is given to search engine thereby reducing the keyword extraction method followed in the above-mentioned search engine-based approach. The total number of search results obtained through search engine and the ranking of the suspected webpage are used to determine the results. The validation of this approach is carried out using three different search engines namely Google, Yahoo and Bing. An approach by Lee *et al.* [8] proposed where the features are gathered by Google's suggestion, web page ranking and wary URL patterns. Approximately 98.23% of phishing websites are detected. An approach based on a weighted token in URL is proposed [9] by Tan *et al.* Identity keyword phrases are extracted as signatures from the webpage. The experiment results achieved 99.20% true positive and 92.20% true negative.

Overall, a search engine–related approach is more effective in phishing detection. However, using a search engine for phishing detection has several disadvantages. It can work only with the webpage that has content in English language, time consuming because Google search engine is involved and bypass if the webpage is composed of image instead of textual content. Thus, it is necessary to use the popularity of websites to support other heuristics properties for phishing detection. A rule-based approach is proposed by Mahmood and Ai [10]. The relationship between the content and URL of a page are extracted. Text matching algorithm is used to test the address of a page resource element together with the URL. Attribute selection-based phishing URL detection is proposed by Carolin *et al.* [11].

Ping *et al.* [12] proposed a deep learning approach in detecting phishing web page where the deep belief networks is presented and the detection accuracy is found to be 89.2%. Wenchuan *et al.* [13] proposed text-based classification using Convolutional Gated Recurrent Unit Neural Network. In the study by Alejandro *et al.* [14], the phishing URLs are detected using recurrent neural network with an accuracy of 98.7%. Liqun *et al.* [15] proposed the NIOSELM approach where the surface level feature, topological, and inheritance of the websites are used in detecting phishing webpages, and the accuracy is found to be 97.5%.

A survey on deep learning in phishing detection is portrayed by Samanesh Mahdavifar and Ali A. Ghorbani [16]. Ishita *et al.* [17] proposed a deep learning approach in detecting phishing webpages with an accuracy of 95%. Tomas Rasymas and Laurynas Dovydaitis [18] proposed detection of phishing URL based on lexical features, word level embedding, and character level embedding using deep learning approach. Manuel *et al.* [19] proposed network traffic classifier using convolutional and recurrent neural network for Internet of Things. Zuguo *et al.* [20] proposed phishing URL detection using deep learning.

18.3   Feature Generation

The heuristic features are extracted from the URL. The detailed feature extraction step is given in Jeeva *et al.* [2]. The architecture of the proposed work is portrayed in Figure 18.2. In our experiments, the data from Phishtank is considered with URLs that has 14 features and one class that specifies if it is a phished or legitimate website. The dataset is preprocessed and all the null values are identified and converted to the average value of the neighbors. The distribution plot of the features is shown in Figure 18.3.

18.4   Convolutional Neural Network for Classification of Phishing vs Legitimate URLs

In deep learning, the convolutional neural network (CNN) belongs to the class of deep neural networks. The Convolutional Neural Network (CNN) has exposed exceptional performance in numerous computer vision and machine learning problems. The advantage of CNN is it inevitably detects the significant features without any human supervision. It accommodates convolution and pooling operations and execute parameter sharing. This allows CNN models to execute on any device and building them universally compliant.

Figure 18.4 shows the traditional neural network is with one input layer, one output layer and one or more hidden layers. Each circle represents a neuron, which has connection to every neuron in the next layer. CNN is a

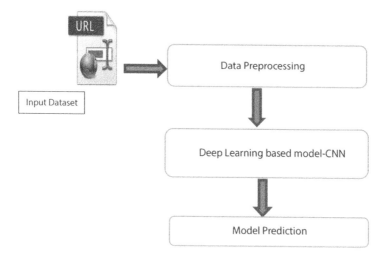

Figure 18.2 System architecture.

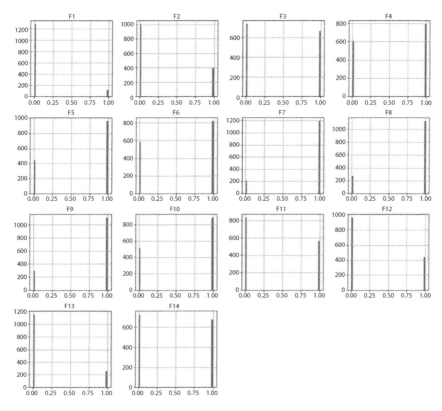

Figure 18.3 Distribution plot of the features.

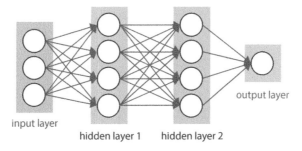

input layer

hidden layer 1   hidden layer 2

output layer

Figure 18.4 Traditional neural network.

form of artificial neural network and is most properly used in image analysis. CNN is also helps in data analysis for classification problems. CNN has hidden layers namely the convolutional layers. The basis of CNN is the convolutional layer. The convolutional layer works like other layers, which accept input and trains and transform the output to the other layer. This is known as convolutional operation. The convolutional layers are used to detect the patterns. This layer combines two sets of information using convolution map and produces a feature map. In each convolutional layer the number of filters to be used must be mentioned. Convolution on each layer can be performed with different filters that produces a feature map. All the feature maps from all the convolution layer can be combined as the final feature map of the convolution layers. The filters are mainly used to detect the patterns. For nonlinearity purposes, the result is passed on to the activation function like Rectified Linear Units (ReLU).

The ReLu activation function is given by: $f(x) = \max(0, x)$ ReLU helps to lessen fading and exploding gradient concerns. It is more competent with respect to time and cost for training huge data in contrast to traditional non-linear activation functions, such as Sigmoid or Tangent functions. Then striding on how much to move the convolution filter is decided. In this paper, we have set Stride to be the default value 1. Then padding can be performed to maintain the same dimensionality. Pooling reduces the dimensionality and in turn reduces the number of parameters. This reduces overfitting and running time of the algorithm. The most used pooling is max pooling. Then we insert fully connected layers to complete the CNN architecture. Training of the network is done like back propagation with gradient descent. During training, Dropout parameter can be tuned to prevent overfitting. Figure 18.5 shows the diagram of CNN, which uses multiple convolutional operations for feature extraction. The model constructed is given in Figure 18.6.

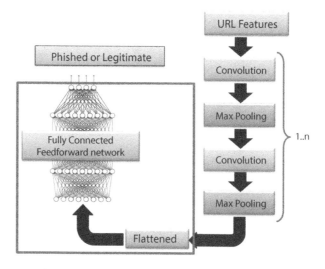

Figure 18.5 Convolution neural network model.

```
Layer (type)                 Output Shape              Param #
=================================================================
input_2 (InputLayer)         [(None, 14, 14)]          0

dense_29 (Dense)             (None, 14, 14)            210

dense_30 (Dense)             (None, 14, 14)            210

dense_31 (Dense)             (None, 14, 12)            180

dense_34 (Dense)             (None, 14, 14)            182

dense_35 (Dense)             (None, 14, 14)            210
=================================================================
Total params: 992
Trainable params: 992
Non-trainable params: 0
```

Figure 18.6 CNN model construction.

18.5   Results and Discussion

The dataset is divided into training and testing, where 80% of the data is used for training and 20% for testing. The result obtained from CNN is shown in Figure 18.7. After 19 epoch, it has found to be 99.64%. The outcome the trained and tested values are used to find out the accuracy of the

```
Epoch 1/100
84/84 [==============================] - 1s 2ms/step - loss: 0.3664 - accuracy: 0.8679
Epoch 2/100
84/84 [==============================] - 0s 2ms/step - loss: 0.1022 - accuracy: 0.9667
Epoch 3/100
84/84 [==============================] - 0s 2ms/step - loss: 0.0229 - accuracy: 0.9964
Epoch 4/100
84/84 [==============================] - 0s 2ms/step - loss: 0.0113 - accuracy: 0.9976
Epoch 5/100
84/84 [==============================] - 0s 2ms/step - loss: 0.0090 - accuracy: 0.9988
Epoch 6/100
84/84 [==============================] - 0s 2ms/step - loss: 0.0072 - accuracy: 0.9988
Epoch 7/100
84/84 [==============================] - 0s 2ms/step - loss: 0.0033 - accuracy: 1.0000
Epoch 8/100
84/84 [==============================] - 0s 2ms/step - loss: 0.0053 - accuracy: 0.9988
Epoch 9/100
84/84 [==============================] - 0s 2ms/step - loss: 0.0018 - accuracy: 1.0000
Epoch 10/100
84/84 [==============================] - 0s 2ms/step - loss: 0.0035 - accuracy: 0.9988
Epoch 11/100
84/84 [==============================] - 0s 1ms/step - loss: 0.0025 - accuracy: 0.9988
Epoch 12/100
84/84 [==============================] - 0s 2ms/step - loss: 0.0010 - accuracy: 1.0000
Epoch 13/100
84/84 [==============================] - 0s 2ms/step - loss: 0.0010 - accuracy: 1.0000
Epoch 14/100
84/84 [==============================] - 0s 2ms/step - loss: 7.8763e-04 - accuracy: 1.0000
Epoch 15/100
84/84 [==============================] - 0s 2ms/step - loss: 7.7947e-04 - accuracy: 1.0000
Epoch 16/100
84/84 [==============================] - 0s 2ms/step - loss: 7.0821e-04 - accuracy: 1.0000
Epoch 17/100
84/84 [==============================] - 0s 2ms/step - loss: 4.2855e-04 - accuracy: 1.0000
Epoch 18/100
84/84 [==============================] - 0s 2ms/step - loss: 3.7000e-04 - accuracy: 1.0000
Epoch 19/100
84/84 [==============================] - 0s 2ms/step - loss: 3.2148e-04 - accuracy: 1.0000
18/18 [==============================] - 0s 1ms/step - loss: 0.0054 - accuracy: 0.9964
```

Figure 18.7 Experimental results obtained using CNN.

dataset. Table 18.1 shows the result of batch loss and accuracy the CNN model for the first 12 epochs.

The graphical representation of the model accuracy and Loss is shown in Figure 18.8. The validation loss is less than the training loss. The loss nearly approaches zero as the epochs are increased and the accuracy almost reaches to 99.64% with a time of 1ms in detecting a phished or legitimate website using URL features. The model is trained and has comparable performance on the test data. The loss and accuracy on the testing data show good performance. The accuracy is also obtained within few epochs as the model has been trained well by the CNN.

Other than classification accuracy Precision, Recall and F1 score, Cohen's kappa, ROC AUC, and confusion matrix are calculated. Precision is the ratio of true positive and the real positive values i.e., the number of URLs that have been identified by CNN as phished to that of the really phished URL in the dataset. The value of precision is high meaning that the CNN has correctly identified 92% of the phished URL correctly. Recall is the ratio of true positive to the total of true positive and true negative.

Table 18.1 Batch loss and accuracy.

Epoch	Loss	Accuracy
1.	0.6855408549308777	0.811904788017273
2.	0.6478201150894165	0.8726190328598022
3	0.5441499352455139	0.8726190328598022
4.	0.37123724818229675	0.8726190328598022
5.	0.23800992965698242	0.8726190328598022
6.	0.18968583643436432	0.8726190328598022
7.	0.1613530069589615	0.8845238089561462
8.	0.13665366172790527	0.9428571462631226
9.	0.11793075501918793	0.9642857313156128
10.	0.10113957524299622	0.9750000238418579
11.	0.084832102060318	0.9785714149475098
12.	0.0697968453168869	0.9797618985176086

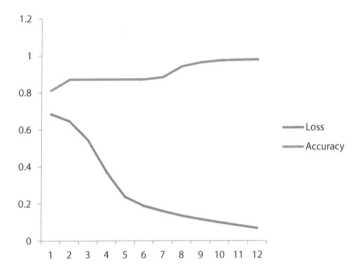

Figure 18.8 Model accuracy and loss using CNN.

Recall value of 1 shows that the CNN model has correctly identified a phished URL. F1 score has given the stability or weighted average between precision and recall with a value of 0.958932. Cohen's Kappa is the reliability measure of the two raters' precision and recall. The value of 0.788465 indicates a substantial agreement between precision and recall. Area under the receiver operating characteristics (AUROC) with the value of 0.989155 suggests that the model is able to classify well between the phished and legitimate URLs. The performance metrics results are portrayed in Table 18.2. Table 18.3 shows the comparison of existing model to the proposed model.

Table 18.2 Performance metrics.

S. no	Metrics	Value
1	Precision	0.921105
2	Recall	1.000000
3	F1 score	0.958932
4	Cohen's kappa	0.788465
5	AUROC	0.989155

Table 18.3 Comparison of the proposed model with the existing method.

Antipishing approaches	Accuracy
Liqun *et al.* (2021)	97.5%
Ishita *et al.* (2020)	95%
Tomas *et al.* (2020)	94.4%
Ping *et al.* (2018)	89.2%
Alejandro *et al.* (2017)	98.7%
Our Approach	99.64%

18.6   Conclusion

This chapter elaborates the study of phishing URL detection. As the pandemic situation prevails throughout the globe, cyberattacks have seen an exponential increase in the financial sector and have led the Internet users becoming targets of cyber threats. The foremost features that differentiate phishing and legitimate is considered and deep learning-based approach for predicting phishing URL is presented. The CNN gives better accuracy and is able to predict and classify the inputs to the specified activity. Using the proposed heuristic features, an accuracy of 99.64% is achieved using this model in detecting phishing URL.

References

1. Rao, R.S. and Pais, A.R., Detection of phishing websites using an efficient feature-based machine learning framework. *Neural Comput. Appl.*, 31, 3851–3873, 2018.
2. Jeeva, S.C. and Rajasingh, E.B., Intelligent phishing URL detection using association rule mining. *Hum.-Centric Comput. Inf. Sci.*, Springer Publications, 6, 10, 1–19, 2016.
3. Abdelhamid, N., Ayesh, A., Thabtah, F., Phishing detection based associative classification data mining. *Expert Syst. Appl.*, 41, 5948–5959, 2014.
4. Jain, A.K. and Gupta, B., A novel approach to protect against phishing attacks at client side using auto-updated white-list. *EURASIP J. Inf. Secur.*, 9, 1–11, 2016.

5. Sonowal, G. and Kuppusamy, K., Masphid: A model to assist screen reader users for detecting phishing sites using aural and visual similarity measures, in: *Proceedings of the International Conference on Informatics and Analytics*, pp. 1–6, 2016.

6. Prakash, P., Kumar, M., Kompella, R.R., Gupta, M., Phishnet: Predictive blacklisting to detect phishing attacks, in: *Proceedings of INFOCOM 2010*, San Diego, CA, March 15-19, pp. 1–5, 2010.

7. Huh, J. and Kim, H., Phishing detection with popular search engines: Simple and effective. *4th Canada-France MITACS Workshop on Foundations and Practice of Security*, Paris, France, May 12-13, Springer Verlag, pp. 194–207, 2011.

8. Lee, J.L., Kim, D.H., Lee, C.H., Heuristic-based approach for phishing site detection using url features, in: *Third International Conference On Advances in Computing, Electronics and Electrical Technology–CEET*, 2015.

9. Tan, C.L., Chiew, K.L., Sze, S.N., Phishing webpage detection using weighted url tokens for identity keywords retrieval, in: *9th International Conference on Robotic, Vision, Signal Processing and Power Applications*, Springer, pp. 133–139, 2017.

10. Moghimi, M. and Varjani, A.Y., New rule based phishing detection method. *Expert Syst. Appl.*, 53, 231–242, 2016.

11. Jeeva, S.C. and Rajasingh, E.B., Phishing URL detection based feature selection to classifiers. *Int. J. Electron. Secur. Digit. Forensics*, 9, 2, 116–131, 2017.

12. Yi, P., Guan, Y., Zou, F., Yao, Y., Wang, W., Zhu, T., Web phishing detection using a deep learning framework. *Wirel. Commun. Mob. Comput.*, (3–4), 1–9, 2018.

13. Yang, W., Zuo, W., Cui, B., Detecting malicious URL via a keyboard based convolutional gated recurrent-unit neural network, journals and magazines. *IEEE*, 7, 1–6, 2019.

14. Bahnsen, A.C., Bohorquez, E.C., Villegas, S., Vargas, J., Gonzalez, F.A., *Classifying Phishing URLs using Recurrent Neural Networks*, IEEE, pp. 1–23, 2017.

15. Yang, L., Zhang, J., Wang, X., Li, Z., Li, Z., He, Y., An improved ELM based and data preprocessing integrated approach for phishing detection considering comprehensive features. *Experts Syst. Appl.*, 165, 1–18, 2021.

16. Mahdavifar, S. and Ghorbani, A.A., Application of deep learning to cyber security: A survey. *Neurocomputing*, 347, 149–176, 2019.

17. Saha, I., Sarma, D., Chakma, R.J., Alam, M.N., Sultana, A., Hossain, S., Phishing attacks detection using deep learning approach. *International Conference on Smart Systems and Inventive Technology*, 2020.

18. Rasymas, T. and Dovydaitis, L., Detection of phishing URLs by using deep learning approach and multiple features combinations. *Balt. J. Mod. Comput.*, 8, 471–483, 2020.

19. Lopez-Martin, M., Carro, B., Sanchez-Esguevillas, A., LIoret, J., Network traffic classifier with convolutional and recurrent neural networks for Internet of Things, journals & magazines. *IEEE Access*, 5, 18042–18050, 2017.
20. Chen, Z., Liu, Y., Chen, C., Lu, M., Zhang, X., Malicious URL detection based on improved multilayer recurrent convolutional neural network model. *Secur. Commun. Netw.*, 2021, 1–13, 2021.

Web Citation

Report by Proofpoint.
http://www.proofpoint.com/us/resources/threat-reports/state-of-phish, 2021.

Part IV

CYBER PHYSICAL SYSTEMS

19

Cyber Physical System—The Gen Z

Jayanta Aich[1]* and Mst Rumana Sultana[2]

[1]Faculty of CSE, Bainware University, West Bengal, India
[2]Computer Science Engineering, Brainware University, West Bengal, India

Abstract

Cyber-Physical System (CPS) refers to a group of relevant systems that can monitor real-world objects and can even manipulate when needed. CPS systems have similarities with IoT, i.e., Internet of Things; however, CPS give priority on the physical, networking, and computational processes which have mutual dependency. As a result of their assimilation with IoT, a new CPS element came into existence. This new CPS element is accepted and recognized as "Internet of Cyber-Physical Things" (IoCPT). Rapid emergence along with evolutionary nature of the CPS has an impact on many parts of people's lives which allows for a greater array of services and electronics appliances, such as e-Health, e-Commerce, and smart homes. In one hand, it connects the cyber and physical worlds; on the other hand, it introduces new security threats. As a result, CPS security has been a discussion for both researchers and businesses. The main characteristics of CPS, as well as the relevant applications, technology, and standards, threats and attacks and role of machine learning (ML) are covered in this chapter.

Keywords: Cyber-physical system (CPS), mechatronics, cybernetics, cyber threats, physical threats, ML (machine learning), supervised learning, unsupervised learning, reinforcement learning

19.1 Introduction

Innovation has changed the manner in which organizations are working these days. It has made our live a lot easier and further more advantageous. So many new technologies invented still date for this purpose. These

---

Corresponding author: aichjayanta9@gmail.com

Rajdeep Chakraborty, Anupam Ghosh, Jyotsna Kumar Mandal and S. Balamurugan (eds.) Convergence of Deep Learning In Cyber-IoT Systems and Security, (399–414) © 2023 Scrivener Publishing LLC

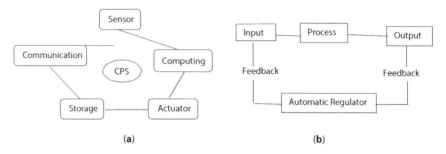

Figure 19.1 (a) Represents the coupling of CPS and (b) represents the feedbacks of CPS.

innovations included a new father in 2006, named CPS, which is basically the close interrelationship between cyber (computing & communication) and the physical (storage, sensing & actuation) components. In this article, we shall discuss one very important notion: Cyber-Physical-System (CPS) which is a bit complex not much. CPS is not a familiar term but its increasing importance for all people in IT and technology.

To understand the meaning of Cyber-Physical-System, it can be better to imagine millions of different technological devices integrate inside a complex ecosystem and connected with digital technology. In other words, Cyber-Physical-System (CPS) are interaction of physical devices which are controlled by software (computer-based algorithms). From smart homes to smart cars-the ease of way we spend our life today is strongly connected to the CPS. The term "Cyber-Physical system", which is also called the Computing System of next-generation, was initially introduced by Ellen Gillin2006. Figure 19.1. a. and 1.b. represents the CPS coupling and CPS feedbacks respectively.

Cyber-physical system includes cybernetics, mechatronics, embedded system, design, artificial intelligence and all the tangible and intangible things that are related to the internet. CPS is our future but still, we are not aware of it very much.

19.2 Architecture and Design

Models that run on simulation describe every details of specific system implementation and architectures often represent systems at a higher level. Architectural modeling is used to incorporate physical factors as elements in specific domains. However, presently there is no mechanism to treat cyber and physical materials parallelly in a more general sense. Because software architectural styles' elements and connectors are insufficient for expressing the different variety of physical components prevalent in CPS and their interactions with cyber entities. Finding a balance between specification and generalization while developing an architectural style is difficult. We need to define three interrelated families that are concerned to the cyber domain, the physical domain, and their interconnection.

19.2.1 Cyber Family

The conventional domain for ADLs is the cyber side of CPS. Standard real-time monitoring and control applications are supported by the components and connectors listed below. The following are the component types:

> *Data Centers:* These components serve as a data link between the system's computing units. These might simply be memory blocks which are passive in a simplistic system. There may be additional information indicating which elements are able to read and write in to the data storage units in a complicated system.
>
> *Computation:* Computation components work with data storage in data store components and update it. Filtering, state estimation, and control components are included in this category.
>
> *Interfaces to Input/Output:* Sensing and controlling the physical world is achieved through implementation of timing functions and computational procedures. Smart sensor software that analyses raw sensor data, for example, falls under this category.

In addition to the computing parts of the software, it is necessary to represent the communication elements in the system in order to reason about software element timing and how it influences the physical behavior of the entire system.

19.2.2 Physical Family

At the architectural level, there are various obstacles in producing a proper functional replica of the physical side of cyber-physical systems. All of the elements needed to simulate the physical dynamics shouldn't be included in architectural models. Similarly, cyber components and connectors correlate to the elements of computer-oriented systems, architectural components and connectors should correspond to intuitive conceptions of physical dynamics. The following are the physical components:

> *Sources:* A source component states power-delivery and source elements for other components. It sends power flow into the system. These components only have output ports.
>
> *Storage of energy:* A component that simulates dynamic parts that conserve energy, such as capacitive and inductive components in electrical systems, is called an energy storage component. These components have ports that allow electricity to be transferred to other sub systems.
>
> *Transducers of the physical world:* Either Power transfer or energy conversion across that happen in different physical domains is represented by transducers. These useful components stimulate systems of multi-domain that have electro mechanical devices.

The following are the types of physical connector:

> *Power flow:* Dynamic coupling occurs as a result of these connectors.
>
> *Shared variable:* The term "shared variable" refers to the fact that the variables in two components are the same. This connector has no directionality connected with it.
>
> *Measurement:* Variables of physical components are identified by measurement connectors. These variables are used as an input of another. These connectors work in both direction and correspond to standard block diagram connections.

19.2.3   Cyber-Physical Interface Family

The cyber-physical interface family combines components from the cyber and physical interface families, as well as new aspects that narrow the difference down between computational and physical systems. There are mostly two types of directed connectors, P2C (physical-to-cyber) and C2P (cyber-to-physical), to simulate interactions between the cyber and physical worlds (cyber-to-physical). P2C connectors can be replicated as simple sensors, and C2P connectors can be modeled as simple actuators [1].

19.3   Distribution and Reliability Management in CPS

19.3.1   CPS Components

Components of CPS can be utilized to detect information [2] or regulate signals. In this connection, components of CPS are further divided into two categories: First component is called the sensing component that can accumulate and precept information, and other component is called controlling component, which can tokenize and manage signals.

A. *Sensing Components:* Sensing components are sensors that accumulate information and pass it to its successor component. They are mostly found at the perception layer. The data are then transferred to another component (actuators) for additional examination and authoritative accuracy. The main CPS sensor components are listed below.

*   ❖ *Sensors:* Gather and store data from real world using correlation technique known as "calibration" which supply accurate data [3]. Data perception is made in a technique, which is based on data analysis.
*   ❖ *Aggregators:* Transmission layer consist of routers, switches, and gateways. The function of aggregator is to process the information, which is received from sensors. Processing is important before making the appropriate decision (s). Data aggregation, however, is built upon the information gathered on a certain goal, which is collected and summed up after a thorough analysis that follows statistical technique. "Online Analytical Processing" (OLAP) is a popular method for information aggregation to report online and process data [3].
*   ❖ *Actuators:* Application layer is the fixed place for actuators, which are the components responsible for making information visible. Adjoining environment needs that information which is the result of aggregators' decision. Action taken by the CPS has certain dependence on a previously executed data aggregation process [2]. Electrical signal is the input and physical action is the output for actuators [3].

B. *Controlling Components:* There is an obvious need to control signals in order to maintain more accuracy and security. Controlling components are mainly used for that. The precise roles are to control to monitor to manage system. System needs to be protected against unintentional accident or intentional penetration. As a consequence, the use of "Programmable Logic Controllers" (PLCs) and "Distributed Control Systems" (DCSs), as well as their associated elements have to be mandatory.

The following is a list of the several kinds of control systems utilized in CPS systems:

Programmable Logic Controller: PLCs (Programmable Logic Controllers) are industrial robust computers that regulate manufacturing process for device labeled as robotic. PLD regulate performance and diagnosis brunch of procedures all owing for greater compatibility.

Distributed Control System: Distributed Control System (DCS) use a central operator supervisory control to distribute autonomous controllers throughout the system.

Remote Terminal Unit (RTU): RTU [6] has a difference with PLCs is that the RTU has no loop as well as no control algorithm. As a result, RTUs are very much suitable for wireless communication.

19.3.2 CPS Models

There are three primary types of CPS models:

Timed Actor CPS: It concentrates on aspects that are the nonfunctional of performance and timing, as well as the functional aspects of behavior and correctness. The filtration based on the "earlier-the-better" approach is the main focus since it allows for the identification of deterministic abstractions that belongs to nondeterministic systems. These models are less likely to be in the hands of state explosion issues, making analytical bounds easier to derive [8].

Event-Based CPS: Before actuation decisions can be made in a model, an event must be identified by the appropriate CPS components. Individual component-time restrictions, on the other hand, fluctuate after taking into consideration the fact of system delay depending on the nondeterministic system induced by various CPS functions, such as sensing, actuating, communicating, and computing [9].

Lattice-Based Event Model [10]: The internal and external event attributes, as well as the event type, are represented in the

CPS events and set a Spatial-temporal feature of any given event, as well as identify all of the components that saw it.

Hybrid-Based CPS Model: This types of heterogeneous system is used for the interconnection between "physical dynamic system" and "discrete-state systems" [11, 12].

19.4   Security Issues in CPS

Despite its many benefits, CPS systems are vulnerable to a variety of cyber and/or physical security risks, attacks, and obstacles because of its heterogeneous character. As a result, these systems may have disastrous consequences, necessitating the implementation of comprehensive security measures. This, however, may result in unacceptably high network overhead, particularly in association with latency. Additionally, constant software, application, and operating system updates should be used to reduce zero-day vulnerabilities. Because cyber-physical security systems are frequently used in critical contexts, the trustworthiness of software and hardware is a major concern. CPS security threats are classified into cyber threats and physical threats.

19.4.1   Cyber Threats

For a variety of reasons cyber risk has been the primary focus of industrial IoT security. From a technical perspective, physical dangers are not the primary concern for IoT security [14]. This involves the transformation of the "electrical grid" into an "Advanced Metering Infrastructure (AMI)," which has ensured the emergence of hitherto undiscovered cyber dangers. Contrasting the attacks, which has a requirement of physical presence and actual instruments, electronic attacks could be launched from any device across the network. Furthermore, the smart meter's interface and interaction with other meters in the NAN, i.e., "Neighborhood Area Network" and "Home Area Network" raises their vulnerability to a variety of distant attacks. Finally, without the proper prevention and defensive actions, electronic attacks are hard to moderate and resist.

As cyber security is not constrained to one aspect, different perspectives must be considered, such as:

Centering Information: This entails safeguarding of data flow during different phases, such as transporting, storing, and processing phases.

Oriented Function: This calls for the "cyber-physical components" of the CPS to be integrated.

Oriented Threat: Availability of data and its integrity as well
as its confidentiality along with the accountability are all
impacted by the oriented threat [15].

Because of the aforementioned flaws, CPS systems are vulnerable to:

Exploitation of Wireless Technology: It necessitates an understanding of the system's structure and, as a result and it
exploiting its wireless capabilities in order to gain remote
access or get control over a system. It could also disrupt all
ongoing operations. As a result, there is a conflict of result
in system [16].

Jamming: In this situation, attackers attempt to disrupt the state
of the device's, and expected actions in order to cause harm
by sending out sequence of de-authenticated and wireless
signals, resulting in the denial of the services [17].

Reconnaissance: One instance for such threat would be when
intelligence agencies conduct operations on Computational
Intelligence (CI) of a nation's. Industrial Control System
(ICS) is also included as an exemplary case in this regards.
This would be done on regular basis, through extensive use
of malware [18]. Because traditional defenses are limited,
this leads to data confidentially being violated [19].

Remote way Access: This is mostly accomplished by attempting
remote access to the CPS infrastructure, resulting in disruptions, financial losses, blackouts, data theft from industry
[20], among other things. Furthermore, Havex Trojans are
consider to be most notorious viruses for ICSs. Sometimes
they might be utilized as weapon to penetrate a nation's
CPS's cyber-warfare campaign management.

Unauthorized Access of Information: Hackers attempt to acquire
unauthorized access to a network via a logical or physical
breach in order to extract sensitive data, resulting in a privacy violation.

Interception: Hackers can exploit existing or new weaknesses to
listen to private conversations resulting in yet another sort of
privacy and confidentiality violation.

Gathering Information: Software companies secretly collect sensitive data save don any given device with the intension of illegally selling this off.

19.4.2   Physical Threats

To preserve the resilience of CPS in industrial domains [21], "Advanced Metering Infrastructure" (AMI) and "Neighborhood Area Networks" (NANs), as well as data meter management systems, have recently been introduced into CPS systems.

Physical threats can be classified depending on the following few factors:

Physical Damage: Stations that generates power are highly secured as different facility types apply multilevel of protection. This is due to the adoption of access restrictions, authorization and mechanisms that enables authentication providing user names and passwords. Next level of security could easily be achieved by making access cards, biometrics, and video surveillance as mandatory at. Because, these physical Devices are well managed, well-manned and well-guarded. Being tamper resistance is must for Smart meters to overcome the loopholes. For an example relying on outage monitoring or perhaps host-based intrusion detection would be a good practice. Tampering at physical level or adversaries' theft is nearly improbable to prevent, but reducing the possibility of intrusion has positive promises.

Loss: The most concerning the case is when a malicious attacker causes many substation failures. A total blackout for several hours in major urban areas could occur when the smart grid is compromised either physically or programmatically.

Repair: It is a self-healing process [22]. The backup resources will be triggered and be automatically reconfigured to carry out the required services. Rapid recovery in best timing is the goal to achieve. Critical components, on the other hand, have either no or limited backup capabilities. As a result, self-healing can take care of severe damage more quickly.

The following are some threats associated with CPS systems:

Spoofing: Spoofing is nothing but the act of design of authenticate source. Sending misleading measurements to the control center is one way to spoof sensors. That is how an attacker becomes capable in spoofing a sensor.

Sabotage: Intercepting legal communication traffic and transferring it to a malevolent third party or disturbing the communication channel is referred as sabotage. CPS components that are being exposed physically anywhere in the power grid might be sabotaged and that could cause interruption in service which ultimately leads to service blackout.

Service Disruption or Denial: Attackers have the ability to physically tamper with any device for disrupt service which has major consequences, particularly in applications that belong to medical sector.

Tracking: Because devices are, an attacker can get access to them and/or attach a Malicious devices could easily be attached to other devices, which are physically accessible. This sort of malicious devices enables attackers to have unlawful accessibility.

19.5   Role of Machine Learning in the Field of CPS

Machine learning is a subfield of artificial intelligence that involved the development of self-learning algorithms to gain knowledge from that data in order to make predictions. Cyber physical systems are described by their ability to accommodate and to learn:

They examine data, collected from their environment and based on the results; they correlate features, learn patterns and make predictive models. In this section we will describe the role of ML in CPS and how ML models are able to with stand from the adverse effect of CPS.

I. Supervised Learning

In supervised learning input variables(X), called features and output variable (Y), called label or a class use an algorithm to learn the correlation from the input to output. Primary motive is to approximate the mapping function such a way that when we enter new input data (X) that we can predict the output variable(Y) for that particular input data. This type of learning is associated with CPS for classification tasks. The following section describes show the following machine learning algorithms can be used in Cyber-physical system.

A. KNN (K-Nearest Neighbor) classification: It is associated with the cyber-physical-social systems (CPSS) for analyzing and mining several data.

B. Classification Trees: To get the benefit from the data mining technique, the classification tree is used for event prediction in a cyber-physical system.

C. Logistic Regression: The most emerging smart-grid, cyber-physical infrastructure, provides a steady, secure, and reliable power system over the current power grid. Using logistic regression technique the system anomalies in smart power grids are identified.

D. Naive-Bayes: Cyber-physical systems are found in industrial and production systems, as well as critical infrastructures. Due to the increasing integration of IP-based technology and standard computing devices, the threat of cyber-attacks on cyber-physical systems has vastly increased. Naïve-Bayes algorithm can be used for the classification of cyberattacks.

E. SVM (Support Vector Machine): SVM, also called the non-probabilistic classifier requires large amount of training set. Nonlinear SVM is used when the data cannot be separated into two classes by drawing a straight line. The kernel function takes low-dimensional feature space as an input and gives output as a high dimensional feature space. SVM can be associated with CPS for the misbehavior detection management of medical IoT devices.

II. Unsupervised Learning

Unsupervised learning is used when the environment has only input data(X) and no corresponding output data are present. Primary motive of unsupervised learning is to model the underlying structure or distribution in the data in order to learn more about the data. In other words, unsupervised learning allows the system to identify patterns within the datasets on its own. The following algorithms are described here:

A. SVD (Singular Value Decomposition): SVD can be associated with CPS, which utilizes network location as context information and used for QoS requirements.

B. PCA (Principal Component Analysis): is used for detection of Cyber Physical attacks, assuring the safety of medical IoT devices.

C. K-Means: This algorithm can be used in connected with CPS for knowledge extraction to increase capability, adaptability, safety and security.

III. Reinforcement learning

Another very useful machine learning algorithm alongside supervised and unsupervised learning algorithm is Reinforcement learning algorithm. This algorithm is concerned with how intelligent agents ought to take actions in an environment in order to maximize the notion of cumulative reward. Figure 19.2 illustrates the relation between machine learning and cyber-physical system.

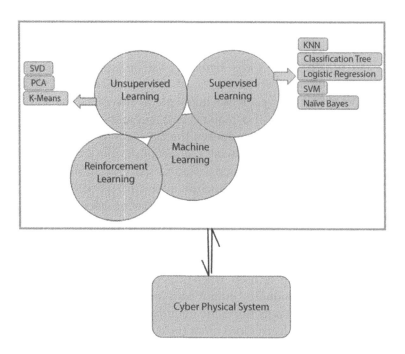

Figure 19.2 Interaction between machine learning and cyber-physical system or how cyber-physical system interacts with machine learning.

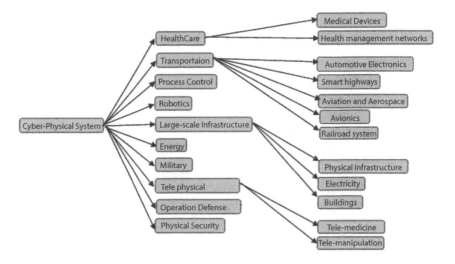

Figure 19.3 Applications of CPS.

19.6   Application

Application of CPS involves to make social interactions more intelligent. This also includes the strong sensing capability; hence wireless sensor networks (WSN) can be an important aspect of CPS. Some applications are shown in Figure 19.3.

19.7   Conclusion

CPS systems are crucial components of Industry v4.0, and by merging the physical and cyber worlds. The goal is to improve the quality of products and the availability and reliability of systems. CPS systems, on the other hand, have a number of security and privacy vulnerabilities that can jeopardize their dependability, safety, and efficiency, as well as obstruct their wide spread adoption. In this chapter, we first discuss the distribution of CPS, and we focus on the main CPS security threats and applications.

References

1. Rajhans, A., Cheng, S.W., Schmerl, B., Garlan, D., Krogh, B.H., Agbi, C., Bhave, A., An architectural approach to the design and analysis of cyber-physical systems. *Electron. Commun. EASST*, 21, 1–10, 2009.

2. Gries, S., Hesenius, M., Gruhn, V., Cascading data corruption: About dependencies in cyber-physical systems: Poster. *Proceedings of the 11th ACM International Conference on Distributed and Event-Based Systems*, ACM, pp. 345–346, 2017.

3. Gubbi, J., Buyya, R., Marusic, S., Palaniswami, M., Internet of things (IoT): avision, architectural elements, and future directions. *Future Gener. Comput. Syst.*, 29, 7, 1645–1660, 2013.

4. S.R. Vogel and S.J. Zack, Method and apparatus providing remote reprogramming of programmable logic devices using embedded jtag physical layer and protocol. USPatent 7,155,711, 2006.

5. Ardanza, A., Moreno, A., Segura, Á., de la Cruz, M., Aguinaga, D., Sustainable and flexible industrial human machine interfaces to support adaptable applications in the industry 4.0 paradigm. *Int. J. Prod. Res.*, 57, 12, 4045–4059, 2019.

6. J.R. Saunders, Automated remote telemetry paging system. USPatent 4,856,047, 1989.

7. Stouffer, K. and Falco, J., Guide to Supervisory control and data acquisition (SCADA) and industrial control systems security, National Institute of Standards and Technology, Gaithersburg, MD, USA, 2006.

8. Canedo, A., Schwarzenbach, E., Al Faruque, M.A., Context-sensitive synthesis of executable functional models of cyber-physical systems. *Proceedings of the ACM/IEEE 4th International Conference on Cyber-Physical Systems*, ACM, pp. 99–108, 2013.

9. Zhang, Z., Porter, J., Eyisi, E., Karsai, G., Koutsoukos, X., Sztipanovits, J., Co-simulation framework for design of time-triggered cyber physical systems. *Proceedings of the ACM/IEEE 4th International Conference on Cyber-Physical Systems*, ACM, pp. 119–128, 2013.

10. Tan, Y., Vuran, M.C., Goddard, S., Yu, Y., Song, M., Ren, S., A concept lattice-based event model for cyber-physical systems. *Proceedings of the 1st ACM/IEEE International Conference on Cyber-Physical Systems*, ACM, pp. 50–60, 2010.

11. Alur, R., Courcoubetis, C., Halbwachs, N., Henzinger, T.A., Ho, P.H., Nicollin, X., Olivero, A., Sifakis, J., Yovine, S., The algorithmic analysis of hybrid systems. *Theor. Comput. Sci.*, 138, 1, 3–34, 1995.

12. Antsaklis, P.J., Stiver, J.A., Lemmon, M., Hybrid system modeling and autonomous control systems, in: *Hybrid Systems*, pp. 366–392, Springer, USA, 1992.

13. Benveniste, A., Bourke, T., Caillaud, B., Pouzet, M., Hybrid systems modeling challenges caused by cyber-physical systems. *Cyber-Phys. Syst. (CPS) Found. Chall.*, 27, 1, 1–22, 2013.

14. Alguliyev, R., Imamverdiyev, Y., Sukhostat, L., Cyber-physical systems and their security issues. *Comput. Ind.*, 100, 212–223, 2018.

15. Cleveland, F.M., Cyber security issues for advanced metering infrastructure (AMI). *2008 IEEE Power and Energy Society General Meeting-Conversion and Delivery of Electrical Energy in the 21st Century*, pp. 1–5.

16. Checkoway, S., McCoy, D., Kantor, B., Anderson, D., Shacham, H., Savage, S., Koscher, K., Czeskis, A., Roesner, F., Kohno, T., Comprehensive experimental analyses of automotive attack surfaces. *USENIX Security Symposium*, San Francisco, pp. 77–92, 2011.

17. Rushanan, M., Rubin, A.D., Kune, D.F., Swanson, C.M., Sok: Security and privacy in implantable medical devices and body area networks. *2014 IEEE Symposium on Security and Privacy (SP)*, IEEE, pp. 524–539, 2014.

18. de Oliveira Albuquerque, R., Villalba, L.J.G., Orozco, A.L.S., de Sousa Junior, R.T., Kim, T.H., Leveraging information security and computational trust for cyber security. *J. Supercomput.*, 72, 10, 3729–3763, 2016.

19. Munro, K., Deconstructing flame: The limitations of traditional defenses. *Comput. Fraud Secur.*, 2012, 10, 8–11, 2012.

20. Mc Daniel, P. and Mc Laughlin, S., Security and privacy challenges in the smart grid. *IEEE Secur. Priv.*, 7, 3, 75–77, 2009.

21. Zeynal, H., Eidiani, M., Yazdanpanah, D., Intelligent substation automation systems for robust operation of smart grids. *2014 IEEE Innovative Smart Grid Technologies-Asia (ISGTASIA)*, IEEE, pp. 786–790, 2014.

22. Davidson, C.M. and Santorelli, M.J., *Realizing the Smart Grid Imperative: A Framework for Enhancing Collaboration Between Energy Utilities and Broadband Service Providers*. Research Program on Digital Communications, Washington, DC, USA, 2011.

20

An Overview of Cyber Physical System (CPS) Security, Threats, and Solutions

Krishna Keerthi Chennam[1]*, Fahmina Taranum[2] and Maniza Hijab[2]

[1]Vasavi College of Engineering, Hyderabad, India
[2]MJCET, Hyderabad, India

Abstract

Academia and industry are deeply looking into cyber physical system (CPS) security attentively from the past few years. Establishing security is the main problem with a wide range of cyberattacks. This chapter focused on segregating research on the CPS security by combining computing, networking, and operations. Analysing the influence of human life in CPS security and identifying the corollary of attacks, models and architecture in CPS. Attacks and threats of various CPS types are analyzed in this chapter. The next-generation future is dependent on the development and usage of technology by integrating computing, communicating, and control of models. CPS strongly focused to avoid challenges of medical care, shipping, and other areas. This chapter provides surveys of CPS research problems and tasks considered for development of CPS and privacy problems, threats, and clarifications for CPS. CPS increases various security challenges with present problems in markets. The main motivation is to identify the security threats related to CPS, challenges, attacks and problems facing, advantages, and drawbacks of the present security system, the main goal is to provide accurate security, reliable, efficient and safe surroundings. In the end chapter, solutions for CPS threats, various approaches for solving upcoming issues are suggested.

Keywords: Cyber physical systems, attacks, retreat, issues, contest

*Corresponding author: krishnakeerthich@gmail.com

Rajdeep Chakraborty, Anupam Ghosh, Jyotsna Kumar Mandal and S. Balamurugan (eds.) Convergence of Deep Learning In Cyber-IoT Systems and Security, (415–434) © 2023 Scrivener Publishing LLC

20.1 Introduction

Latest trend of cyber-physical systems (CPS) seeks the physical convergence and cyber areas in regular life. CPS scale system firmly with cyber level and physical systems. The cyber area is completely related to the digital area, which can compute, communicate, and order using automatic programs. Physically, the system is similar to multiple Internet of Things (IoT) sensors [1], where CPS is related to hardware (HW), software (SW), actuators, embedded systems (ES), sensors, and much more related to humans and machines. CPS system is firmly similar to future generations related to network system uses in distributed systems and IoT by merging physical systems with sensors and actuators by controlling the computer elements since these are useful in CPS systems to develop information and communication technology.

A CPS is an intelligent computer-based system used to control or monitor the work of algorithms. The component used for fabricating smart networked systems includes processors, sensors or actuators, software systems, and communicating devices. These physical devices (for which IoT is used to create worldwide connectivity) are mapped with the virtual components (computational world) to create an abstract model for information flow with guaranteed performance in safety critical applications. CPS system can be realized with dynamic control, information service and time sensing, with the help of deep conglomerate techniques, like computing, communication, and control. The components of CPS are mobile and satellite networks, sensors or actuators, radiofrequency identification (RFID), and IOT [2], system of systems, big data, cloud and embedded systems. Essential features of CPS are safety, performance, and interoperability. Security in CPS is supported by using the components defined in the model depicted in Figure 20.1.

The characteristics used to understand the problem include decentralization, heterogeneity, privacy policies, and an untrusted environment. For creating a holistic secured view, features like diverse security goals, nature of attacker and its complexity must be recognized. CPS systems usually feel the adjoining surroundings or network, with the intention to prepare, monitor, and deal with the physical world.

Security goals for CPS are created by using a detailed analysis of security policy, risk analysis, safety and security requirements. Safety requirements are recognized along with hazard analysis to generate the security policies. Security requirement works on the input collected from threats and vulnerabilities.

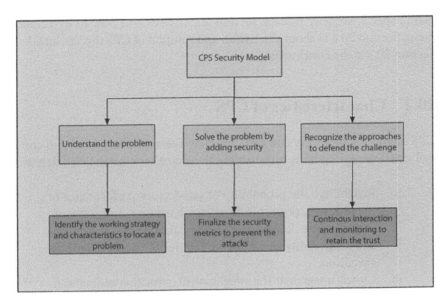

Figure 20.1 Problem identification in CPS model.

20.1.1 Motivation of Work

CPS continuously integrated with high demand frameworks like smart grids, healthcare, supply chain, telephone, agriculture, and military are the interesting objectives for malicious attacks for different reasons like money, crime, military secrets, politics, and homicide. Accountability of CPS is destinated to manage risky attacks opposed to such systems. Various security reasons are destinated depending on integrity, confidentiality and reachability. The CPS system developed to understand the advantages and the benefits and facilitate the system more easily; it is a mandatory service to provide security of these systems internally or externally, passively or actively from any feasible attacks. The main motivation to identify the CPS security threats, challenges, attacks and problems facing, advantages, and drawbacks of the present security system, the main goal is to provide accurate security, reliable, efficient, and safe surroundings.

20.1.2 Organization of Sections

Section 20.1 discussed the introduction and motivation for identifying this research. Section 20.2 discussed the characteristics of CPS using attributes and its functionality. Section 20.3 is types of CPS; section 20.4, main aspects, security threats; section 20.5, issues and how to overcome them. Section 20.6 is about discussion and solution of CPS threats, attacks. Section 20.7 is the conclusion.

20.2   Characteristics of CPS

CPS methodologies have emerged as a new alternative to model and control smart energy systems by satisfying the characteristics as listed below:

  i.   Reliability: The probability of satisfactory performance of the task with respect to firmware, hardware, and software.
  ii. Autonomies: Robustness under unexpected conditions and adaptability to subsystem failures for smooth and safe execution.
  iii. Closely integrated: The integration of estimation and substantial energy components through network communication.
  iv. Resource constraints: Every physical component is restricted with cyber capability and resources.
  v.   Large scale network: Collaborating electronic gadgets to create a distributed network.
  vi. Handling Complexity at different scales: Reducing the time critical complexity of the components with probable granularity of time and spatiality.

The details of the attributes and their functionality for managing CPS are depicted in Figure 20.2. Major challenges of CPS are quality of

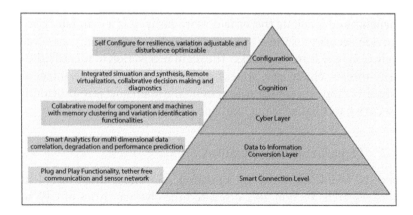

Figure 20.2 Attributes and functionality of CPS.

communication, data transfer rate, sustainability, design validation, and interoperability. Designing a distributed CPS with integrated platform overcoming the gaps and challenges is a difficult task. This forces one to rework on connecting services with radically new concepts extracted from different layers of Figure 20.2.

With the rapid modernization, the need emerges to work on collaborating different system designs by assigning responsibilities for allocating physical devices and system components. The emerging changes must be adaptable for coupling disciplines without enforcing the use of new strategies or tools for analysis.

20.3   Types of CPS Security

CPS addresses security concerns for CPS and Internet of things (IoT) devices by smoothly mapping them by abiding with security constraints. Various security conditions that can be targeted include integrity, authentication, confidentiality, availability, privacy of data and systems, accessibility and authorizing trust between IoT and CPS [3, 4, 7, 8]. IOT and CPS rely on features like reliability, safe execution, consistency, dependability, interaction, and coordination as depicted in Figure 20.3 to work on for making a trustworthy system.

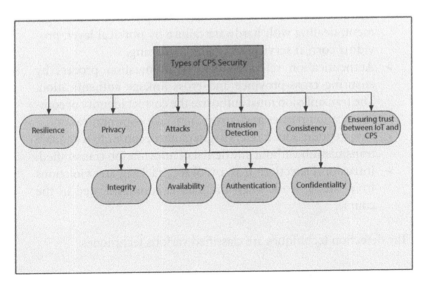

Figure 20.3 Types of CPS security.

➢ Resilience: The concept of resilience is to make a system reliable or quick recoverable. In automating, the CPS resilience metrics used for computation includes qualitative and quantitative simulating architectures, vulnerability calculation, conception, and reporting processes statistics. To ensure resilience of CPS, a cross discipline analysis over open issues and addressing the cybersecurity threats is mandatory.

➢ Privacy: It is a feature added to increase the authenticity of accessing data. New privacy enhancing technologies are adapted to minimize the negative impact on the utility of CPS. Privacy acts as a key concern for design, development, and operation of CPS.

➢ Attacks: Physical or malicious attacks permit an assessment to critical assets, ensuing damage or compromise of information, while cyberattacks may cause physical breakdowns, resulting in real world significance.

➢ Data confidentiality is the capability in protecting the security while transmitting the data and for storing the data as well to avoid the illegal access from other parties.

➢ Integrity assigns from the data changes which may not be certified from different users and the deficiency in integrity leads to fraud access.

➢ Availability refers to ease of use when needed. Keeping highly equipped resources in CPS system needs the listed characteristics: Timely system updates, power load management, dealing with hardware failure by physical layer, providing correct service, and right processing.

➢ Authentication refers to the communication process by ensuring cross-province and cross linkage authentication. The transmission must authorize the correct identity of communication parties and ensure non-fake communication.

➢ Non-repudiation: It refers to guaranteed, committed and safe transmission without any denial of information transmitted.

➢ Intrusion Detection: It is a tool for tracking any violations from the network when the data is communicated in the course.

The detection techniques are classified various techniques:

• Signature-based-detection: It operates by investigating the patterns transmitted during communication like data flow or network traffic, or malware. Patterns are regarded as signatures. If stored patterns of the system are insufficient then identification of new signatures becomes tedious.

- Anomaly-based detection: It is used to overcome the pit-falls existing in signature-based detection. The deviated based system, ML is followed by constructing a scheme with similar activities, against with fresh identified patterns are contrasted. This mode is at an upper hand since it generates skilled configurations and requirements.

➤ Reputation-based-detection: It helps to recognize the potential threat by measuring the scores using reputation. This helps to prevent threats and zero-day attack. The foremost functionality of the IDS is to examine the data pertaining to the network conduct and diagnose the intrusions, so as to shield the system.

20.4   Cyber Physical System Security Mechanism— Main Aspects

Cyber-physical system retreat processes are dynamically adaptive to the corporeal environment and are assisted by the coupling of framework, where context refers to the conventional environmental situations and conditions that either regulate an application's reaction or an event of an application. Context can include that of the system (example: CPU or wire-less network status, etc.), the user (example: position, sentiment, medicinal history, etc.), the physical environment (e.g. disaster, lighting, thundering, temperature, weather, etc.), and the time. In CPS, the main focus is on security, the security framework consists of the collection of contextual components that contributes to characterize the structure of an entity, whose charge affects the choice of the furthermost appropriate controls (measures) or the conformation of those panels to shield information system from unauthorized access, utilization, revelation, interruption, variation, or destruction in order to provide concealment, reliability and obtainability.

The security significant contextual attributes standards influence the selection of the most appropriate panels which in chance control the likelihood of convinced threats to concealment, truthfulness, and obtainability being realized. Thus, security in the milieu of context awareness has three main aspects like sensing security, cyber security, and control security.

In sensing security, we need to form context discovery, context acquisition to ensure a trusted environment, say use of Trusted-Platform Module

(TPM), which is a comparatively reasonable hardware constituent used to simplify construction of trusted software systems. Thus, achieving the TPM functionality of confirming to the honesty of software working on a sensor to a distant verifier. Cyber Security: Security related to communication and computing falls under its purview. The network CPS accepts for creating the fusion of data networks and commits to the rear entities to consider the reply actions. Various protocols in communications in inter- and intra-CPS security, which are active and passive users, need to include context, which means context-aware managing keys techniques, context-conscious mutual authentication technique and context-conscious privacy protection technique should be an intrinsic part. Also, context-aware encryption, digital signature, and access control solutions.

Control security is partitioned as feedback and actuation security. Actuation security aims to ensure that actuation happens under the suitable authorization. Feedback security refers to confirming that the control systems of CPS, which offer the obligatory feedback for achieving protected actuation.

In Figure 20.4, the main aspects of security viz., security sensing, control security and cyber security, their interplay in the normal workflow

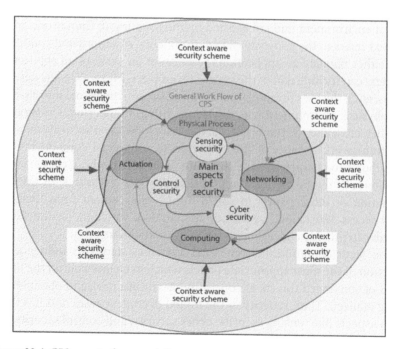

Figure 20.4 CPS security framework features.

of a CPS wherein right from procuring data from sensors which is physical resources, collecting physical data in-network which is networking, to accurate calculated results from physical collected states direct the controller for identifying the accurate commands which is computing. Physical process actuation networking computing is depicted.

20.4.1   CPS Security Threats

The classification of threats in CPS with an intension to damage the system is listed out in Figure 20.5. CPS systems are inclined to numerous cyber, corporeal, layer based, infrastructure based, physical and security threats.

20.4.2   Information Layer

It is a threat to the information used for data transmission. The subclassification under this category is as follows: CPS flow must be protected to ensure nonvulnerable infrastructure. Information layer threats includes authentication-attacks, cross-network and routing attacks, distributed and DoS attacks, exposing client privacy information, malicious code control network and DoS attacks, path selection error, flood and channel attacks.

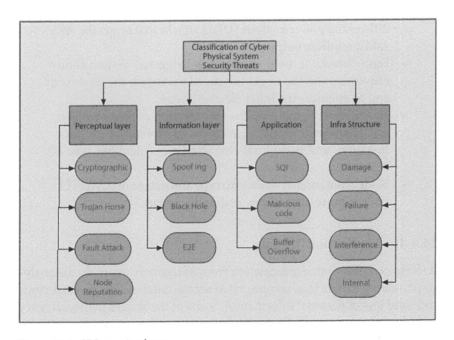

Figure 20.5 CPS security threats.

- E2E: deals with every authentication and threats from bottom line, mankind keys using existing available encipher algorithms, DoS and DDoS attacks. It protects personal information or profile data shared in a large network.
- Black hole: deals with Packet drop, selective or not forwarding packets to neighbouring nodes. Other types of wormhole and grey hole can also be a part of Hole attack category
- Spoofing: It is an address attack of disguising a communication and pretending to be a trusted source.
- Sabotage: the traffic communication of blocking processes and forwarding to a node, which is a malicious or disrupting the transmission process.

20.4.3 Perceptual Layer

It deals with limited computing resources related to memory utilization or physical environment

- Cryptographic: It deals with the deliberate outbreaks by cyber or hardware layers, which are collected, administered, synthesized, transmitted, and deposited over dispersed hardware gadget. Example of cryptographic confidences is differential power analysis (DPA) attacks that target the AES AddRoundKey output.
- Fault attack: It uses deliberately triggered responsibility movements on the target beneficial to retrieve the password and re-engineer the inner electric circuit.
- Hardware Trojan horse: The classification of this is by physical (corrupted chips), activation (performance or functionality), and behavioral characteristics (identifies type of destructive nature).
- Node reputation: It deals with type and nature of devices like node capture, fake nodes, and node outages.

20.4.4 Application Threats

It works on collection of information from a large network to do the analysis pertaining to data loss, unauthorized access, database attacks, malicious code and loss of personal information. Some of the attacks in this category include control network DOS attacks, perceptual data interfere attacks, control command forgery attacks, viruses and Trojans, cloud computing service threats, and vulnerability and resonant attacks.

- Buffer overflow: It stores the program's intended behaviour and prevents normal functionality. It uses function-pointer manipulation to reconstruct password, modify content, and perform software vulnerability exploitation.
- Malicious code: It uses malignant code to client intrusion's operational code and damage the network. It hides the details without invalidating the intermediate steps.
- Structured Query Language (SQL): It helps to access database applications using SQL queries to do content manipulation and manage structural changes.

20.4.5   Infrastructure

The protection of the infrastructure (grid, sensor, server, protocols, etc.,) is a highly sensitive and critical threat to the environment. The types of threat under this category include physical injury, equipment let-down, link failure, electromagnetic meddling, and internal threats. Physical threats: It is a danger progressed in the manufacturing domain used to uphold the robustness of CPS, and also to observe data meter management systems. Physical layer threats include node seizure, denial of facility attacks, node regulator, passive attacks, clock synchronization bouts, crash spells, exhaustion occurrences, unfair competition, eavesdropping, tampering, and intervention.

- Physical Damage: Some physical devices can be damaged easily because of less protection or well planning. Example smart meters are tamper resistant but transmission lines are susceptible to sabotage and disruption. However the tendency of the attack and its impact can be reduced to mitigate the risk.
- Loss: The loss in the communication because of single point failure in transmission. This can be avoided or reduced by increasing the availability of resources.
- Repair: It is a fast recovery or self-healing process used to replace or repair the erroneous component to proceed with safe execution of the system.

20.5   Issues and How to Overcome Them

- CPS works on the analysis made from the system behaviour. Significant efforts were made to ensure end-to-end QoS. To ensure QoS, the awareness on the working of MAC layer protocols, Transport layer protocol and traffic flow used at the network layer is required.

- CPS application generates large volumes of streaming data, making interpretation difficult. To deal with environmental changes and complex computing communication with respect to restricted resource inheritance, autonomous resource management techniques with promising feedback schedules can be used to guarantee flexible QoS interpretations.

- Power management is an issue, which is dependent on the network lifetime and performance. Controlling the CPU energy consumption and the residual energy utilization of sensor nodes by experimenting on different voltage techniques may ease out the problem.

- Network layer issues: Heterogeneous networks work on different network security structures, which makes them adaptable, compatible and consistent to different protocols and technologies. Security tasks at the network layer include identifying network layer substantiation, resource admittance control, transmitting data sincerely, securely and private access and routing. The consistent security mechanism includes hop-by-hop encryption, mutual authentication among nodes, security everywhere, assuring network connectivity and cross-network authentication. For transmission of data, concepts used for security include accommodating, managing secret keys, and cryptographic algorithm selection.

- Collaborative layer solutions: It fetches useful data for analysis and uses it to identify malicious information for securing the system. Further, maintaining the data privacy and security, receiver and retailer is compulsory for certification. To enhance security of CPS high confidentiality of efficient encrypted data is made mandatory.

- Application control layer solution: It works on the principle of providing final security destinated with facilities given exact operation. The common services include protection of user privacy, prohibiting unauthorized access and access control, securing system and upgrading system policies.

- Privacy protection technology: Node communication may end up with privacy disclosure. The focus of privacy protection is on video privacy data encryption along with maintaining confidentiality of data via encryption, multipath transmission and concealment.
- Sensing Layer: threat under this layer is node control, tampering and frequent interference. The security solution measures include authentication, transmission spectrum like direct sequence transmission spectrum or frequency hopping transmission spectrum, message priority, intrusion detection, and recovery.

20.6   Discussion and Solutions

Extendable and distancing CPS security to accommodate the threats to develop systems. Formerly, the CPS threats are divided into physical, communications and application models but most of the research is developing to assure the system. Clearly this discussion talks about the recommended results of various security threats and various issues involved in CPS security with possibility options in development. [10] Show the overall monitor system operations with dynamic hardware and software security policies with the help of communication channels and protocols. Combining the hardware attacks and software attacks causes false positives or issues and eliminate the security policy. [11] Researched about transferring information, protecting against kernel level malware and various other security modules. Based on a series of system and CPU, overhead of the system is researched in [12] by adding the PUF contents with the basic model. The PUF is to identify the error correction in digital figure prints and produce secret keys in a secure way.

To avoid vulnerabilities, SD-CPS [14] secures the data without decryption. Gupta, Keerthi et al. [5, 6, 26] discuss a regularity-based procedure for identifying coordinated wormhole attacks in wireless sensor networks, which maintains security in protocol for every node. Encryption and decryption methods are implemented in routing protocols. Cardenas et al. [15] identify or detect attacks from damaged systems and focused on authentication and access control mechanisms. Yampolskiy et al. [9] propose an early warning OSN worm identification method to identify the

Table 20.1 Comparison of CPS security solution, narration and other relevant research.

Source	Solution types	Characterization
[10, 11]	System safety Hardware anchor key	HW, SW and SoC with high security and productivity.
[12]	PUF	Fingerprints uses for unique ID of a semiconductor
[13]	WSO2 CEP solution	Combined models for multi agents systems
[26]	DPA	Providing access to encrypted data and plain data avoiding users
[14]	Network access detection	Instead of using SDN switches and controllers using SD-CPS
[5]	Wormhole attack detection algorithm	Wormhole tunnels and bandwidth of frequency tables in WSN
[15]	Control System attack detection	Guarding and closing system accessing illegally.
[16]	Pre-forecast	CPS Emulator and interpolation procedure established on a never ending loop for computing system state progression eventually
[18]	Anomaly code detection- Early threatening OSN worm detection system	Identifying the users from Maximum range algorithm
[22]	Smart city	Distributed block chain network established on SDN controller for smart city similar problems
[24]	Smart grid	DHCD method to analyse and minimise FDI attacks
[25]	Smart healthcare	CPS, health-CPS, based on Cloud storage and big data learning scheme

Table 20.2 CPS security hazards with analogous results.

	Cryptography threats	Fault attack	HW Trojan horse	Node reputation	E2E	Hole attack	Spoofing attack	Buffer over flow	Malicious code	SQL
[10][11]	✓	✓	✓	✓	×	×	✓	✓	✓	✓
[12]	✓	✓	✓	✓	✓	×	×	×	✓	×
[13]	✓	✓	×	✓	×	×	×	×	×	✓
[7]	✓	✓	✓	✓	✓	✓	✓			
[14]				✓	✓	✓	✓			✓
[5]	✓			✓	✓	✓				
[15]	✓	✓		✓	✓	✓			✓	✓
[18]					✓	✓			✓	
[19]		✓		✓	✓		✓		✓	✓
[20]		✓		✓	✓	✓			✓	✓

(Continued)

Table 20.2 CPS security hazards with analogous results. (*Continued*)

	Cryptography threats	Fault attack	HW Trojan horse	Node reputation	E2E	Hole attack	Spoofing attack	Buffer over flow	Malicious code	SQL
[21]		✓		✓	✓	✓	✓		✓	
[22]		✓		✓	✓	✓	✓	✓	✓	✓
[23]			✓	✓	✓	✓	✓		✓	✓
[24]				✓	✓			✓	✓	✓
[25]	✓	✓		✓	✓				✓	✓

method of propagation of multiple worms, the surveillance of the network was strong to check the worm propagation. The implemented model has various problems like deployment and node caching and raw data filtration with the network. Handling over flow of buffers and attacks on flow boards produces better presentation than former methods like bandwidth. Sharma *et al.* [23] have SDN method and was developed by using block chain and has many issues like large-scale IoT issues. This architecture role is developing and preventing threats, protecting data and controlling access, cache-flooding, ARP spoofing and DoS, and DDoS attacks and migrating the attacks in the network as discussed in Li *et al.* [24]. The data which is preprocessed and encrypted using privacy methods in the health CPS based on the hierarchical permissions in security discussed in Zhang *et al.* [25]. The distributed file storage is effective in storing data, with maximum throughput while uploading or downloading data, maximum error tolerance while using data, with various access controls and access data with optimum speed and changing to data in huge data disks or volumes in health data [17] as shown in Tables 20.1 and 20.2.

20.7 Conclusion

CPS security is within the environment though its recent research area from other works. The multiple sensors, data models, generating new data and accessing the data, analyzing the data, processing the data from different run time environments. This research paper differentiates the threats, problems, and trials in CPS security and compares the various security challenges and provides solutions for various challenges. The recent trend of security is CPS surveys in security and challenges. Hazards and results of security in CPS and related problems are discussed. Further outlook information technology expands the CPS security scope from merging the IoT and different sensors. Interacting with different systems must be secure with the environment. CPS environments have different layers and have threats that conclude the security improvement for the systems. CPS has huge security in smart cities, IoT, healthcare, and grids. The CPS security is more important in smart areas.

References

1. Kumar, J.S. and Patel, D.R., A survey on internet of things: Security and privacy issues. *Int. J. Comput. Appl.*, 90, 11, 20–26, 2014.

2. Niraja, K.S. and Rao, S.S., RFID and biometric authentication framework for secure access to IoT based smart home. *Test Eng. Manag.*, 83, 9461–9469, 2020.

3. Lu, T., Lin, J., Zhao, L., Li, Y., Peng, Y., A security architecture in cyber-physical systems: Security theories, analysis, simulation and application fields. *Int. J. Secur. Its Appl.*, 9, 7, 1–16, 2015.

4. Jabbar, M.A., Samreen, S., Aluvalu, R., Reddy, K.K., Cyber physical systems for smart cities development. *Int. J. Eng. Technol.*, 7, 36–38, 2018.

5. Gupta, G., Frequency based detection algorithm of wormhole attack in WSNs. *IJARCET*, 4, 7, 3057–3060, 2015.

6. Keerthi, C.K., Jabbar, M.A., Seetharamulu, B., Cyber physical systems (CPS): Security issues, challenges and solutions. *2017 IEEE International Conference on Computational Intelligence and Computing Research (ICCIC)*, pp. 1–4, 2017.

7. Jabbar, M.A., Prasad, K.M.V.V., Aluvalu, R., Reimagining the Indian healthcare ecosystem with AI for a healthy smart city, in: *Emerging Technologies in Data Mining and Information Security. Advances in Intelligent Systems and Computing*, vol. 1286, A.E. Hassanien, S. Bhattacharyya, S. Chakrabati, A. Bhattacharya, S. Dutta (Eds.), Springer, Singapore, 2021.

8. Zhu, B., Joseph, A., Sastry, S., A taxonomy of cyber attacks on SCADA systems, in: *Proceedings of 2011 IEEE International Conferences on Internet of Things, and Cyber, Physical and Social Computing*, Dalian, China, pp. 380–388, 2011.

9. Yampolskiy, M., Horvath, P., Koutsoukos, X.D., Xue, Y., Sztipanovits, J., A language for describing attacks on cyber-physical systems. *Int. J. Crit. Infrastruct. Prot.*, 8, 40–52, 2015.

10. Jin, Y. and Oliveira, D., Trustworthy SoC architecture with on-demand security policies and HW-SW cooperation, in: *Proceedings of the 5th Workshop on SoCs, Heterogeneous Architectures and Workloads (SHAW-5)*, Orlando, FL, 2015.

11. Oliveira, D., Wetzel, N., Bucci, M., Navarro, J., Sullivan, D., Jin, Y., Hardware-software collaboration for secure coexistence with kernel extensions. *ACM SIGAPP Appl. Comput. Rev.*, 14, 3, 22–35, 2014.

12. Al Ibrahim, O. and Nair, S., Cyber-physical security using system-level PUFs, in: *Proceedings of 2011 7th International Wireless Communications and Mobile Computing Conference (IWCMC)*, Istanbul, Turkey, pp. 1672–1676, 2011.

13. Vegh, L. and Miclea, L., Secure and efficient communication in cyber-physical systems through cryptography and complex event processing, in: *Proceedings of 2016 International Conference on Communications (COMM)*, Bucharest, Romania, pp. 273–276, 2016.

14. Kathiravelu, P. and Veiga, L., *SD-CPS: Taming the challenges of cyber-physical systems with a software defined approach*, 2017, [Online]. Available: https://arxiv.org/abs/1701.01676.

15. Cardenas, A.A., Amin, S., Lin, Z.S., Huang, Y.L., Huang, C.Y., Sastry, S., Attacks against process control systems: risk assessment, detection, and response, in: *Proceedings of the 6th ACM Symposium on Information, Computer and Communications SecurityHong Kong, China*, pp. 355–366, 2011.

16. Sanchez, B.B., Alcarria, R., De Rivera, D.S., Sanchez-Picot, A., Predictive algorithms for mobility and device lifecycle management in cyber-physical systems. *EURASIP J. Wirel. Commun.*, 2016, article no. 228, 1–13, 2016.

17. Rathore, S., Sharma, P.K., Loia, V., Jeong, Y.S., Park, J.H., Social network security: Issues, challenges, threats, and solutions. *Inf. Sci.*, 421, 43–69, 2017.

18. Meera, A.J., Kantipudi, M.V.V.P., Aluvalu, R., Intrusion detection system for the IoT: A comprehensive review, in: *SoCPaR 2019: Proceedings of the 11th International Conference on Soft Computing and Pattern Recognition (SoCPaR 2019)*, 2021.

19. Rathore, S., Sharma, P.K., Park, J.H., XSSClassifier: An efficient XSS attack detection approach based on machine learning classifier on SNSs. *J. Inf. Process. Syst.*, 13, 4, 1014–1028, 2017.

20. Khalid, A., Kirisci, P., Ghrairi, Z., Thoben, K.D., Pannek, J., A methodology to develop collaborative robotic cyber physical systems for production environments. *Logist. Res.*, 9, article no. 23, 1–16, 2016.

21. Kim, N.Y., Ryu, J.H., Kwon, B.W., Pan, Y., Park, J.H., CF-CloudOrch: Container fog node-based cloud orchestration for IoT networks. *J. Supercomput.*, 74, 12, 7024–7045, 2018.

22. Sharma, P.K., Rathore, S., Park, J.H., DistArch-SCNet: Blockchain-based distributed architecture with Li-Fi communication for a scalable smart city network. *IEEE Consum. Electron. Mag.*, 7, 4, 55–64, 2018.

23. Sharma, P.K., Singh, S., Jeong, Y.S., Park, J.H., DistBlockNet: A distributed block chains-based secure SDN architecture for IoT networks. *IEEE Commun. Mag.*, 55, 9, 78–85, 2017.

24. Li, B., Lu, R., Wang, W., Choo, K.K.R., Distributed host-based collaborative detection for false data injection attacks in smart grid cyber-physical system. *J. Parallel Distrib. Comput.*, 103, 32–41, 2017.

25. Zhang, Y., Qiu, M., Tsai, C.W., Hassan, M.M., Alamri, A., Health-CPS: Healthcare cyber-physical system assisted by cloud and big data. *IEEE Syst. J.*, 11, 1, 88–95, 2017.

Index

Also of Interest

Check out these published and forthcoming titles in the "Artificial Intelligence and Soft Computing for Industrial Transformation" series from Scrivener Publishing

Advances in Artificial Intelligence and Computational Methods for Transportation Safety
Edited by Naga Pasupuleti, Naveen Chilamkurti, B. Balamurugan, T. Poongodi
Forthcoming 2023. ISBN 978-1-119-76170-9

Cognitive Intelligence and Big Data in Healthcare
Edited by D. Sumathi, T. Poongodi, B. Balamurugan and Lakshmana Kumar Ramasamy
Forthcoming 2022. ISBN 978-1-119-76888-3

Convergence of Deep Learning in Cyber-IoT Systems and Security
Edited by Rajdeep Chakraborty, Anupam Ghosh, Jyotsna Kumar Mandal and S. Balamurugan
Published 2022. ISBN 978-1-119-85721-1

The New Advanced Society
Artificial Intelligence and Industrial Internet of Things Paradigm
Edited by Sandeep Kumar Panda, Ramesh Kumar Mohapatra, Subhrakanta Panda and S. Balamurugan
Published 2022. ISBN 978-1-119-82447-3

Digitization of Healthcare Data using Blockchain
Edited by T. Poongodi, D. Sumathi, B. Balamurugan and K. S. Savita
Published 2022. ISBN 978-1-119-79185-0

Tele-Healthcare
Applications of Artificial Intelligence and Soft Computing Techniques
Edited by R. Nidhya, Manish Kumar and S. Balamurugan
Published 2022. ISBN 978-1-119-84176-0

Impact of Artificial Intelligence on Organizational Transformation
Edited by S. Balamurugan, Sonal Pathak, Anupriya Jain, Sachin Gupta, Sachin Sharma and Sonia Duggal
Published 2022. ISBN 978-1-119-71017-2

Artificial Intelligence for Renewable Energy Systems
Edited by Ajay Kumar Vyas, S. Balamurugan, Kamal Kant Hiran Harsh S. Dhiman
Published 2022. ISBN 978-1-119-76169-3

Artificial Intelligence Techniques for Wireless Communication and Networking
Edited by Kanthavel R., K. Ananthajothi, S. Balamurugan and R. Karthik Ganesh
Published 2022. ISBN 978-1-119-82127 4

Advanced Healthcare Systems
Empowering Physicians with IoT-Enabled Technologies
Edited by Rohit Tanwar, S. Balamurugan, R. K. Saini, Vishal Bharti and Premkumar Chithaluru
Published 2022. ISBN 978-1-119-76886-9

Smart Systems for Industrial Applications
Edited by C. Venkatesh, N. Rengarajan, P. Ponmurugan and S. Balamurugan
Published 2022. ISBN 978-1-119-76200-3

Intelligent Renewable Energy Systems
Edited by Neeraj Priyadarshi, Akash Kumar Bhoi, Sanjeevikumar Padmanabam, S. Balamurugan, and Jens Bo Holm-Nielson
Published 2022. ISBN 978-1-119-78627-6

Human Technology Communication
Internet of Robotic Things and Ubiquitous Computing
Edited by R. Anandan, G. Suseendran, S. Balamurugan, Ashish Mishra and D. Balaganesh
Published 2021. ISBN 978-1-119-75059-8

Nature-Inspired Algorithms Applications
Edited by S. Balamurugan, Anupriya Jain, Sachin Sharma, Dinesh Goyal, Sonia Duggal and Seema Sharma
Published 2021. ISBN 978-1-119-68174-8

Computation in Bioinformatics
Multidisciplinary Applications
Edited by S. Balamurugan, Anand Krishnan, Dinesh Goyal, Balakumar
Chandrasekaran and Boomi Pandi
Published 2021. ISBN 978-1-119-65471-1

Fuzzy Intelligent Systems
Methodologies, Techniques, and Applications
Edited by E. Chandrasekaran, R. Anandan, G. Suseendran, S. Balamurugan
and Hanaa Hachimi
Published 2021. ISBN 978-1-119-76045-0

Biomedical Data Mining for Information Retrieval
Methodologies, Techniques and Applications
Edited by Sujata Dash, Subhendu Kumar Pani, S. Balamurugan and Ajith
Abraham
Published 2021. ISBN 978-1-119-71124-7

Design and Analysis of Security Protocols for Communication
Edited by Dinesh Goyal, S. Balamurugan, Sheng-Lung Peng and O.P.
Verma
Published 2020. ISBN 978-1-119-55564-3

www.scrivenerpublishing.com

Printed and bound by CPI Group (UK) Ltd, Croydon, CR0 4YY

27/10/2024

14580174-0005